Colonial Cinema and Imperial France, 1919–1939

Colonial Cinema and Imperial France, 1919–1939

White Blind Spots, Male Fantasies, Settler Myths

David Henry Slavin

The Johns Hopkins University Press
Baltimore and London

© 2001 The Johns Hopkins University Press
All rights reserved. Published 2001
Printed in the United States of America on acid-free paper
9 8 7 6 5 4 3 2 1

The Johns Hopkins University Press
2715 North Charles Street
Baltimore, Maryland 21218-4363
www.press.jhu.edu

Library of Congress Cataloging-in-Publication Data

Slavin, David Henry.
    Colonial cinema and imperial France, 1919–1939 : white blind spots, male
fantasies, settler myths / David Henry Slavin.
        p. cm.
Includes bibliographical references and index.
    ISBN 0-8018-6616-2 (alk. paper)
    1. Motion pictures—France—History. 2. Imperialism in motion pictures.
3. France—Colonies—Africa. I. Title.
    PN1993.5.F7 S587 2001
    791.43′658—dc21

00-011757

A catalog record for this book is available from the British Library.

To my parents
Irving Slavin (1915–2001) and Jeanette Slavin

Contents

Illustrations

Preface

French film companies of the 1920s and 1930s produced dozens of films about the Foreign Legion and other colonial themes. The films reflected the usual tensions between art and commerce, but because they were made on location in North Africa, the task of attracting a mass audience and financial backing was complicated by an equally urgent need for logistical support. French authorities in the Maghreb provided such support but exacted a price, influencing content and manipulating the message to promote their policies over competing colonial stratagems. This interplay is one aspect of the overall role of colonial cinema as an expression of the interaction of cultural hegemony and political power.

All narrative fictional film is well suited to influencing attitudes subtly and indirectly. Stimulating eye and ear, the medium legitimates assumptions about the world shared by audience and filmmaker. Fixated on romantic love, it opens a vast terrain for investigating gender. Colonial cinema goes a step beyond the simple love story, however, because in the colonial setting gender and race are inextricably intertwined. Occasionally, a film of this genre did protest aspects of colonialism, indicating that blind spots could be dispelled and cultural hegemony contested, but broad challenges to the colonial order were extremely rare.

This study examines the racial and gender subtexts that were rife in colonial cinema, unstated assumptions that remained closer to the surface than those of more mundane cinematic fare. The subtexts fostered blind spots that camouflaged the injustices of the social order. Of course, exotic, escapist fare diverted attention from all harsh social realities. But themes of loss of identity were often the focus of colonial films—identities that depended on and were defined by racial privilege and male dominance. Defense of superior status deflected the energies of the European laboring classes in the metropole and in Algeria away from confronting ruling elites and helped maintain social control.

This book has had a long gestation, and the acknowledgments of colleagues and others in my life may seem inordinately lengthy. For this I beg the reader's indulgence. Kathryn Amdur of Emory University, a colleague and friend for a decade, generously gave her time to read articles and a draft of this manuscript. Her incisive comments helped me sharpen my historical logic. For even longer, Len Berlanstein of the University of Virginia has been a calm voice of support and sound advice on what seemed never-ending frustrations about writing or searching for a job. My dissertation advisor, Hans Schmitt, taught me the difference between historical scholarship and polemic (to the extent that I learned from his counsel). A published version of my dissertation will yet, I hope, join his shelves of works by former students. For now, this small homage will have to suffice.

Michael Miller of Syracuse University consistently encouraged me. He and Dudley Andrew, now at Yale, read a preliminary draft of the manuscript and suggested ways to overcome its limitations. Tom Conley of Harvard gave a strong vote of confidence to the resulting draft. Richard Holway, editor at the University Press of Virginia, shepherded the project for a year and helped place the manuscript with the Johns Hopkins University Press. There, thanks to executive editor Henry Tom, it was approved with minimum delay. I am grateful to him, to Michael Lonegro, his assistant, and to Dennis Marshall, copyeditor, for their advice and patience, as well as to Alexa Selph and Joel Ward.

My status as an adjunct, compelled over the years to glean academia's fields without the perquisites of tenure-stream tillers of its soil, severely restricted my access to support staff. A rare exception was the assistance I got from Elizabeth Adams, who spent many hours compiling this book's bibliography. My thanks to her and to the Georgia State University History Department for allowing her to help me. When I submitted the final manuscript, I was able to walk the distance from my office to the Press because, by a fortuitous coincidence, the Johns Hopkins History Department had hired me as a visiting assistant professor. I am grateful to the chair, Gabrielle Spiegel, for the opportunity to teach at Hopkins. My current employer, Knox College, nurtures and supports all its faculty, regardless of status. Dean Larry Breitborde and my chair, Penny Gold, have put at my disposal resources to help me put the final touches on the manuscript. Thanks also to Gene Lebovics, Joe Miller, and George Ross, and apologies to those unnamed.

In 1989 I returned to Paris to delve into the Third Republic's school textbooks and determine what children learned about France's colonies. The Bibliothèque Nationale's archivist, M. Christian Amalvi, guided me through its extensive collection to the most representative texts.

The American Council of Learned Societies fellowship I received in the fall of 1991 gave me time to write a preliminary essay. On three occasions I won a place in summer seminars funded by the National Endowment for the Humanities. These stimulating stints sustained me financially and intellectually. Dudley Andrew and Steven Ungar, who directed "Cultures of the Popular Front" at the University of Iowa, in 1991, encouraged me to launch this project. At Harvard in 1998, Susan Suleiman's seminar "War and Memory: Postwar Representations of the Occupation and World War II" provided structured time and inspiration to rewrite the draft of this manuscript. Georgetown University professors Voll, Sonbol, Haddad, and Esposito led an institute in 1999, "Islam: Heritage and Prospects," which deepened my awareness of the Muslim dimensions of the Maghreb.

Throughout this work my emphasis has been on the themes and unstated messages of the films rather than on the filmic or visual artistry. Of course, the power of the messages comes from their subliminal, preconscious effects on many senses. Since blind spots tend to short-circuit conscious, rational thought, the visual impact of the films on racial assumptions is particularly strong. But I felt that, given my training, drawing the connection between plot themes and broader issues of cultural politics was the best contribution I could make. Others more expert in the study of film per se are, I am sure, already at work on studies that will confirm and challenge this book's assertions.

Given my focus, advertising posters seem more useful as illustrations than still frames taken from the films. The posters are composites of what the producers thought were the films' most captivating scenes or story elements, and thus they offer visual evidence of audience reception. Procuring the posters required the kind cooperation of many individuals. My search for poster art was proving futile until my colleague and friend Patricia M. E. Lorcin, then at Rice and now at Texas Tech, put me in touch with Lyle Cohen of the Retro Gallery in Houston. He contacted M. Jean-Louis Capitaine, owner of Ciné-Images, Paris, and encouraged his colleague to help me. M. Capitaine generously loaned me color transparencies of the posters; his diligent assistant Alexandre Boyer ensured that they reached me. William Ball, a Johns Hopkins environmental engineering professor with an ecumenical interest in the humanities, photographed several of these posters while in Paris. Jay Van Rensselaer of Johns Hopkins expertly converted color slides to black and white prints. It is a shame that the cost of color reproductions is prohibitive for a scholarly work such as this one, since the colors are striking. But Mr. Van Rensselaer has digitized the color images, and I will make them available to fellow researchers upon request.

Family and friends have given me crucial support to enable me to complete this project. My parents shared what resources they had to help me though lean times. Their generosity was crucial to my finishing this work. Even more important were the democratic, egalitarian values and commitment to social justice that they passed on to me. For their financial help and the moral compass their example provided, I dedicate this book to them.

In a book on film, it is relevant to invoke one with special meaning for me, Mario Monicelli's *The Organizer* (*I compagni,* 1963). A virtual celluloid guide to Antonio Gramsci's theory of cultural hegemony, the film revolves around the workers of a Turin textile mill and a professor who helps them organize a strike and who embodies Gramsci's concept of the organic intellectual. I have known just such people all my life, and their example inspired me to play this role in the world. My father is one, as is Charles ("C") E. Wilson. Theodore William Allen, independent scholar and author of *The Invention of the White Race,* is another who for several decades lent me his patient, critical, yet nonjudgmental, ear as I have extrapolated his "line" and, most recently, applied it to France, Algeria, and the world.

Rich Barnett of the University of Virginia and Chuck Holtz of Berwyn, Pennsylvania, for many years have been my morale officers and mainstays of emotional support. For at least as long, Mike Perna of CUNY Hunter College has kept up a steady stream of encouraging letters. Lisa Tracy, an old friend and fellow alumnus of Oberlin College, now an editor at the *Philadelphia Inquirer,* applied her formidable skills, keen mind, and good humor to help me cross that crucial threshold where the chapters of a book come together as a coherent whole. To all these people I owe lasting thanks and can only hope they value my friendship as much as I value theirs.

Furling my sails at odyssey's end brings to mind the final words of another organic intellectual, quintessentially American albeit fictional. Huckleberry Finn concludes his adventures by saying, "And so there ain't nothing more to write about, and I am rotten glad of it, because if I'd a knowed what a trouble it was to make a book I wouldn't a tackled it and ain't going to no more." In the climactic scene of his book, one of the great moments in American literature, Huck decides to defy respectable white society and "steal Jim out of slavery again." His "existential leap," as Ted Allen has called it, is an example to everyone who is committed to social justice. "All right then," says Huck, "I'll go to hell. As long as I was in, and in for good, I might as well go the whole hog." Although Huck resolved to put down his pen forever, his example and that of my mentors, comrades, and friends inspires me to keep on writing about the consequences of racial and gender inequality, to go the "whole hog," to "leap" again.

My father died in March 2001, just six months short of the time when I could have put this book in his hands. Passionately committed to science and to building a rational, just society, he was above all a dedicated teacher—a rebbe, or rabbi. In his own Yiddishkeit culture, to be so named is the deepest honor, and that is the judgment of all who knew him. He was thwarted from practicing his true calling by the political climate of the 1950s, and he was happiest when, long after he retired, he was finally able to teach. My father was a great soul, and I am proud to be his son.

Colonial Cinema and
Imperial France, 1919–1939

1 | Cultural Hegemony in French-Algerian History

On the streets of Paris, 17 October 1961, thirty thousand demonstrators against the Algerian War were converging peaceably on several gathering points in the city when the police attacked. Thousands of ragtag Nanterre residents had made their way through the posh suburb of Neuilly, across the Seine on the Pont de Neuilly into the elegant Sixteenth Arrondissement to rally at the Place de la Concorde. There *les flics* charged, wounding dozens and tossing them senseless into the river. Battered, bullet-riddled corpses washed up on the banks downstream. On the Boulevard Bonne-Nouvelle, border of the Second and Tenth Arrondissements, the protestors held their ground for an hour. Police dispersed them by firing point-blank into the crowd. A doctor treating the wounded on the scene saw a heap of bodies lying next to a group of prisoners. At Place de l'Etoile, hundreds who emerged from the Métro with their hands in the air were forced under a gauntlet of batons as police loaded them into vans. In the Latin Quarter, police hunted down hundreds more. The vans carried 11,538 to a sports stadium on the edge of the city. Greeted by another gauntlet of truncheons, left without food, water, or medical attention, but carefully scrutinized by police spies, their leaders were culled. It was rumored that some were tortured to death in the cellar of police headquarters. The rest were sent to internment camps in Algeria; 177 were never heard from again.

That evening, officials announced three deaths and hundreds of arrests in "incidents" around the city, but an internal police report, kept secret for twenty-five years, estimated the true toll at 140 dead. The leftist press raised an outcry, but inquiries were squelched and, although thousands witnessed the afternoon's events, the public was kept in the dark. The detainees were released without being charged or tried, and

1

they dispersed back to the ghettos where they lived in near-complete isolation. Total dead and "disappeared": 317.[1]

The victims were Algerians. "Subjects" of France for a century, bestowed with the rights of citizenship by the Fourth Republic, they had taken to the streets to speed up talks with the Front de la Libération Nationale (FLN) provisional government and demand the revocation of a curfew the police had imposed in their neighborhoods and cafés. The French metropolitan Left, deeply conflicted over the war, did nothing in the face of this clear case of racial discrimination. The French Communist party (PCF) in particular was anxious to avoid confronting the government. Socialist faculty and students at the Sorbonne staged a small protest on Toussaint (1 November), issuing a manifesto that compared French passivity with "Germans who did not react to Nazism's atrocities." But this solitary rally was merely "for appearances' sake."[2]

A crack in this wall of silence and denial appeared after the ultras in the Algerian settlers' camp formed the Organisation Armée Sécrète (OAS), which between November 1961 and February 1962 carried out 450 bombings in Paris in a last-ditch effort to stop the peace talks. An explosion in André Malraux's apartment on 7 February blinded and maimed a four-year-old girl. The next afternoon, ten thousand demonstrators defied a police ban and rallied at the Place Bastille. Aware that the ultras had sympathizers within the ranks of the police who were hindering the investigation, the angry crowd skirmished with officers for several hours. Suddenly the police massed and charged, trapping hundreds on the steps leading down to a gated and locked entrance to the Charonne Métro station. Another police rampage erupted; a company just returned from duty in Algiers displayed the greatest savagery. Hurling wrought-iron tree guards, marble-topped café tables, and bodies on the people below, they killed four men, three women, and a sixteen-year-old boy. Hundreds of demonstrators and 140 police were injured. The next Tuesday, half a million people joined the funeral cortège and laid the victims to rest in Père Lachaise, the cemetery that held the Left's martyrs since the Paris Commune.

Of that day's speakers, only a Catholic (CFTC) union official, Robert Duvivier, mentioned the events of 17 October, a little more than three months earlier. Local FLN leader Mohammed Saddok was in the crowd listening, and he grew so embittered by the "choice of deaths" (8 French lives versus 317 Algerian) that he half-wished someone would throw a grenade. A historian has observed that "Charonne remains in the French collective memory while oblivion covers October 1961 . . . the victims of the 17th are drowned in the memory of the French."[3]

It remains an open question whether a vigorous protest of the initial curfew would have restrained the police. Police prefect Maurice Papon was accused of inciting the police attacks, but he escaped accountability. However, in 1998 he was convicted of crimes against humanity for turning over the Jews of Bordeaux to the Nazis, a law applying only to acts committed by agents of the Vichy regime and specifically exempting soldiers and police who fought the Algerian War. Papon's Paris record was taken up in the press to buttress the case against him, yet it also shed light on the juridical double standard that remains a disturbing feature of the French legal system.[4]

The events of 17 October and Métro Charonne reflect the racialization of French life, an underlying theme of this book. During the interwar years, mass culture, and particularly film, legitimated racial superiority under the guise of a discourse of dominance that invested Frenchness with innate superiority. Racial superiority justified subordinating Algerian rights and aspirations, withholding the Rights of Man from an "inferior" people. Like the portrait of Dorian Gray, stereotypes allowed the French to attribute to Africa their own deformities and insecurities. The staunchest defenders of the Enlightenment's universal standards of human rights, the Left, took up the Algerian's cause only with the greatest reluctance and willfully avoided the fact that France and Algeria shared a common fate.[5]

This study situates colonial cinema in a context of cultural hegemony and social control. It focuses on several dozen French films set in North Africa, supplemented by evidence from fan magazines, picture postcards, popular fiction, school textbooks, colonial exhibitions, and unwitting or intentional transmitters of stereotypes, such as parliamentary lobbyists, colonial soldiers, settlers, tourists, and motion-picture actors, writers, and directors. Colonial film reflected and reinforced the machinery of cultural hegemony, noncoercive social control, and the underlying politics of privilege. Occluding realities "as plain as the nose on your face," film legitimated the racial privileges of European workers, diverted attention from their own exploitation, and disabled impulses to solidarity with women and colonial peoples. Racial interests conjoined French workers and elites, allowing workers to feel more

"French." While colonial film of the 1920s supported policy goals in Morocco, and those of the 1930s praised the Foreign Legion, its more subtle, lasting impact was to normalize the exploited-yet-privileged status of European workers in the metropole and the Maghreb. The Left in general and the French Communist party in particular tried to uphold antiimperialism and repudiate racial superiority, but in the face of anticolonial uprisings, the spread of fascism, and threats to the Soviet Union, the PCF and the Left recoiled from its stand on race. The twists and turns of the Left on issues of gender and race demonstrate how the French became white.

Modernization homogenized French classes, corporate groups, and political constituencies into undifferentiated *citoyens* (citizens). Workers, peasants, artisans, and shopkeepers wrestled with conflicts between traditional identity and adaptation to modernity. By disseminating colonial mythology, film helped Frenchmen transcend narrow identities and redefine themselves as bearers of civilization to the colonized. As they moved from opposition to governance, the parties of the Left abandoned antiimperialism. For the Radicals this transition came in 1899 when they formed their first government. Most anticolonial socialists went communist after the split at the Tours congress in 1921. The rump joined with the Radicals in the Cartel des Gauches electoral coalition of 1924–26 and supported the war against the Riffian Berbers of Morocco.[6] In Algeria, conflicts between settler-based Marxist parties and native nationalists and between secessionist and assimilationist wings of the nationalist movement complicated the factional disputes. The PCF was the last in the line of left parties to reverse its stand on North Africa. Despite antiimperialist injunctions by the Third International in the 1920s, the PCF's shift of position in the 1930s amounted to a tacit defense of the empire.

The Maghreb indelibly marked France's passage through the twentieth century, and recent scholarship is challenging earlier views of colonial-metropolitan interaction as unidirectional. Reversing polarities highlights the impact of the colonies on the metropole. However, the to-and-fro flow of capital and administrative/military personnel, migrant labor and tourism, commodities and raw materials hid unacknowledged, socially constructed inequalities imposed on Algerians. Willful amnesia, selective recognition, male fantasies, and white blind spots distorted French vision and produced a full-blown politics of denial.

Europeans faced sanctions as racial transgressors if they "declined the stereotypes." Accusations of race treason, for instance, often accompanied charges of Communist treason against the nation.[7]

The Left's expediency and dislocated praxis serve as a touchstone for the overall evolution of social privilege in France. Algerian settler society racialized French politics, and the pied-noir working class, committed to racial supremacy over the natives, hamstrung the metropolitan working-class parties' efforts to implement programs for social justice. Two congruent streams of thought, Antonio Gramsci's theory of hegemony and Theodore William Allen's history of the invention of the white race in seventeenth-century Virginia, suggest theoretical underpinnings for understanding the role of racial and gender privilege in France and the role of cinema in France's culture wars of the first half of the twentieth century.

In Gramsci's view, hegemony derived from dual consciousness. The industrial proletariat's revolutionary conception of the world "which manifests itself in action . . . in flashes" coexists uneasily with a mindset that it "inherits from the past and uncritically absorb[s]." This contradiction

> influences moral conduct and the direction of will. "Man-in-the-mass" displays a "contradictory state of consciousness [that] does not permit of any action, any decision or any choice, and produces a condition of moral and political passivity. . . . The contrast between thought and action, i.e. the co-existence of two conceptions of the world, one affirmed in words and the other displayed in effective action, is not simply a product of self-deception [*malafede*]. Self-deception can be an adequate explanation for a few individuals or . . . groups . . . but it is not adequate when the contrast occurs in the life of the great masses.[8]

Gramsci's dialectical view of consciousness is consistent with concepts such as white-supremacist democracy and white workers as exploited members of a "master race." The New York Irish who resisted the Civil War draft with an armed insurrection and mass murder of African Americans is one example of white blindness and dual consciousness based on social privilege through which capital constructs inequality; another example is the white South African miners who stopped employers from training blacks for semiskilled jobs by mounting an armed general strike in 1922 under the banner "Workers of the world unite and fight for a white South Africa." As Gramsci and Allen would concur, such groups mobilize white workers in defense of racial prerogatives, and, by undermining class solidarity, they serve the interests of the owning classes and reduce the conditions of the white worker along with those of color.

For Allen, the "white race" is an invention of the Anglo-American plantation bourgeoisie to solve the problem of social control. Allen sees "a true paradox at the core of American history, the paradox embodied in the 'white' identity of the European-American laborer, wherein the social class identity is immured. Perhaps so many of our historians have failed to see the paradox because they conceive of the 'white race' as a phenomenon of nature." In historiography as in working-class activism, the white blind spot and cultural hegemony preclude alternative interpretations of history or social justice. Capital manufactures consent by occluding alternatives to the rule of the market, while privilege imbues racial identity with force of habit by sustaining it over several generations and elevating it, like the market itself, to the realm of natural law, immune from human control.[9]

Both Gramsci and Allen examine how capital maintains power in the face of waxing proletarian political strength and periodic upheavals. Both civil society and white-supremacist democracy are forms of rule that incorporate racially privileged workers as capital's intermediate strata to rationalize, administer, and repress. Privileged yet exploited, the workers that Gramsci and Allen describe are implicated in the "underdevelopment" of the South, be it southern Italy or the southern United States, because they perceive the landless rural poor, Calabrian peasant or black sharecropper, as the threat to their interests, rather than the backwardness foisted on them by the national elites.

Gramsci's essay "The Southern Question" and Allen's work complement and reinforce each other. Despite different historical roots, the Mezzogiorno (Calabria, Sicily, and Sardinia, where Gramsci was raised) and the postbellum South were products of the capitalist world market. Both contained large estates worked by sharecroppers or landless laborers and were attached to urban, proletarian, industrial Norths. Just as white Americans believed in black inferiority, so northern Italians of all classes agreed that Mezzogiornans were innately inferior. As Gramsci observed, "the socialist party was largely the vehicle of this bourgeois ideology among the northern proletariat." In the United States, white and black workers were virtually the same class, but the social gap of privilege created an unbridgeable racial chasm. So, too, Algeria's incorporation into France gradually added a racial dynamic to class conflict in the Hexagon.[10]

An integral part of France, Algeria became a site for the construction of a white race in which elite and working class shared a culture of dominance that denied the universality of Enlightenment ideals and, on the basis of innate cultural traits, denied the rationality of the natives and transformed the Rights of Man into conferred privileges. The settlers, locked in power struggles with native elites, modern nationalists, and reformers in Paris, took the lead in constructing the bonds of race. The culture wars shaping French national identity, working-class politics, and gender relations—all were racialized, while a "white blind spot," a discourse of denial, rendered the racial realm invisible, forbidden to scrutiny and immune to analysis.

French essentialist culture in the past century asserted the innate superiority of Frenchness. Muslims and Jews were depicted as aliens threatening to overrun and undermine "True France." Settlers, soldiers, lobbyists, tourists, and film directors projected images of Maghrebin subjects to the metropole through a distorted lens of movies, magazines, postcards, popular fiction, textbooks, and exhibitions. Archival sources such as police reports on French leftists and labor unions, Maghrebin nationalists, and immigrant laborers attest to the French both using and being manipulated by these images. Even those with gender and class grievances conformed to the norms of the master race. The disobedient risked being branded as racial renegades. Film and other products of mass consumer culture provided authoritative rationales for social inequalities that in other circumstances might have been seen as intolerable injustices.

Lording it over Arab, Berber, and Jew, wealthy colons and impoverished flotsam of Spain, Calabria, Sicily, and Malta solidified into a master race. Playing "the race card" in Paris, they blocked Algerian reform by appealing to white solidarity to hold back what they saw as the hordes of barbaric, fanatical Muslims, protecting their privileged status, at least until Charles de Gaulle came to power in 1958.

To understand why colonial reform failed in the waning years of the Third Republic, it is necessary to examine how a white supremacist regime emerged in Algeria during its early years. From its outset in 1870–71, the Third Republic was implicated in the creation of the Algerian settler "race." By currying the support of the settlers against the metropolitan monarchists, the Republic's creators instituted settler rule and legalized the exclusion of natives from citizenship. A Code de l'Indigénat, a Black Code, restricted the human and civil rights of natives and erected a privileged status for settlers. From their position of advantage, the settlers dispossessed natives of vast tracts of urban, farm, grazing, and forest land. French colons grew rich and their prosperity attracted impoverished immigrants from Spain, Italy, and Malta. Together they developed a consciousness of themselves as a "new race." However, in 1870 Paris bestowed citizenship on Algerian Jews, a decision that sought to fulfill the Enlightenment's legacy and provide allies for colonial rule. The decree incensed the settlers, who viewed the Jews as natives, and their rights as a dagger pointed at the heart of their privileged status. The pied-noir poor saw Jews as economic competitors and exploiters, and mounting anti-Semitic violence in Algeria galvanized and amplified the Dreyfus Affair riots in French cities. A virtual insurrection erupted, which Paris neutralized by granting unprecedented rights of fiscal autonomy to the three Algerian *départements*. These concessions and a fear of servile insurrection by Arab and Berber peasants cooled pied-noir anti-Semitic ardor, and by 1901 the unrest had subsided.

One-tenth of Algeria's population, rich and poor alike, shared the egocentric illusion that their happiness and status depended on the immiseration of the native majority. The settler state, which emerged in the wake of the Kabyle Revolt of 1871, led by Sheikh Mohammed al Muqrani of Constantine, had incubated during the decades following the French invasion of 1830. The counterinsurgent warfare of 1830–47 shattered Algerian society. The French army reduced the population of 3 million souls drastically, and in 1876 it had not yet recovered, standing at 2.46 million.[11] Settlers devastated the native peasantry, expropriating land and then inducing the impoverished Algerians to till their former holdings for wages. Since the natives worked for one-quarter the pay of Europeans and at comparable levels of productivity, a preference for indigenous labor arose. A decree of 1849 imposed special taxes, *impôts arabes*, on all except those employed as sharecroppers *(métayers)* or wage workers on European estates, and the Second Empire conscripted labor through a corvée. Native population climbed once the peasants determined that child labor increased family income.[12]

Proletarianization of native labor squeezed small-scale European farmers and concentrated landholdings. The "pioneers" retreated to the urban areas, and new arrivals settled in the four big cities without ever going out to the *bled* (the bush, or outback). The colon elite deputized "poor whites" as policemen and overseers, whose job was to protect property that did not belong to them. Out of a matrix of race privilege arose a system of social control that insured labor discipline on the estates and precluded class solidarity between rural native and urban European poor. In the early days of the Third Republic, the settler elite, led by a deputy to the Chamber in Paris, Dr. Auguste Warnier, erected a Code de l'Indigénat restricting day-to-day activities of Muslims. This Black Code handicapped the native people economically and educationally and prevented them from competing on equal footing with the propertyless settler poor. Its obverse effect was to make French citizenship a privilege for whites only.[13]

Ratified by the Chamber in Paris in 1874, the code had by 1881 grown to a list of thirty-three infractions that applied only to native Algerians, or were more serious when committed by them. It authorized settler-controlled local governments, *communes mixtes,* and justices of the peace, *juges des paix,* to handle such cases without trial or right of appeal. Refusing to perform transportation service, fire patrol, night-guard duty, or other corvée was cause for arrest; all Europeans were exempt except prisoners. Natives required special permits to sell goods in a market, hold public banquets, or travel on pilgrimage. Fines were levied for not giving or knowing one's patronymic, not reporting marriages or births, and for firing blank cartridges from rifles, a custom at weddings and *fantaisies* (horsemanship displays celebrating feasts and saints' days). Until repealed by the French Senate in July 1914, a law against *gredins* (rascals), ostensibly to curtail vagabondage, required natives to obtain travel passes for all movement. An Arab or Berber man violating the code was fined, and jailed if he could not pay. If he did not pay his taxes, his wife was put in restraints. Convictions for infractions of the code averaged twenty-five thousand a year from 1883 to 1914; the authorities imprisoned offenders an average of three days per violation.[14]

The code was the logical outgrowth of burgeoning settler power. Decades of collective reprisals had obliterated Muslim property relations, crushed the native elite, and left the Third Republic without indigenous agents to act on its behalf. Jules Cambon, who served as Algeria's governor from 1891 to 1897 and as foreign minister in many pre-1914 cabinets, pointed out that "once the Turkish authorities had disappeared . . . there was not a day that we did not try to destroy the 'grandes tentes' . . . because we found them to be forces of resistance

... as a result today we are faced with a sort of human dust *[une sorte de poussière d'hommes]* on which we have no influence and in which are produced movements completely unknown to us. We no longer have any authorized intermediaries between ourselves and the indigenous population."[15]

Thus pulverized, Algerian society gave way to white racist democracy. Regardless of class, Europeans acquired prerogatives over all natives, and racial categories distorted class structure. The Chamber of Deputies naturalized all Algerian-born Europeans in 1889, inadvertently reinforcing the association of race privilege with French citizenship. To protect their privileges, the poor whites *(petits colons)* accepted from their "betters," the elite *grands colons*, the role of agents of social control. Concentrated in the cities, the pieds noirs came to dominate urban society, while the army drafted their sons to protect the estates and vineyards of the *blédards*, the "Boer" farmers of the outback. Cambon was not the first prominent republican to criticize this emerging racial hierarchy. After visiting Algeria in 1892, Jules Ferry, architect of France's imperial expansion, questioned the settler's fitness to rule, observing to the Chamber that the new Algerian lacked "the virtues of the victor. [It is difficult] to convince the European settler that there are rights other than his own in an Arab country and that the native is not a race to be taxed and exploited to the utmost limits."[16]

Ferry's sympathies fell short of taking responsibility for alleviating the natives' misery. As Charles-Robert Ageron, the preeminent historian of Algeria, pointed out, "anticolonialists before 1914 were more concerned to humanize the colonial regime than to repudiate it." Criticism of the settlers continued. Charles Jonnart, another leading figure in colonial circles who had served as Algeria's governor, admonished the Chamber in 1893 that leaving the 3.5 million Arabs in the settlers' hands "would mean exposing natives to a denial of justice and to . . . exploitation." A series of eight articles by journalist Paul Bourde appeared in *Le Temps* in May 1912 and made a strong impression on public opinion. After two decades of settler rule, he concluded, "the privileges of the colons make impartiality impossible for our African administrators and force them to take a stand against the natives." Yet the *"Algériens"* in the Chamber convinced their colleagues, as they had convinced the pied-noir poor, that reform would open the floodgates to social equality and threaten the settlers' security. When the Indigénat came up for renewal, usually every seven years, they stymied all efforts at reform and intransigently opposed equal rights until the bitter end of Algérie française.[17]

The Roman Catholic hierarchy in North Africa lent indirect support to the settler cause. Cardinal Charles Lavigerie founded the White Fathers and Sisters in 1868 and charged them with converting the Berber Kabyles. They studied Arabic and the Qur'an, learned the Kabyle dialect well enough to write a Berber dictionary, and ministered to a flock that proved impervious to Christianization. Lavigerie tacitly admitted failure in the 1880s by shifting the focus of the Pères Blancs, the White Fathers, to the abolition of the slave trade in central Africa. The cardinal supported the army as an essential protection against "Muslim fanaticism" and rebellion, and his priests provided the military with excellent intelligence. But he opposed army control of colonial policy, and before he died in 1892 he reluctantly shifted from a pro-Berber policy to support for civilian rule. A curious symbiosis developed between the monarchist clergy and Opportunist Republican authorities, grounded in their common commitment to imperialism and preserving settler prerogatives.[18]

Despite their anticlericalism, for the public intellectuals delineating Algeria's racial boundaries, religion demarcated the color line and culled Berbers and Jews along with Arabs from the "new Latin race." One of the earliest to define the racial divide was Nicolas Auguste Pomel (d. 1898), a senator from Oran; his thirty-five scholarly monographs carried weight in France. Academician Charles Humbert declared that religious taboos separated the races too much to permit intermarriage. Jules Harmand, a naval doctor and diplomat, appealed to Paris to protect the defenseless natives. He drew on the authority of two of his friends, sociologist Gustave Le Bon and anthropologist Lucien Lévy-Bruhl, who argued that a *mentalité prélogique* prevented the natives from absorbing all but the most rudimentary understanding of European culture. Another influential voice was Louis Bertrand, classics professor of the Lycée d'Alger. Author of thirty histories, including a biography of Saint Augustine, columnist for *Revue des Deux Mondes,* and a novelist who wrote in the pied-noir dialect and created the picaresque character Pépète, Bertrand was elected to the Académie Française in 1925, filling the seat vacated by the death of Maurice Barrès. Seeing race war looming on the horizon, he claimed that African conditions had produced a new breed, the "Afro-Latins," who would unify, revitalize, and prepare Europe for the coming cataclysm with Islam. His book *Le Sang des races*

(1898) distinguished Arabs from Berbers but ruled out fusing the natives with the new race and obliterated the achievements of Islamic civilization. By 1898, the prestigious Société d'Anthropologie de Paris, founded by Paul Broca, was also promulgating the notion of an "African European," another variation on the name for this new race.[19]

According to Charles-Robert Ageron, "the violence of anti-Semitism . . . [was] incontestably one of the major characteristics of Algerian political life."[20] The New Latin Race's appearance coincided with the rise of a populist anti-Jewish movement. An active anti-Jewish front was already operating in Algeria when the Dreyfus Affair exploded in France. Anti-Jewish organizers in fin-de-siècle France devised an electoral strategy to outbid the better-organized Left for peasant and working-class votes and enabled the construction of a dominant-race, national identity by excluding the "impure" Jew. Pied-noir anti-Judaism predated the anti-Dreyfusard movement by a decade, and the settler advance guard went far beyond the tame tactics of the Hexagon. The pied-noir press urged physical extermination of the Jews, pogrom-like attacks occurred intermittently, and the entire corps of elected officials openly declared their anti-Semitism.

Anti-Semitism erupted throughout Europe at century's end, emanating from the tsarist empire. The arrival of emigrants from Russia's Pale of Settlement in industrial and imperial centers like Paris and Vienna produced dislocations that stimulated anti-Judaism. Algerian anti-Semitism, however, formed an independent epicenter, as officially tolerated and locally sponsored as the tsardom's, but grounded in the unique status of Algeria's Jews and the separatist impulses of the settlers. United in a desire to block Jewish assimilation, the heterogeneous pieds noirs vacillated between identity as French citizens and identity as New Latin "whites." Their racially based anti-Judaism thus had autonomous roots that fed the anti-Dreyfusard movement in the metropole as well as white Algerian separatism. In this sense, Algerian anti-Semitism foreshadowed interwar Poland's, where efforts to uproot the centuries-old Jewish minority acted as a racial "social cement" to rejoin the historic nation.[21]

Because they were natives and citizens, Jews threatened the basis of settler dominance, the association between French citizenship and race. The decree conferring French citizenship on Algerian Jews had been authored by Adolphe Crémieux, justice minister of the provisional regime of 1870–71. Crémieux had promulgated the regime's basic laws and designed its Algeria policy; he was also a Jew, and presided over a charitable foundation, the Alliance Israélite Universelle (AIU). By attaching his name to this one law among many he wrote on Algerian policy, his enemies implied special pleading. In fact, Léon Gambetta and his other Opportunist Party moderate republican colleagues had joined Crémieux in sponsoring the bill and ushering it into law. Indisputably "native," Algerian Jews had lived in North Africa since the Roman diaspora; a second wave arrived in 1492, expelled after seven centuries in Muslim Spain. The AIU helped this thoroughly Arabized, Sephardic Jewish community to convert its cultural orientation to France. Once citizens, Algerian Jews had access to free public schooling, and the Republic relieved the AIU of educational tasks, accelerating the process of shedding Arabic civilization. Consistent with its traditions, Algerian Jewry transferred its loyalty to its new, stronger protector, an obligation that readily translated into electoral support for Algeria's Opportunist party. Government-financed local religious authorities that administered each sect's charitable and devotional activities *(the consistoires)*, mobilized Jewish voters in the Algerian elections.[22]

Thus anti-Judaism among the pied noir was racial, electoral, and economic. Radical-socialist anticlericals united with antirepublican Roman Catholics, the latter hurling hoary medieval slanders of deicide at the Jews, while the former propounded a "socialism of fools" and accused Jews of exploiting whites, stealing jobs, cheating in trade, and siding with the elite in elections. The Jewish petite bourgeoisie did indeed hold decided competitive advantages. Citizenship freed them of restrictions faced by most Muslims. Straddling the native and colon worlds, speaking both Arabic and French, Jewish merchants built ties to French export houses and sold to all three communities in Algerian towns. But colonial films were first made in Morocco, not Algeria, sponsored by its French resident-general, Louis-Hubert Lyautey. Reflecting Lyautey's policy of constructive colonialism, incorporating native elites as junior partners in governing the country, the early movies were glaringly paternalistic, but they sympathetically portrayed Arab culture. The colonial war of the mid 1920s discredited Lyautey, and the idea of recruiting Muslim elites to participate in French endeavors lost ground. Filmmaking shifted to Algeria, where the settlers had imposed themselves as the agents of social control.

We come full circle, back to 17 October 1961, amnesia, and moral lassitude. Anti-Semitism took two forms in France, anti-Judaism and anti–Arabo/Berberism. Edward Said has explored the "white blindspot" that separates the two in French memory and has suggested studying Ernest Renan's racialism because it connects them. French efforts to bring war criminals to trial ignored the connection until 1998, when the trial of Maurice Papon, avatar of both anti-Semitisms, brought to light his role in the 17 October 1961 massacre.[23]

It is fruitful to explore why these links are obscured. One of the first acts of the Vichy regime was to abrogate the Crémieux Decree of 1870 conferring citizenship on Algerian Jews. The Vichy measure placed Algerian Jews in extreme peril, rendering them vulnerable to the first step in the process of deportation and extermination. This concession to the pied-noir community again revealed the settlers' role in racializing Frenchness. The Resistance disputed Vichy's view of Jews as unassimilable—that is, not "white"—but neither camp reflected on whiteness per se, and both drew a color line excluding Algerian natives. Among dirt-poor Algerian whites such as those who appear in Camus' novels, race immured class consciousness and at the same time boxed in metropolitan policy. Reforms in North Africa had to be achieved along racial lines to protect white privilege within French citizenship. Patriarchy, powerful in its own right, reinforced racial superiority.

In summary, loyalty to the civilizing mission and master-race helped tie French working people to the ruling elites, fulfill their longings for respectability, and integrate them into the social mainstream. The Left chose to avoid coming to grips with the deeply seated prejudices and assumptions about colonial peoples in mass culture and popular consciousness. The Left's politics of avoidance in the colonial arena opened the door to compromises on a wide front and undermined its overall quest for social justice. Inequalities of wealth and power, not simply stereotyped ideas and culture, alienated metropolitan workers from colonial peoples and stifled their internationalist impulses. Racial ties to the settler thousands overrode more abstract solidarity with the indigenous millions.

This book, combining cultural studies with archivally based research on the French Left, the working class, and France's North African empire, steers a middle passage between culture as a social mirror, on the one hand, and as a fully independent shaper of consciousness, on the other. The ideas of a civilizing mission and a master race tied the Left and the working class to the ruling elites' colonial policies, but this culture stemmed from the material conditions separating metropolitan workers from colonial peoples. Gender inequality, expanding leisure activity, persistent small-scale production, and shifts from blue- to white-collar occupations combined to neutralize class struggle, and since the 1930s race has become an ever more prominent factor in this combination.

Without taking into account the strain placed on their tenuous contacts with the Maghreb's nationalists, the working-class parties allied with the procolonial metropolitan middle classes. As a consequence, scattered voices advocating anticolonial alternatives were given little hearing, and the Popular Front's heirs have been unable to resolve racial tensions that are as rife in contemporary France as in the rest of Europe.

Through its anti-Jewish and anti-Muslim activities, pied-noir Algeria and its offshoots in Morocco and Tunisia fostered racial supremacy in North Africa and galvanized race-based politics in metropolitan France. The Dreyfus Affair, resistance to reform, anti-Semitic politics of the late 1930s, and Vichy's revocation of Algerian Jewish citizenship were steps on a road to collaboration with the Final Solution that in turn created a climate of collusion with or indifference to the suppression of Vietnamese and Algerian independence through internment camps and mass bombings of civilians.

The interaction of imperial myth, the cult of the Foreign Legion, male supremacy, and cultural essentialism was cemented in place during the period between the Rif War and the Spanish Civil War. Attitudes toward North Africans reflected in the popular culture helped produce a "white" identity in France and altered the history of French workers, women, and the Left. The Left's relations with Maghrebin nationalists from 1924 to 1939 bequeathed a colonialist legacy that exerted its pull on France's internal affairs during Vichy, the Vietnam War, the Algerian War, and in recent reactions to non-European immigrants.

2 The Form of Rule in Cultural Context

White supremacy, anti-Semitism, and settler nationalism thus impelled *cinéma colonial* toward the settler weltanschauung, and colonial film came to inhabit the settler's moral universe. Film also revealed conflicting strategies for imperial control, often reflecting policy debates over association versus assimilation of colonial peoples. The emergence and erosion of the alliance with traditional elites that the governor-general of Morocco, Marshal Louis-Hubert Lyautey, carried out from 1912 to 1925 can be traced through film. As settlers migrated from pied-noir Algeria, they supplanted the old elites as agents of social control and agitated for more power. Colonial film discourse illustrated and helped construct a culture of racial dominance, of whiteness, that settler elites used during the interwar years to unite the North African European community across class and ethnic lines in defense of racial privilege. White power forged the identity and loyalty of the settlers, enabling them to beat back the impetus from Paris and from indigenous nationalists to reform Algeria's governance.

Whiteness, its boundaries marked by anti-Semitism as well as anti-Arabism, also tied metropolitan opinion to settler interests. Even the poetic realist films of the Popular Front era, with their celebration of the common man, legitimated racial double standards when they took up colonial themes. Applying the inconsistent logic of the white blind spot, as well as willful ignorance, they presented women of color as self-sacrificing saviors of white men, and contrasted European women as agents of their destruction.

Paradoxically, while filmmakers declared their commitment to verisimilitude in portraying colonized peoples, their depictions of native life, accurate or not, were incidental to stories that reflected the worldview and mind-set of Europeans, colonial and metropolitan. Chinua Achebe,

16

Edward Said, Albert Memmi, and other "outsiders" corroborate the view that the European culture of dominance reflected unease with the inequalities of status and power by attributing Europe's sins to peoples of color. In *Heart of Darkness,* Conrad shows the European soul irresistibly drawn to the Dark Continent. So, too, the Maghreb drew orientalist French painters, writers, tourists, and filmmakers toward a Heart of Light: the shimmering, ultraclear light of the Mediterranean littoral; the merciless glare of the Saharan sun.

Stories of Light and Darkness

After all is said and done, colonial films are melodramas, simple stories of individual lives and loves. But they are suffused with racial and gender privilege. These political realities made their greatest impact on film during the interwar years, when cinema's role in representing "the people" and constructing national identity achieved its widest influence. In her efforts to apply Gramsci to film, Marcia Landy suggests that cinema is a resource for probing the ways history is used to create "folklores of national identity." For Gramsci, language, culture, and politics interact and work through folklore to form nation and state. Grounded in folklore, mass cultural forms depend on melodrama to transmit a "commonsense" worldview. "In its excessive affect (emotion), Manicheanism, obsession with justice, fixation on victimage and verbal and physical violence, melodrama addresses every conceivable form of social antagonism."[1]

Melodramas displace the public sphere onto the private and also indicate symptoms of social crisis by raising gender-identity issues and tensions in sexuality that are tied to social as well as psychic ills. Their "persistent binarism in public and private spheres" leads to two subgenres, the woman's film, which deals with conformity and rebellion within the family and gender relations, and the action film, which focuses on the social order and subordinates the domestic sphere.[2] French films blur the demarcation between the two, expressing binarism within a single film. Thus French action melodramas often contain scenes of (frustrated) domesticity.

Colonial film borrowed themes and images from precursors. These included orientalist painting, illustrated magazines, colonial novels, dioramas and panoramas, and tourist postcards. In Paris, the ever-fascinating Musée Grévin wax museum displayed colonial tableaux. Love affairs occupied the spotlight in most films; colonial cinema used history and politics as backdrops, highlighting the role of the "white" woman in Africa. Colonial novels and cinema reacted to challenges to male dominance in France by portraying the white woman as an agent of destruction of the white man's mission, while the woman of color serves him and redeems him. An opposing discourse promoted by "paternal" colonialists and "maternal" feminists presented white women as the vessels of the civilizing mission. Immune to *le cafard,* the mind-wrenching homesickness that led to mental illness and violence against whites or natives, white women were suited to "moral conquest" of the colonized better than white men. Moral conquest implied that the Dark Continent's immorality threatened to swallow white men. Fears of pollution and corrosion displaced fascination with exotic Others. As Chinua Achebe observed, "the West seems to suffer deep anxieties about the precariousness of its civilization and to have a need for constant reassurance by comparison with Africa."[3]

Didactic tales of the perils of miscegenation, based on novels written by colonial military officers or settlers like Pierre Loti, figured prominently in the films set in Africa. *Roman d'un Spahi* (1881), Loti's prototypical tragic and popular novel, was twice adapted to film in the 1920s. Jean Peyral, a peasant lad from the mountains of the Cévennes, is drafted for five years of military service and posted to a colonial Spahi regiment garrisoned in Senegal's port of Saint Louis. Wrenched from his idyllic life and his fiancée, Jean is seduced by Cora, a *métisse* (mulatto) "of such a white type that she looked Parisian. . . . The wife of a rich man . . . she had been to Paris." When Cora takes another lover, Jean goes on a suicidal binge, but Cora's servant girl Fatou-gaye saves him. She forsakes her people, the Khassonké, to live with him. Fatou fills the sexual needs Cora awakened in him; his fiancée remains an abstract love, a symbol of patriotism and racial purity. Trapped by Africa and his own lust, he worries that "his dignity as a white man [was] soiled by contact with this black flesh." Jean's racial and sexual transgression incurs the ire of his officers and his fiancée's father. He blames Fatou, and when she steals his watch, he whips her and drives her away; then, ashamed of his brutality, he resolves to become a model soldier. At the end of his tour, he wins his sergeant's stripes, but King Boubakar-Ségou of Djagabar declares war and Jean is obliged to perform one last act of redemption. But Fatou has born him a near-white son and, as the regiment marches into the interior, she shows him the boy. His love for the child is instantaneous and he determines to return to Fatou after one last visit to his aged parents. On patrol, however, Boubakar's advance guard ambush his unit and, shades of *Rolande*, kill all the Spahis. Fatou finds Jean's body and, in despair, she strangles the baby, filling his mouth with sand to still his cries and burying his head in the sand to hide his face. Then she poisons herself, and the vultures descend on the three bodies.[4]

With an intimate knowledge of the land and its peoples, Loti vividly described exotic places while cruising the realms of his own emotional distress; male protagonists like Peyral served as pseudonymous alter egos. Fatou's African suttee was the logical extension of Loti's view of the dark-skinned woman: she was an intellectual and moral inferior with no meaning or existence outside her white lover, redeeming herself through enhancing his position, exalting his ego, serving his needs, and quieting his unease about the inevitability of death. In their portrayals of colonized women, films imitated this self-immolating devotion. It was taken for granted that the Fatou-Gayes of film would reject or betray their own people or deny their own needs out of adoration of a white man, just as Scheherezade of the *Arabian Nights* staved off the king's ax by revealing women's wiles to him and betraying her sex. In *L'Occident* (1927), Hassina carries a message for reinforcements from her lover, Lieutenant Cadière, to his naval vessel and helps defeat a Berber uprising. Josephine Baker, in *Zouzou* (1934), steps aside for her blonde friend Claire, to form a "natural" (i.e., white) proletarian family with her adoptive brother Jean (played by Jean Gabin). As Papitou, in *La Sirène des tropiques* (1927), too, Baker acts out of selfless devotion for the engineer she loves; and as a fantasy character in the mind of an author in *Princesse Tam Tam* (1935), she reunites him with his estranged French wife. Films about the Foreign Legion, such as *La Bandera* (Julien Duvivier, 1935), *Le Grand jeu* (Jacques Feyder, 1934), or *Sarati le Terrible* (1923 and 1937) about a settler in Algiers, fit the same pattern.

Postcards from the Edge: Cinema's Precursors

Illustrated magazines and picture postcards first appeared in 1889 and relied on new industrial technology, photo-offset printing. Transitional intermediaries, they linked early forms of vicarious tourism, such as orientalist painting, exotic novels, and travel literature, with colonial film. The Paris Exposition of 1900 inaugurated the postcard's golden age, with 100 million printed by 1910 in an industry that employed thirty thousand workers. Identified with tourism, postcards (*carte postale*) purveyed exotic and erotic images of North Africa. But the cards were also put to other uses: unions used their own images to win support for strikes, and the Communists distributed grisly photos of French atrocities as graphic protests against the Rif War of 1925. Colon and French photographers—often war veterans like Marcellin Flandin, whose career spanned the 1920s—shot photos that were reproduced in dozens of French and Algerian printshops, sold to tourists and settlers, mailed back to France to be placed on mantels or in desk drawers of French homes. As growing numbers of French tourists and Algerian migrant workers crisscrossed the Mediterranean, so did a brisk trade in postcards. The market for cards in the North African tourist trade lagged behind, but expanded with, the French market.[5]

Postcards whetted consumer appetites for exotic documentary films. The anthropologic "Scènes et types," a particular category of card shot on location, depicted scenes of daily life emphasizing the timelessness and backwardness of Arab North Africa. Postcards and illustrated magazines—French versions of *National Geographic*—brought readers information about non-European life; but images of preindustrial technology, poverty, and quaint, anachronistic or barbaric customs distanced the viewer psychologically and emotionally. Studio stills prefigured narrative fiction film, their dressed sets telling stories in one frame instead of many. Native women with breasts exposed were paired in suggestively Sapphic poses and rendered acceptably scientific by intermingling the pornographic with more sedate images. Senders often ignored their content, since they were no more explicit or lewd than those circulating in France. The same banal greetings are found on them as on other cards.

The postcard illustrates the colonial double bind: "picturesque" Algerians depended on tourism, which invented the picturesque, and tourism perpetuated the "backwardness" that legitimated French dominance. Even the most naturalistic of the "Scènes et types" were posed, with a stultifying formality that hints at the consumer's need for these impostures. Behind the cards, especially the nudes, lurked colonial coercion. Products of the dislocated margins of native society, the women faced a camera, behind which leaned a white male photographer. Behind him, figuratively speaking, we can glimpse the colonial official, the officer, the gendarme, and the disruption of native life.[6]

> The heyday of picture postcards, 1900–1930, corresponds to the height of settler colonialism in Algeria, to the period when the settlers established their *de facto* hegemony in Algerian affairs. . . . On the postcards we see inscribed the rigidification of social boundaries. In constituting the Algerian subjects as objects, "scènes et types" by their nature are stereotypes, the cards testify to a hardening of colonial arteries.[7]

The virtual gendarme image is helpful in seeing how photographers were able to cater to the male fantasies expressed in pornographic cards, the desire to remove the veil, to penetrate the harem. Filmmakers refashioned the pictorial strategies the photographs derived from orientalist painting. Images from postcards, magazines, and expositions, combined with the plots of colonial novels, created a potent synergy. The Arab woman, the *moukère,* was "manless," instantly available and giving herself entirely, sacrificing even her life for the colonizer. This myth supplanted myths of "empty lands" and bold pioneers, which held little appeal to French working people, recently departed from farms and villages.

Under close scrutiny, the orientalist male fantasy crumbled. "Beautiful from afar, horrible from close by, Africa deceives the white: this theme of 'lost illusions' is ubiquitous."[8] Early feminists of the 1890s subjected the status of women in Algeria to such scrutiny. Hubertine Auclert lived in Algeria and concluded that seventy years of French rule had degraded the moukère. She argued that if Frenchwomen had the vote, they would not permit child marriage, which she condemned as "child rape," or polygamy "in a territory under French control." An advocate of the vote for Arab women as well as men, she opposed the racial superiority of the colons and, astutely, the nostalgia of the Arabophiles, who saw Muslim society as encased in amber. Yet her campaign hardly affected colonial policy and expressed French feminists' own blind spots, since conditions endured by Frenchwomen, who could not vote, hold property, or take a job without permission from a father or husband, were no shining example. Nor did solidarity arise with workingwomen, in factories or households, who faced the threat of hard times forcing them into prostitution.[9] If anything, Auclert's critique reinforced the perceptions of Muslims' "immutable otherness" and hence the collective identity of the settlers as racially and culturally superior.

Faithful to the Radical Party, which after the Dreyfus Affair shifted from antiimperialism to defense of the empire, Auclert adopted its rhetoric of moral conquest, as did socialist leaders such as Jean Jaurès. An associate of Marguerite Durand, publisher of the daily *La Fronde,* Auclert was among those who preached a "relational" or "maternalist" feminism. Emancipation would arise from society honoring women's existing gender roles as wives and mothers. They pleaded for suffrage on grounds that they could carry out peaceful penetration and the civilizing mission more effectively than white men. Isabel Eberhardt, the "passionate nomad" who lived and died in North Africa at the turn of the century, adopted Arab male dress and was recruited by Lyautey for intelligence missions in Morocco. She exemplified feminism's link with colonial advocates of indirect rule. Just such a strange alliance produced *Itto* (1934), a film directed by a French feminist with a Berber woman as a central character, played by a French actress who spoke the Chleuh dialect.[10]

The paternalistic vision of European women engaged in "moral conquest" was shunted aside after the settlers had forced Lyautey into retirement in the midst of the Rif War (1925–26) and expanded the domain of direct racial rule. Filmmakers wore out their welcome in Morocco and returned to Algeria for locations to shoot their colonial films. The shift began in the late 1920s, by which time the bobbed-hair flapper *(garçonne)* had aroused the ire of both Roman Catholics and maternal feminists: the former were ridden with "abortion anxiety" and the latter targeted the "new woman" for egocentrically refusing to do her duty as wife and mother. Eugenicists joined the backlash, accusing the flapper of neglecting the "biological regeneration" of France and forfeiting the population race with Germany. As the boyish flapper-look went out of fashion and a softer, more traditionally feminine style came into vogue, colonial film rewrote the racial roles of female protagonists. Selflessness in native women was taken for granted by writers and directors, whose European male characters pursued the white woman to the point of self-destruction. Racial coding thus reinforced film's harshly critical view of Frenchwomen, sent them a disapproving message about their comportment, issued silent appeals and veiled threats to return to traditional ways, and heralded a broad reassertion of rigid gender roles.[11]

Dark-skinned rescuers and white destroyers racialized the love-triangle cliché of melodrama. In *L'Atlantide* (1921, 1932), a serving girl, Tanit-Zerga, sacrifices her life helping a French Legion lieutenant, Saint-Avit, escape the clutches of Antinéa, Atlantis's Circe-like white queen. In *Le Grand jeu* (1934), Jacques Feyder used one actress to play two roles—a Parisian sophisticate who abandons the hero and a "nativized" prostitute in Sidi Bel Abbès, Algeria, headquarters of the Foreign Legion, who tries to save him. The one actress/two roles strategem suggested that racially charged polarities resided in each woman, as did the nearly universal use of French actresses in walnut-stain makeup to play non-white roles. Julien Duvivier's *Pépé le Moko* (1937) both transcended and reinforced the cliché, while other poetic realist films of the Popular Front era bristled with hostility to white women even in the absence of a colonial plot. Duvivier's *La Belle equipe* (1936), an allegory of the Popular Front, featured a self-centered woman who destroys male bonds of solidarity. A similar character appeared in *Gueule d'Amour* (Jean Grémillon, 1937). Male protagonists, played by the proletarian populist everyman Jean Gabin, are supported by friends in a "united front" of white male bonding. Grémillon's film ends with Gabin's character murdering the woman after she seduces his best friend, an army buddy who then helps him escape to Algeria to join the Foreign Legion.[12]

French misogynists shared with Muslim patriarchs the view of female sexuality as powerful and destructive, an irony lost on French orientalists, who found the safest women farthest from home. Barred from access to the Muslim private sphere, they extrapolated what was known of family life in the eighteenth- and nineteenth-century Egyptian and Palestinian urban upper class to conclude that Muslim women were powerless child-brides isolated from public life and denied status as consenting adults. In fact, endogamous cousin-marriage, retention of property rights by women, even their role as bearer of *'ird*, the burden of family honor and shame, gave women power in the home. Both aspects of this blind spot served the ends of white-male dominance.[13]

Beauty and the Beholder's Eye

Orientalism counterposed the imperviously unchanging Arab family with the West's dynamic family. American mass production, consumerism, and advertising introduced new standards of female beauty conforming to the new age. Magazines targeted at movie fans ran photo-essays of beauty contests, which "although never so widespread as in the United States, had become a French institution by the mid 1930s, as had the [movie] fan club."[14] Photos of judges running measuring tapes over women's bodies, looking for "ideal" proportions, and rows of disembodied legs and torsos in bathing suits testify to Fordist standardization. Publicity photos of French and American starlets suggest templates restamping Frenchwomen's looks, and Busby Berkeley musicals evoke spectacles of motorized, industrial-age harems. Arbiters of fashion wrote pompous articles authorizing a new regime of women's style using the commandist, passive voice of official decrees. After Anita Loos's *Gentlemen Prefer Blondes* appeared in 1928, France's popular film magazine *Ciné-Miroir* launched a "Grand Inquiry" and found that "it is decidedly an avowed fact, a consecration: men prefer blondes." In interviews, male directors and actors suggested that blonde hair and complexions showed up better in black-and-white photography, as if modern technology conspired to favor white skin.[15] Racial assumptions overtly surfaced when beauty discussions turned to *"le tanning"*: "See the charming Rochelle Hudson [photo], her brown color adorned by the sun's rays to a beautiful coppery hue which the young women now envy. But she protects her charms from remaining in the sun too long, because while one looks for warm tones, those tones are no longer liked [in fashion] which make us look like métisses."[16]

Beauty standards erased nonwhite women or patronizingly exploited them for colonial ends. At the Paris Exposition Universelle of 1937, there was a "Miss Outre Mer" beauty contest to determine the most beautiful métisse of "France overseas": the winner, from Guadaloupe, was described as having "skin as pale as ivory," but one contestant was disqualified as too white to compete. Color was not so much the issue as which races were mixed; felicitous combinations would help France overcome her population gap with Germany. Before 1914, General Mangin had conceived of a *force noire,* native troops drawn from the empire, as "economical cannon fodder." At the Paris Peace Conference, Premier Clemenceau had insisted on the "unlimited right of levying black troops to assist in the defense" against Germany. Nationalist French eugenicists Alexis Carrel and René Martial searched for the best races with which to interbreed to close the birth-rate gap with Germany. They condemned "racial anarchy" but believed in good as well as bad racial combinations. Algerians were beyond the pale, so to speak. Among colons, one in four marriages joined couples of different nationalities, but rarely did they intermarry with Arabs, Berbers, or Jews.[17]

In keeping with the settler outlook of most colonial novels, films preached the perils of miscegenation. *L'Esclave blanche* (Augusto Genina, 1927), *La Symphonie pathéthique* (Mario Nalpas, 1928) and *La Croix du Sud* (André Hugon, 1931) expand the theme of white women fleeing the tyranny of an Arab husband set forth in 1911 by Charles Géniaux's novel *Le Choc des races*. After the Yen Bay Insurrection of 1931, novels about Indochina featured interracial lovers falling from grace. The influential pied-noir novelist Jean Vignaud published *Maison du Maltais* in 1926, which Henri Fescourt adapted to the screen within the year. It was remade in 1938. Fescourt faithfully followed the novel's plot: a Maltese sponge fisherman living in the Tunisian port of Sfax marries a Bedouin Arab girl and is ruined by his defiance of social convention. The Arab wife raises their son, Matteo, as a Muslim. He, too, meets a Bedouin, Safia, marries, and settles in his father's house, but Safia runs off to Paris with a Frenchman, a dealer in pearls, Chervin. Matteo steals his father's hoard of pearls, follows Chervin to Paris, and uses his wealth to ruin the dealer. Avenged, Matteo takes Safia back to Sfax and sequesters her in his father's house, the House of the Maltese. Pierre Chenal's 1938 remake transformed the story. Safia is a French prostitute, Chervin an archeologist who takes her back to Paris, where she assimilates and becomes a wife befitting a sophisticated intellectual. To protect Safia and his daughter, whom Chervin thinks is his, Matteo nobly sacrifices himself. When he realizes he can neither assimilate nor return home, he commits suicide. Fescourt focused on miscegenation; Chenal, a Belgian Jew by birth, interpreted the story as a tragedy of deracination.[18]

Jean Vignaud's *Sarati* and Incest: Oedipus in Algiers?

In *Sarati le Terrible* (1919), Vignaud's novel about race, displacement, and forbidden sexuality, a pied noir's incestuous feelings undo him. In short order, the novel was turned into a film that was successful enough to inspire a remake in sound. The plot is the quintessential expression of the *pied-noir tragique*, a play for sympathy by dressing up as a tragic figure a most odious colon. Sarati is a petty tyrant lording over downtrodden dockers and coal loaders of the Algiers waterfront, a crossroads of races. He has become rich by exploiting Arab and African laborers as a recruiter–straw boss, shaping up crews for loading coal to fuel ships' boilers, and as a landlord of a cheap *hotel-garni,* or hostel. Brandishing a club that he carries like an extension of his personality, he terrorizes his tenants and workers and wields the kind of power and privilege impermissible in France. The story opens with Sarati in his fifties; his powers have declined, but he is still feared. Remédios, a former mistress, keeps house for him and has raised his orphaned niece, Rose. Now a pretty young woman of sixteen, Rose evokes the one speck of human feeling in Sarati's otherwise brutish life.

A young Breton of aristocratic demeanor becomes a lodger and a coal carrier, the meanest job on the docks. Like many European misfits and dangerous men, Gilbert has entered the shadow world of North Africa to hide, to atone, and to expiate a sin. Sarati instinctively understands this and senses an opportunity for gain. He cleverly exploits his police contacts and ferrets out the secret of Gilbert's past. The young man's near-murderous clash with his brother over a woman was part of a disorderly life of gambling, debt, drunkenness, and debauchery. He disappeared and broke his rich, widowed mother's heart. Sarati sees a way to exploit the information and capitalize on the mother's distress, but the scheme backfires. By keeping Gilbert close to watch him, Sarati brings him into contact with Rose. Her maturing womanly feelings fix on Gilbert; but he is nine years older, and at first he treats her like a child. As they draw closer, Sarati grows jealous, then obsessed, and he declares his desires to Rose. She recoils in horror and flees with Remédios, the housekeeper, to a refuge.[19]

Rose sends for Gilbert, tells him what has happened, and he asks for her hand. Sarati refuses his consent, but Rose holds title to her father's land (originally stolen from the Berber Kabyles, of course) and is independent of her uncle. Sarati relents, gives his blessing, and then discovers that Gilbert has engineered his downfall. Gilbert and the harbormaster Hudelo have invested in two steam cranes and loading machinery; the mechanization, which only incidentally ruins Sarati, will put the coal heavers out of work. The unemployed, says Gilbert, with all the sensitivity of a born colonialist, "are needed more on the land, anyway."[20]

Sarati turns violent in defeat. He contemplates murdering Gilbert, then taking his own life. At the wedding, the Muslims stare as men and women dance together "like dogs." Their severe faces provoke Sarati to a club-swinging rage. Afterwards he embarks on a three-day spree of drunken debauchery in the red-light district, venting his fury on the prostitutes and native workmen. Emerging from his stupor, he wanders to the honeymoon cottage, sees Gilbert walking on the beach, sneaks in to find Rose sleeping, and contemplates murder-suicide to be with her for eternity. Overcome with despair, he slashes his throat instead, crumpling in a heap at the foot of the stairs. As blood oozes to the floor, the last sound he hears is Rose dreamily murmuring Gilbert's name. In the film, Sarati knifes Gilbert in a dramatic battle on the waterfront, but the younger man wins. Sarati drowns himself. Gilbert and Rose are safe.

A pied noir himself, Vignaud propagated the settler cause by implying that the rough work of conquest that lay the ground for the civilizing mission required just such atavistic qualities as his sexually obsessed, abusive colon demonstrates. A lout who ruthlessly exploits every opportunity for gain and dominance, Sarati takes on a patina of tragic nobility under Vignaud's pen. Such brutes were necessary in the early stages of colonial rule; a barbarian, but *our* barbarian, Vignaud suggests. He elicited sympathy for Sarati by telling the story entirely from the colon's point of view. When Remédios returns to the hotel a week after helping Rose escape, she finds Sarati in a sorry state and apologizes for leaving him to do his own cooking and cleaning. From his inverted perspective, Vignaud elevates Sarati's despicable traits to the stature of tragic flaws. Rose's rejection is tantamount to Sarati's treatment of his workers; spurning him strips away his racial superiority and crushes his manhood in one fell swoop. Vignaud then recasts him as a working-class underdog. "How spitefully . . . she had spoken to him! Caesar [Sarati] did not treat Ahmet as badly as she treated him. And so she wouldn't see any more of him? She forbade him to speak to her in the street or on the quay? She was ashamed of him before the coal heavers, was she? There was nothing for him to do but . . . prowl like a dog through the corridors and rooms of his house, among the Kabyles and negroes."[21]

Sarati le Terrible was the first of Vignaud's many colonial novels to win literary prizes and become bestsellers. It was popular enough with French readers to prompt Louis Mercanton to adapt it for the silent screen in 1923, and André Hugon released a remake in the summer of 1937 to an audience familiar with the story and with two other Vignaud novels made into silent films, *Maison du Maltais* (1926) and *Vénus* (1928). Pierre Chenal remade *Maison du Maltais* in 1938 in a poetic realist style. Vignaud wrote a history of Algeria in 1947, and his literary reputation lent credibility to this venture. The cumulative effect of his writings was a cogent message that the pied-noir community's identity and fate were inextricably tied to those of France. Like Pierre Benoit, author of *L'Atlantide*, Vignaud popularized the view that colonial lands were there for the Europeans' taking and that violence was an unavoidable by-product of colonial progress.[22]

The story line of *Sarati* followed a common plot element of silent film and literature of the 1920s that pitted an older man against a younger rival for the affections of a young woman. In such "oedipal narratives," the former bested the latter through superior experience to win the love of a woman young enough to be his daughter. Widespread among the French bourgeoisie since the Renaissance, such marriages continued to be the norm because of the loss of young men in the Great War and "archaic features . . . of gender and family." Women's economic dependency, sequestration from political life, Catholic patriarchy, and the Napoleonic Code reinforced legal inequality and wide discrepancies of power in daily life. Bourgeois society tolerated male adultery and perversely justified state-sanctioned, institutionalized prostitution as reinforcing family life by siphoning off inevitable male lust from "good" women to "bad" ones.[23]

Vignaud added a wrinkle to the plot: real incest presented as a tragic flaw to overcome the reader's repugnance. Incest precluded Sarati's triumph, but by subtly implying that it was preferable to miscegenation, Vignaud introduced the colons' racially polarized worldview. Yet his viewpoint contained a striking blind spot, a peculiarly Mediterranean flavor to Sarati's sexual impulse that strongly indicated the commonality in the cultures surrounding the sea. "Patrilineal endogamy" or "cousin marriage" to the father's brother's daughter (FaBrDa) was more prevalent in Mediterranean cultures than elsewhere in the world. Proscribed by Roman Catholicism, Orthodox Christianity, and Islam, such marriages were tacitly accepted to prevent fragmentation of landholding in a region that for millennia suffered from a dearth of arable land. In his study of Algeria, anthropologist Pierre Bourdieu pointed out that the practice strengthened family ties over larger social units. Women as well as men remained within their kinship group, and a subordinate but semiautonomous female society developed, a closed world that exerted influence through child rearing and magic beliefs expressed through rituals. Women trained children in the formulaic expressions that made up most conversation, set phrases that imparted a dignity and reserve to behavior but hid self and inner feelings from outsiders, even from family, behind a veil of politeness. Despite victimization within this old order, Algerian women carried out "effective, secret and underground resistance" to any modification. Similar gender structures evolved in Calabria and Sicily, characterized by Edward Banfield as "amoral familism."[24]

Vignaud's *Notre enfant, l'Algérie* (1947), like an outdated history of the American West, unrelentingly promoted the myth of brave settlers conquering an "empty land" and marginalized or erased the "natives." Although 90 percent of the Europeans ended up in Algeria's cities, Vignaud described them as "pioneers" and, as with *Sarati*, encouraged sympathy with the settlers' most deplorable acts with the rationale that "the first *colons* were not saints but without knowing it they were heroes."[25] He acknowledged the natives only in their role as the colons' hewers of wood and drawers of water, grinning fools or hapless victims cringing under the clubs of men like Sarati. An anachronism who had outlived his time after serving a valuable purpose, Sarati was Vignaud's tragic figure crushed in the onrush of mechanization.

Vignaud's natives have no life of their own. Like Conrad, whose pen turned the Fang people into the skeletal wraiths of *Heart of Darkness*, Vignaud attended to natives only to contrast their passivity with the dynamism of the Europeans who developed the land. "Timelessness and immobility" characterized the Algiers Casbah. Vignaud remarked that when the Popular Front raised the native minimum wage to European levels in 1936 (from 40–60 francs per day to 70–80), natives stopped working as soon as they had earned enough for subsistence, whereas Europeans finished out the week. He devotes individual chapters to settler heroes: Charles Foucault, General Laperrine, and the Foreign Legion. Algeria was "another California," as illusory a vision as the French view of Morocco as the former "granary of Rome." He alluded to the riot at Sétif on V-E Day (8 May 1945)—the one autonomous native action he described—but omitted the fact that the army and settler vigilantes had killed thousands in the ensuing months. Fueled by land hunger and famine, Sétif had been the native nationalist response to victory over Nazism; French repression dashed all hope of reform. Yet with stunning myopia, Vignaud concluded that "it would suffice to glance at the harvests to be reassured of the future; they announce a new century of prosperity."[26]

Despite differences in point of view, Vignaud's works are bound by a common nostalgia with the film *Itto* (1934), which focused on a native holdover from the past, the Sheik Hamou, who led the resistance to the French in central Morocco from 1914 to 1919, and with *Bourrasque* (The squall) (Pierre Billon, 1935). With its title suggesting a sudden gust of wind blowing over the moral order of the colonial universe, *Bourrasque* represented the debate over colonial policy of assimilation, thinly disguised in a cinema melodrama. Marcel, a young colon, falls in love with a young woman on a ship bound for Algiers. She is Arab, but so completely assimilated that Marcel mistakes her for a Parisienne. Only her name, Ayada, reveals her identity; she is the daughter of an Arab officer of a Spahis colonial regiment and niece of his father's old friend and adversary Belkacem, a *q'aid,* or local judge and notable. Marcel's father, Pierre Bardet, a coarse, brutal patriarch like Sarati, represents the old colonial order and opposes mixing of the races. He has chosen a blonde settler to be his son's bride, and when Marcel refuses to marry her, Pierre banishes him. Yet he respects Belkacem, who is noble and heroic but also represents an outmoded tradition. Contrasting q'aid and colon with the young lovers symbolizes the passing of the old colonialism. Ayada is modern, yet when she steps on Algerian soil she dons her robes to greet her uncle and becomes a moukère again.[27]

To save her son's happiness, Madame Bardet sheds her timid deference to her husband and claims that Marcel is the son of the q'aid. This revelation devastates the old colon, dispossessing him of the son who was to carry on his identity as man, father, and white. Marcel dons Arab clothes, participates in a *fantaisie,* an Arab display of horsemanship, and forgets that he is to meet the young Frenchwoman whom his erstwhile father has arranged for him to marry. Marcel rejects the life the old colon prepared for him and sets out for Oran on his own, and his leap into manhood includes marrying Ayada. If he was the q'aid's son, the union would uphold the quintessentially Mediterranean tradition of cousin marriage, and Marcel would become the bearer not of modernity but of old ways. But the outcome is ambiguous. Belkacem assures Bardet the boy is legitimate and, gravely insulted by his former friend, he turns the colon away from his door forever. In the film's political allegory, the marriage of Marcel and Ayada symbolizes an alliance of liberal colonialists and the native elite. But Ayada is so assimilated that her Arab-ness is present only in her style of dress; Marcel, too, is made by his clothes. The film promises that race mixing and assimilation will solve the colonial problem, but in reality the elder Bardet was not outmoded and remained the most forceful voice of the settlers.[28]

A druidical sense of the magical powers of place pervades the French colonial myth in novels and film and imparts to them a forbidden sexuality that fascinated artists and audiences alike. André Gide's protagonist in *The Immoralist* (1901) is immobilized in Biskra, a town deep in the Algerian heartland: "I had great steadfastness of mind . . . that's what makes real men—I have it no longer. . . . This climate is what's responsible . . . this perpetual blue sky. Here any exertion is impossible, so closely does pleasure follow desire. . . . I can't leave of my own accord. Something in my will has been broken."[29]

Inès, the dark-skinned mistress of *Pépé le Moko,* pleads with her Paris jewel-thief lover to stay with her in the old quarter of Algiers and not make his self-destructive mad dash to the ship to be with the white woman he loves. What have I done wrong? she pleads, and Pépé replies: It's not you, it's this place; it's the Qasbah. In *Maison du Maltais,* the Tunisian Matteo, feeling uprooted when he is forced to remain in Paris, ritualistically kills himself. Julien Duvivier reverses the genders in his 1929 adaptation of *Maman Colibri,* a play from 1904, in which Countess Irène falls in love with her son's best friend, a dashing lieutenant of a colonial regiment of Spahis; their difference in age suggests oedipal incest. They run off to Africa, where he abandons her for a younger mistress. Returning home, she begs her husband's forgiveness and settles down to a normal life of caring for her younger children. Her return to France marks her return to her senses, so to speak, as if a spell has been broken—as if a magical African aura has worn off.[30]

Where *Bourrasque* addressed miscegenation elliptically and *Maman Colibri* and *Sarati* hinted at or gingerly discussed incest, *Simoun* (1933), an obscure film, linked taboo sexuality directly with Africa. Laurency, a colon abandoned by his wife twenty years before, has never seen his daughters. He sends for them. The eldest, Clotilde, resembles her mother so closely that the father loses touch with reality and declares his love to her. She flees into the desert. Laurency's moment of mad desire begins on the night of the start of the season of the *simoun,* the hot, sand-laden wind that blows out of the desert and drives men mad, overwhelming the moderating effects of the *harmattan,* the cool, moist wind from the sea. Similarly, in *L'Atlantide* also, the desert plays a major role. Lieutenant Saint-Avit, hypnotized by the drugs and beauty of the Circe-like queen of the lost city of Atlantis, murders Captain Morhange, his friend, mentor, and father figure. Drawn inexorably back to the scene of his oedipal crime, Saint-Avit disappears into the Sahara in a sandstorm that covers his tracks from his rescuer-pursuers. In French colonial films, the Sahara, heart of light, releases the European soul's heart of darkness.

Themes of miscegenation, patricide, self-immolation, and incest in settler-identified colonial films evoked a moral universe through which settler society expressed its collective will. Possessing the woman and controlling the land, an interactive, metaphorical synergy of dominance, linked white settler to the metropole. Mythic North Africa was a virgin land containing virgin women, the lure of the land being amplified by the allure of the women. The myth stimulated impulses to dominance and overpowered bonds of working-class solidarity. It erased the native male, rendering him invisible, and distracted attention from the harsh reality that both the land and the women were "not virgin, but widowed."[31]

Settler political leaders could also make Muslim men highly visible when it suited their purposes. In their effort to block the reforms of Algerian governance proposed by Senator Maurice Violette, a former governor of Algeria and later Léon Blum's Popular Front minister for colonies, they cited polygamy, unequal inheritance, and sequestration of women as immutable practices of the Muslim male. Paul Cuttoli, senator of the Algerian Département of Constantine, argued that since Muslim law was "based exclusively on the exorbitant and archaic principle of masculinity," Muslim men could never relinquish their male privileges and assimilate, hence never could become French citizens. Cuttoli's concern for Muslim women scarcely meant he had been converted to the ideas of Hubertine Auclert. Feminism's hidden colonialist assumptions left it open to manipulation by *faux féministes* like Cuttoli. His adversaries in the Senate, even Violette, shared his underlying outlook, as evidenced by the way they studiously ignored three obvious points of rebuttal: the Catholic position on divorce contradicted French law, but the law required no Catholic to "repudiate his personal status"; France had conferred French citizenship on Senegalese Muslims who practiced polygamy; and the Code Napoléon harshly subordinated French women. Violette revealed his own paternalism in his claim that "the natives of Algeria know . . . they will not really count as men until . . . [they are citizens] and no longer only subjects." Algerians were denied rights granted to Senegalese because, to hold the loyalty and win the vote of the working-class pied noir, settler elites created a racial regime that conferred on poor whites, not the old Muslim elite, the tasks of social control.[32]

In the 1920s and 1930s, an era when film arguably exercised its greatest influence, interpretation of film texts can reveal the contours of French cultural identity and power relations. Mindful of subaltern as well as dominant readings of such texts, and of the rule that "popular culture can simultaneously subvert and reproduce hegemony," we can employ the device of the "integrated reader" to analyze the films in question. This abstract audience attributes meanings to the text that the reader spontaneously considers perfectly natural but that are derived from the "integration propaganda" unconsciously adopted by writers and directors. In the absence of opinion polling, which began in the late 1930s, audience reception must be extrapolated through film reviews and letters to film magazines. They provide direct and indirect evidence of the ways in which film narratives reflected and influenced political opinion and movements. Colonial film was one of the sources of impressions of the colonies common to all the French—one that the metropole shared with whites in the overseas possessions. Reinforced by the gendered discourse of melodrama, colonial film strengthened awareness of race as defined by the settlers.[33]

The earliest narrative colonial film and one of the first to be remade with sound was *L'Atlantide*. The film obliquely refers to an incident in the Sudan in July 1899, when France was still disturbed by the anti-Dreyfusard coup and the confrontation with the United Kingdom along the Nile. Two junior officers, ordered by Paris to rendezvous with Captain Marchand at Fashoda, spread a reign of terror across the Sahel. The captain in command seems to have gone mad and set himself up as king of Lake Chad. A column commanded by Colonel Maurice Klobb marched east from Senegal to investigate, and the two units met on Bastille Day. The captain ordered his native troops to open fire, and Colonel Klobb died in the first volley. A few weeks later, the two officers were killed by their own men. The second in command was a lieutenant, the son of General Charles Chanoine, the minister of war in Henri Brissot's cabinet who had busily covered up the high command's role in framing Dreyfus and who then abruptly resigned in October 1898, bringing down Brissot's ministry and precipitating the unrest that led to the anti-Semitic riots in France and Algeria. Klobb's murder intensified the debate over civilian-military relations at the heart of the Dreyfus Affair. For the Left, it revealed the evil consequences of the absence of civilian control. The Right believed that the press had seized the opportunity to discredit the army.[34]

L'Atlantide is a "story,"[35] a cultural narrative mixing history and myth, public and private life, fantasy and reality, surrealism and psychology. The tale of a young officer who, under the influence of drugs, the desert, and a mysterious woman, murders his superior, it implanted a paradigm for colonial films that followed. Weaving together on the screen the underlying assumptions of gender, race, and class, it both legitimated and disturbed the social equilibrium of interwar France.

3 | Heart of Darkness, Heart of Light
La Mission Civilizatrice and
Le Cafard in L'Atlantide

The French imperial realm in Africa encompassed the arid and desert regions of the Maghreb, Sahara, and Sahel. Gleaming sun and sand rather than foreboding jungle characterized the "dark" continent in France's imperial "mythistory." Nevertheless, its ideology followed a pattern that contemporary cultural criticism has made familiar: erasure of subjugated peoples' achievements and substitution of derogatory stereotypes that bolstered white superiority.[1] One film that so effectively displaced history with myth it has recast popular culture also has displayed remarkable vitality and longevity. L'Atlantide, based on an equally mythomaniacal novel of the same name, is set in the heart of the vast Sahara. It couples the legend of Atlantis with Foreign Legion officers on a *mission,* a word Roland Barthes called an "imperial manna term." Both ingredients fired the imaginations of French audiences; combined, they were mesmerizing.

The story expressed French fascination with people of color, profound unease with Europeans' place in Africa, and deep fears of the polluting effects of contact on European racial and personal identity. As Chinua Achebe noted in his critique of Conrad's Heart of Darkness, "the West seems to suffer deep anxieties about the precariousness of its civilization and to have a need for constant reassurance by comparison with Africa."[2] And, he might have added, to blame its victims: the term le cafard (homesickness) excused French savageries and produced a white blind spot, a state of denial and willful ignorance of the dark side of colonialism.

The career of Pierre Benoit, who wrote the novel in 1918 and died in 1962, spanned the colonial era from its zenith to the loss of Algeria. His story retains its appeal. Albin Michel continues to publish new editions of the novel and the film was remade for a fourth time in 1992.

35

L'Atlantide: The veiled figure on the poster is a Tuareg nomad. Among the Tuareg, men not women wore veils, mainly as protection against desert sands. This poster announces the 1932 version of the film, made with sound eleven years after the spectacular silent film. It is based on a novel that offers the Tuareg as last claimant to the Berber Myth—that Berbers, as "imperfectly Islamicized" descendants of Europeans, would ally with the French against the Arabs. But the eyes above the veil seem hostile, overshadowing the backdrop map of France's African empire. *Credit:* copyright Galerie Cine-Images, Paris

The story glorifies France's "civilizing mission," excuses colonialism's destructive impact, and superimposes the Greco-Roman myth of Atlantis gleaned from Plato on the Tuareg, the "fierce" nomads who ruled the inner Sahara. The last Berbers to be conquered by France, they were the last repository for the Berber myth. Benoit ignored their Islamic past and rewrote their history to conform to mythology. His story also was an encomium to the martyred White Father missionary Captain Charles de Foucauld, who spent sixteen years among the Tuareg, and as an apology for the Affaire Voulet-Chanoine, an embarrassing colonial excess entangled with both the Fashoda incident and the Dreyfus Affair.

While new editions of the book left the text rooted in its time, the films evolved through successive remakes. The original film premiered in 1921 and was rereleased by the producers in 1928; directed by Jacques Feyder, it faithfully reproduced Benoit's narrative. When Georg Wilhelm Pabst remade the film version in 1932, movies had crossed the silent-sound divide, and he produced English, German, and French versions simultaneously. His script downplayed specifically French aspects of Feyder's screenplay, ascribing Freudian motives to the European characters and stripping the Tuareg of any remaining Berber, Muslim, and Maghrebbin cultural traits. The result was a more racially polarized film than Feyder's, an unintended consequence of Pabst's effort to widen its appeal to German- and English-speaking audiences. But the antipodal racialism also expressed a hardening of race and gender roles, an outgrowth of unconscious pessimism about colonialism's future and Europe's prospects for continued world dominance.

Even to cognoscenti of colonialist fiction, this story is not well known outside of France. As the 1932 film opens,[3] a scholar is delivering a lecture on Plato's Atlantis, speculating that it lies buried in the Sahara rather than under the Atlantic. The camera angle widens, and the viewer sees that he is talking to a radio microphone, not a live audience. The scene shifts to two French officers listening to the broadcast at a desert outpost. Lieutenant Ferrières is skeptical, but Captain Saint-Avit makes an astonishing claim. "I have been to Atlantis . . . two years ago with Captain Morhange. . . . There I killed him." Sent to explore the routes from Tunis south into the Sahara, Saint-Avit continues, they were actually on an intelligence mission to gather information on the Tuareg.

The scene fades to a flashback, and without any further narration Saint-Avit's story unfolds. The two officers (Saint-Avit at that time is a lieutenant) and their guide join a caravan heading into the desert. As they ride their camels, they speculate about the Atlantis legend. Saint-Avit reveals his youthful impulsiveness. Morhange, mature and steady, expresses the view that the Tuareg were once Christians. He wears the cross of a Père Blanc priest, and Benoit modeled him on Charles de Foucauld, an intelligence officer who became a missionary to the Tuareg and was killed by them in 1916. Middle- and long-distance shots of the caravan, the rocking gait of camels, and the open desert intersperse the dialogue, consciously imitating the 1921 film's use of the undulating dunes and craggy rocks, of which one critic said, "There is one great actor in *L'Atlantide,* the sand."[4] An austere, virgin wilderness awaits the intrepid French officers to penetrate and tame with their civilizing hand.

Suddenly their guide points; a shield with a cross-shaped design lies in the sand. "Tuareg!" he exclaims. Saint-Avit rushes off and finds a Targui lying among the rocks. He gives the black-clad figure water, and as Morhange and the guide ride up, the caravan leaves them behind. The Targui seems ill, but as they help him to his camel, he stealthily pulls up his veil. The guide leads them through a gorge to an oasis, where they camp. At dusk, the officers find the guide dead, run through with a spear. When they confront the Targui, he says simply, "he was Châamba; Châamba are enemy." Dependent on the assassin to show them the way, the officers are powerless. That night, they are attacked and, in the flurry of rifle shots and spears, separated. Overwhelmed, Morhange shouts the Legionnaires' cry for aid, "Saint-Avit! A moi!"[5] The screen goes dark.

Saint-Avit regains consciousness in the deep shadows of an underground room and sees the Targui who lured them into ambush kneeling before a small altar. He introduces himself as Cegheir ben Cheik, the only Tuareg man that the movie names. Saint-Avit asks whether he wants a ransom. No, replies Cegheir, you would come back with soldiers and machine guns; you will stay. Saint-Avit stumbles outside into a narrow, winding, windowless street that is typical of precolonial urban design in North Africa and the Middle East. He spies a man in a Legion officer's cape and limps after him, shouting "Morhange!" But it is a Tuareg who turns, laughing. Others squat on the ground, chanting; next to them, an old-fashioned gramophone plays the movie's theme, Offenbach's "Orpheus in the Underworld." This juxtaposition of underground room and angular play of light and shadow in the street suggests Greek myths of Orpheus's descent into Hades or Plato's metaphor of the cave, with the Forms casting their shadows on the walls.[6]

The feverish Saint-Avit faints in the street, and Tanit-Zerga, the queen's servant, helps him back to the room and nurses him. He awakens in a sumptuous room in a palace with a bevy of serving girls who pamper him. A dandified, mustachioed European in formal evening clothes minces into the room. He introduces himself as Count Velosei, hetman of Jitomir, although he hardly looks the part of a Cossack chief. He speaks cryptically of Queen Antinéa. Another European appears, a Norwegian ship captain; how he came to the middle of the Sahara, two thousand miles from any coast, is never explained. Heavily drugged from smoking *kif* (hashish), the sailor mumbles incoherently about when "she" will call for him. He ignores Saint-Avit, but when the guards summon the Frenchman to the queen, in a jealous rage the captain leaps at his rival's throat. Saint-Avit fends off the befuddled man, who warns, "You will finish up just like me."

Saint-Avit enters the queen's chamber; young women, diaphanously clad, dance to the tune of a small orchestra playing cello-like instruments. At the center of the room, Antinéa sits playing chess with Tanit-Zerga, who smiles longingly at Saint-Avit and withdraws. The lieutenant hardly notices her; he is mesmerized by the queen. A pet leopard lying near her snarls and she growls in reply: she is a man-eater and Circe; the kif and hashish give her magical powers over men. Leading Saint-Avit to the chessboard, she bids him play. The music gets wilder as she checks him again and again, losing pieces but in the end checkmating him. Abruptly she leaves, and the scene shifts to the Norwegian ship captain's deathbed. The count directs his funeral; Tuareg pallbearers carry the body through the palace corridors. They bow before the monumental stone bust of Antinéa that is the set's centerpiece, an imitation of Muslim prayer that was inadvertently but deeply offensive to the Tuareg since it implied they were idolaters.

After the funeral, Count Velosei gets drunk and shows Saint-Avit a clipping from *Le Figaro*, dated nineteen years before. It reads, "Tuareg Prince Marries Well-Known Dancer," Clemantinéa. As the Norwegian foretold, Saint-Avit falls under her spell, smokes kif, and begins to murmur, "I have a feeling I shall be called to her today." But unbeknownst to Saint-Avit, the queen has been holding Morhange in the palace and has fallen in love with him. Fretfully, she calls for her African fortune-teller to throw the bones to help her decide what to do. The old crone's reading is a cryptic message that "He will come back." (Only at the end of the film do we discover that it is Saint-Avit, not Morhange, who will fulfill the prophecy.) Antinéa summons Morhange and tries to seduce him. The warrior priest, his cross prominently displayed on his chest, spurns her. European patriarchy triumphs over gynarchy, despite the "unnatural" ruler's Medusan gaze and Circe-like ways. In a rage, she orders Morhange to leave her.

Saint-Avit has witnessed the quarrel from behind a screen without discovering the man's identity, and he emerges as Morhange leaves. Antinéa kisses Saint-Avit seductively, then weeps and says, "if you love me, you will kill the man who has insulted me." As if in a trance, Saint-Avit picks up a mallet, stalks the receding figure, and strikes a mortal blow. He turns over the fallen man and, before Morhange dies, they have one moment of anguished recognition. The young man has killed his elder and replaced him in the affections of a deified woman, a re-enactment of the Oedipus myth. Thus the script cleaves to Greek myth leavened with Freudianism and misogyny.[7] Pabst accented Brigitte Helm's Nordic blonde looks to sustain his classical theme. One critic described her as "hieratic . . . *onduleuse,* capricious, majestic, with an Oriental soul and the fine profile of Athens."[8]

In contrast, Tanit-Zerga, loyal and submissive to her European, helps Saint-Avit escape by disguising him in Tuareg robes and enlists the aid of Cegheir ben Cheik, who, for reasons of his own, provides them with water and camels. As they leave the palace, Saint-Avit notices a little boy playing with an amulet and a cross; the cross is Morhange's. Nearby, a body lies wrapped in a shroud. Saint-Avit pulls back the sheet and sees Morhange's face. Again stricken with grief and remorse, he is led into the desert by Tanit-Zerga. They ride until they run out of water and the camels die. On their last legs, they find a watering hole, but the well is dry and Tanit-Zerga soon dies. He covers her with sand and stumbles on, hallucinatory mirages of oases and the sea clouding his brain. Saint-Avit collapses in the sand, but as the camera focuses on his prostrate form, the cruciform shadow of a low-flying plane passes over him like a benediction. Like the radio in the first scene, this shadow emblematically links him with the modern world and signals that he has regained contact with an outpost of Western civilization.

Astounded by the tale, Ferrières suggests Saint-Avit lie down and rest. But the troubled narrator wanders into the courtyard of the fort just as the *méhari* (the camel cavalry) bring in a captured Targui. It is Cegheir. He greets Saint-Avit with the traditional "Peace be with you." The captain tells the troopers that he knows the man and orders them to release him. As Cegheir rides off, Saint-Avit smiles a secret smile. He is registered as missing at the next roll call, which prompts Ferrières to lead a patrol to look for him. The méhari follow two sets of camel tracks, but the wind picks up and begins to cover the trail. As it builds to a sandstorm, they are forced to dismount, and finally they take shelter behind their camels. Ferrières, his cape whipping in the wind, shouts to the desert, "Saint-Avit! Saint-Avit!" The only reply is the howling wind and blowing sand. The film ends with a shot of the stone bust of Antinéa filling the screen.

Pierre Benoit: Between Berber Myth and Settler Power

Pierre Benoit, whose hand penned the Atlantis-in-the-desert tale, was born in Albi, in the Midi, in 1886. The son of an officer, he was six years old when his father was assigned to North Africa. Pierre spent his formative years in the pied-noir colonial milieu, attending lycée in Algiers. The curriculum of such schools ignored Arabo-Berber history, glorified the French conquest, exhorted native pupils to love France, and reminded the sons of the colons that they bore responsibility for civilizing their lesser brethren. Since European and Muslim children sat in the same classrooms, the double messages reinforced one another through awkward proximity.[9] Benoit's childhood was steeped in stories of French encounters with the Tuareg, the Apaches of the Sahara. The European scramble for Africa had just begun when several Tuareg were brought to Algiers in 1876 under arrest for murder and theft. Their presence caused a sensation. After the charges were dropped, they offered to guide White Father missionaries across the desert to Timbuktu. Bishop Lavigerie agreed, but French and Arab authorities insisted the priests sign waivers before they left Algiers for Ouargla, the jump-off point for the trek. Three months later, the French post at Laghouat confirmed their deaths. Father Louis Richard bought their effects from Arab traders who led him to their graves. Exhumation revealed they had been stabbed, shot, then decapitated, which a Muslim would do only to an infidel: dismembered, a Muslim was unable to enter heaven and would haunt his murderer forever. Luring Europeans to their deaths in the deep desert became a Tuareg modus operandi. The next victims were the men of a military mission dispatched by the French government in 1880 to survey a route for a trans-Saharan railway to link Algeria with France's West African colonies.

The nomadic caravanners, not surprisingly, saw this expedition as an invasion. Tuareg guides led Colonel Paul Flatters and his men far off-coùrse, exhausted their supplies, and drew them into an ambush. The colonel was killed and all the camels captured. Eighteen hundred miles from the Mediterranean, the soldiers could find neither food nor water, and the eleven remaining Europeans died eating poisoned dates, a false Tuareg peace offering. Out of seventy-seven Senegalese *tirailleurs* (riflemen), a handful of survivors straggled back to Tunis. Their confession that they cannibalized their dead to fend off starvation traumatized the French public. Saharan exploration, henceforth associated with the Flatters party's grisly fate, stopped for fourteen years.[10]

The French army finally breached the Sahara from the south. Timbuktu, the historic entrepôt of the caravan trade at the Bend of the Niger, the northernmost point of river's arc, fell to Colonel Eugène Bonnier. The loss of this vital center of what remained of desert commerce prompted a Tuareg counterattack in January 1894 in which Bonnier and one-half of his men died. With Anglo-French rivalry in Africa heating up, perennial indifference to colonial affairs turned to zeal, inflating the colonial lobby's influence in the French parliament. A shady adventurer, the marquis de Morès, generated momentum for wider engagement in the region, building prestige for the anti-Semitic groups that backed him by organizing an expedition that left Algiers in 1896 to complete Flatters's route. His party was lost in the desert, never heard from again, and apparently shared Flatters's fate. Bowing to growing demands to avenge Bonnier and Morès, the army assigned General Louis Archimbaud to retake the Niger Bend. Amid acclaim for the general's pledge to "kill as many Tuareg as possible," another expedition was sent to seize Lake Chad, and Captain Jean Baptiste Marchand set out from his base in the Congo to capture the eastern Sudan. Arriving at Fashoda in July 1898, just before the battle of Omdurman, Marchand confronted the much larger Anglo-Egyptian expedition and almost precipitated a war. The Fashoda Incident overlapped the Dreyfus Affair, producing a general political crisis in fin de siècle France.[11]

Swept into the ebb and flow of great power rivalries, the Tuareg became the object of the Berber myth. This self-serving array of half-truths concocted by French advocates of indirect colonial rule convinced the metropole policymakers that the Berbers hated their former overlords, the Arabs, and held an affinity for Christianity that made them potential allies of France's colonial enterprise. A faction of the colonial lobby that came to be led by Marshal Louis-Hubert Lyautey, the resident-general of Morocco, composed of military officers, civilian bureaucrats, and a few liberal-minded colons, used the myth to justify ruling through the traditional elites and a policy of paternalistic regard for Islamic culture. Inspired by the idea of *la plus grande France* and "100 million Frenchmen," buoyed by Lyautey's success in "housebreaking" the old elite,[12] proponents of indirect rule gained support, but the Saharan uprisings in 1916, the protracted Rif War of 1921–26, and Lyautey's forced retirement were disillusioning. The search for protégés to assist overextended colonial ambitions slowed.[13]

Lyautey ruled Morocco by meticulous research of local customs and dispensation of favors to manipulate the rural tribes. However, his tactics supplemented but never supplanted military occupation. The other faction of the *parti colonial,* Algerian settlers and their allies in the metropole, advocated direct settler rule. Although they referred to themselves as whites, the settler definition of race deemphasized genetic phenotypes, such as hair texture, melanin content, and facial features, that Anglo-American white supremacists employed to differentiate categories they themselves had invented. French racialism drew on the ideas of right-wing ideologues like Louis Marin, who posited True France, the *pays réel* rooted in the "soil" of rural life, as opposed to the *pays légal* of sordid Third Republic politics. North Africa's colons claimed that innate cultural superiority justified extending privileges to all European settlers, even the poorest pied noir, and excluding all natives from citizenship. The wealthy colon elite elevated the polyglot immigrants from Spain, Italy, Portugal, and Malta to racially superior status and drew them into a united front against native equality. Together they blocked any effort to reform Algerian governance or differentiate natives by class or status, a costly intransigence since it hampered the army's ability to control the outback through the use of Lyautey's methods of manipulation and favoritism.

By incorporating the Berber myth into their fantasy, the author and directors of *L'Atlantide* entered a contested political terrain. The myth itself had a history; a variety of interest groups had modified it to justify their positions on the nature of colonial rule. The French army first encountered the Berbers of the Kabyle, the highland littoral southeast of Algiers. During Abd el-Qadr's war of resistance (1830–47), the Kabyles had remained aloof, prompting military and colonial circles to imagine them as potential allies. Ethnologists, noting the prevalence of red hair and green eyes among Kabyles, concluded that they descended from the Celts and hence were cousins to "nos ancêtres les Gauloises." Roman Catholics like Bishop Lavigerie, who had delivered his priests into the clutches of the Tuareg, believed the Berbers had been Christians whom the Arabs had converted by the sword and who would return to the fold. But missionaries failed to win even a handful of converts, discouraging Catholic Kabylophiles. The Second Empire sought its allies within the Arab elite, and the Third Republic turned to the settlers, offering them virtual home rule in return for support against the monarchists. Settler domination provoked the al-Mokrani revolt, whose epicenter was Kabylia, which again became a guerrilla stronghold in the 1954–62 war of independence.[14]

Traces of another myth can be found in *L'Atlantide:* the widely accepted Hamitic hypothesis ascribing African achievement to the work of "Hamites" from Europe or Asia. In one regard, if the Berbers were the long-lost Hamites awaiting Europe's redemption, the myths complemented each other. On the other hand, Count Arthur Gobineau's writings had raised the fear that African primitive blood was more potent than the blood of the outsiders and had caused them to degenerate. For Pierre Loti, too, colonialism posed the danger of polluting the white race. In *Roman d'un spahi,* he associated whiteness with inherent moral superiority and described his soldier, Peyral, as "de pure race blanche." Everything African was black in countenance and soul. Peyral's Khassonké mistress, Fatou-gaye, is "roughly equivalent to his yellow-haired dog."[15] Loti judged Hindu, Arab, and Persian imitation of the West as a mark of decline, since these peoples had achieved high civilization before Europe. But "Kaffir and Hottentot" had no culture, so imitating the West was progress for them.[16] If the Tuareg in *L'Atlantide* were a degenerate race of whites, their decline took place in the decade between Feyder's and Pabst's films. The former accorded them a far more active role in his film than the latter.

As the settlers consolidated their rule of Algeria, they Africanized Islam and cast down Muslims into the "people without history." Some colons and a few pan-Arabists declared that there were no Berbers at all, only successive waves of Arab migration; Berber language was corrupted Arabic, and "a Berber is simply a man who has never been to school." Others saw no Arabs, only Berbers Arabized to varying degrees.[17] In either case, the settlers attributed all civilization in the Maghreb to the Romans and claimed the empire as their patrimony. In his handbook on colonial warfare, studied by all French officers, General Bugeaud asserted that his "civilized" infantry campaign had defeated Abd el-Qadr's cavalry, proving the efficacy of "Roman" over "barbarian" tactics. Streets in Algerian cities were renamed for French or Roman generals. Tourist postcards ignored the sites of the Islamic past. The colonial city government of Bône (Annaba) restored Saint Augustine's church at Hippo and let Muslim quarters decay. Even in Lyautey's Morocco, settlers caught the Roman fever and pressed for a disastrous agricultural policy promoting wheat production. The rationale—Mauritania had been the "granary of Rome," but the Muslims had let it go to rack and ruin—defied historical evidence that Arabs were among the world's most proficient dry farmers. By erasing the Islamic period and banishing natives into historical limbo, the settlers legitimated their claims as heirs of Rome and hence as the master race.[18]

The Tuaregs and the Missionary: The Story of Charles de Foucauld

The French encounter with the Tuareg resurrected the Berber myth in a form most palatable to the settlers, since the people of the desert were far removed from Algeria's centers of population and power. In black robes, turbans, and veils, their gazelle-hide shields decorated with crosses, they evoked French fantasies of medieval Christian knights. *Tuareg* is an Arabic word meaning "abandoned by God," a testament to their protracted resistance to Islam and Arab encroachment. Tuareg call themselves Kel Tagelmoust, "the people of the veil," since men not women cover their faces.[19] Tuareg Berber and Bedouin Arab caravans plied the Sahara by half a dozen routes, one of them through the Hoggar Mountains. For a millennium, the caravans linked Mediterranean and West African cities. According to Ibn Khaldun, by 1400 A.D. the nomads made these annual crossings using more than twelve thousand camels on each route.[20]

The transatlantic slave trade diverted African trade to the coasts, and nineteenth-century European imperialism disrupted the African termini of Saharan commerce. Between 1898 and 1903, Britain destroyed the states of Hausaland on the lower Niger, and in 1903 France captured the Sudanic city-states of Kano and Sokoto, also dividing the thousand-year-old state of Kanem-Borno with Germany, completing West Africa's economic reorientation. Impoverished Saharans such as the Tuareg turned outlaw in response to this marginalization, and the decline of Ottoman suzerainty over the Sahara and the Barbary coast accelerated the slide toward anarchy, banditry, and piracy. With their inaccessible mountain strongholds as bases, the Tuareg used their knowledge of the desert to dominate inhabitants of the Sahara's fringes, exacting tribute and raiding or trading depending on which offered the best return. Tuareg clans exacted *ghefara,* or tribute, from travelers for safe passage, but did not honor one another's protection. Rather than storming caravans by frontal assault, raiders infiltrated them, learned their weaknesses, and isolated victims. As in the case of the Flatters mission and the fictional *L'Atlantide,* they sometimes offered themselves as guides to those low on food and water, then led them into ambush. Caravans were loosely knit, and in order to save their own skins, the *kofflé* (line) would abandon a caravanner who fell victim.[21]

French attempts to impose order worsened the chaos since the French ignored signs that the anarchy of the desert stemmed from long-term economic decline. To conquer the Sahara, the army assigned General Henri Laperrine; he created the méhari, and for seven years this camel corps fought the Tuareg for control of the central Saharan oases. The Ahaggar clans submitted in 1905 after several stinging defeats, and the French helped Moussa ag Amastane (in Arabic, Musa Wa'q al-Mustah), leader of the peace party, become king *(amenoukal),* by promising to restore trade and prosperity. After freeing the African slaves and the *harratin,* the serfs who had maintained the *foggaras* (watercourses), the French sank artesian wells, which flooded the oases, bred malaria, and lowered the water table. Date palms, whose fruit was the staple food of the oasis dwellers, began to die. Garrison troops strained the oases' resources, since the army requisitioned thousands of camels to carry supplies and mount patrols, further impoverishing the inhabitants and thus fomenting more banditry.[22]

As the guns of August sounded in 1914, Egyptian nationalist Mohammed Ali Duse noted in an editorial, "It may be that the non-European races will profit by the European disaster. God's ways are mysterious."[23] Germany smuggled money and supplies to the Riffians, encouraging them to raid French Morocco. Libyan Arabs ambushed an Italian army of four thousand men in March 1915. Native auxiliaries turned on them and few survived. Captured arms were distributed throughout the desert, and fighting spread from the upper Nile to the Atlantic. Moussa's Ahaggar, fed up with broken French promises, joined the insurgents of the Ajjer Tuareg clans, who with the aid of Turkish officers had already begun to besiege French forts. French outposts were withdrawn to the oasis garrisons, and Laperrine, France's expert in desert warfare, was reassigned from the Western Front back to the Sahara. His troops stamped out resistance by 1918, although southern Tunisia did not submit until 1921. The general died in a plane crash in the Sahara in 1920.[24]

Benoit's Captain Morhange, a name that recalled a battlefield of the early months of the Great War, is modeled on Captain Charles de Foucauld, the Père Blanc missionary and former colonial cavalry officer who died in the 1916 Tuareg uprising. A classmate of Laperrine at Saint-Cyr, in 1883–84 Foucauld had disguised himself as a Jewish merchant to reconnoitre secretly the interior of Morocco for army command in Algeria. He resigned his commission, took vows, and in 1901, set up a hermitage at Tamanrasset, which doubled as a French listening post in the Ahaggar. In 1916, Foucauld refused to repair to the French fort fifty miles to the south. Saharan troops fortified his dwelling with a moat and drawbridge and left him well armed, but despite the precautions, a Tuareg *harka* captured him on 1 December 1916. Undoubtedly, the Tuareg intended to take Foucauald hostage, but they were surprised by a French patrol and, in the ensuing firefight, the young Targui guarding the prisoner panicked and shot him dead. The imperialist press spared the details and made him a martyr to the civilizing mission.[25]

The story of Foucauld's dissolute youth and call to God in middle age invited hagiography. The French Right canonized him, and Benoit's invocation of his legend was only the first of many. Léon Poirier made a film of his life, *L'Appel du silence*, with full access to family papers and 100,000 francs raised through small donations from thousands of French Catholics. Although it premiered in 1936 amid the leftist upsurge surrounding the victory of the Popular Front, the film drew the second highest box-office attendance of the year.[26] The dutifully reverential reviews described Foucauld as "one who understood the soul of the native and became the victim of fanatical murderers." Foucauld had vigorously promoted the belief that Berbers were crypto-Catholics because, in their "associational" form of worship, *m'rabout* (marabout) saints interceded for sinners. To Foucauld, Islam was France's enemy, and he urged a Tuareg policy emphasizing conversion. He deplored the use of Châamba Arabs to conquer the Tuareg, which inadvertently encouraged the spread of a reformed, "Protestant" Islamic orthodoxy requiring that the Qur'an be read in the original Arabic. Among the Tuareg, the Châamba presence propagated both faith and language, and Foucauld compiled a dictionary of Tamahak to preserve and protect Tuareg cultural life from corrosive, corrupting Arab influences.[27]

Foucauld was wrong; the Berbers proved as impervious to Christianity as the Arabs. By his own admission, he converted only three people in his fifteen years in the desert: an elderly woman slave, a dying infant, and a male teenager. His abrasive, antisocial, and ascetic personality probably got in the way of proselytizing, but other Christian missionaries, too, had little success among Muslims, who tended to see the doctrine of the Trinity and the divinity of Jesus as inconsistent with monotheism. The White Fathers and Sisters, the Pères Blancs and Soeurs Blanches, working among the Kabyles abandoned the goal of conversion by 1900 in favor of mutual understanding and education.[28]

Benoit's Eclectic Mythology of the Sahara

From the pied-noir milieu, Benoit extracted a concoction of facts, legends, and stereotypes about the Tuareg and mixed them with Greco-Roman mythology. He became an amateur archaeologist, and in 1906 did his military service in a Zouave (colonial infantry) regiment. On leave, he indulged his avocation by inspecting Roman, Christian, and pre-Roman ruins in the Algerian desert. He attended the University of Montpellier, where his allegiance to empire and preoccupation with Christian devotional ideals took root. Arriving in Paris in 1910, he fell in with right-wing politico-literary circles and became a protégé of Louis Barthou, Charles Maurras, and Léon Daudet. While he never joined the Action française, he was an ardent sympathizer and dedicated his first book to its leading light, Maurice Barrès.

Benoit was mobilized in August 1914 and sent to the front. Many young writers of his circle died under fire, but after months in the trenches Benoit fell ill and was forced to spend the spring of 1915 in hospital. While recuperating, he wrote his first novel, *Koenigsmark,* which reflected the Manichean, anti-German views of his literary and political circle. Benoit finished *L'Atlantide,* his second novel, just after Armistice Day. It struck a resonant chord with a wide audience that welcomed escapist fare as a relief from the war's nightmares. The imagined Sahara and its denizens fascinated the public, and the novel became a bestseller.

Marcel Prévost, editor of the *Revue de Paris*, serialized the book, and with the support of Barrès it won the Académie française prize for 1919.[29]

The most striking character of *L'Atlantide* is Antinéa. To prevent discovery of her dystopian Shangri-la, the Circe-like queen captures, seduces, bewitches, and kills European explorers and turns them into electroplated statues. She is so reminiscent of the title character in H. Rider Haggard's *She* that Benoit was accused of plagiarism. But Benoit insisted that his inspiration was the funerary statue of Cléopâtra Séléné, queen of Numidia, who was the daughter of Marc Antony and Cleopatra VII, the last Ptolemy to rule Egypt. Benoit had come across her tomb on one of his youthful archeological trips. The man-devouring white woman became a fixture of his subsequent forty novels; each of them has a lead female character whose name begins with the letter *A*, to commemorate his native Albi and as a cryptic symbol of Eve, the Alpha woman, source of man's mortality and immortality. Here, too, Benoit anticipated social stresses of the 1920s, when conservative commentators railed at the bobbed hair and short skirts of the French flapper, accusing them of undermining the family and ruining France.[30]

Benoit's literary fantasy tapped French desires for escapism, stirred unnamed fears of a deracinated, unmoored gender system, and stimulated a familiar male colonial obsession with racializing womanhood. The popularity of this mixture of escapism and sexual anxiety that marked all of Benoit's work can be judged by the number of screen adaptations, and by that criterion Benoit rates as the most popular writer between the wars. Five of his novels became silent films, three of them remade in sound versions during the 1930s, two remade again in the 1950s. Two more novels and a movie script joined his film credits in the 1930s, although the settings were more exotic than colonial. Benoit's output outdistanced even the perennially popular works of Emile Zola and Pierre Loti.[31]

Beginning in January 1918, Benoit had done some cursory research, reading Plato's *Critias*, orientalist scholarship on the Tuareg, and histories of Christian North Africa. He cast aside the Tuareg's own legends of sirenlike women who lured travelers into magical mountains whose peaks moved around and married each other. Elaborating a synthetic mythology that imagined Plato's Atlantis swallowed by sand, not sea, he drew on the Hamitic hypothesis to depict the desert-dwelling Tuareg

The two posters for the silent-film version of *L'Atlantide* (1921) were these unusual art nouveau/art deco portraits of Antinea, the Mistress of Atlantis; by Manuel Orazi (d. 1934), they have the look of works by Beardsley and Klimt. These posters emphasize the erotic aspects of the story; by contrast, the sound version's poster has a decidedly imperial focus that suggests African hostility to Europe. *Credit:* copyright Galerie Cine-Images, Paris

as descendants of the mythical kingdom's inhabitants. Stripping the Tuareg's historical and cultural identity, he made them the human backdrop that lent exotic reality to his fantastic storyline.[32]

Films Made and Remade

Feyder's *L'Atlantide* reawakened fascination with the Berber myth, and film reviews reinforced the image of the *indigènes* as "a race who evoke the Tuareg, horsemen of unknown origin, of noble blood, both European and Asiatic."[33] One critic claimed "the story has become . . . a new myth." Another expressed the hope that the film would inspire French pioneers, evoke a desire to leave "our narrow horizon, thirst for fresh air, escape toward the *bled*."[34] Mistinguett, the famous *chanteuse réaliste*, or torch singer, popularized the story in a song.[35] Feyder's pathbreaking film, the first feature shot on location (although on the Sahara's northern rim, not in the inaccessible Ahaggar), cost a million dollars to produce but was such a box office sensation it quickly grossed immense profits and started a wave of filmmaking in North Africa. Almost every silent movie with a colonial theme was remade with sound in the 1930s.[36]

Pabst's 1932 version departed from Feyder's original film, removing contextual references to France and North Africa. Pabst's dehistoricized story emphasized psychological nuances and ascribed the characters' motivations to internal, emotional drives rather than external commitments to colonial conquest. While distancing his film from overt French colonial propaganda, Pabst's Freudianized interpretation of Greek mythology associated it more closely with broader traits of European racial identity.

Feyder's 1921 film alluded to the Tuareg, Islam, and French valor. Rife with colonial propaganda, it nonetheless explained the motives of the characters more clearly than Pabst's story line. For instance, Feyder's Tuareg guide, Cegheir ben Cheik, tells Saint-Avit he is helping him escape because "the Prophet allows once in one's life duty to give way to pity, and I remember that you have saved my life." Pabst's Cegheir is a murky presence whose motives and actions are cloaked in mystery. Feyder made his Tanit-Zerga more "indigenous" and resolute than Pabst's character. She accomplishes the escape nearly single-handedly, since Saint-Avit's shoulder is injured in an earlier scuffle with the guards. She saddles the camel, lowers Saint-Avit down the wall by rope, and ingeniously signals Cegheir with a firefly lantern. When she dies, a mirage of her birthplace appears before her eyes: "Gaô is there . . . I see it! The town of the hundred domes, of the blue gum trees!" Feyder's palace is grandly Egyptian in style, whereas Pabst used stark, curving, white walls. The strange Russian count in formal evening clothes appears only in Pabst's film, replacing a turbaned Targui librarian who tells the officers that Antinéa is a descendent of Queen Clito of Atlantis and the Queen of Sheba. The electroplated, gilded mummies of her lover-victims that line the corridors of Feyder's palace are all "famously missing" African explorers.

Pabst gave his queen, Brigitte Helm, an accessible, European past and attributed her seductions to psychological powers rather than pharmacology. Pabst's Morhange, played by Jean Angelo in both films, resists Antinéa more out of maturity and firm grip on his European male identity than out of priestly faith and virtue. Pabst ended his film with Saint-Avit following Cegheir as if impelled by an unconscious compulsion; both are swallowed by the sandstorm, while Lieutenant Ferrières' voice—beckoning the captain back to the rational European world, perhaps?—is drowned by the wind. In contrast, Feyder had Ferrières ride off with Saint-Avit and Cegheir, as if on a new mission to the Tuareg.

Pabst's film unfolds like a Freudian dream; the characters may be all in Saint-Avit's mind, expressions of his own personality. Freud's interpretations of Greek mythology predominate: the oedipal triangle lies at the core of Pabst's plot. The cave-like cellar in which Pabst's Saint-Avit is imprisoned suggests Freud's adaptation of Plato's cave metaphor. Moreover, the stark, white-walled streets of the Tuareg village, the ominously shadowy palace corridors, the unreal Europeans such as the Russian and the Norwegian replacing Tuareg characters, Helm's pale beauty . . . all these inflect Pabst's Freudian frame of reference with the racial dichotomy of "primitive" versus "civilized" minds. Pabst reserves complex emotions and motivations for the European characters, as if only a "complex" society breeds complex minds susceptible to complexes. He reduces the Tuareg to automaton palace guards, inscrutable denizens of the village, and dancing girls whose motives are unreadable. He attributes the simplest motives to the two natives who speak: Cegheir kills the guide because he is "enemy"; he will not ransom the officers because they will bring more soldiers; he allows Saint-Avit to leave to pay back the debt of saving his life; and the reference to Islamic law is downplayed. Tanit-Zerga's feelings are similarly simplified: gone is her longing for home that in Feyder's film gave nuance to her reasons for helping Saint-Avit; in the Pabst version, she is simply a colored girl who automatically falls for the first white man she sees, not the distant Morhange whom the queen has reserved for herself but the younger man closest to her in age.[37]

The circumstances under which the two directors worked, as well as idiosyncracies of style, determined the results of their efforts. Feyder had been a newcomer when he began his project, and his producers at Aubert studios had blanched at his estimates of what the extravaganza would cost. They kept strict control of his budget and warned him against tampering with Benoit's plot, which was still fresh in the minds of the French public. Feyder's three-hour epic thus faithfully recreated Benoit's novel. The actors had arrived in Algiers with the novel in hand, but Stacia Napierkowska, Feyder's Antinéa, had given him headaches. A lithe dancer when he hired her, she had arrived on location thirty pounds overweight and had to be filmed under wraps, so to speak. Her sensuality contrasts with Helm's cold remoteness, which was one way in which Pabst's work lacked "Frenchness." His seventy-five-minute film was made simultaneously in French, English, and German versions, a common practice during the early sound era, when invading

U.S. subsidiaries set the tone of movie making in Europe and before the triumph of sound allowed a distinctive, national French cinema to re-emerge.[38] Given the feelings of the immediate postwar period, Feyder had approached the matter of one French officer murdering another circumspectly, soothing ruffled patriotism by blaming the crime on *le kif* and *le cafard*. Pabst may have applied Freudian symbolism to kif. Antinéa induces dependency through the suckling-like act of smoking, an oral fixation and attachment to the mother's breast, as well as the chemical effects of the drug. In a state of regression, Saint-Avit cannot restrain his id. His murderous rage unleashed, he reverts to the savagery that Freud and ethnologists of his day associated with the "primitive mind."[39]

Although the critics proffered high marks to both films for verisimilitude, neither was shot where the events were supposed to have taken place, in the central Sahara. Where they were made helps explain their audience appeal. Working in the deep desert was technically feasible for both directors, but it would have been financially prohibitive, so they took their crews to Touggourt, an oasis town on the northern rim of the true desert. The end of the Biskra-Constantine rail line, it was the jumping-off point for the trans-Saharan rally that Citroen sponsored in 1923 to advertise his cars. Thereafter the town was included on the auto touring clubs' regular Algerian circuit. A nearby fort, whose French complement had been overrun and massacred during the al-Mokrani revolt of 1871, proved ideal for the scenes of Saint-Avit's return to civilization.[40]

The film crews thus joined a stream of wealthy tourists who had been swarming over Algeria for several decades in search of the exotic. André Gide visited Biskra in 1895 and 1896 and was invited to a private, Arab home, where he watched secretly as dozens of African, Arab, and Jewish women exorcised demons by dancing to exhaustion. Invariably, Gide was the only European to witness such intimacies, and he contrasted his experience with the show put on for tourists by the notorious Ouled Nayle—"holy prostitutes" who made their home in Biskra. He suspected that "the paid guides show the [tourists] a trashy Africa in order to protect the Arabs, who like calm and secrecy, from intruders. For I have never met a single one of them in the neighborhood of anything interesting. . . . The hotels are full of travelers, but they fall into the trap set by the quack guides and pay dearly for the falsified ceremonies tricked up for them." Thirty years later, Wyndham Lewis disgustedly deplored the "Baedekered blight" that had descended on the entire region.[41]

In light of these remarks, comments about "primitive natives" who played as film extras sound willfully ignorant. George Root, Pabst's publicity flack, described them as having the "admirable instincts of primitives who felt no self-consciousness under the eye of the camera." Jean Angelo assumed in 1921 that the locals had never seen a camera. The q'aid advised that they be shown a movie to give them an idea of what would be expected. Feyder had one especially flown in from Paris—a sad melodrama that, as he remarked with some dismay, provoked laughter all the way through. But since none of these local men understood French, the film probably bewildered them, and they simply were showing appreciation for the efforts to entertain them. Napierkowska, who was raised in Scutarie near Istanbul and knew some Arabic, had a more open mind. When passing caravans harassed the camera crew and tried to destroy equipment, she noted that the local people believed the *roumi* (infidels) "had no right to steal with images a part of the sky." The vandals seemed well aware of the camera's function. Abd el Kader ben Ali, an Algiers café owner who played Cegheir, shrewdly squeezed Feyder for bonuses by threatening to quit at strategic moments.[42] In Morocco, Lyautey's native-affairs officers might have roundly excoriated such stereotypes, but Feyder and Pabst were far removed from their influence. Even in Morocco, a leftist director, Jean Benoît-Lévy, made the film *Itto* in 1934 and promoted the notion that in front of the camera "primitive peoples, . . . like children," were "natural actors." Yet the Berber clan he hired as extras had played in six earlier feature films; they had ten years of acting experience. The Berbers even dubbed his crew *les Ait Cinéma* (the film clan), hybridizing language and the idea of kinship.[43]

Le Cafard

Willful ignorance of colonialism's disastrous consequences, obscured or rationalized by exaggerated emphasis on the positive results of the mission to uplift, had a darker side, a blind eye to brutal outrages and massacres. Colonial officers conveniently and often shrewdly attributed their adventurism, defiance of orders, brutality toward enlisted men, and depredations of civilian populations to attacks of le cafard (homesickness); the term *le cafard* connotes nostalgia, uprootedness, and perhaps suppressed memories of slaughter and domination, as do Kurtz's last words in *Heart of Darkness:* "the horror, the horror." However, French officers like Laperrine and parliamentary deputies treated le cafard as a real illness, caused by too much sun, which "boils the blood and calcifies the brain." The only antidote was *le pinard* (army ration wine).[44]

For Pierre Benoit's generation, the murder of one French officer by another brought to mind the deeds of two real-life Kurtzes. As we saw in chapter 2, Captain Paul Voulet and Lieutenant Charles Chanoine in 1898 went on a rampage in the western Sudan; they had used *goumiers* (irregular mercenaries) to plunder local inhabitants while forcing them to act as bearers. To summarize the story again, when Paris dispatched Colonel Maurice Klobb to investigate and Voulet ordered his men to fire on Klobb's troops, the colonel died in the first volley. Voulet then declared himself king. When he began shooting his own men to restore discipline, he and Chanoine were murdered by their mutinous troops. The army and the press attributed Voulet's and Chanoine's acts to *la soudanité,* a sub-Saharan version of le cafard. *Le Temps,* reporting Klobb's death on 21 September 1899, concluded, "The irreparable act was committed in one of those moments of mental aberration which the strenuous life of torrid Africa seems to encourage." Klobb's death became entangled in the Dreyfus Affair. Chanoine was the son of General Charles Chanoine, who was minister of war in the Brisson cabinet and whose sudden resignation in October 1898 brought down the ministry. With the domestic crisis compounded by the confrontation with the British at Fashoda, the Right claimed that the Radicals and the new Waldeck-Rousseau cabinet were trying to use the murder to impose more civilian control of the army. To avoid reopening the wounds of the affair, the government encouraged the press to sweep the whole sordid business under the rug.[45]

Lost in the shuffle of domestic politics were the deaths of thousands of Sudanese and the many times that number who were made homeless and destitute. The colonial system itself set the tragedy in motion. Paris abdicated decisions to junior officers on the spot, whose heads were filled with amoral, white-supremacist notions. Their one advantage over the Africans was the destructiveness of their firepower. The huge expanse of territory from Senegal to Lake Chad was occupied by four thousand troops, who relied on bearers to transport everything, disrupting the economic life of the region with demands for labor. Moreover, the African tirailleur recruits, who expected booty as part of their pay, plundered the rural areas. As in the Sahara, French imperial control brought economic chaos, the French invasion provoked resistance, and governments trying to bring officers to heel were accused of undermining the army.[46]

As the first narrative colonial film shot on location, Feyder's *L'Atlantide* invited imitation, and in the decade that followed, other directors made the trek to the Maghreb to try their hand at surpassing its magnetic combination of escapist adventure and patriotic mission. Before Pabst remade the film, cinéma colonial had emerged as a genre with established conventions. He steered those conventions in the direction of racial polarization and cultural dichotomy between European and African, civilized and savage, advanced and primitive. Feyder's emphasis on exoticism gave way to white superiority as justifying dominance. But before that shift occurred, a dozen or more films made in Morocco, under the guiding hand of Lyautey, offered a more nuanced, respectful view of Islamic North Africa's peoples, albeit one still drenched in paternalism. Location proved crucial because Lyautey and his staff, powerfully influential in Paris, advocated including the Moroccan elites as junior partners in governing the Sherifian empire, a form of rule that diverged sharply from that of the Algerian settler regime.

In a sense, the imaginative world of exotic fiction mirrored the political realities of locale. Magical notions of the evil effects of place, a hallmark of fairy tales, pervade colonial film and literature. *L'Atlantide*'s Antinéa draws her occult powers from her mysterious kingdom. André Gide, an anticolonialist, concluded *The Immoralist* with Michel transfixed—by the boy he had taken as a lover and by the peculiar, translucent North African light. The four friends who come to rescue him are drawn into his paralysis. The Heart of Light mirrors the *Heart of Darkness*, which, as Chinua Achebe points out, conveys the message that "Kurtz . . . foolishly exposed himself to the wild irresistible allure of the jungle."[47]

4 | French Cinema's Other First Wave

The Political and Racial Economics of Filming the Colonies

The first wave of French filmmaking, the years before the Great War, is described by Richard Abel as a time of immense technological and artistic innovation. Another early wave sent film to the empire, as the colonial lobby quickly grasped its efficacy as a means of influencing public opinion. Appeals to the nation to support the colonial mission instilled a sense of cultural and racial superiority that common people could share with their "betters." Thus film joined other forms of mass entertainment and leisure in creating cultural cohesion, and colonial film drew upon crucial ingredients of the Third Republic's social "cement," the binding aggregates that welded the cultural hegemony of its elites.[1]

Colonial cinema captured imaginations and promoted empire by associating modern arms, machinery, and medicine with European superiority. The colonial lobby sponsored or encouraged the production of a flotilla of travelogues and documentaries, which whetted the public appetite for the feature films that followed. Publicity campaigns stimulated a consuming interest in the exotic and created a receptive market. At home and abroad, colonial films successfully competed with Hollywood productions. Allusions to the colonies lent an ominous note, an exotic flavor, or an air of mystery to other films, set in France. Although only 5.5 percent of all feature films made between the wars were set in colonial locales and focused on colonial themes, they were inordinately influential. Based on experience filming in French Africa in the 1920s, a new generation of directors, Jacques Feyder, Jacques de Baroncelli, and Léon Poirier, broke with the international, imitation-American style fostered by Pathé, the largest French production company in the industry's early years, and began making more culturally specific films. The colonies thus were a formative component of French cinematic nationalism.[2]

58

Travelogues, Documentaries, and
Anthrodramas: Vicarious Tourism

Some of the earliest first-wave films were ethnographic travelogues that wedded cinema to empire. The Lumière brothers brought back to Paris in 1897 the first footage of Algeria and Tunisia. Unlike slightly disreputable and low-brow one-reelers or nickelodeons, such real-life scenes *(actualités)* attracted middle-class audiences and included documentaries that stimulated interest in the overseas empire. Publicist François Laurent, expressing the colonial lobby's bitterness and hopes, proclaimed in 1912 that "the geographical film . . . helps link the colonies to the mother country. It shows us all the outlets offered to French enterprise by our vast overseas possessions. . . . It shows the mighty endeavors of our engineers over there and reminds us of the Frenchmen sacrificing themselves to an ideal without even hoping for a little encouragement from a mother country so often ungrateful because it is ignorant. Cinema will be the best emigration agency of the future."[3]

Within two years of inaugurating the French protectorate, Marshal Lyautey used film in Morocco's pacification, arranging a film screening in 1914 as a beau geste to the sultan's notables and Muslim religious leaders. As a phonograph in the background played "La Marseillaise," a newsreel showed Bastille Day military formations on parade at Longchamps in the Bois de Boulogne, Paris; shots of naval squadrons, submarines, planes, railroads, and automobiles followed. According to one officer present at the event, it "stupefied and dazzled" the Moroccans. One notable, with more resignation than acrimony, ruefully remarked, "The French have conquered everything but death."[4]

Albert Sarraut, a leading spokesman of the colonial lobby and minister of colonies in several interwar cabinets, struck a practical note. It was "absolutely indispensable," he declared in 1920, "that a methodical . . . propaganda by word and visual image *[l'image]*, journal, conference, film and exposition be activated in our land among adults and children." Integrating film into a school curriculum offered a "lively, expressive and practical" means of overcoming French youth's ignorance of the colonies.[5]

While he was governor-general of Indochina from 1920 to 1922, Sarraut created a *mission cinématographique* to put his ideas into practice. This team of filmmakers made travelogues of daily life and historical sites such as the imperial capital at Hué, depicting Vietnam's traditional economy efficiently using domesticated buffalo, elephants, and water transport to cultivate rice and sugar. Projecting an image of a tranquil, stable society of contented, hardworking adults and happy children—of a people, "little and brown, minutely polite, whose skin is the color of old wax"—the films implied that Indochina awaited development, and subtly invited French capital investment. But by 1922, Sarraut's attempt to create a film industry in Indochina had failed. Distance to France raised production costs, film stock reacted badly to the hot, humid climate, and the Vietnamese were poor actors. They posed and became self-conscious in front of the camera. Even the animals were skittish and cantankerous. But idealized travelogues continued to be shown, primarily for the edification of French schoolchildren. At the cinema in the Paris headquarters of the Indochina Information Agency on rue de la Boétie, a pretty street lined with trees and art galleries, Ilya Ehrenburg took in one of these films in 1932, a year after France suppressed the Yen Bay peasant insurrection. While newspapers, he pointed out, were covering the execution of thirteen Annamite rebels, the trial of a French foreman for beating to death a Vietnamese factory girl, and forced labor on the rubber plantations, "on the screen, life is as pretty as the . . . paintings in the neighboring galleries."[6]

Since the moderate Left embraced the colonial consensus, it allowed itself to be misdirected by such travelogues. The League of the Rights of Man (LDH) praised France's "mission of spreading . . . the ideas which have made it great. . . . Carrying science to peoples who are ignorant of it, giving them roads, canals, railroads, autos, telegraph, telephone, organizing among them health services, allowing them to know at last the rights of man . . . is not a labor of imperialism, it is a task of fraternity." Albert Thomas, a leading socialist, a founder of the LDH, and avid colonialist, also supported colonial film. He sought backing for films by Abel Gance, and when Jacques Feyder, after his success with *L'Atlantide,* wanted to film another Pierre Benoit novel, *Le Roi Lépreux* (The leper king), on location in Vietnam in 1925, Thomas interceded. He asked the socialist governor, Alexandre Varenne, to press the Bank of Indochina to underwrite a loan of 200,000 francs to Feyder, saying, "I believe a film by him will have immense propaganda value for Indochina." The bank refused, and Feyder abandoned the project. *Ramuntcho,* made in 1937, was the only French feature film produced in Indochina.[7]

Africa proved a more successful film locale than Southeast Asia. Its accessibility enabled French filmmakers to satisfy the French fascination with exotica and desire to see "authentic and primitive" Africa, part of a wider obsession that included Paris's enthusiastic reception to Josephine Baker and Afro-American jazz. Africana thus exploited the same vicarious tourism that made westerns as popular in Europe as in the United States, and French-made African pictures competed effectively with U.S. studio output. French moviegoers were more sophisticated than before the Great War, however, and directors could no longer pass off the park at Fontainebleau as a pristine rain forest. But financial backers balked at the expense of going to Chad or the Niger, so directors kept down costs by accompanying European explorers on African expeditions. Touted as "missions," these exploits were infused with a heroic aura and redemptive glow. Using *autochenilles*, half-track vehicles invented by Citroen engineer Georges-Marie Haardt, seven motor caravans crossed Africa in the mid 1920s. Five transcontinental airplane crossings were made as well. From Touggourt in Algeria (where *L'Atlantide* was filmed), Haardt and Louis Audoin-Dubreuil crossed the Sahara in 1922–23 to the Niger River. In 1926, the team's Croisière Noire, or trans-Africa expedition, crossed the desert again and reached the Indian Ocean through equatorial Africa. Meticulously planned and supplied by depots along the route, Haardt's feat handed Citroen a stunning public-relations coup.[8]

Whether the irony registered with audience or filmmaker, *La Croisière noire* inadvertently revealed the dependence of Western machines on native labor. Scenes showed hundreds of African porters dragging the Citroens through swamps, hacking paths for them through jungle, and floating them across rivers on rafts. African animists, termed *fetishists*, are shown presenting as gifts to the expedition a fascinating assortment of religious and art *objets*; in the final scene, the camera triumphantly recorded a display of hundreds of these objects that Haardt's party delivered to the Trocadero museum of ethnography in Paris. The narrator calls them *butin* (booty), and as James Clifford has pointed out, this scene inadvertently revealed its own commodity fetishism for these objects, projected onto the Africans. In a more critical film of French colonialism, Marc Allégret recorded novelist André Gide's voyage to the Congo in 1927, a documentary that served as Allégret's apprenticeship.[9]

The colonies challenged directors to break the shackles of theatrical convention, leave the studio, and develop a unique filmic art form extracted directly from life, as different from theater as the stage was from painting. So believed Léon Poirier, the romantic imperialist who filmed *La Croisière noire* and who, in 1936, made the biography of Father Foucauld, *L'Appel du silence*. He began his career making orientalist fantasies in Nice for Gaumont Studios, imitating the theater in his earliest films to legitimate the medium to the middle class. In the mid 1920s, Poirier sought for the maturing cinema its own identity. France, with its "marvelous colonies," offered a new generation of cinematographers "all that is needed for exotic cinema to carry the mark of French genius."[10]

Not content to document French exploits, Poirier, Allégret, and other directors of the 1920s captured the lives of indigenous peoples on film, mixing messages of racial paternalism and common humanity. Profoundly affected by *Nanook of the North (Nanouk l'Esquimaux)*, they turned out "anthrodramas" like *Snouk, l'Homme des glaces (Snook, Man of the Ice)*, and *Razaff le Malgache (Razaff the Madagascan)*. "It is more moving to see a good documentary than a bad drama," said Stacia Napierkowska, the leading lady of *L'Atlantide*, upon her return to North Africa in 1923 to make *In'ch'Allah*. "I cried when I saw Nanook." After the Croisière Noire expedition reached Madagascar, Poirier made *Amours Exotiques,* hiring local actors to tell a folk tale of a young man who uses trickery to win the hand of his lover by faking his own death and rising up at his funeral. *Ciné-Miroir*'s review of *Amours Exotiques* concluded that in the "dark continent" love often serves base instincts, but "hearts suffer and love in the same manner in all latitudes." *Siliva the Zulu,* a 1928 Franco-Italian production filmed with local Zulu talent, also told a tale of a frustrated suitor. A rival poisons Siliva's goats, wiping out his bride-price, and a shaman, in cahoots with the rival, blames Siliva for a drought that is devastating Zululand. The villagers are about to kill him to cleanse his sacrilege and bring the rain, when Siliva's fiancée exposes the conspiracy of rival and shaman, for which her father, the king, banishes them. The documentary style of these films left the ambiguous impression that they represented Zulu or Madagascan culture as a whole, rather than folk or fairy tales, and juxtaposed the superstition-ridden, magical-thinking "they" to the scientific and rational "we," the European audience.[11]

Travelogues never questioned the inevitability of the white man's dominance, but they did voice doubts about the myth of progress. "If white men bring political violence, alcohol, taxes," declared a film on New Guinea, "the *pygmées* will surely regret their coming!" Big-game hunters heedlessly slaughtering wildlife, an icon of European superiority, were filmed with armies of native "bearers" carrying the supplies and high-powered rifles. As with films of the auto rallies, these films carried the double message of dominance and dependence. A film that showed captive baby gorillas, no doubt orphaned by such "hunters," expressed surprise at their docility, thus demonstrating the overall ignorance of Africa. Fascination with actualités continued, but by the late 1920s "fetishist" dances and white hunters were old hat. "We have seen all that in *La Croisière noire*," reviewers complained, reserving praise for camera operators who thrilled audiences by taking dangerous chances filming wild animals up close—or appearing to; and therein lies a tale.[12]

One American producer found a solution to the jaded audience reaction. A U.S. film crew spent fourteen months in Uganda shooting *Africa Speaks*, a film that Ilya Ehrenburg attributed to the fertile imagination and inventive promotion of Columbia Pictures owner Harry Cohn. Audiences were bored with the faked deaths of war movies, and Cohn decided to film death *pour tout de bon* (for real). He outfitted the Colorado Africa Expeditions' explorers Paul Hoeffler and Harrold Austin and sent them, via Mombasa, to Uganda to film "curiosities" of the Congo basin. There the Colorado team met an expedition that had left Dakar in 1931 and traversed the Sahel grasslands en route to Djibuti on the Somali coast. From the safety of circular brush enclosures called *boma*, guarded by bearers armed with pikes, the crew filmed lions hunting antelope and Massai hunting lions. In one grisly scene, the camera trained on a porter being mauled by a lion. Ehrenburg claimed that white audiences in the United States, inured by years of lynchings, were amused. London and Berlin moviegoers also got their money's worth, but European sensibilities gradually awakened and there were protests.

At first, Cohn told reporters the scenes were real, shown in the interests of science: the Ugandan was no more to be pitied than the antelope. But studio lawyers warned that the scandal he was creating for the sake of publicity could make legal problems for Columbia, so he changed his tune, claiming editors had superimposed two bands of film in a new, secret technique. Before the sensation died down, Columbia netted $500,000 in only three months. The mystery writer Georges Simenon, who had retraced Gide's Congo voyage, returned to Paris in time to see *Africa Speaks*. His pithy response to the trickery *(truquage)* and hullabaloo was, "Yes, Africa speaks to us; it says *merde*—and we deserve it!" Yet Georges-Henri Rivière, of the Paris Trocadero Ethnology

Museum, praised the film's respect for native cultures. He pointed to its explanation of the custom of the Sara Kyabe, or Ubangi, who first put disks in women's lips to discourage Arab slave raiders from stealing and selling them. In his judgment, the film avoided mockery, badinage, and ridicule, took the natives on their own terms, and made a valuable contribution to ethnologic studies.[13]

Lyautey and the Rise of a Franco-Moroccan Film Industry

Such knitting together of travelogues and anthrodrama story lines fell short of achieving the stunning box-office success of *L'Atlantide* (1921), which inspired ambitious directors to try their hand at colonial fiction and made filming on location de rigeur. In the popular imagination, Morocco and the Sahara remained wild, insecure, and untamed; in reality Marshal Lyautey's residency helped film companies overcome logistical problems: they preferred to work in Moroccan locales, where the architecture and folk ways gave them ready-made sets and low-cost labor for movie extras. A rare symbiosis emerged. The elements of precolonial society that remained intact, due in no small measure to Lyautey's policy of indirect rule, enabled filmmakers to use them to compete with Hollywood spectaculars. Lyautey maintained support in Paris by manipulating French opinion through sophisticated media campaigns, not least through film. In turn, directors acknowledged their debt to him in screen credits and publicity articles. The symbiosis exercised subtle yet powerful influences on film themes and content, contributing to France's colonial "mythistory,"[14] shaping cultural identity, and adding to the aura of infallibility around Lyautey himself.

Lyautey masterfully manipulated a wide range of contacts in the mass media in France to create a climate of opinion favorable to his policy of indirect rule. Assisting French film production was part of his broad strategy to build a reputation as France's infallible expert in colonial affairs and thus ensure minimal meddling from governments at home or settlers in-country. His prestige was fatally damaged by the Rif War, the surprise attack by the Berbers of the northern, Spanish zone of the protectorate. Ten weeks after fighting erupted, the veil of secrecy shrouding Lyautey's propaganda machine lifted for the first time in twelve years. A letter written by his secretary Paul Vatin-Perignon on 25 May to the marshal's nephew Pierre had been intercepted and sent to *L'Humanité,* the Communist (PCF) daily, which published it on 10

June, the day after PCF deputy Jacques Doriot had read it to the Chamber. Since Pierre had complained to the police that his mail was being tampered with and had unwittingly verified Vatin-Perignon's signature, no one challenged its authenticity.[15]

The letter called on Pierre to mobilize his "team of agents" on the Paris "front"—editors and "well-oriented" journalists of conservative papers and mass-circulation dailies—to repair the general's reputation. It revealed the complicity of the Cartel des Gauches coalition, including Léon Blum and Paul-Boncour, leaders of the Socialist SFIO, in the policy decisions that had led to the war. Phillippe Berthelot, a senior official in the Ministry of Foreign Affairs and one-time private secretary to Aristide Briand, had kept the Socialists up to date, and from October 1924 on they knew as much about Moroccan events as did Premier Herriot. Doriot accused Lyautey of master-minding the Right's policy of supporting the new premier, Paul Painlevé, for the duration of the war. Police investigators, convinced that a conspiracy was afoot, actually found that the handful of Communists living in Morocco were working-class settlers with no access to Lyautey's mail. So the source of the letter remains a mystery, but it was a sign that the *maréchal* was losing his grip on events.[16]

Before the letter exposed his hand, Lyautey had neutralized political backlash against his covert management of opinion by openly sponsoring film productions. Film crews needed his native-affairs officers to scout locations, secure transport, and enlist aid from the q'aids in the area. Directors who heeded ethnographic tidbits fed to them by officers measurably enhanced the verisimilitude of their films, and Paris film critics, in turn, touted the films' realism. Moroccan notables protected film crews from molestation and enabled filmmakers to recruit thousands of extras for spectacular battle scenes. Moroccan customs such as fantaisie horse riding lent themselves to work for movie extras. At gatherings to honor a saint's holy day or a visit by the sultan, hundreds of horsemen would mass at one end of an open plain and gallop wildly toward the spectators, suddenly draw up their mounts, wheel, and fire their antique flintlock muskets in the air. The displays attracted tourists, and none of the participants confused such pageantry with military training. Yet *Ciné-Miroir*'s critic V. G. Danvers conflated the two, declaring that "whatever tribe they are from, the Arabs love war. . . . [It is] under their skin . . . they love simulated combat." Like other public-relations flaks, Danvers romanticized Moroccan customs to promote films and, disingenuously or not, reinforced positive impressions of the traditional elite, which helped Lyautey cultivate attitudes in France that supported his policies in Morocco.[17]

Colonial officials joined publicists in helping directors by using their good relations with the pasha of Marrakech and other powerful noblemen of south-central Morocco to mobilize cheap labor. The leading families used their influence with the Chleuh Berbers to enable director Luitz-Morat to employ twelve thousand extras. Chleuh menfolk, many with their own horses, spent three days shooting a battle scene for Luitz-Morat's 1921 film *Au Seuil du harem*. René Jeanne, a critic who reviewed the film, described the post-production festivities, adding an exotic, romantic note that reinforced the images viewers would see on the screen. Chleuh notables treated the director and crew as honored guests, serving them a traditional "Arab" banquet of whole roast lamb, chicken stuffed with figs and dates, eaten by hand from great copper plates and followed by mint tea, poetry, and dance. Thus the film crew "experience first-hand the Arab [*sic*] life, sleeping on the ground, eating *mechoui* [lamb] without forks." In 1922, Luitz-Morat made *Sang d'Allah*, a film that subtly yet sternly cautioned Europeans against meddling in Moroccan mores and customs. For the interior scenes, the sultan opened his palace in Marrakech, even his private apartments. Lyautey enlisted the king's "obliging collaboration," encouraging him to visit movie locations and welcome film crews to his palaces as guests. This cooperation, critic René Jeanne assured his readers, meant that the films of 1922–23 would show "Morocco without embellishment or artifice . . . grim and foreboding, medieval in values and bearing but definitely nearer than we believe to modern life . . . its inhabitants so ferocious when they do not know one, but so sweet, ingenuous, and hospitable when one gains their confidence."[18]

Lyautey's officers and the sultan's government officials enabled French directors to produce spectaculars à la Cecil B. DeMille. With labor costs close to nil and real palaces available, French filmmakers were freed from the usual production-expense restraints and could stage huge battles, sumptuous interior shots, and lavish garden scenes. Moreover, film tapped the Moroccan labor market without disrupting traditional economic relations. Hiring extras a few weeks a year expropriated no land and employed notables as recruiters, reinforcing their role in rural society. Officers, notables, and filmmakers achieved a rare symbiosis, and respectful portrayals of Morocco's traditional elite popularized Lyautey's policy in France. But when the Rif War broke out in April 1925, it smothered the burgeoning industry and in September forced Lyautey to resign. Sultan Mawlay Youssef died in 1927, and settlers, whose influence had grown with their numbers, demanded access to rural labor and asserted their own ideas about how to run Morocco.

Before the film ventures ran out of steam, Lyautey had imprinted them with his fine hand. He assured directors E.-E. Violet and E. B. Donatien "the most complete and efficacious cooperation of all civil and military services, French and native" for *Les Hommes nouveaux* (1922). His enthusiasm smacks of self-promotion. The film featured Lyautey's role at Settat in 1907, a battle in which, as an aide to General d'Amade, he distinguished himself by defeating an uprising against French encroachments in Morocco. The film's didactic side, like that of *Sang d'Allah,* showed the French public that settlers must follow the army's instructions about respecting local customs or they would be liable to provoke just such an embroglio with the natives. In the movie, Amédée Bourron, a lowly laborer, is saved by Lyautey at Settat, and through drive and sheer force of will he becomes a wealthy colon. But his rudeness and obsession with business drives his young wife away and she succumbs to the attentions of a French officer. The officer, after being wounded in a later battle, dies in her arms. Her heart twice broken, she returns to France. Bourron gives in to despair, but the character based on Lyautey inspires him to rededicate himself to developing Morocco. In *Les Hommes nouveaux,* Settat takes its place at the crossroads of myth and history. The film concealed the battle's context—the conflicts over colonial policy.[19]

Historically, the battle of Settat concluded the colonial lobby's initial attempt to maneuver France into seizing Morocco. The French army had just occupied Oudjda, on the Algerian border, incensing Moroccans, who had forced Sultan Aziz to abdicate. His less-compliant brother Hafid had mounted the throne and called for mass resistance. In response, Paris landed forty-five hundred troops on the Atlantic coast near Casablanca, and the expedition marched inland to the Chaouia region around Marrakech, ostensibly to punish the assassins of Dr. Emile Mauchamp and put down riots that erupted in the wake of his murder. Mauchamp, who had done much to contain epidemic disease, had also loudly voiced his contempt for Islam's "fanaticism and ineluctable decadence." In his clinic at Marrakech, he had been surrounded by a mob, which fell on him with sticks, stones, and swords. Chaouian peasants seized the chance to protest a rail line that hauled rock to construct the port at Casablanca but which French engineers had run through a Muslim cemetery. At Settat, French troops routed Hafid's forces, but parliament, led by the still-anticolonial socialists and Jean Jaurès, forced the military to withdraw. Hafid was brought to heel, nonetheless. He had to borrow from the French-run state bank to pay indemnities imposed by France, and he sank into debt. The corporations and banks of the Comité du Maroc made him sign the same mining law imposed on Aziz, and by 1908 European contractors had acquired full subsoil rights.[20]

Hafid had changed nothing, and in 1911, Zayn, a third son of Sultan Mawlay Hasan, rose against him. This time, the colonial lobby led by Algerian deputy Eugène Etienne orchestrated a press campaign that invented an entire French colony in Fez. Mendacious dispatches claimed the city was under seige, luridly detailing what the plight would be of the children and women if they were not rescued. Forcing Aristide Briand out of office, the colonial lobby maneuvered the government of the inexperienced new premier, Ernest de Monis, into an invasion, putting twelve thousand troops under Lyautey's command. To protect its national interests, Germany reacted, sending the gunboat *Panther* to Agadir and precipitated what came to be known as the Second Moroccan Crisis. A cynical transfer of several million people of the Cameroons from French to German rule temporarily resolved the situation, but the "Panther's leap" began the countdown to August 1914 and the start of the Great War. In their effort to remain independent, Morocco's rulers had briefly but fatally altered the course of European affairs. But it took sixty years to unseat the keystone myth of German aggression as the sole cause of the Great War, and that myth was cemented in place, in part, by the assumption that France was protecting its nationals from Muslim fanatics when it invaded Morocco. French Communists were among the first to challenge the myth. During the Rif War, they harped on the connection between Moroccan "adventures" and European-wide war. However, the European powers had recently signed the Locarno Treaty, promising to resolve disputes among themselves without resorting to war. Ironically, as the "Spirit of Locarno" descended on Europe, it allowed France and Spain a free hand to conduct their military operations in the Rif.[21]

Celebrations of French imperial mythistory were one type of film made under Lyautey's aegis. Another familiarized French audiences with Morocco's traditional culture, at least at elite level, by retelling old Moroccan tales, legends, and stories. Skillfully etched versions of the clumsy anthrodramas made in other colonial areas, they occasionally used Moroccan actors in leading parts and were set before the colonial era. One early production, *C'Était écrit* (1920), is a tale of a rich noble's son charged by the pasha with suppressing a revolt of his kinsmen. They convince him to lead their uprising instead. Defeated, he refuses the intercession of the pasha's niece, whom he had freed, and he accepts his punishment because "It Is Written."

In'ch'Allah, directed by Franz Toussaint in 1923, retells another legend. An invasion of *roumis* (infidels) ruins an old nobleman, Bakir, who discovers an ancient document prophesying that the Sherifan empire will be saved by a beautiful young woman. Convinced that the manuscript has summoned his daughter Zilah, a dancer played by Stacia Napierkowska (Feyder's star in *L'Atlantide*), Bakir follows her south. But the evil q'aid Sliman desires her and sends seven men to kidnap her. Sliman's younger brother Said slays all seven and rescues Zilah. Bakir finds them, reveals the parchment that predicted Said's deed, and convinces the young man to help Zilah fulfill her destiny. Together they overthrow the incompetent sultan and his consort Djahilah, who had intrigued with Sliman to hand over the empire to the infidels. Zilah and Said enter the capital in triumph, and the people proclaim her sultaness. She invites Said to rule by her side, but he returns to the desert: the prophecy did not include him. Once again: "It Is Written."[22]

A new director bringing his own powerful Paris political connections arrived under Morocco's skies to make films under Lyautey's auspices. René Le Somptier, recipient of the Legion d'honneur, secretary to a cabinet minister, and confidant of Aristide Briand, had been charged with several sensitive missions to Africa. The films he made in 1924 paid homage to Lyautey, but they also seemed to favor settler rule. In *Les Terres d'or*, a Spahi veteran becomes a colon farmer after being wounded and disfigured in the Great War. A love triangle develops, and his fiancée, unable to endure the rigors of pioneer life, returns to Paris. He marries a Moroccan, an inversion of the French stereotype since she proves more capable of love than the European female. The virgin land lured; the male-less woman allured: the script's erasure of Moroccan men emphasized the director's message. French audiences saw a virgin land that was, as in the Americas, not virgin but "widowed."[23]

Le Somptier's second film, *Les Fils du soleil* (June 1924), an ambitious, eight-part serial, honored Lyautey. The credits read, "The major-

This poster for *Les Fils du soleil* (1924) shows one of many cliff-hanger end-ings of the eight-part serial. The rebel emir's half-naked executioner is about to behead Youssef, Arab friend of the hero, Hubert. Both are officers of the foreign legion. Armed horsemen sit on their mounts in the background. The poster used vivid colors—a yellow and pink sky, the executioner in red and green—to lend dynamism to the figures. Brave Youssef, jaw set, eyes fixed, prepares to die. Will Hubert and the Legion ride to his rescue? Don't miss the next exciting episode. *Credit:* copyright Galerie Cine-Images, Paris

ity of Morocco today recognizes, thanks to the prodigious efforts of Marshal Lyautey, that France and its sons are . . . friends come to col-laborate in the great effort of civilization."[24] The film alluded to so many contemporary events, the hints can hardly be accidental. Le Somptier named his young hero Hubert, like Lyautey, and made him a graduate of the French military academy, Saint Cyr, again like the marshal. Hu-bert is engaged to Aurore, but a "cosmopolitan financier," Baron de Horne, also desires her. A suggestively anti-Semitic character, de Horne plots with his half-breed *(métis)* henchman to destroy Hubert by fram-ing him for theft. Cashiered and disgraced, Hubert joins the Foreign Legion and goes off to fight dissident Moroccan tribes. Meanwhile, back in Paris, the baron secretly buys arms to supply an emir leading a "rebellion" (a real emir, Abd el-Krim, led the Riffians and founded an independent Islamic republic). In a bit of familiar silent-screen villainy, the baron ruins Aurore's father, the marquis, to get the girl in his clutches. She flees to Morocco to find Hubert, but is carried off by the emir. Bringing reinforcements to a besieged French garrison in the nick of time, Hubert defeats the emir, rescues Aurore, exposes Baron de Horne's plots, and is reinstated to his former rank. In the midst of saving the day, he finds time to act out a subplot dramatizing Lyautey's favorite theme, cooperation between French and Moroccan elites. Hubert befriends a Moroccan captain in the French army (his name is Youssef—the same as the reigning sultan, whom Lyautey had hand-picked in 1912 after forcing the intractable Hafid to abdicate). The emir's men capture Youssef, but Hubert saves him while his head is literally resting on the chopping block.

Lyautey extended every courtesy to the film's director. He arranged for the sultan to open his palaces and the royal gardens in Rabat for some scenes, visited the set several days in a row to ask if the crew had everything they needed, and stayed to watch the shooting. The marshal's friend and ally al Glaoui, the pasha of Marrakech, once again supplied thousands of extras, Chleuh Berbers no doubt, and Lyautey ordered up units of *tirailleurs Sénégalais*, Spahis, and four Legion regiments to oppose them in the staged battle scenes.[25]

The secret arms deal is the plot-thickener of this French *Perils of Pauline*, with its broadly drawn anti-Jewish and anti-Muslim stereotypes. It is a theme drawn from actual events. After France had joined Spain in its war against the Riffians, Louis Berthon, a Communist deputy, revealed to the Chamber and the press that he had met Abd el-Krim's brother M'hmed in 1923, quite by accident, in a Paris café. M'hmed admitted he was shopping for arms and hinted that Lyautey might be encouraging the dealings in hopes of influencing the Riffians and discomforting the Spanish. The Sûreté Général reported that no French arms dealers were involved, but Berthon pointed out that noninterference gave tacit approval.[26]

Before Berthon's revelations in May 1925, few outside the intelligence services knew of these byzantine machinations. But Le Somptier was well-placed to have access to such information. Settlers in both Morocco and western Algeria strenuously opposed these dealings, which were part of Lyautey's strategy of co-opting regional leaders that had proved so effective since 1912. That he would fail to "domesticate" Abd el-Krim was something no one in France knew in 1924. Perhaps Le Somptier circulated the story simply to spice up his script. But another possibility is that his powerful allies wanted to embarrass Lyautey or warn him to put a stop to his dangerous game. Lyautey clearly did not retaliate, and whether he knew, or how he reacted, is unknown; perhaps the film's flattering portrayal blinded him to its other edge. In any case, General Miguel Primo de Rivera, the Spanish dictator, believed France was meddling, and in 1924 he showed reporters captured ammunition and spent cartridges from late-model French weapons. He warned the French they could not control Abd el-Krim and, after withdrawing Spanish forces to a few coast enclaves, watched as tensions mounted between France and the Rif. The clash came in April 1925, led to Lyautey's disgrace, Franco-Spanish cooperation, the destruction of the Rif Republic, and, in May 1926, to Abd el-Krim's surrender.[27]

The Rif War: Pivot Point of Political and Cultural Change

After the 1918 Armistice, Moroccan events again, as in 1911, impinged on Europe's internal affairs. The Riffian Berbers, denizens of the northern highlands and Mediterranean littoral, the region ceded to Spain by the act of Algeçiras of 1905, inflicted an unmitigated military catastrophe on their would-be conquerors. At Anwal (Anual, in Spanish) in July 1921, eight thousand soldiers of Spain's Army of Africa died at the hands of an indigenous uprising organized by the prominent and respected local leader Mohammed Abd el-Krim. For five years, Abd el-Krim's movement gradually pushed the Spanish into coastal enclaves around the ports of Ceuta and Melilla. The Spanish constitutional monarchy collapsed under the weight of the military disaster—an investigation that threatened to expose scandalous corruption and cowardice among the "Africanista" army officers—and an abortive Communist insurrection in the Vizcayan cities. A military junta won King Alfonso's support and "pronounced," that is, launched a coup d'etat.

The leading figure of the Pronunciamiento, Miguel Primo de Rivera, was known to oppose the war and was expected to extricate Spain from the bloody mess in Morocco. Instead, he suppressed all opposition and allied with the Africanista officers in an all-out effort to win. That strategy failed, but Abd el-Krim's growing power actually worked to Primo's advantage. The Rif Republic, the independent Islamic state that Abd el-

Krim founded in 1924, threatened not only the protectorate but also France's position in Algeria, economically as well as militarily. Riffian migrants were crucial seasonal labor for estate owners in the Oranais, in western Algeria, and Abd el-Krim's agents, organizing under the nose of Legion headquarters in Sidi bel Abbès, urged or intimidated workers to return to the Rif to join the crusade. The settlers pressed for action. Lyautey blockaded the Rif from trade with the northern region of the French zone on which it depended for grain. Backs to the wall, the Riffians attacked south, taking Lyautey completely by surprise, overrunning French blockhouses, and menacing Fez. Taking advantage of the sudden setback to the erstwhile hero who had become the main obstacle in the way of widening their prerogatives in Morocco, settlers demanded his removal.

At the time of the Riffian attack, the Cartel des Gauches, the leftist coalition of Radicals and Socialists that held power, had just undergone a cabinet crisis. The premier had been Edouard Herriot. Now, Horace Finaly, chairman of the Banque de Paris et Pays Bas (Paribas), coordinator of the corporate investment consortium in control of Morocco and kingmaker of the Cartel, designated Paul Painlevé as Herriot's successor, assenting to Painlevé's plan to offer up Lyautey as scapegoat for a war that was provoking protests throughout France. Lyautey would be eased out and replaced by Marshal Philippe Pétain, a trusted ally since 1917. Pétain's task was to broker an alliance with Primo de Rivera to crush the Rif Republic, with a minimum loss of "white" troops and maximum advantage to French settlers.

The Rif War laid a crucial stepping-stone on the path to racialization. It soured the goodwill that had accrued from the colonial contribution to the war effort in 1914–18 and it put the entire Left on the defensive as "race traitors," particularly the Communists. Because of the Leninist and Comintern calls for colonial independence, the Right condemned "Asiatic" Bolshevism for unleashing colored hordes for an assault on the West. A widening circle of fascist or far-right writers, party spokesmen, and leaders of the *ligues*, the extra-parliamentary, mass-based, right-wing formations, repeatedly charged a Bolshevik plot was afoot.

French Communists, never entirely committed to the rights of colonial peoples, accused party leaders of turning them into "vulgar spies." The antiwar protests shifted away from antiimperialism to the inflationary effects of the war, a step that narrowed the scope of class struggle to the domestic front. The Socialists of the SFIO, who had refused to break with their Cartel partners over the war and who had indeed begun to supplant them as the leaders of the moderate Left, abstained from voting against war taxes to pay for military operations. They justified themselves with rhetoric that came directly from the pens and mouths of the petits colons: Muslims understood only force; to negotiate would be viewed as a sign of weakness; the Communist program of fraternization with the Riffians and military evacuation of Morocco would invite another imperialist power in, or worse, a massacre of colons.

The Political Economy of the Interwar World Cinema Market

The Rif War shut down the Moroccan film industry, and it never regained its former glory. In its prewar heyday, however, it complemented the protectorate's role in France's imperial system. War debts to the United States and Britain, and the Bolshevik expropriation of billions in French-held tsarist state bonds, had turned the world's largest creditor into a debtor. As a "rentier state," reaping interest on loans rather than profits from industrial raw materials, France suffered after 1918. But Morocco's state bank and budget remained firmly in French control and continued to float loans from French banks to fund large-scale public-works projects that went to French corporations, a revolving door that helped France revive her status as a world creditor. Moroccan film paralleled Morocco's role in the wider economy. Beset by U.S. competition, the French film industry found a haven in Lyautey's Morocco to produce films that could recapture audiences bedazzled by Hollywood.

A "fragmented, atomized and vulnerable . . . atelier system" of production hampered the French film industry's ability to compete. Its most formidable competitors were the eight giant U.S. studios, which made three-quarters of all American films. The six biggest French producers made 166 films, one-ninth of the 1,300 films made in France in the 1930s; 285 were produced by companies that made only one film. Exhibition, too, was decentralized. In 1939, three chains each owned 100 theaters; the rest of France's 4,800 movie houses were mainly single-theater family businesses. Distribution was haphazard. A film would premiere at a downtown Paris theater, the length of the run to be determined by the film's success, then move to provincial theaters, which typically screened a movie for one week. Theater owners chose which films they would show, and their regular clientele loyally attended once a week, whatever was playing. A fringe group would join the weekly crowd for box-office sensations like *Modern Times* or Marcel Pagnol's *César* (1936), attending only perhaps a few times a year. Mass audiences of the 1930s diluted the discerning tastes of the 1920s and watched anything from masterpieces to *navets* (turnips), flops often cooked up by speculators.[28]

The U.S. studios' vertical integration, from screenwriting to theater distribution, led to economies of scale that enabled them to recoup production costs at home and undersell Europeans in their home markets. The Italian cinema had gone bankrupt in the early 1920s, and one-third of French films failed to break even, making it harder to find backers for subsequent projects. The absence of large companies, which could offset flops with hits to keep their books in the black, also hurt French film technically: it lagged three years behind the Americans in converting to sound, which measurably added to production costs. Another problem for the French was that skilled workers in sound, lighting, and camera work lacked steady jobs, and they were further handicapped by having to use outmoded and incompatible equipment. Together, these difficulties were sinking the French film industry. In 1929, 85 percent of the world's sound films came from the United States, even though Hollywood studios were facing bankruptcy, receivership, or internal reorganization. They held on to their dominant position and competitive advantage with a "brutally single-minded" penetration of Europe. The Motion Picture Producers and Distributors of America, the U.S. cartel and lobby headed by Wil R. Hays, evaded French quotas on foreign films by setting up French subsidiaries to make "quota quickies," their own turnips, to offset imports of American-made hits. Efforts to limit imports extended to the empire. The Cinematographic Act of 1927 censored "unsuitable" films in "primitive societies," which included rural Algeria.[29]

Paradoxically, silent-era Franco-Moroccan films gave birth to a vision of the Orient that breached racial stereotypes. The economic exigencies impelled them to create a distinctive product that could compete with U.S. films. Implicit and explicit criticism of American film stereotypes was a leitmotif of French film critics during the interwar years. Critics praised French filmmakers for their truthful depictions of Africa; they in turn used their access to Africa to compete with American studios. Critic René Jeanne examined the role of "Negroes and Red-Skins in the cinema" for the popular film magazine *Ciné-Miroir* in 1922, asserting that since most films were American and Americans did not like blacks, people of African descent rarely appeared in film. "Redskins" were held in higher regard because they perfectly complemented the cowboy, and their "habitats" [sic] contained great scenic beauty. Jeanne wrongly concluded that the western was on the wane since Native Americans were dying out and therefore would vanish from screen. "Moreover, these last representatives of a dying race may rightly think they have other things to do before meeting the Great Spirit than attacking stagecoaches for the greater profit of Hollywood moguls." American directors would then have to make films about the Eskimo to cater to the American taste for the exotic.[30] Jeanne's anticipation of the extinction of Native American nations expressed the social-Darwinist view that such eradications were part of the natural order, rather than a consequence of a market economy and bourgeois social system.

The French reception of *L'Atlantide* contrasts with that of *The Sheik*, which premiered in the United States in October 1921, almost simultaneously with the opening of its French counterpart in Paris. *Ciné-Miroir* devoted its entire first issue to Feyder's film, and never reviewed *The Sheik*.[31] Theirs was not the only prognosis that missed the mark; even Cecil B. DeMille had predicted that it was so boring it would flop. Paramount executives were almost as pessimistic. They had bought the rights to Edith Hull's novel of a miscegenational affair between an English-woman, Lady Diana Mayo, and Sheik Ahmad Ben Hassan, because, after first publication in England in 1919, by 1921 it had sold a million copies in the United States. But they worried that it was too controversial. Lady Diana's brother calls the hero a "damned nigger," and Hull filled her book with lurid passages alluding to rape by brutish Arab men: "She was alone in an uncivilized country among a savage people with no protection of any kind." Their concern was fueled by the Ku Klux Klan's use of D. W. Griffith's film *Birth of a Nation* to recruit tens of thousands of members and by NAACP protests of screenings in many cities. The plots of both *The Sheik* and *Birth of a Nation* pivoted on rape-and-rescue fantasies. In both films, white actors played the nonwhite characters, and in both cases public reaction made little distinction between the actors and the roles. After *The Sheik*'s premier, a British embassy official in Washington swore an oath to the press that no proper English lady would allow herself to be compromised by a "wog."[32]

Actor Valentino overshadowed the film. His stardom owed to women, who composed three-quarters of his audiences. He was a "woman-made man." Visiting London and Paris in the fall of 1923, he was greeted with enthusiasm, and Paris put three limousines at his disposal so he and wife Natasha could go on a shopping spree. "He was the idol of millions," *Ciné-Miroir* wrote in 1929 on the third anniversary of his death.[33]

Taking advantage of Anglo-American stereotypes that French racial and sexual attitudes were more liberal than their own, Hull had set the novel and its sequel in the French Sahara. But the film was shot on location in Yuma, Arizona, as was the United Artists' sequel, *Son of the Sheik* (1926), based on Hull's second novel and starring Valentino as father and son. This time, *Ciné-Miroir* was not caught off guard: it devoted seven consecutive issues entirely to the film. Dozens of still photos accompanied scene-by-scene descriptions of the plot, all its "frothy fribble, desert storms, dancing girls, and fights against overwhelming odds." Feyder's *L'Atlantide* had made French filmmakers aware of the profitability of North African locales; the success of *The Sheik, Robinson Crusoe, Solomon and Sheba, The Thief of Baghdad,* and other Anglo-Saxon imports now awoke them to the vulnerability of "their" Moroccan resources to American imitations and challenged them to compete. Moreover, if it was not galling enough to find the American Southwest fobbed off as the "French" Sahara, the sheik, like Tarzan, turned out to be an English nobleman. So the French imbibed the story's racialism but also used it as a convenient foil to claim that French productions were more sensitive to the nuances of Muslim society.[34]

Feckless, American-produced "Foreign Legion movies" did not look right. Even John Waters's *The Spahi* (1928), a film made in Arizona but with a compelling plot, could not dress up the Southwestern desert to imitate the Sahara. Concern for accuracy compelled Rex Ingram to shoot the exteriors for his 1925 movie *The Arab* in Tunisia and the Algerian town of Biskra, but he used only two American actors as leads, recruited the rest of his principals from Paris, and engaged hundreds of extras on location. His *Garden of Allah* (1927) was also made with a French company; only one other American film was produced in the Maghreb. Costly logistics, ignorance of local conditions, uncooperative French officials, and obdurate native notables created insurmountable obstacles for U.S. film crews.[35]

American subsidiaries in Paris in the early years of sound, bent on penetrating all European markets, produced French, German, and Italian versions of English films. Georg Pabst imitated this practice in making *L'Atlantide*. Paramount's sound-film studio in the Paris suburb of Joinville made 150 French talkies and 150 in other languages during its

lifespan from 1930 to 1933. Hollywood's Paris colony spoke a unique
language, an English-French pidgin jokingly called "le Paramount." The
"cosmopolitan" direction of the industry led French right-wing intellectuals to recall nostalgically the glory days of French silent film. Literary critics around the Action française organization promoted the
stereotype that New York Jews ran Hollywood, railed against "Jewish
imperialism," and called on right-wing deputies to purge foreign influences.[36]

By mid decade, sound was producing distinctive national cinemas
around the world. French film revived artistically and critically, enter-
ing its "golden age." Paramount-Joinville folded in 1933, but the French
film industry was unable to take full advantage of the opportunity to
catch up with the technology or business organization of Hollywood
studios. The biggest French studios, Gaumont and Pathé, also went bankrupt, while vertically integrated U.S. film factories, by maintaining high-
quality production values, standardized output, and ferociously cut-
throat marketing tactics, continued to dominate the world film market.
By the Popular Front era (1936–38), Hollywood was striding across
France again, peddling its fantasy world. "At the time of the Popular
Front, MGM's trade journal *Voice of the Lion (Le Lion Vous Parle)* was
rallying thousands of little [French] children in Laurel-Hardiste fan
clubs." And the most popular film in France in 1938 was the fairy tale
Snow White, Walt Disney's first feature-length cartoon.[37]

French critics who praised the colonial genre's authenticity and sen-
sitivity heaped scorn on the ridiculous American attempts to depict the
Maghreb. The two versions of Hollywood's rendition of Christopher
Wren's novel *Beau Geste* met with particularly scathing attacks. The
French government protested the films' depictions of life in the Foreign
Legion, and the Legion high command banned both the 1928 original
and the 1938 remake from release in French North Africa. And the film
magazine *Pour Vous* scoffed at *Garden of Allah*, a 1936 remake of Rex
Ingram's film starring Marlene Dietrich and Charles Boyer, for its crude
stereotypes and inappropriate costumes. But *Beau Geste* was an early
sound film; and *Garden of Allah* (although *Pour Vous* neglected to mention the fact) was one of the first films shot in color. Thus both of these
films singled out for attack represented American technological break-
throughs that threatened to overwhelm French competitors.[38]

Pour Vous reasserted the superiority of French portrayals of North
Africa in 1938, pointing out that, in Hollywood films, "one can be cer-

tain to see a lascivious dancer surrounded by frenzied extras decked out in turbans with false beards. Misunderstanding of the Islamic world, of its mores and true poetry, is one of the most tenacious errors of American cinema."[39]

As anticolonial resistance emerged and economic competition with U.S. film incited cultural nationalism in France, the message in the film medium became more essentialist. Films fostered a French identity synecdochically conflated with "whiteness" and "European-ness," consigned women to their "proper" place, dichotomized the world into West and East, categorized ethnolinguistic groups in social-Darwinist terms, and sought to project a view of Western society that transcended class realities. Initially, Lyautey had widened his influence by projecting a heroic imperial past and an image of a civilizing mission that enriched the metropole while improving the lot of the natives. But settlers who landed on Africa's shores seeking to dominate, not cooperate, eventually undermined his project. As filmmaking in Morocco declined, directors went to Algeria, not back to the studios, and the Foreign Legion adopted Lyautey's methods of using logistical support to influence film content and indirectly shape French public opinion.

Renovating the national cinema preoccupied directors, critics, and audiences of all political persuasions. *Pour Vous* conducted a "referendum," or poll, in 1939, asking readers to rate the commercial value of movie stars. French audiences admitted only two foreigners, one female and one male, into the top-ten list, neither of them Americans. Actors outpolled actresses by 33 percent[40]—a preference for male stars that benefitted the colonial genre, with its distinctively masculine world. Rugged manliness joined realistic North African settings in the arsenal of weapons defending against American exports. The pride in Lyautey's preservation of the glories of Muslim civilization, expressed earlier by *Pour Vous*, echoed with unintended irony. French colonial film did not condone lynch terror or rationalize genocide, as had *Birth of a Nation* and westerns, but it remained steeped in cultural imperialism: in a final analysis, French directors availed themselves of access to the North African settings by right of conquest.[41]

Films Promoting Assimilation

French liberals, who reserved for Muslims the bottom of the cultural ladder, patronized Africans and Afro-Caribbeans. The Tarzan novels found a mass audience in France in the 1930s, when fifteen of them, nearly the entire series, were translated. At once adolescent, male escapist fantasy and sharp critique of modern life, Edgar Rice Burroughs's plots condemned slavery and King Leopold's brutal Congo regime, yet assumed the natural superiority of whites. Those who condemned other nations' imperialism but viewed France's colonial role as essentially benign found Burroughs appealing.[42]

The Africans who embraced the canons of French culture as taught by the Third Republic's schools, dubbed *évolués,* were accepted as "little Frenchmen" but discouraged from voicing their own cultures or reshaping that of France, as every group "within the hexagon" had done since the Middle Ages. Arabs and Berbers of the Maghreb, however, resisted Frenchification, were branded fanatics, denigrated as inherently inferior, and stereotyped with a blend of culture and genetics. Algeria contained the largest European population in the empire, and settler democracy subjugated all natives to the will of the "New Latin Race," with the rights of French citizenship reserved nearly exclusively for whites. Moroccan settlers marched across the same fault line when they forced Lyautey out and pressured Paris for an Algerian form of colonial rule. As sympathetic treatment of Muslims in French colonial film waned, Moroccan locales lost their appeal, and directors shifted production to Algeria, where they made film after film about the Foreign Legion. The few films still preaching racial cooperation or respect for traditional, elite Muslim culture looked out of place and anachronistic.

As French tastes for the exotic became jaded, new formulas revived the box office. One scenario, often used in Josephine Baker's films, involved a colonial who assimilated French culture and achieved success but lost a measure of fulfillment in the process. Georges Milton, who played Bouboule in popular, escapist comedies, incorporated this cliché into *Bouboule 1ère, le roi nègre* (1934). Pursued by jewel thieves to Senegal, he is captured by cannibals, whose chief gives him the choice of marrying his daughter or ending up in the pot, a marvelous colonial fantasy: avoid becoming *boeuf bourgignon,* and in Africa the white man becomes a king. Complexities of social hierarchy and class conflict at home were simplified in a fictional "colonial society divided into a caste of masters (big and small) and a multitude of inferiors *(soushommes)."* The tribe helps Bouboule foil the thieves, a curiously mixed message, and he returns to Paris with the jewels, a rich man, accompanied by Toto, a six-year-old African boy supposed to be his (adopted?) son. Child and man debark from the ocean liner dressed in identical camel-hair over-coats and suits, complete with matching canes and bowler hats. Audiences did not look for meaning from Georges Milton, but here is either a deliberate satire or an unintentional revelation of the paternalistic rigidity of French notions of assimilation.[43]

If one image expressed the ambiguities of French views of Africans, generically labeled Sénégalais, it was "Bonhomme Bana," the trademark advertisement of Banania, a hot-cereal mix of banana flour, cocoa, and sugar. Clever marketing compensated for nutritional deficiency. A label introduced in 1917 displayed a tirailleur Sénégalais and a slogan "Y'a bon!"—African pidgin French for *C'est bon*. A prototype of the character appeared in a collection of war stories by Claude Farèrre, the author of a paean to Lyautey, *Les Hommes nouveaux*. Dimba Fatimata, a tall (six feet, six inches), wiley, lovable overgrown child, steals horses' oats to eat because they are so tasty—"Y'a bon!" The story fairly exudes paternalist reciprocity: African sacrifices oblige "us" to "civilize" them. A realistic, natural, portrait of the soldier on the Banania label in his red *chéchia*, or fez, with blue tassel and Zouave uniform expressed an affection, even respect, fitting for the historical moment when African and Maghrebin troops were incurring heavy casualties on the Western Front, and the French public was grateful for their contribution to the war.[44] But wartime experience with Africans faded, and Banania became a Sambo image, like Aunt Jemimah, Uncle Ben, and the face on the box of Cream of Wheat, advertising products for domestic pleasure, cooking, or cleaning that epitomized "servility with exceptionally natural cheerfulness." Postwar France, after proposing to repay North African and African veterans by granting French citizenship, reneged on the commitment. The Banania figure became more abstract and stereotyped in the 1920s, an object of parody for Dadaists. Léopold Senghor, the leading poet of negritude, vowed to wipe the smile off every poster and box.[45]

A Confusing Interregnum

In summary, films made in Morocco bore Lyautey's mark. His influence rested on the firm economic foundations of Morocco's role in the French imperial system, which in turn shored up France's place in the world market. Moviemaking and tourism combined to exploit his legacy. Film scenes of ocean liners debarking passengers at modern, well-equipped

North African ports acted as thinly disguised travel posters for the Com-
pagnie Transmediterranée.[46] Moroccan productions helped French film
companies compete with Hollywood and preserve their share of the
home market.

Lyautey boarded ship at Casablanca in September 1925, unseated by
the settlers and their allies in Paris over his failure to contain the Riffians. As the port he had built sank below the horizon, so did his twelve
years' service to the empire and his unequaled influence on colonial
affairs. No government official greeted his landing at Marseille, and
he retired quietly to his estate. Sultan Mawlay Youssef, willing tool of
French development and the traditional elite's intermediary with French
corporations, died in 1927. His teenaged son Sidi Mohammed suc-
ceeded, relegated by the French to an even more ceremonial role than
his father. The infant Franco-Moroccan film industry never recovered
from Lyautey's fall from grace and Mawlay Youssef's death.[47]

Mohammed spent the first four years of his reign in a gilded cage,
strictly controlled by two French protégés, his tutor Si Mammeri and
his grand vizier, who indulged his fascination for technological toys. On
his first state visit to Paris in 1929, Mohammed spent his evenings at
private movie screenings. The head of the Loew's Metro company in
Paris closed its flagship theater, the Madeleine, to honor the king with
a private screening of *Broadway Melody*. Through Si Mammeri, the king
told the press it was "Magnificent! Pages would be needed to explain
it all and still the storyteller could not succeed." The next evening, at
Cinéma Mont-Doré, he watched French films, staying on until 2.00 A.M.
The program included *Vénus*, based on a novel by Jean Vignaud about
Franco-Algerian high society. *Ciné-Miroir* described the king as a "clois-
tered slave of the protocol of another age," movies being his only window on "reality." In fact, the French residency had been doing all it
could to keep him isolated from what it considered dangerous influences.
Never a patron to moviemakers, Mohammed was content to *watch*
film—and, to the chagrin of the French film industry, mostly American
productions, at that.[48]

Thus the late 1920s ushered in a confusing interregnum for colonial
cinema. The Franco-Riffian war and the fall of Lyautey had marked a
watershed in the racialization of French politics. French conservative
opinion makers redefined Europeans as the dominant race and intermingled race and class. Confused and intimidated, the Left capitulated
to the new racial order. In the world of cinema, settler political pres-

sure, the advent of sound, and U.S. competition were drawing movie sets into the culture wars defining "True France."

Films respectful of Islamic culture were going out of style. Directors began shifting locales to settler-dominated Algeria, focusing scripts exclusively on Europeans and rendering North Africans invisible. An entire subgenre emerged to glorify the Foreign Legion as the "thin white line" holding back Arab barbarians, an unseen "enemy" at Western civilization's gates. The Legion mystique magnetically drew filmmakers to the unit's headquarters at Sidi Bel Abbès in Algeria. But the final shift was still a few years away, after French cinema definitively breached the sound barrier in 1930. In the late 1920s, colonial cinema's message swung back and forth between Lyautey and the Legion.

The young king also went through a transformation. When his French administrators insisted that he sign the Berber Dahir of 1930, they provoked the first urban, mass protests in Morocco. The king seized the moment of the *dahir*, or royal decree, to act as interlocutor between the protectorate and the new forces of nationalism, carving out for himself a more independent role than that of his father.

5 | Tourists, Rebels, and Settlers
French-Moroccan Film in Decline,
1926–1931

Narrative film, tourism, picture postcards, and novels of the early 1920s had subjected Morocco to the French gaze and put it on display. Taking advantage of sumptuous palaces, ancient ruins, splendid natural scenery, and cheap labor, directors had followed in Cecil B. DeMille's footsteps, thrilling audiences with spectacular vistas of battle sequences filmed with hundreds of movie extras and romantic interludes set in exotic "oriental" palaces and gardens. These films competed with aggressively marketed Hollywood exports largely because the French colonial presence obviated costs for labor and set production. They promoted the mix of paternalism and mutual respect, cooperation and manipulation that Resident General Louis-Hubert Lyautey and his Native Affairs Bureau (BAI) had been using to maintain order in the protectorate since 1912.

Romanticized versions of Morocco's traditional tales of outcasts revealed to be lost sons of kings or nobles, which cautioned against inflicting injustice on the poor and lowborn, adapted the aristocratic high culture and legitimated it by highlighting the old elite's value to Lyautey's system of indirect rule. Scripts derived from tales of resistance to foreign invasions by *roumi* (infidels) depicted a golden age in a dim past when Europeans were the barbarians. Part of Lyautey's broader labor to win French respect for Morocco's aristocratic traditions, these racially enlightened but still orientalist themes were framed within efforts to preserve a way of life that French conservatives felt they were losing in the metropole. "True Morocco" was going the way of "True France"; urbanization, white settlement, and market forces were undermining the old order of rural notables, which until the Rif War had enabled the seemingly benign paternalism of French "protection."

After the Rif War, Moroccan films reflected the tensions between those

84

colonialists who wanted to preserve the old order and those who wanted to sweep it away. Three melodramas, all released in 1928, that revolved around love affairs still expressed undertones of the racial conflict that marked the policy debates in Paris.[1] *La Comtesse Marie*, which though filmed in Spain incorporated documentary footage shot in Morocco, subtly appealed to race to foster right-wing, corporatist solidarity; a counterpoint, *Dans l'Ombre du harem*, challenged stereotypes of Muslim marriage customs by holding a mirror to the hypocritical behavior of European men; *L'Occident* endorsed cooperation between the races and reiterated the message that collaboration remained on European terms. The latter was the only one of the three that was made on the scale of prewar films.

After a three-year hiatus, *Cinq Gentlemen maudits* was shot in 1931, the crew arriving in Morocco soon after an urban mass protest movement had been quelled. One of the last films made on location in Morocco, it combined documentary footage with a story line that blended illusion and reality. The film wove a metaphor of French experience in a bid to show French audiences that what tourists thought they saw in Morocco was not what it seemed. Colonialists thought they were interacting with "True Morocco." Yet, by blinding them to the rapid changes they themselves were introducing, that concept fostered the illusion that Muslim society was timeless.[2]

The Rise of the Petits Colons in Morocco

The resident-general who replaced Lyautey in October 1925, Théodore Stéeg, had been governor of Algeria. He relaxed Lyautey's restrictions on the petits colons' freedom of action and encouraged Algerian whites to immigrate. Racial tensions rose, while pastoralism and subsistence farming declined. These undercurrents surfaced in film, with new realities intruding on idealized reconstructions of the past. Directors found the "old Morocco," the rural outback and seminomadic herders that served as backdrop for films, less accessible than a few years before. In the cities, restive, native nationalists were raising their first challenges to French authority. Heads of noble landowning families and rural notables, the assiduously cultivated junior partners of Lyautey's system of indirect rule, lost status and power as French capital changed rural life and Europeans settled the bled. Wage labor displaced tenantry, promoting migration to the cities and loosening the grip of notables and clans on rural society. Tribal banishment no longer threatened dire consequences if a transgressor could find work in Casablanca or Marseille.

The colons who came after the Rif War were less tolerant and more exclusive than those who settled when Lyautey was in charge. Most came from Algeria, where intolerance and contempt were hallmarks of pied noir/native relations and where Maurice Violette, who replaced Stéeg as governor, met with "bristling opposition" when he tried to extend native political rights.[3] Settlers reduced all indigenous people, irrespective of class, gender, or ethnicity to an undifferentiated mass of hewers of wood and drawers of water. To them, the most degraded white represented Western civilization and hence was superior to the noblest Muslim, whose culture was an obsolete evil, to be erased entirely. Street names of Algerian colonial towns like Bône (Annaba) and postcards sold to tourists evoked the history and monuments of Roman and Christian antiquity or the accomplishments of French colonialism, grafting ancient to modern and erasing memory of the intervening Islamic millennium. "Algériens" emigrating to Morocco outnumbered European settlers and brought with them a keen sense of their prerogatives as "lords of humankind." Coveting the lands and laborers of Morocco's old elite, they opposed protections of native rights proposed by Paris, the residency, or the big banks of the colonial lobby.

Filmmakers still influenced by Lyautey and the BAI reaffirmed their respect for Moroccan traditions and pointed out the absurdities of the settler view, but the influx of settlers increased pressure to adopt Algerian ways and negate Morocco's culture. Films made in Morocco after the Rif War reflected changes in colonial policy and form of rule. They mounted a rearguard action on the culture front, but Algerian films, which glorified the settlers and the Foreign Legion as heroes holding back the barbarians at the gates, supplanted them.

When Théodore Stéeg had taken charge of the protectorate in October 1925, some 66,000 Europeans, mainly French citizens, lived in Morocco, chafing under Lyautey's authoritarian, paternalistic protection of Moroccans. He had distrusted settler demands for democracy as a restraint on his freedom of action and as an excuse to dominate the natives through predatory speculation and landgrabbing. Stéeg, asserting French parliamentary control, was more responsive to French settlers than to native Moroccans. Before he retired in 1929, Stéeg expanded the settler advisory council's power and eased the way for more colonization; by 1931 they numbered 115,000, a 42 percent increase.

Subsequent residents-general gave freer rein to the settlers, but, reluctant to play the role of pioneers and "Indian fighters," immigrants concentrated in the cities, as in Algeria. In 1937, Europeans were 14 percent of Algeria's population, 9 percent of Tunisia's, and 4 percent of Morocco's.

Stéeg had earned a reputation for pro-native reform in Algeria, but in Morocco he encouraged European settlement through farm loans and irrigation assistance. By the late 1920s, the Moroccan farmland with the best rainfall had fallen into colon hands, and Stéeg built dams and concrete-lined irrigation courses as a way to aid farmers of modest means develop small-scale intensive agriculture such as fruit and vegetable cultivation. Although the Great Depression and urban settlers' demands for water and electricity slowed these irrigation projects, Stéeg created a central fund to finance ongoing storage-dam construction. By the mid 1930s, the government had settled French veterans and official immigrants on 1,750 farms, totaling 250,000 hectares, and private individuals had bought another half million hectares.

Settlers wanted autonomy, tariff protection, and integration of Morocco's economy into France's sphere, all violations of the Open Door policy of the 1906 Act of Algerçiras that aggravated the effects of the 1929 economic crisis. Lyautey had supported large-scale wheat farming because it restricted the number of settlers. To appease the colons already there, other colonial planners went along with him, and a myth arose that the land had gone to seed because of the Arabs' poor agronomy and that France could restore "Mauritania, the granary of Rome." In fact, Arab farming techniques suited a climate that had become far drier than in Roman times. And despite its need for expensive water subsidies, the colonial wheat lobby was strong enough in March 1923 to overcome the resistance of the metropole's powerful farm lobby and win the Chamber's approval for a tariff-free quota on Moroccan wheat imported to France.

Tariff policies extended French protection to settlers, a key support for colonial agricultural production. Paris exempted the entire empire from a 1.3 percent tax on agricultural products in February 1925, and in April 1928 Raymond Poincaré's conservative government created a duty-free French customs union. With this measure and with the onset of the Great Depression, settlers and natives both became economically dependent on the metropole. The crop not being able to compete on the world market with Russian or American grain, was dumped on the metropole, driving down the price of the grain produced by depression-wracked French farms. Opposition to Moroccan wheat subsidies grew with the grain surpluses, Moroccan wheat farming collapsed, and the myth of the "granary of Rome" disintegrated in the face of production costs that rose above world and even French levels. Colon farmers and merchants had wrested subsidies from parliament, but paradoxically the extension of credit drew them further into debt to the French banks that controlled the colonial investment consortiums. The white racial solidarity that installed settler dominance over the natives also enabled French finance capital to dominate the wheat farmers of the Maghreb and the metropole.[4]

La Comtesse Marie

Colonial film expressed contestations over race contained in these policy debates, and its subtexts landscaped the cinematic terrain with expectations of race war or racial cooperation. *La Comtesse Marie* appealed to white racial solidarity against nonwhites, in part by subtly invoking Western literary antecedents. Like the Rif War that surrounded the love story at the film's thematic center, the movie was a Franco-Spanish production. Studio Albatros, of Paris, invested 750,000 francs in a joint venture with Sociedad Julio César, of Bilbao, hiring Spanish director Benito Perojo and a mixed French and Spanish cast to film this melodrama in Spain. Louis, an army lieutenant who happens to be a grandee—one of the few hundred great noble landowners of Spain—meets Rosario, a young, poor, seamstress, in Madrid. He falls in love with her and proposes, but before they can marry, she falls ill, and Louis's regiment is called up for duty. Intercut with documentary footage, the film shows Louis heroically rallying his men in the thick of bitter fighting at the battle of Tetouan. The army informs his mother, Countess Marie, that he is missing and presumed dead, while Rosario, alone and penniless, bears Louis's child. She is too proud to beg, but the baby falls ill, and in desperation she goes to the countess, claiming to be Louis's wife. The kindly aristocrat takes her into the family palace. Louis's cousins, Clotilde and Manolo, who the intertitles say "hides a soul most vile beneath a correct exterior," conspire to seize the family fortune by proving that the baby is illegitimate. In the Rif, Louis has been captured. After suffering months of starvation, forced labor, and other torments, he bribes a guard to help him escape. Still wearing a dirty, tattered Riffian djellaba, he returns, like Odysseus, incognito to his manor. Discovering his presumptuous cousins' schemes, he reveals himself and drives them out. His tortuous ordeal—his odyssey—softens his heart, and the sight of his son rekindles his love for Rosario. They marry and go on honeymoon.[5]

This fantasy of love across Spanish society's chasmic class divisions drew on the real history of the war. After the victory at Anwal in July 1921, the Riffians held several hundred Spanish soldiers captive, compounding the army's humiliation. Mounting public concern over the prisoners' plight forced the government to ransom them. Through the good offices of the omnipresent Basque steel magnate Luis Echevarrietta, in January 1923 it paid Abd el-Krim the equivalent of $1 million for their return. The deal convinced the coterie of generals around King Alfonso that the parliamentary regime was ineffectual, and they hatched a plot to overthrow it. The pronunciamiento of September 1923 installed a dictatorship, headed by General Primo de Rivera, who promised to extricate Spain from the Rif. Instead, he maneuvered France into the war and, by dreadful sacrifice of men and treasure, held the protectorate. In the process, his traditional Spanish praetorian regime evolved into a "new state," coping with industrialization and modernization through "fascism from above." The film was as corporatist as the "new state," delivering the message that Spaniards of all classes, like the countess and Rosario, had suffered in common through the war and had persevered to achieve happiness by uniting against foreign enemies and domestic plotters. Luca de Tena, who wrote the script, was director of the monarchist Madrid daily *ABC*, the semiofficial mouthpiece of the regime, and had accompanied Primo on the Moroccan campaigns of 1923–26 as his "house journalist."[6] Primo's son, José Antonio, founded the Spanish fascist party, the Falange.

La Comtesse Marie allegorizes Spain's Rif War. It recalls Cervantes' "Prisoner's Tale" in *Don Quixote,* where the prisoner retells the story of his capture and years-long imprisonment by the Moors. The film identifies the hero with Primo de Rivera, also a grandee, and alludes to the trials of Odysseus, with noisesome suitors plaguing his house while he is away at war. Primo's secret police alleged that enemies within were plotting coups and assassinations and used the threat of conspiracies to eradicate Spain's Communist Party, drive the anarchists underground, and force liberals into exile in France. When the government stepped up military operations, crackdowns in 1924 smothered dissent.[7] The war revived the memory of the millennium-long struggle to reconquer

Spain from "the Moors" and infused it with modern race doctrine. Primo's regime adopted late-nineteenth-century cultural trends that had extirpated Spain's Moorish legacy to assert her Europeanness and repudiate the adage that "Africa begins at the Pyrenees."[8]

Roman Catholic patriarchal corporatism straddled the Pyrenees, and the Rif War infused it with racialism. The French press buried Lyautey and acclaimed his replacement, Marshal Philippe Pétain, as it had in 1918. It lauded him as preserver of his (metropolitan) troops and savior of the settlers. In fact, Pétain shifted the brunt of the fighting to North African troops, cynically adapting to Morocco the project of a force noire, the World War I plan to use the colonial army to aid France against Germany. In a preface to a popular military history of the Rif War published in 1928, Pétain had celebrated solidarity in battle: "French of France and Overseas French, brothers in arms, share this glory with pride." His use of the term *Français d'outre-mer* referred to citizens of the empire, a category that included Senegalese, but few Algerians. This subtle evasion implied that, despite their sacrifices, Pétain conceded no obligation to expand their rights.[9]

Pétain orchestrated military cooperation and built bridges to Primo and Francisco Franco, who was engaged in a parallel and equally cynical enterprise, building an African mercenary force from the Riffians he defeated in 1926. Along with his *Tercio extranjero,* the Spanish Foreign Legion, these Moorish *regulares* (professional native soldiers) became his shock troops in the coming civil war, accomplices in the fight against communism and liberalism. Their officers spurred them to terrorize Republican troops and civilians, among whom they acquired a demonic reputation. Remarkably, the Right embraced them, while simultaneously claiming the legacy of the medieval Reconquista against the Moors. In the uprising of 18 July 1936, the author of *La Comtesse Marie,* Luca de Tena, became a key conspirator. He arranged Franco's flight from exile in the Canary Islands to Morocco and the Nazi airlift of his shock force, the Praetorian *Tercio* and the regulares, across the straits to strike the first blow in Spain. In 1939, Pétain became the first ambassador to Franco's new state; a year later he took the helm of the Vichy regime, which fostered anti-Semitism, conjured "Asiatic Bolshevism," and drew on white-supremacist racial solidarity to disguise the class hierarchy of "True France." The Right created a different Muslim Orient from the Left—one that selected the Maghrebin traits that suited its political agenda and confirmed its worldview, yet shared assumptions of European superiority. The seeds of Franquist and Pétainist politics were germinating in *La Comtesse Marie*.[10]

Dans l'Ombre du Harem

Other films still voiced Lyauteyiste discourse, validating "True Morocco" or mourning its passing. *Dans l'Ombre du harem* hinges on the clash between unvarnished Muslim patriarchy and the hypocrisies of Western marriage, challenging the assumptions that Moroccan values were dissolute, backward, and decadent and that French treatment of women was entirely progressive. Based on a play by Lucien Besnard (a "Boulevard crime story with oriental dress and sets," it opened in Paris in 1927), the 1928 film echoed Lyautey's admiration for Morocco's traditional elite and support for its role as interlocutor of French imperial control. It targeted the male settlers' blindness to their double standard on monogamy and the stereotype of the lascivious oriental potentate, but its sympathies lay less with Muslims than with European women married to bounders. Isabelle, in *Dans l'Ombre du harem*, is such a woman, in such a predicament. Her husband, Roger, is an engineer in an unnamed Muslim country under French rule. They live in a modest cottage of European design across the road from the palace of an emir, Abd en-Nacer. Roger catches a glimpse of the emir's favorite wife, Djebellen'nour, and plots her seduction. Roger does penetrate the harem but is caught and the pair are brought before the emir. Abd en-Nacer imprisons his wife and plots an intricate revenge against Roger. His men kidnap the European couple's son, and as ransom Abd en-Nacer demands Isabelle for one night. Roger confesses his infidelity to Isabelle—he has no choice—and she goes to the emir to save her son. Expecting a cruel oriental chieftain, she finds instead a wise man who is moved by her courage and "moral beauty" to release the boy without forcing her to his bed. Roger begs her forgiveness, but, her trust broken, she refuses to live with him or to divorce him, finding solace only in raising her son.[11]

Plays like Besnard's were published regularly in the popular biweekly *Petite Illustration*. One-quarter of the twenty-six plays and novelettes appearing in the magazine's pages each year during the interwar years contained orientalist themes or plot elements. Besnard, who had lived in Morocco and fell under Lyautey's sway, was one of the few playwrights whose work was translated to the screen. Critical reaction took predictable lines. On the left, *Comoedia* critic Etienne Rey attributed the intense curiosity about the colonies to France's growing cultural diversity. Besnard had "studied the Muslim soul" and had revealed the "divergent concepts of love" and the resentment of those forced to submit to French control. *Le Figaro*'s Robert de Flers read the play as a premonitory encounter foreshadowing an impending race war. Abd el-Krim's aggression, he warned, "ought to make even the most indifferent aware of the problems posed by the awakening of Asia and Africa mobilized by Bolshevism against Western Civilization."

Many public figures of the French Right, such as Maurice Muret, Henri Massis, Louis Marin, Pierre Taittinger, and moderates such as Albert Sarraut, had adopted this racialized view of global class struggle. Lothrop Stoddard's *Rising Tide of Color* swayed this influential circle to place the Rif War within the context of a social-Darwinist vision of the future. First published in the United States, it was translated into French in 1925. *Petit Illustration*'s own critic held the view that Emir Abd en-Nacer showed French audiences "an Islamic soul complex and closed, composed of instincts both primitive and refined, of generosity and ferocity *(dureté)*, of righteousness and trickery *(ruse)*. Such a great q'aid, whom the political wisdom of a Lyautey won to our cause, served as model for M. Lucien Besnard."[12]

Besnard anointed European women as bearers of civilization to the natives, preaching a feminist message that cropped up again in *Itto* (1934), the last Lyauteyiste film. Isabelle touches the emir's sense of honor, dissuading him from revenge. Her honor prevents her from divorcing Roger or living with him again, and she plunges him into domestic limbo, fitting punishment for Roger, who honors Christian monogamy more in the breach than in the practice. During their ten-year marriage, he had betrayed her before, once with her closest friend. Moral hypocrisy mixed with orientalist fantasies lead him to seduce Djebellen'nour's sister and use her to lure the emir's wife to him. "Christian women are poor lovers compared to the daughters of Allah," he says at one point; Christian women demand loyalty and put pride before love. "An oriental woman . . . abases herself before the whims of the man . . . even [the whim] of another woman."[13]

Engineers loomed large in colonial mythology, and Besnard bared a dark side of Roger's profession. Although his preface disclaims the setting as a "philosophical place," Besnard later says Roger works for a phosphate mining company in Sla (Salé), a town near Casablanca. Its operations destroy the emir's orchards and farms, and the stereotype of a capricious oriental potentate thus fades before the picture of a man justifiably angered by the despoliation of his land and home. Besnard's movie-scene style challenged audiences along with his content, since middle-brow snobbery exalted theater and disparaged film. Cutting each act of his play into three or four rapidly shifted tableaux, he imitated film technique, reversing the source of inspiration.[14]

Film itself expressed the conflicting reactions of critics to *Dans l'Ombre du harem*. The movie *L'Esclave blanche* (The white slave) premiered in December 1927, seven months after Besnard's play opened in Paris and seven months before it arrived on the screen. It took an antithetical view of racially divided marriage and morals. Mary Watson, a young English heiress vacationing at an elegant resort, falls in love with Benver Bey, an "oriental man of the world." They marry, and he takes her to his European-style palace in North Africa. But her happiness sours as "the abyss of incomprehension that separates the races is revealed in all its terrible depths." Mary complains that she feels cut off from the outside world so the Bey puts his limousine at her disposal. But its doors lock from the outside. The chauffeur drives her to town, and through the window she hails some acquaintances and invites them to dinner. The bey cancels the soirée, saying, "It is not the custom of his race." Realizing she is a prisoner, she explores the palace for an unguarded exit, discovers the bey's's first wife, Fatma, sequestered in an apartment, and faints in shock. When she recovers, Mary helps Fatma to escape with a young man she loves, but the bey and his horsemen chase them down, kill the lover, and imprison Fatma. A young doctor, Warner, rescues Mary. In his car, they leave their pursuers far behind, but the automobile gets trapped in the sand. The bey rides up, his flintlock aimed, just as the tires grab, the car lurches forward, and his startled horse throws him to his death. Warner and Mary reach the port and embark for the safety of Europe.[15]

The contest between Benver Bey and Warner embodies the conventional triumph of superior Western technology and values over oriental despotism. It mirrors *Dans l'ombre*'s reversal of roles, where Roger's lasciviousness and duplicity, traits usually assigned to the Arab male, provokes the troubles. In the film version, the play's harsh condemnation of Roger is mitigated by reconciling the couple. Roger's attempt to rescue Djebellen'nour from the emir's dungeon pandered to a favorite male fantasy of fiction, cinema, and picture postcards, the prisoner of

Although produced for the 1939 sound remake of *L'Esclave blanche* (The white slave), this poster conveys the sense of the original 1927 silent film. The main character, Mary Watson (played by Viviane Romance in the sound remake), is depicted in two costumes symbolizing the change from European society heiress to "white slave" in the harem of Muslim nobleman Benver Bey. Both the "Arab" headdress and the European-style hat are thinly veiled, a suggestive mirroring of women's status in both France and North Africa. *Credit:* copyright Galerie Cine-Images, Paris the harem. The fantasy was more pronounced in the film, where the harem is a seraglio of a dozen women, than in the play, where the emir quotes Qur'anic proscription on the number of wives and admonishments to equal treatment.[16] On the other hand, *L'Esclave*'s women do not compete for the attention of a white man, they unite to escape the clutches of their common oppressor. Fatma presumably desires monogamous love and emancipation from an arranged, child-bride marriage, and Mary's help was a role touted by French women travel writers and feminists as the special contribution European women made to the civilizing mission.[17]

Roger's invasion of the emir's home was more than metaphorical. The French followed conquest and occupation of the land with attempts to reform the Muslim family by freeing women from the veil and arranged marriage, which in turn became symbols of resistance. Roger is above Muslim law, immune to recourse even from an emir. A native police chief makes this point, and is portrayed as a dignified and reasonable protector of the emir's rights, not a stereotypical cardboard Arab villain. Besnard presents Roger's violation of law and custom as an individual act, yet implies that extraterritorial immunity was a cornerstone of white privilege. Phantasmic "rescues" in both films strip the native woman of her cultural identity and encase her in colonial cliches of sexual fantasy. In reality a traditionist-griotte, she could "lie up a nation," that is, keep alive the histories of Northwest African peoples, and help them resist or accommodate European domination. Film reduced rich linguistic heritages to a few cries, except in *Sirocco* (1930) and *Itto* (1934), where native women spoke at length in Arabic or Berber and aroused curiosity and suspicion among French reviewers.[18]

The theme of irreconcilable incompatibility of French and Arab culture recurs in films made in Algeria. Implicit rejoinders to Besnard, they reflect the viewpoint of the petit-colon defense of race privilege. *La Symphonie pathétique* (1928) was filmed in the Algerian Sahara. Zetzaia, the daughter of a European mother and an Arab father, carries the mixing of race to a second generation when she falls in love with a French aviator. His squadron leaves, her Arab uncle imprisons her, and several years pass before she can send the Frenchman word of her predicament. He has married, but out of love and duty he rescues her and takes her to New York. The intrigues of a friend of his wife reveal that he is married, and Zetzaia dies of shame. He overcomes his despondency and gains a new lease on life when his wife presents him

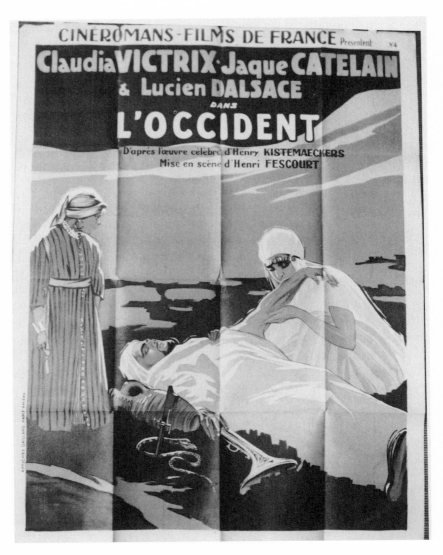

L'Occident (1928): Lieutenant Cadières, disguised in a burnous, has been bitten by a snake; he lies on the ground, dunes in the background. Next to him is the snake that Hassina has now killed with her dagger. Watched by her sister, she sucks the snake poison from his arm. The poster highlights the stereotype of the dark-skinned colonial woman as rescuer of the white man literally lost in the colonized world. *Credit:* copyright Galerie Cine-Images, Paris with a child and he returns to the bosom of his monogamous family. Zetzaia's fate is preordained; she comes to bad end because she is métisse and cannot reconcile her mixed heritage.[19]

L'Occident

Implicit contestation of race continued with *L'Occident*, released in September 1928. Based on Henri Kistemaeckers's play, which had opened in Paris in 1913 during the protectorate's halcyon days, it projected hopes for cooperation between the races. Albert Capellani, an emigré French director working in the United States, adapted it to the screen in 1918. Recognizing that the scenario was a proven moneymaker, Henri Fescourt remade it in 1928 and again in 1937. Its reincarnations reveal changing attitudes toward race; the 1928 version incidentally disclosed recondite economic features of Moroccan film production, since it acquired help from French authorities to deploy army units and native "dissidents" for battle scenes.

The fictional plot revolves around a rebellion incited by a q'aid, Tayeb el Hani, a ferocious enemy of France who resembles the real Riffian leader Abd el-Krim. A squadron is dispatched to Moroccan waters to quell the revolt, and Lieutenant Cadière is assigned to reconnaissance. As night falls, he slips ashore disguised in the burnous of a q'aid and makes his way to the rebel encampment. Hassina, a young woman of a nearby village, is out walking with her little sister and finds him asleep on the ground. Seeing a cobra slithering toward him, she adroitly throws her knife and kills it, but not before it strikes. She sucks the poison from his arm and, after a long night on the brink of death, he recovers. Once he is himself, he thanks her in her language, which he speaks fluently. She has fallen for him. His cloak recalls a prophecy a sorcerer made to her that she would marry an emir. She pledges her love. When the rebels discover him and close in, he reveals his identity to her and enlists her to slip through their lines and report his position to the squadron. Returning with a company of marines commanded by his friend Ensign Arnaud, she comes to his rescue a second time. Taking refuge atop a fortified hill, the marines fight off several assaults by Tayeb's men, who wound Hassina and carry off her sister Fathima. Reinforcements arrive, put the dissidents to rout in a big battle, and, as Hassina is evacuated on a stretcher, the marines stand on parade and salute her. Cadière brings her to Toulon, the fleet headquarters, to live with him.

But the fate of her missing sister, Fathima, clouds Hassina's happiness. No one knows Tayeb has smuggled the girl to Toulon, where he exhibits her as a dancer in sleazy waterfront bars while plotting an uprising to avenge his defeat. Donning a disguise, he seeks out Hassina and convinces her that the message Cadière had asked her to carry had trained the ships' guns on Fathima's hiding place and killed her. Hassina agrees to seduce Arnaud and run off with him. Arnaud is betrothed to the squadron commander's daughter but thinks he loves Hassina. Cadière discovers the love triangle, dissuades Arnaud from deserting, and uncovers Tayeb's hiding place. By threats and bribes, he thwarts the q'aid's plot, forcing him to relinquish Fathima, and Tayeb's uprising is defeated in a spectacular battle. Reunited with her sister, Hassina falls into Cadière's arms; they marry, adopt Fathima, and live happily ever after.[20]

For the battle scene, Fescourt took pride in the authenticity he achieved by using real soldiers and Chleuh Berbers as "native extras." To stage the scene, Fescourt hired J. Roger-Mathieu, a correspondent who had covered the Rif War, and deputized him "general of the dissidents." The reporter had just returned from Réunion Island, in the Indian Ocean, where France had exiled Abd el-Krim, and had helped the Riffian leader write his memoirs. Fescourt also won the cooperation of Resident-general Stéeg and General Vidalon, the commander in chief of Morocco. Vidalon instructed the local commander of Marrakech, General Huré, to assign two battalions of infantry, two cavalry squadrons, and two artillery batteries to film duty. El Hadj Thami al Glaoui, pasha of Marrakech and long-time ally of the French, recruited local Berber clansmen, the Chleuh, who had acted as extras in films since the early 1920s. Al Glaoui promised his utmost cooperation and sent word for his men to assemble, but the next day scarcely 150 answered this "first call." Roger-Mathieu told those who did show up that he needed two thousand men the following morning, that he "would pay them directly," and that Al Glaoui would be displeased if they did not deliver on his promise. The speech brought out hundreds more, who took part in filming skirmishes over the next two days. For the climactic battle, they hired a troop of horsemen who had come to the Marrakech Fair to perform a fantaisie. The Legionnaires and other French units deployed on the peak of a rocky hill, while Roger-Mathieu issued his order of the day to the Chleuh: "La formation de combat: le pagaie"— a disordered mass charge. Fescourt's screenplay called for a furious countercharge by the Legionnaires, routing the Chleuh, who "played their parts to the hilt." The disciplined French predictably inflicted a "fictional massacre [on] the dissidents," and they fled.[21]

The reporter's account presents a rare glimpse of filmmaking in a colonial setting. With the help of a police officer and a Spahi sergeant who spoke Chleuh Berber, Roger-Mathieu issued instructions to the extras, most of whom spoke neither French nor Arabic. Fescourt was amazed at their ability to carry out the most intricate directions, and he was able to film the big battle sequence in only two days. One young horseman rode to the location with his wife in the saddle behind him. While he joined the battle, she watched the day's shooting sitting in the shade of an automobile, admiring its interior. At the end of the day, he picked up his pay and they rode off to the south (one almost expects him to be carrying a Screen Actors Guild card). For the Chleuh, working as movie extras became a windfall source of day labor, with the cash assuaging the indignity of "defeat."[22]

In his memoirs, Fescourt admitted to pangs of conscience about his conscious imitation of Hollywood's cavalry-and-Indian battles. Imagining what real Native Americans felt when they played extras in movies, he considered how the conventions of the western reduced all non-Europeans to savages and overpowered attempts at honest portrayals. "The idea never occurred to the managers of this warlike spectacle," he said, "that perhaps among the crowd of retreating Moroccans were some secretly offended at the role they had been given to play."[23] Fescourt had been preoccupied with the ordinary tribulations of filmmaking and blind to such painful ironies, but they were not lost on imperialists such as Mussolini, who backed the production of *Scipio Africanus*, a film celebrating Rome's destruction of Carthage. In January 1937, Il Duce visited the set on location in Tripoli; as he looked on, Libyans, only recently subdued by Italy, played Hannibal's soldiers, and mock Roman Legions routed them for the cameras.[24] In retrospect, Fescourt concluded, the script of *L'Occident* was banal and the film's commercial success far outweighed its artistry. His relations with Claudia Victrix, the unphotogenic actress who played Hassina, were soured by "artistic differences," a polite way of saying she could not act. Since she was the wife of her producer, Jean Sapène, he put up with her. He was enchanted by the marvelous scenery and moonlit aromatic gardens of Marrakech, Mogador, and Tananaout, but his peace of mind was disturbed by accidents, poverty, and disease. Typhus struck Marrakech, and "every morning around seven we crossed paths with native burial parties, rapid funeral cortèges."[25] Concerned for the inhabitants, yet willfully ignoring France's role in disrupting local life, he attributed their woes to Morocco's timeless "backwardness," a predilection sanctioned by officers and settlers alike.

Fescourt remade *L'Occident* in 1937, and again army, navy, and colonial authorities put troops and ships at his disposal. This time he shot only a few scenes in Casablanca, filming the rest in Bou Sâada, two hundred kilometers south of Algiers. He revised the script, reworking the illiterate Hassina into a Sorbonne student and évolué played by Madagascan actress Rama-Tahé, herself light-skinned and thoroughly assimilated into upper-class Parisian society. Q'aid Tayeb was transformed from dissident into bandit, anticolonial resistance was criminalized, and the battle was reduced in scale to a *razzia,* or raid. In 1928, the naval bombardment was justified because the rebellion obstructed "progress." In the 1937 film, Tayeb's men burn Hassina's village, and the q'aid hatches a plot to blame the French. When she discovers that Tayeb killed her family, Hassina kills him, an "Arab" act of revenge suggesting that, despite her assimilation, Hassina retained her atavistic culture. Interracial love and marriage seemed less conceivable and more distant in 1937 than in 1928. Although the love triangle still complicated the later version, and Ensign Arnaud still chose honor over love, the fleet sailed with Cadière and Hassina unreconciled. *Pour Vous*'s reviewer remarked, "Only the question of rapport between East and West has not been decided."[26]

The changing rural economic landscape accounted in part for the changes in Fescourt films. Roger-Mathieu's speech to the Chleuh "first call," mixing individual incentive with communal admonition, proletarian wage with feudal obligation, reflected the transition. In the early 1920s, tribal horsemen gave their time to a film as a service to Al Glaoui, but in 1928 Fescourt paid them wages. As underdevelopment spread, farmers and nomads lost land and herds, and Moroccan film lost its sponsors, Lyautey and the king. In the 1930s, directors chose Algerian Saharan film sites, which were more arid and sparsely populated than Morocco; the Algerian economy had been disrupted by French occupation of Tuareg oases. As was apparent in films like *L'Atlantide,* film work could count on few hands. Smaller scale and altered content marked the shift to Algerian locales in early sound-era remakes.

As tourism, that two-edged sword, widened the impact of French market forces, it also enabled North Africans to cope with the disruptions of French economic penetration. Tourism commodified the picturesque, producing vicarious tourism, a vast industry of which film was a branch. Millions of advertising posters, product labels, and picture postcards posed, recorded, and reproduced overt images of white control and sub-liminal messages of white dominance. Mock battles reenacted at colonial expositions were antecedents of film. The 1893 Expo's producers brought a group of Pai-Pi-Bris, of Dahomey, to Paris, divided them into two armies, and had them fire their antique flintlocks at each other until the powder ran out. The Lumière Brothers dispatched one of their cameramen, Félix Mesguich, to North Africa to record images already made popular by the expos, illustrated magazines, and travel literature. In Biskra, Mesguich produced the first film footage of a fantaisie, hiring a unit of irregular local troops in French service at 7 francs per man for the entire assignment. But two were accidentally killed in the filming. Their families demanded 2,000 francs compensation, and Mesguich absconded, fearing Lumière would not pay. Eventually, the relatives received 5,000 francs in damages.

Another pioneer of Algerian film, Raoul Grimoin-Sanson, arranged a similar mock battle, and a French general supplied several thousand horsemen. Pathé Cinéma won exclusive rights to exhibit similar scenes on film at the Marseille Colonial Expo of 1906, boosting its dominant position in the distribution of all films. The Colonial Exposition of 1931 and the Colonial Pavilions of the 1937 World's Fair tempered the zoo-like, carnivalesque atmosphere of earlier shows. Visitors were forbidden to throw money at colonial performers, as was customary, but the more tasteful displays of the 1930s retained a diorama-like quality. The 1931 Exposition imported whole villages and set artisans to work under the gaze of the European spectators. No interaction was allowed, reinforcing the unequal status between observer and observed.[27]

An example of the dialectics of commodification appeared in *Ciné-Miroir*, which sent a woman reporter to Senegal to answer the question "Are Blacks Photogenic?" In Dakar, her film crew shot scenes of the townspeople dressed in their best clothes—red and green jackets and hats with black pants—then motored to a nearby village where they found the women weaving or preparing manioc, or cassava, in front of their houses. When the women saw the cameras, they all went inside and shut their doors; one woman came out to explain that the crew would have to pay to film them. "You understand, missy, other directors *(metteurs en scène)* come here, take photos and give *matabich*, 15 francs per woman. If you want to do the same you must also give *matabich.*" The reporter translated this word as *gratuity* or *gift (pourboire; cadeau)*; where once a moral economy of the poor had operated freely, now it was embedded in a context of tourism and racial overlordship. Sénégalais were photogenic, she concluded, but curiously, the photo of a muscular, nearly nude young man that accompanied her story had been cropped from an earlier issue of *Ciné-Miroir,* where the caption accompanying the photo had identified him as a Zulu warrior. While Dakar market women bartered their images as the entry fee into the world economy, an interchangeable image sold magazines in France.[28]

Tourism, Film, and the Berber Dahir of 1930

Tourism and filmmaking were symbiotic: as tourism impelled greater demand for verisimilitude in film, film whetted the French appetite for vicarious tourism, and shooting on location turned filmmakers into tourists. One of the last films to be made in Morocco, Duvivier's *Cinq Gentlemen maudits* (1931), was caught up in these dialectics and in the nationalist reaction to them. The calculus of governance was already delicately balanced and extremely complicated. The protectorate had to ensure large investors' profits, privilege the petits colons, prop up the native elites, employ the new urban middle classes, and meet urban and rural development needs. Lyautey had modernized Casablanca's port, created an administrative capital at Rabat, and built roads between cities where there had been none. New government buildings, power plants, and warehouses blended modern function with traditional design features like white facades and tile roofs that kept buildings cool in the Moroccan sun. The French considered Moorish urban design equal to the accomplishments of Andalucia, and Lyautey's urban planner, Henri Prost, preserved monuments, mosques, and whole quarters of the old cities. He restored Casablanca's canals, watercourses, market districts *(medinas),* and the university quarter *(medersa).* As more Europeans visited and settled, Prost "Haussmann-ized" the city, clearing great swaths of slums to allow crowd and disease control, a preoccupation of colonialists everywhere. European districts were created by zoning areas where building codes required indoor plumbing, low walls, slanted roofs, and other design elements that interfered with Islamic customs (e.g., the seclusion of women). The rest of the city retained its

flat-roofed, high-walled structures with internal courtyards, which without formal apartheid segregated the traditional elites from the French
quarter.[29]

This de facto, rather than de jure, segregation of Casablanca blurred
boundaries; in 1930, nearly twenty-five thousand upper-class Muslims
and Jews lived in homes of mixed architectural design in the European
quarter. In older, working-class quarters of the city, Portuguese and
Spanish laborers lived among Moroccans. The poorest arrivals, Arab
and Berber rural emigrants, set up "bidonvilles"—slums made up of
cardboard-and-tin shacks—on the outskirts. Prost declared these slums
the most serious problem facing colonial policymakers in 1931. They
were springing up throughout the colonial world as a result of rural
impoverishment, but he made no connection between the expanding
flow of French capital into Morocco and the economic dislocation of
the slum dwellers.[30]

Protectorate officials invited urban land speculation by honoring
French over Moroccan land titles. A dahir promulgated in the sultan's
name in 1927 declared "French settlement" sufficient justification for
expropriating Moroccan-owned land, and the placing of such judgments in the hands of French courts further encouraged speculation.
But tourism curtailed the drive to remake Moroccan cities through real-
estate dealings. As Lyautey recognized, preserving the "flavor" of old
Morocco was not just an aesthetic duty, it was an economic necessity.
"Since the recent, intense development of large-scale tourism, preservation of a country's beauty takes on economic significance of the first
order. To attract large-scale tourism is to gain everything for both public and private budgets. The tourist does not come to a country where
there is no longer anything to visit."[31] "Authentic" picturesque cityscapes attracted tens of thousands of French visitors via the liners ply-
ing between Le Havre, Bordeaux and Marseille and Algiers or Lyautey's
new port facilities at Casablanca. Colonial films included travel-poster
scenes of protagonists disembarking such vessels full of hope or being
carried away in despair.[32]

Although the movement to rescind the Berber decree pitted urban
nationalists more against the residency than against the *makhzan* (the
sultan's government, shadowed by French officials), the colons had in-
stigated changes in customary law that precipitated the outburst. Concerned that rural courts validate their land titles, issue clear documents
and deeds, and enforce labor contracts, they pressed for Berber justice

to be reconciled with the French legal system. Wherever possible, questions of title were to be brought under the jurisdiction of French courts. Thus the decree conformed with the Berber policy devised by Lyautey's aides, which favored rural Berber clans over Arab-dominated cities but also encouraged French investment and turned rural clans into a wage-labor force. By making French law preeminent over both Berber traditional law and Qur'anic *shariy'a,* the decree went far to undermine the traditional rural Berber way of life that it was ostensibly designed to preserve.[33]

First introduced as part of the pacification strategy, Berber policy evolved into a means of social control that coincided with the economic needs of the settlers. Lyautey had accepted the submission of Middle Atlas Berber clans to France rather than the sultan, through whom he issued a dahir in 1914 declaring Berber autonomy inviolate. As one residence official remarked, "The Berber race is a useful instrument for counteracting the Arab race . . . and the *Makhzan* itself."[34] Maurice LeGlay, the main advocate of Berber policy, argued in 1921 that France should try to abolish Islamic instruction and replace the Arabic with the Roman alphabet in Berber schools. Franco-Berber schools grew in number from five in 1923 to eighteen in 1931; they tried to de-Islamicize the Berbers, eliminate "foreign" Arab influences, and curtail the intrusion of *fqih,* itinerant Arabic language teachers of the Qur'an. Just before issuing the 1930 decree, the protectorate began restricting travel permits to fqih bound for Berber regions.[35]

As their population rose, the settlers kept the Algerian precedent in mind. White clerks and petty officials *tutoyé*'d (addressed in the familiar *tu*) native doctors and lawyers in both countries, and school textbooks thinly disguised their contempt for Islam. The only official editions of government decrees were the French versions; unofficial Arabic translations appeared weeks later. However, pieds noirs had concentrated on preventing natives from acquiring skills that created racial competition for jobs. Morocco's settlers needed natives who understood French, both as foremen with technical skills for urban work and as overseers with a knowledge of basic agronomy who could supervise agricultural laborers and increase productivity of the land.[36]

In promulgating the decree on 16 May 1930, Resident-General Lucien Saint intemperately remarked that it represented the first step toward the introduction of French justice. The comment aroused the nationalists, as did the Roman Catholic bishop's inflammatory claims about conversions and the revival of clerical proselytizing. The "revolt" against the decree began with boycotts of French goods and reached a crescendo in July and August with "pray-ins" at the mosques, which led to arrests and provoked mass demonstrations that spread to the old cities of the Sharifian empire, Salé, Rabat, Fez, and Marrakech. French authorities, accustomed to regarding the cities as their strongholds and the bled as an arena of dissidence, were rattled by "dahirium tremens" and disoriented by the leaders of the movement, who were young, French-educated évolués they had considered allies in the colonial enterprise. Urban merchants who did not relish the idea of doing business in Berber areas under Berber customary law and were being ruined by a flood of Japanese imports in the first year of the Great Depression, joined the youth. The French experts on Muslim mores and customs trained under Lyautey were nonplussed and embarrassed to be caught by surprise, but once the revolt's religious character emerged, they judiciously withdrew their forces and allowed the makhzan to handle the task of quelling it and restoring order.[37]

At first, the rural, clan-based Berbers remained aloof from the fray, but the dahir forced them to choose between their traditional rights and Muslim orthodoxy. Their notables' role as viable intermediaries for French rule was by this time defunct. Urban nationalists had supplanted old elites as the colons' competitors.[38] The Berbers sided with the students and *ulamaa*, the council of religious scholars, and subscribed to its Islamic reform movement, or Salafiyyah. Facing unprecedented unity of his subjects, urban and rural, Arab and Berber, the sultan intervened in the fall and struck his name from the most offensive clauses of the decree. Stepping out of the gilded cage in which the residency had kept him, he remade himself as a more independent interlocutor between the French officials and the nationalists, who institutionalized their victory by founding the National Action Bloc, or Kutlah.[39] Neither the king nor the Kutlah wanted to overthrow French rule; they wanted to stymie the settlers:

The Moroccan nationalists complained loudly of cultural assimilation and . . . the complaints were genuine. But on closer inspection it will become clear that what [they] really wanted was *more* assimilation for themselves, in the form of an open door to [French] universities, and *less* for the lower classes, by the elimination of the French language from their schools. What concerned them most was the education of a Moroccan elite (themselves) in sufficient numbers to restore control of their country to native leadership (their own).[40]

Although allied with the Kutlah, French socialists in Morocco noted the self-serving aspects of its Plan des Reformes. "Freeing a nation," they admonished in May 1934, "does not necessarily mean freeing its proletariat. . . . We do not want the Moroccan workers to be sacrificed to the appetites of a few young bourgeois." But the socialists, mainly low-level civil servants, had a stake in legitimating colon privileges. The North African Interfederal Socialist Congress of 1926 expressed a desire to raise natives "to the level . . . of the parent state." Successive meetings held true to assimilation, not anticolonialism, as their goal.[41]

Pressed by colon demands for contract and property law reform to put Morocco on the Algerian path toward settler privilege and rule, French authorities heedlessly upset complicated and delicate balances in the native legal system. The miscalculation reaffirmed the wisdom of Lyautey's advice to respect indigenous culture, and Lucien Saint held his post until 1933, temporarily setting back the advocates of direct rule and blunting the drive to a settler state as the residency proceeded more slowly with its plans to impose French contractual law.

Cinq Gentlemen maudits: Five Damned Tourists?

Within months of the restoration of calm, Julien Duvivier's crew arrived in Morocco to film Cinq Gentlemen maudits. Saint permitted the director to make mildly subversive jibes at settlers and at suggestible naifs who believed the stereotypes of native Moroccans. Like the mysterious veiled woman and the blind beggar around whom the story pivots, nothing in the film is what it seems. The protectorate's complex interplay of groups, veiled objectives, and hidden meanings created an atmosphere for the mystery and drove forward the plot.

The film opens with ten minutes of strange but fascinating documentary scenes: a tannery works in Fez, the laborers calling out to one another as they go about their tasks; the sights and sounds of an open-air market and other activities of daily life; muezzin in minarets sonorously calling the faithful to prayer; boys chanting recitations of the Qur'an to their teacher. In a scene that seems to be part of the documentary, a veiled woman gestures to a blind beggar, who nods in reply.

Deception charges the air. No narrative voice or translation is heard, but the addition of sound to the typical sights of travelogues was new.

The scene shifts to an ocean liner bound for Morocco, and the film introduces its hero, Jacques Le Guérentec. A naive, impressionable, wealthy young Breton, he has met four British Royal Air Force officers and Françoise, the niece of a rich colon. The pilots befriend him. Jacques falls in love with the girl, setting the stage for a bildungsroman, a story of a youth achieving manhood through a test of his courage and resourcefulness. Before they disembark at Tangier, Duvivier includes an odd scene of a deck-tennis game in slow motion, with the ball acting as if on a tether and keeping time to the music. This trompe l'oeil special effect hints at his intention to deceive.

From Tangiers, Jacques and his friends travel to Moulay Idriss, a holy city that unbelievers must leave by nightfall. An Islamic brotherhood, the Aissawa, celebrates a *moussem,* or saint's day, and the friends watch Berber horsemen firing rifles in the air as they perform a fantaisie. Fascinated and appalled, they look on at a great gathering of men dancing in line to flute and pipes, at fire-eaters, at men flagellating themselves, and lines of women dancing to the beat of drums, long hair flying wildly, dervish-like. The blind beggar and the veiled woman appear, and one of the Brits tries to pull off her veil. As she backs away, the blind man leaps forward, knife drawn, but two native constables are near and they put him in restraints. He points to the Europeans and counts them off one by one, saying, "You will die in this order before the moon is full." At the Europeans' insistence, the policemen translate his curse but scoffingly dismiss it. The constables drive the beggar-sorcerer away.

In a Casablanca night club that night, the five companions get drunk, and one of the pilots disappears. Police arrive and conclude he has fallen off the patio wall and into the bay below. They restrain the four from diving in after him since the tide assuredly swept him out to sea. One of pilots points out that the blind sorcerer had marked the drowned man as the first to die, and they return to the colon's house, shocked and sobered. In the morning, the second pilot on the sorcerer's list returns to Europe to take part in an air show. The next day they read a newspaper item: his plane had crashed and he was killed. That night, a shadowy figure, camouflaged behind a sheaf of grain, slips past a guard watching the colon's fields, creeps up to the house, and drops a note through the window of Jacques's room: it urges him to go to the Roman ruins nearby if he wants to find out what is happening to his friends. Later still, a figure clad in caftan and Arab slippers steals into Jacques's room and reads the note. In the morning, Jacques takes Françoise riding, and at the ruins they stumble on the body of the third pilot, a dagger in his back. The native police conclude that the murder was the work of bandits. At dinner, Jacques is so shaken he cannot eat, but the colon derides his fears. After Françoise berates her uncle for insensitivity, he consults a scholarly tome on Moroccan sorcery, which dismisses the country's magic as the morbid superstitions of a backward society. Strawber, the last of the four pilots, is satisfied, but Jacques remains skeptical of glib rationales; his anxiety is unabated.

The next night is the full moon, and to distract Jacques, the colon takes them to a hotel in Fès. But a native funeral party passes under the hotel window, casting a pall over their evening. As Jacques sits writing out his will, Strawber receives a phone call that leaves him shaken. Jacques follows him to his room, finds him holding a pistol to his head, and gently takes away the gun. Strawber explains that he has gambled and lost a million francs; he cannot pay and has no way out but suicide. Seeing a way to keep his friend alive and stave off the curse, Jacques writes Strawber a check, to their mutual relief.

Alone on a sightseeing stroll the next morning, Jacques by chance catches sight of the sorcerer. Screwing up his courage, he trails the ragged man through the streets. The same sights and sounds as filled the opening sequences now seem more intelligible and less fearsome as seen through Jacques's emboldened eyes. He follows the beggar up a flight of stairs into a courtyard where, blind no more, he is arguing with Strawber, two of the other pilots, and the veiled woman—unveiled; she is blonde and French. Jacques steps into their midst and demands an explanation. The thieves fall out. The pilots confess that Strawber concocted this scheme to get Jacques's money and that Strawber killed their companion, the other pilot, to silence him. Strawber insists the murder was the work of bandits, but lets slip that he was the caftaned, slippered figure who slipped into Jacques's room and read the note. His hand exposed, Strawber flees, with Jacques in pursuit across rooftops and through the market of Fez. They fight around the tannery, scattering Moroccans by the dozens. Jacques knocks out Strawber, and his newfound courage wins Françoise's heart. As the film ends, they embrace.[42]

Duvivier's film arrived in theaters in time to capitalize on the huge drawing power of the Colonial Exposition. Eight million visitors were being captivated by the scaled-down replicas of the empire's life and architecture, comfortably nestled in the Bois de Vincennes. Reviewers of the film, although fascinated by the opening sequences, complained that they were too long, as if "the excellent hors d'oeuvre nearly becomes the meal." Film scholars have concurred; the "boulevard mystery" (the documentary opening) seems disjointed from the colonial setting, as if the exotic surroundings distracted Duvivier and overpowered the story. These critiques underrate his uncanny skill at manipulating the audience through innovative sound imagery and audacious trick photography. The absence of narration was also significant. It created an anti-travelogue that took advantage of the attention attracted to the Paris Exposition yet disturbed the European ease with the colonial environment. Indeed, Duvivier reversed the powerful subliminal effect of the Exposition, which

> projected a vision of a greater France by wrapping native cultures within the high culture of European France. This enclosing worked in two ways. First, wrapping colonial cultures gave them legitimacy in the eyes of Europeans by relating them to European icons. Second, it set the aesthetic and political guidelines for the creation of an imperial culture, one neither purely metropolitan French nor devoid of nativeness, but dominated and circumscribed by the setting in the capital of Greater France. . . . [Moreover] a non-Western civilization that can be approached by subway, picnic basket in hand, loses stature and awesomeness. Its glories seem easily appreciated and readily fathomed.[43]

Within the film, the setting wraps the Europeans (or, to use a term more fitting for film, *frames* them). Of the various well-known types of French character, the one most convinced that Morocco is a place filled with superstitious natives and bizarre dangers is a Breton Bretonnant, an impressionable country bumpkin from a backward, superstitious part of France—a character filmgoers would easily recognize. Yet, if the audience shared Jacques's prejudices, Strawber's confidence game tricks them. The film holds a mirror to French stereotypes, while conveying other messages that cast their own reflections. A multilayered *mise en abŷme,* the filmmaking process frames and captures images as if they were transcribed from picture-postcard "Scènes et types," appropriating Morocco and wrapping it in celluloid technology so as to treat

French audiences to an elegant object lesson. As with the Colonial Exposition, chaired and guided by Lyautey, so with the film. Both send mixed messages of tolerance and superiority.

Duvivier made four colonial films that, chameleon-like, took on the political coloration of his location hosts. *Maman Colibri* (1929), made in Algeria, celebrated the Foreign Legion; *Bandera* (1935), made in Spanish Morocco, he dedicated to General Francisco Franco; *Pépé le Moko* (1937) was told in the poetic realist style of the Popular Front era. *Cinq Gentlemen maudits,* based on a novel by André Reuze, was a remake of Luitz-Morat's film released in September 1920. In a dispute over screen rights, Luitz-Morat had Duvivier's film seized at its Paris premier, one of many tribulations the younger director faced making his version of the story. As with other films, silent and remake treatments contain suggestive contrasts. In the silent film, native actors played the veiled woman, a seller of magic charms, and her father; no hireling of a European, he delivers a genuine curse. The four conspirators in Duvivier's film are English, imparting a pronounced anti-British tenor to his version. British and American support for German demands to revise the Versailles Treaty had been growing, and the former allies seemed unreliable. Better to trust a force noire and Morocco as part of the empire of "100 million Frenchmen" to ensure against German revanche. Anglo-American sympathy enabled Germany to evade reparations that France relied on to pay its war debts. A financial crisis struck in July 1926, on the heels of the Rif War. Within two years, inflation and devaluation wiped out the savings of small proprietors holding state war bonds, a catastrophe laid at the feet of Britain, "perfidious Albion," not tax resistance by big business or the inequitable tax structure.[44]

By poking fun at the belief that Muslim fanatics were lurking behind every bush ready to slash the throat of any unlucky infidel who happened by, the film performed a public-relations service to the tourist industry in the wake of the urban revolt of 1930. After the stabbing at the Roman ruins, the colon consults a volume on his bookshelf, *Sorcellerie et Magie au Maroc,* a stage prop that recalls an influential book by Dr. Emile Mauchamp, who believed Islam was inimical to progress and rational discourse. The doctor's murder in Marrakech in 1907 precipitated the ensuing French invasion and the battle of Settat, in which Lyautey distinguished himself and won the right, five years later, to implement policies Mauchamp likely would have despised.[45] The film's last scenes bring tourist and native worlds together, reassuringly to the tourist. The Europeans are the perpetrators of the violence, fraud, and deceit. As Jacques and Strawber fight, smashing stalls, wares, and crockery, Fez street vendors run away without protecting their goods. And the fantaisie scene, with its galloping riders firing their antique muskets into the air, unmasks the source of battle scenes in earlier films as ritual mock combat, not warfare by fierce tribal cavalry.

The privileged status of whites is also ridiculed; antiheroic stereotypes tarnish their image. The jovial, good-natured colon, played by Harry Baur, is loutishly insensitive to the natives. On a tour of his estate, his guests see a long line of Arab laborers toiling in a field, cutting wheat with sickles. "How do you like my combine?" he asks, cynically equating men with agricultural machinery. He laughs when a lone "dissident" with a flintlock shoots at him from a tree stump in the distance: the sniper is hopelessly out of range. At their spacious home, his wife complains shrewishly and incessantly that the servants are stealing from them. The couple take no part in the conspiracy, remain placidly unruffled by the strange goings-on, and not the least unnerved by taboos.

Settlers resented this image of "wealthy clodhoppers" *(cul-terreux)* living a life of ease on the backs of the natives. They saw themselves as "honest hardworking men of the soil" developing the land and its people, hammered by debt, and looking for neither bailouts nor a fast buck.[46] Since debt pressed the European farmers to sweat native labor, reality lies in combining the two pictures. But the colons wanted to have their cake and eat it, too. They pressed for short-term aid to carry them through the Great Depression and help them meet their obligations. They lobbied Paris to convert their consultative assembly into a legislature, but proposed to exclude the Moroccans, 98 percent of the population, from the vote. Despite the Open Door guaranteed by the Algeçiras treaty, they wanted subsidies, protective tariffs, integration into the French economy, and the right to bargain for trade agreements with other countries. French-educated Moroccan nationalists blunted this settler drive for direct rule, while French administrators refereed a hybrid system, maintaining a precarious balance among French investors, settlers, nationalists, and colonial elite. The various factions subjected this inherently unstable regime to repeated tests of strength.[47]

In the protectorate, nothing was what it seemed, a facet of colonial rule that Duvivier captured on film. A shadow government of French bureaucrats manipulated the sultan from behind the scenes, writing decrees that he rubber-stamped. They superimposed French legal structures and defrauded the Berbers of their land in the name of protecting Berber rights. French planners rebuilt a "timeless, authentic" Morocco to their own specifications and perceptions, much as the Colonial Exposition had built a model of the Angkor Wat temple. Tourists debarked from newly built quays to splendid cityscapes that hid tin-shack Bidonvilles on city outskirts, teeming with displaced urban dwellers and rural refugees. Urban nationalists and settlers fought an invisible struggle for mastery of the rural poor, displacing the rural elites but leaving imperial rule intact. The quirky idiosyncrasies of *Cinq Gentlemen maudits* mimicked Morocco's real state of affairs. The sorcerer and the veiled woman appear in the opening sequences, calling into question the authenticity of the documentary, and the "gentlemen" who appear to be interacting with the real Morocco are actually playing an elaborate ruse. Another layer of meaning excludes all but Europeans from an active role in the plot; the Moroccans are imposters, hired police, or ninepins to be bowled over in the final melée. In a sense, Duvivier exposed one blind spot while falling prey to another. A scrim curtain, the theatrical world's veil, hides a deus ex machina that Duvivier reveals in part, inviting audiences to question their expectations of exotic scenery, people, and places and casting doubt on all other films coming out of Africa. His style reflected a new trend in cinema, expressing the unknowability of the colonial world.

> In sum, moments in the French films displaying handheld camera work, natural lighting, figures outside the camera's range of focus, shots lacking an inscription of a narrative trajectory, absence of blocking for figure movement, abrupt changes in image tonality, conflicting spatial cues, nonprofessional actors, and the lack of subtitles for African speech appear to be essential features of the genre. Rather than simple technical flaws attributable to an undercapitalized national film industry, such stylistic peculiarities are understandable as symptoms of the very project of cinéma colonial, which endows the colonial world with particular kinds of affect through an association with phenomena that exceed the representational capacities of the official culture. Unlike, say, American films set in North Africa (e.g. Gary Cooper vehicles such as *Morocco* [von Sternberg, 1930]), the distinctiveness of cinéma colonial resides less in a depiction of the conventionally exotic, however much on display, than in an attempt to provide the viewer with more unsettling forms of experiences.[48]

French filmmaking in Morocco declined after the Rif War of 1925–26 and virtually disappeared after protests against the Berber Dahir of 1930 erupted in Moroccan cities. Franco-Algerian films of the 1930s eliminated crowd-pleasing, spectacular battle scenes, which marked the climax of Franco-Moroccan silent-era films. Remakes transformed the native into an anonymous, often invisible "enemy." Labor shortages and other changes in the Maghreb's economic landscape, the waning of Lyauteyiste and *associationiste* influence, settler voices growing louder in the Chamber of Deputies and other Parisian corridors of power, the colonial army command's concern with control and security—all contributed to the shift in location and to the change in representations of the relationship between colony and metropole, native and settler.

French anxiety over worlds lost and won in its fictional, orientalized Africa projected similar feelings toward the onset of industrialization and modernization in France itself. The entire political spectrum greeted Taylorism and Fordism with intense debate and profound ambivalence; technocratic solutions attracted both the Left and the Right, which were equally repelled by the dislocations of "rationalization." *A Nous la liberté*, René Clair's cinematic vision of the factory's dehumanizing effects and of technology's potential to liberate humankind, ran the gamut of French reactions to industrialism.[49] It, too, was released in 1931, against the backdrop of the Colonial Exposition. Heaping their hopes, fears, and sins on Africa, the French discovered in white superiority a solace and a crutch in an uncertain and rapidly changing world.

French Colonial Film before and after *Itto*, 1934

From Berber Myth to Race War

Lyauteyisme breathed its last with *Itto*, a stunning film that chronicled Berber resistance to French colonization. Made in 1934, it was the last and arguably the best of the Moroccan-based productions, but it was also a film with differing if not conflicting agendas. Its backers and writers were enlightened imperialists of Lyautey's coterie, interested in celebrating his strategy for colonial social control. The directors, Jean Benoît-Lévy and Marie Epstein, an early, influential woman filmmaker, perfected a semifictional, semidocumentary style pioneered by colonial docudramas. Mingling French actors and Berber-speaking nonactors translated by French subtitles, *Itto* achieved unusual nuance and sensitivity to the visual aspects of everyday life of the peoples of the Middle Atlas. Well-rounded Berber characters contrasted with the caricatures of nonwhites that Hollywood paraded across the screen. The film looked right, and Benoît-Lévy believed he had depicted the Berbers authentically. But his own attitudes led inadvertently to a condescendingly superior tone. It was left to Epstein to impart the egalitarian feminism that emerged as the film's unique and significant strain.

Critics and scholars who have admired the anthropological insights of *Itto*'s portrait of Berber life remain skeptical about the attached Romeo-and-Juliet love story.[1] Despite appearances, the biography of the Berber woman Itto and her betrothed was historically accurate, while the anthropology was steeped in a variant of the noble-savage stereotype, the Berber myth. Resurrected and transplanted from Algeria, where it had been applied to the Kabyles, the myth suited Lyautey's imperial strategy. Maurice LeGlay, one of the colonels who comprised the resident-general's *équipe* of advisers on native affairs, formulated the Berber policy as part of a strategy of indirect rule. He also authored the novels from which *Itto* was drawn and had participated in the military campaigns against the real-life Itto's father. Other Lyautey intimates helped bring the project to the screen, and by sponsoring a film that encouraged respect for Morocco's elite as helpmates to French rule, they drew a page from his own handbook on influencing colonial policy. *Itto*'s credits pay homage to the film company's benefactor, Si Abdallah al-Glaoui, the pasha of Marrakech, and Conseiller Indigène. In 1914, his noble family had recruited its Chleuh followers to defeat the Zaian branch of these Middle Atlas Berber clans. Pacification took seven years, then al-Glaoui began helping film directors to employ Chleuh as movie extras. *Itto* presents the history as a textbook success of Lyautey's policy. In fact, mistakes and setbacks marred the Zaian campaign, and the film's real success was in projecting, one last time, the myth of Lyautey's infallible leadership.

The Berber Myth

Lyauteyisme gave the French public different impressions of Muslim society than Algerian settlerism. It idealized Moroccan customs and traditions, romanticized the nomadic regions, and promoted the Berber myth, a self-serving array of half-truths concocted to explain the origins of the Maghreb's earliest inhabitants and convince the metropole that these indigènes could be allies out of hatred of the Arabs and affinity for France.[2] The fantasy ensnared home governments and colonial administrators alike, complicating the task of controlling the diverse Maghrebin communities. Though the need for military occupation continued, colonial strategists clung to the Berber myth, which distorted perceptions of politico-cultural reality, foiled development, and, ultimately, undermined French rule.

The first subjects of the myth, the Algerian Kabyle, had disappointed the French bitterly, but Lyautey's version of the myth proved more sophisticated and useful. Berber speakers comprised one-half of the population of Morocco (compared with one-quarter of the population in Algeria), and Lyautey claimed to have paved the way to a secure Morocco by "conquering the Berber soul" and protecting their *vie intime,* clan customs, and traditions from external intrusions.[3] A Directorate of Native Affairs, staffed by a team of officers who studied Arabic and Berber language and customs, by 1919 had instituted a form of rule based on the notion that Berber social characteristics set them apart from the Arabic speakers: like the Kabyles, the Berbers were the original inhabitants who had resisted invasions from mountain strongholds and remained independent of the sultans. Beneath an Islamicized veneer, they preserved the superstitions, customs, rituals, and beliefs of earlier faiths. Insofar as they were Muslims, Berbers were "frank schismatics," whose customary law superseded shari'ya—Qur'anic law.[4]

Berber customary law shared traits with ancient Roman and French patriarchal codes, especially regarding the status of women. Although Islam's shari'ya unites law and religion, Berber practices were often the exact opposite of those prescribed by Arab custom and Qur'anic directives. Berbers resisted the rule of powerful chiefs and the makhzan, the sultan's state, because they exercised an instinctive democracy through the *djemâ'a,* the clan council. While outside enemies brought clans together, the djemâ'a could not resolve matters of family honor, hence the frequent clan feuds. Historian Edmund Burke III concludes that "by 1919 the essential traits of the Berber myth had been sketched in, and the myth itself given a wide diffusion. By 1919 as well, all of the essential policy decisions had been taken on which the completed edifice would be erected between the two wars. The foundations for France's Berber policy in Morocco were laid prior to 1919 under Lyautey."[5]

Lyautey's first step was to have the Berbers of the Middle Atlas submit to the *dawla,* the protectorate administration, not the makhzan. In return, he guaranteed that Berber law and custom would prevail over shari'ya. Native-affairs officers researched the exact nature of customary law, and he pressed the sultan to issue a dahir in September 1914 setting forth (in the vaguest terms) Berber rights to their own judicial regime.[6]

LeGlay Reinvents the Berber Myth

Benoît-Lévy and Epstein, each holding a distinctive point of view, were surrounded by a team of Lyautey's former subordinates, who collaborated to script and produce the film. As the credits state, the film was "drawn entirely from the works of Maurice LeGlay," an accomplished writer whose ten novels and mémoirs were based on his experiences in the war against the Chleuh. LeGlay had been an instructor with the first French military mission to the sultanate in 1910; in the protectorate's formative decade, he became Lyautey's chief advisor on native affairs and a principal advocate of the Berber policy. LeGlay devised the notion that the country was divided into *bled Makhzen,* land of order, and *bled s siba,* land of dissonance. His research convinced Lyautey that the Arabs had never conquered the Middle Atlas Berber clans nor interfered with their internal affairs, and that the makhzen had exacted tribute only as a pledge of obeisance to the sultan. This view justified intervention to restore order, but ignored the fact that Europeans had been smuggling guns to local clan leaders for decades in an effort to extract mining and other concessions, disrupting the balance of power in key regions, and creating the anarchy the French later sought to suppress.[7]

LeGlay imported to Morocco a myth first applied to the Kabyle of Algeria, an exercise in wishful thinking derived from Captain Charles de Foucauld, the Père Blanc missionary, intelligence officer, and apostle to the Saharan Tuareg. More interested in weaning Berbers from Islamic "fanaticism" to make them political allies rather than Christians, he stressed their militarized, patriarchal clan democracy as much as their heterodox beliefs. Lyautey embraced LeGlay's views, and a reminiscence from his retirement revealed his "secret": "I always supported the Berber element over the rather degenerate Arab element. . . . The Berber element will never be understood except by a soldier." Like the British after the Gurkha wars of 1815–16, the French justified recruiting Berber mercenaries with a warrior-race mystique.[8]

The Film Based on LeGlay's Writings

Several of LeGlay's books mythologized Lyautey's signal success, the submission of the Chleuh-speaking Berbers of the Middle Atlas after years of resistance under their leader, Itto's father, Moha ou Hamou el Zaiani. Through his clansmen, the Ait Zaian, Hamou mobilized an uprising in central Morocco just after the start of the Great War. French forces, stretched paper thin and overextended by the needs of the Western Front, kept control of Morocco, and a grateful government promoted Lyautey to marshal. In the twilight of Lyautey's life, the film based on LeGlay's novels was an encomium to the old man's achievement, and by enhancing Lyautey's prestige, LeGlay may have cast a hopeful eye to reexerting influence over colonial policy.

Itto's opening credits succinctly announce its main theme. It is "the story of the submission of a tribe in the Atlas Mountains."[9] More than half the film's running time takes place in the Berber milieu, and the story unfolds from the points of view of Hamou, Itto, and her betrothed, Miloud. In the first scenes, Hamou rallies hundreds of his followers to his cause and urges them to take up arms against the French. His main ally, Hassan, Miloud's father, pledges his support. A French plane appears overhead, and Hassan's men shoot it down, wounding the pilot and stranding him behind enemy lines. Taking the aviator hostage, Hassan sends Miloud under flag of truce to the French camp to fetch a *toubib,* an army doctor who becomes a central character. In real life, Lyautey regarded such officers as key agents of pacification. Dispatched to treat the flyer's wounds, the doctor discovers an outbreak of anthrax among the sheep of Hassan's clan and inoculates the flocks, averting a disastrous economic blow to the clan. Hassan vows to resist the French no longer, and Hamou accuses him of betrayal. Miloud defies his father and tries to rejoin Hamou's forces, but Hamou's men ambush Miloud and leave him for dead. The army doctor finds him, saves his life, and wins his loyalty. The French defeat Hamou in battle while Itto is giving birth to Miloud's child. Torn between father and lover, she joins Hamou in his fortress, to be gunned down by *goums,* Moroccan mercenaries fighting for the French, in a last stand.[10]

To encourage French audiences to identify with the Berbers, the film interweaves their stories with those of the French protagonists, but in his novel *Itto* (1923), LeGlay centered on the conflict between daughter and father, whom LeGlay portrayed as blinded by ambition and concern with his own power, even though his followers would have benefitted from French rule. Hamou spoke for those Zaiani who saw France as an evil empire and believed the prophecy of the clan's marabout, or spiritual guide, Ali-Amhauouch, who told them they would never be vanquished as long as they held their ancient fortress at Tidikelt. At a clan assembly, Itto advocated peace, accusing Hamou of manipulating the prophecy and lying. Arrested and condemned for lèse-majesté, she escaped to the French lines. Later, Hamou's men (not French goums, as in the film) shot her. After their pacification, the Zaian came to revere her as a marabout in her own right and buried her in a tomb near the key Middle Atlas stronghold town of Khénifra. Dissident nomads made pilgrimages to her shrine and came in contact with French officers, ideas, and works. The reconnaissance pilot shot down over Tidikelt, whose life she had saved, also visited her grave. For LeGlay, Itto reflected a Berber spirit of cooperation and tolerance antithetical to Arab Muslim fanaticism, and she remained a force for assimilation even after her death.[11]

The Chleuh Resistance in Historical Context

Hamou's war was part of a decade-long effort to fend off French encroachments. In 1912, Lyautey deposed Sultan Hafiz and pressured the *ulaama* (assembly) of Fez to proclaim in his stead a compliant younger brother, Yussef, who became an "exquisite French marionette brought out for command performances."[12] When the Great War broke out, and Paris ordered Lyautey to send his reserves to the Western Front, rural resistance flared. Aided by money, supplies, and advisers from Turkey and Germany, Abd el-Malik, in the Rif, and Raisuli, in the Gomara, roused followers to raid from the safety of the neutral zone governed by Spain. El-Hiba, a *rogui,* or pretender to the throne, rallied the south. Ali-Amhaouch held sway in the Middle Atlas, ably seconded by two other leaders, Moha ou Said, and Hamou, baron of the Zaian clan and father-in-law to the deposed Sultan Hafiz. This personal stake made Hamou the first to rise.

With help from Pasha al-Glaoui of Marrakech, Lyautey prevented the regional movements from coalescing around a single leader. Liberally supplied with French weaponry, Glaoui clansmen kept el-Hiba at bay, cut off from the Zaian. General Paul Henrys checked Hamou by reinforcing the French stronghold at Khénifra. But Henrys anticipated that a general French evacuation, necessary to bolster strength on the Western Front, would invite heavy attacks so he applied LeGlay's Berber policy and tried to appease/accommodate Hamou while isolating him from other centers of anti-French resistance. By the fall of 1914, Hamou's attacks were dwindling, even as Henrys's reserves were still embarking for Europe. However, Colonel René Laverdure impetuously launched an unauthorized assault on Hamou's mountain camps on 13 November, and on the road back to Khénifra his column was ambushed. Hamou's men killed 613 French, including Laverdure, and captured two batteries of field artillery. Although the encounter went unnoticed in France, where the army was laboring to stop the Germans at the Marne and Ypres, it was a stunning defeat. According to Lyautey, Khénifra nearly fell, jeopardizing the French position throughout Morocco.

By preventing the local uprisings from coalescing and igniting a regional war, Lyautey probably helped contain the Tuareg when they took up arms to expel the French eighteen months later and swept across the Sahara. A Turkish-supported Tuareg thrust across Libya toward Suez would have strengthened the hand of the Arab Revolt vis à vis the

British. Although fighting on opposite sides of the European conflict, Tuareg and Arabs would have been helping each other's bid for independence. So Lyautey's tactical success had far-reaching consequences. Yet pacification had required brute force. Peaceful penetration, bestowing the benefits of civilization and currying the nobles' favor, had broken down in the Middle Atlas. Exerting even greater military pressure after the Armistice of 1918, Lyautey finally cracked Zaian unity. Hamou was killed in the spring of 1921 in a skirmish between his resistance fighters and Zaian collaborators. The system Lyautey put in place paid handsome dividends elsewhere in Morocco, but the events mythologized in *Itto* revealed serious flaws in its workings.[13]

Lyautey's System and the Making of *Itto:* Benoît-Lévy's Folly

The core of Lyautey's system, a native-affairs officers' training school headed by Colonel Henri Berriau, required that the trainees *(stagiaires)* take 140 hours of language instruction in Arabic and Berber and 84 hours of Arabic literature, culture, and law. The trainees wrote theses that expanded French knowledge of the customs and practices of the clans and earned the equivalent of a master's degree in ethnology. Graduates became *hakim,* or advisers, defending clans against settler predation. They drew fire from European-controlled chambers of commerce, which pressured Berriau to remind his men that settlers were, as he put it, "indispensable for the realization of our native program . . . for the native, the initiator, stimulator, living example" of enterprise and development. Berriau's bureau drew on surveyors and engineers for technical support, but most crucial was the medical staff.[14]

Berriau, born in 1870 and sixteen years his commander's junior, was protégé, intimate, and one of a team of colonels on Lyautey's staff since his first general command on Algeria's tense Moroccan border in 1903. Director of political affairs and intelligence services, Berriau was treated by Lyautey as a surrogate son. Lyautey disapproved of his marriage to Simone, an actress and long-time mistress, but she became a stalwart helpmate, learning nursing and, probably in the school Berriau had founded, the Chleuh dialect. Berriau died during the influenza pandemic of December 1918; he contracted the disease while recovering from wounds he received in a skirmish. His death affected Lyautey deeply.[15]

Lyautey regarded the army's doctors as military assets of the highest order, and within weeks of his arrival in Morocco in 1912 created Groupes Sanitaires. Enemy wounded were treated with the same care provided his own troops. As he wrote to his mentor General Joseph Gallieni, with four more doctors he could release four battalions from the duty of suppressing revolts. Doctors assigned to rural clans worked with local q'aids and made French political authority palatable. They traveled the length of the country, and Lyautey consulted them on political matters because they were astute, independent observers. "The role of the doctor as agent of penetration, of attraction, and of pacification is a most solidly established fact," he concluded. The film magazine *Pour Vous* quoted this remark in its first article on *Itto*.[16]

Other protégés of Lyautey completed the work of transferring LeGlay's novel to the screen. Georges Duvernois, who wrote the screenplay, had been subprefect of Constantine when Lyautey earlier, had been stationed in Algeria. After serving in 1906–7 as Premier Georges Clemenceau's chief of staff, he became secretary-general of the protectorate. Etienne Rey collaborated on the dialogue. His successful book in 1912 had defended the French occupation of Morocco. Enlisting in 1914, he became Lyautey's morale office—in fact, his "right arm," implementing the marshal's plan to improve the morals of recruits by organizing throughout Morocco 150 "soldiers' parlors"; partly financed by the YMCA, these were modeled on its reading rooms. Berriau's widow, Simone, took the role of Itto. An actress from the Opéra Comique, she quite likely was the only Frenchwoman who spoke Berber fluently.

Also associated with the *Itto* production were Lyautey's adjutants in the Zaian campaign, General Paul Henrys and Colonel Henri Simon, who reached out to the technocratic, well-oiled rural administrative machine they had left in place, which still maintained order by subtly combining bribery, good intelligence, force, and respect for local customs, although no longer able to protect tribes from economic exploitation by colons. Thus when the *Itto* expedition—seventy-five actors and technicians, twenty-two cars, three lighting and sound trucks—set out from Marrakech in April 1934 under the protection of Pasha al-Glaoui, local French officers took them in hand. An unofficial "special-effects department" for the crew, they provided logistical support, negotiated with local notables for extras, and even built fifty kilometers of road to haul equipment to locations at the high plains village of Taliouine. Director Benoît-Lévy himself studiously ignored every aspect of the production process that did not fit his preconceived notions. Like tourists the world over, he saw what he was programmed to see: in his case, "primitives" who were "natural actors."

> Natural actors are those who approach closest to nature; they are creatures whose minds have not been cultivated, who have kept their psychological reflexes independent of any control by will or reason. Children are the screen's ideal natural actors, but I have found the same freshness of mind, the same innocence, in the Chleuh of the Atlas. The primitive life led by these nomad warriors kept their intellectual development at the level of that of a normal child who has not yet felt the impact of reason and education.[17]

Benoît-Lévy was ignorant of Chleuh history, but he believed in "universal civilization," accepting French anthropology's codes that humans are the same whether in the Atlas Mountains or in a French town. Lucien Lévy-Bruhl, Michel Mauss, and Daniel Rivet, founders of the Ethnology Society and the Musée de l'Homme, no longer saw non-Europeans as innately inferior but as "primitive," "prelogical" peoples with an "aversion to rational thought" who could catch up with modern societies by imitation. Through this lens of disingenuousness, Benoît-Lévy saw the Chleuh as uncorrupted by modernity, although they were in fact old hands at filmmaking and had integrated it into their world. The Chleuh called *Itto*'s cast and crew *les ait-cinéma,* the "cinema clan," an appellation that could more aptly be applied to themselves. They had acted in a dozen films in the 1920s; in assessing their performances in *L'Occident* (1927), Henri Fescourt declared that, despite language barriers, Chleuh extras readily followed the most complex directions. Indeed, *Itto* inadvertently revealed Chleuh adaptations to colonialism. Miloud, played by a local shepherd named Ali Ben Brick, recovers from his wounds, swears allegiance to France, and loiters around the French camp—a Berber version of the trading-post Indian of westerns. Despite the sophistication of the Chleuh, North Africa remained devoid of film-processing studios, both a reflection and a result of the underdevelopment the French imposed on the overall Maghrebin economy. In order to review the daily rushes, filmmakers had to send raw film by auto to an airstrip, fly it to Paris, and return it by the same elaborate route.[18]

Itto's French and Russian Cinematographic Influences

Itto's directors belonged to two of French cinema's founding families, and their connections assured them technical and financial backing. Benoit-Lévy's father led the Pathé company from 1906 to 1908; a Paris lawyer, he had acquired two hundred theaters for Pathé and secured its dominance in French film distribution. Epstein's brother, Jean, worked with Pathé before he struck out on his own and "bequeathed" his sister to his former partner. A cinematic visionary, Jean developed theories of editing *(montage)* that paralleled those of Sergei Eisenstein and Vsevelod Pudovkin. Debates over film theory and semiotics flew between Moscow and Paris. Soviet influence in France matched the impact of Abel Gance's *La Roue* (1922 and 1926) in the USSR. Epstein went to work for Films Albatros, whose Russian emigré owners made it Paris's leading production company. From 1924 to 1927, he directed a string of commercial successes, his work converging with simple, direct, Soviet-style "psychological documentary." Pudovkin's *Mother* (1926) noticeably influenced his *Finis Terrae* (1929).[19]

Jean continued to work with Benoit-Lévy, and Marie wrote scripts for him. Her trademark was to hinge the plot on a scene with a single powerful image. In an early film for Albatros, *Le Lion des Mongols* (1924), Jean collaborated with nomadic emigré actor-screenwriter Ivan Mosjoukine, who cross-pollinated French and Soviet cinema theory and technique and had collaborated with Lev Kuleshov and Pudovkin in a crucial experiment revealing the artifice and "truth" of film. Intercutting scenes of a bowl of soup, a woman in a coffin, and a girl playing with a teddy bear with virtually identical closeups of Mosjoukine's near-expressionless face created a powerful illusion. When they varied the length of the closeup, audiences "saw" strong emotional responses on the actor's face: pensiveness over the forgotten soup, grief at the death, delight with the happy girl. Pudovkin's film biography of Pavlov, *The Mechanism of the Brain* (1925), later demystified the "Kuleshov effect" as a Pavlovian manipulation of audience and actors, which he used in *Storm over Asia* (1929), his masterwork about the Buryat Mongol revolt during the Russian Civil War that rivals Eisenstein's best work. The Jean Epstein/Mosjoukine collaboration also merits scrutiny as precursor to *Itto*.[20]

In *Le Lion des Mongols*, a film that takes place in a fantastical Mongolia and a surreal Paris, the Russian starred as Roundghito-Sing, a young prince who falls in love with a captive princess, Zemgali, and helps her escape the clutches of the Great Khan. In a fierce fight, he throws the evil usurper out of a window, but the uproar arouses the guard and he is forced to flee into the Gobi. There he encounters a French film company making a movie. Anna, the star, is a Paris-educated Mongol whom M. Morel, the banker financing the picture, wants as his mistress. She convinces the director to hire Roundghito and take him back to Paris, where Anna's attentions arouse Morel's jealousy.

The banker tries to corrupt the prince by introducing him to the soft, elegant Parisian life and to control him by lending him money. He proves susceptible, even under the stern eye of Kavalas, the hardy warrior who is his faithful companion. One day, Roundghito finds Morel forcing himself on Anna; reminded of the princess Zemgali's plight, the enraged prince attacks the roué. Morel wounds him with a shot from his revolver, but before Morel can fire again Kavalas appears, knocks the pistol from Morel's hand, and strangles him. To evade the police, Roundghito and Kavalas mingle with the crowd at a costume ball in the hotel, but they are arrested. Roundghito's torn costume reveals a lion tatoo on his chest; by this mark, Anna discovers that he is her brother and that he had survived the palace coup in which an evil pretender killed their father, the legitimate khan, and forced her into exile. Kavalas slips away and reappears with a retinue of Mongol notables, who announce that the usurper has died and that Roundghito is heir to the throne. Back in Mongolia, his coronation is followed by marriage to Zemgali.[21]

Exotic fantasies were common enough in the early 1920s to constitute a genre of French film, but Mosjoukine's script for *Le Lion des Mongols* cast a decidedly antiimperialist shadow. Morel personified imperialism in using his financial power to bend Anna and Roundghito to his will and in resorting to force when money fails. Perhaps to make the Mongol hero and French villain more palatable to French audiences, the film employed fantastical juxtapositions of the Mongol palace and the Hotel Olympic costume ball, reflecting the avant-garde's influence on film. Surreal pyrotechnics thus paved the way for the revolutionary fire of *Storm over Asia*.[22]

Le Lion's Mongolia is a Shangri-la stereotype of "timeless Asia." The characters travel to Paris to overthrow the past. The real Inner Asia had undergone years of revolutionary upheaval, which Pudovkin traveled south to capture in his film. Released throughout Europe in 1929, *Storm over Asia* impressed critics and audiences with its truthfulness and power, increased their receptivity to the semidocumentary style, and anticipated *Itto*. But the iconoclastic Pudovkin had little sympathy for Benoit-Lévy's paternalistic, self-congratulatory theory of natural actors. The Russian called extras "casual players" and revealed the tricks he played to evoke naturalistic performances from them. He wanted a look of rapture on faces of the onlookers in a scene where they see a rare silver-fox fur, so he hired a Chinese conjurer, filmed the fascinated expressions on the faces of the "casuals" watching him perform, and joined this footage to his takes of a trader buying the fur. In order to direct casual actors, he said, "one must be cunning . . . invent thousands of tricks to create the mood in the person and to catch the right moment to photograph him." Pudovkin claimed no great understanding of the Mongols. Those he used in his film were "absolutely uncultured people who did not even understand my language . . . [yet they] easily compete, as far as acting honors are concerned, with the best actors."[23]

A commissar, or political-affairs worker, named Ashirov acted as Pudovkin's information source and, in much the same way that French officers aided *Itto*, arranged logistics, recounted folk tales, and described everyday scenes of Buryat life, such as the customary greeting of visitors to a *yurta*, the nomads' circular felt tent. The commissar helped Pudovkin set the tone of the film. Playing the lead was Inkizhinov, a trained actor and assimilated Mongol who spoke Russian better than Mongolian. He took pains to reconnect with his culture and learned to ride Mongol-style at a Red Army cavalry school. His own father played the father role in the film, and Pudovkin filmed the old man in his own home. Keeping stereotyped Mongol habits (e.g., hissing sighs to punctuate speech, blowing the nose in the fist, scratching) to a minimum, Pudovkin instead indicated emotion with shy smiles ("reasons for smiling"), a deliberately narrowed range of movement, and sudden furious explosions of energy.[24] Although he parroted Soviet myths, gave off an air of superiority, and manipulated his subjects, Pudovkin also treated them as creative collaborators in depicting their own history.

Filmed on location around the lamasery of Tomchinsk in the Buryat Soviet Republic and based on an incident from the Civil War, Pudovkin's *Storm* tells the story of a humble trapper who catches a rare silver fox but is cheated of his prize by an English merchant. Joining the partisans, he is captured; British occupation troops order him shot. In a brilliant sequence, a smart-stepping British Tommy escorts the shuffling, disheveled, listless trapper, Bair, to an execution site, carefully skirting a mud puddle that Bair stumbles through. But when the soldier is forced to look Bair in the eye, his resolve crumbles: he botches the shooting and cannot bring himself to deliver the coup de grâce. Leaving Bair for dead and dragging his rifle as he trudges back through the same puddle he had so primly avoided, his leggings come undone.[25] Bair's effects are presented to the general, who finds an amulet certifying that Bair descends from Genghis Khan. Rescued and nursed back to life, Bair is pressed into service as a figurehead. Acquiescent and apathetic until a young peasant partisan begs him for mercy but is executed before his eyes, Bair escapes and rejoins the guerrillas, who are gathering their forces, symbolized by Pudovkin's intercuts of lowering clouds breaking out in a thunderstorm when the Mongol's uprising begins to drive out the British.[26]

Itto's precursors also include three distinctly Lyauteyiste films made in Morocco by Jacques Séverac. In *L'Ame du bled,* a 1929 film that recalled Moroccan films of the early 1920s, a q'aid turns away from anti-colonial resistance and rallies to France out of friendship for a colon. *Sirocco* (1930) retold a legend in which the kidnapped infant son of a pasha grows up to become a dangerous bandit chief; captured and nearly executed, he escapes, dropping an amulet proving his origin; the pasha seeks him out and blesses the son's marriage to the young woman he loves. *Razzia* (1931), another old tale, is about a bandit siege in 1318 and a marabout's daughter held hostage to force the town to open its gates; her fiancé organizes resistance, saves her, and puts the bandits to flight. In all his films, Séverac mixed a documentary travelogue with native legends and used Moroccan actors Abslem ben el Kébir and Leila Atouna, a stunning dancer, to play leads. But the dialogue, spoken in Arabic without subtitles, baffled French filmgoers. A reviewer found *Sirocco*'s images of Morocco fascinating and Atouna charming, but the "shrill cries and bawling intonations" were incomprehensible and unsettling; the reviewer speculated that the language was gibberish invented for the film. With the Maghreb's rich linguistic heritage thus jokingly dismissed and without *Itto*'s financial and political backing, Séverac's films fared badly. Commercial and critical success arrived when he changed his point of view in 1936 with a film glorifying the French colonial army.[27]

Audience Reaction to *Itto*

In the 1930s, French promotion and distribution of films was haphazard at best, in sharp contrast with the American system of major film studios with large advertising budgets and networks of distributors. Despite the vicissitudes of distribution, *Itto* did well with the general public at the box office, and met with an even warmer response among intellectuals. *Pour Vous* kept the film in the public eye by printing reactions to the film in its letters column, "The Audience Speaks." To judge from the readers' letters, *Itto* generated an extraordinary reaction, stimulating more audience comment than any other film in the decade. The fourteen letters printed in four issues of *Pour Vous* offer ample anecdotal insight into attitudes toward the film. These French viewers were receptive to the Berber characters and identified with them. They were delighted to learn how the Chleuh lived and hear the Berbers speak their own language. Since dubbing was available but despised in France as spoiling the actor's personality, *Itto*'s creators avoided Séverac's pitfall by using subtitles.[28] The only complaint on this score was that white print was hard to read when it appeared against a light background such as a white *jelaba,* the hooded, woolen outergarment worn by Berber men. Only two readers made the common mistake of referring to the natives as Arabs, not Berbers, and more than half referred to the Chleuh by name. The letter writers were not only well informed: half of them had associations with the Maghreb. There were comments from colons living in Casablanca, Fez, and Algeria, and a retired colon living in Cannes wrote a long review, saying he had lived in Morocco; others indicated an intimate familiarity with the land.

While they avoided typical pied-noir usages—such as calling themselves Algerians, using *Arab, native,* and *black* as interchangeable terms of contempt—they presumed to speak for all the people of the Maghreb and expected to be treated as the arbiters of the truthfulness and accuracy of the film. *Pour Vous*'s metropolitan readers deferred to them in the ongoing exchanges about the film, but assessments were contradictory. The Cannes retiree faulted the film for not glorifying the military, while a woman colon felt that the army doctor's story covered up the brutalities of conquest.

The letter writers wanted interesting plots, characters, and locales, but they were also concerned with the ongoing rivalry with Hollywood, and they compared *Itto* with *Lives of a Bengal Lancer,* an American-made, Kiplingesque spectacle of war and male bonding that opened in France at the same time. Audiences judged the French film better at showing the ethnography of the indigènes and approved the three-dimensional portrayal of the Berbers. Some viewers complained that the French characters seemed undeveloped, cardboard cutouts, if compared with the colorful British in *Bengal Lancer,* played by Franchot Tone and Gary Cooper. Ironically, French national pride led readers to defend the French film's sensitive portrayal of a people who had risen against France. That Hollywood's *Bengal Lancer,* a superficial "Hindu operetta," monopolized the attention and box office receipts incensed a writer who signed herself as "Pierrette of Paris," especially since French artists were given so little credit. For all its limitations and blind spots, therefore, *Itto* was a potent antidote to the creed of race war being disseminated by right-wing public intellectuals, most of whom came from within Lyautey's own political circle.[29]

The Yellow Peril and the End of Lyauteyisme in Film

Despite genuine admiration and affection for Moroccan civilization, Lyautey's monarchist affinities wedded him to the Fédération Républicaine (FR), the party dedicated to preserving Roman Catholic, small-town society. Values embodied in a racially superior, culturally essentialist belief in "True France" aligned the FR with the extraparliamentary ligues and Action Française. Personal ties linked Lyautey to the FR's power brokers Louis Marin and François de Wendel. The ancestral estates of all three families lay near Nancy, in Lorraine, and had been occupied by the Germans in 1870 and 1914. Their views were expressed by editors like Maurice Muret, who wrote for de Wendel's newspapers, and Henri Massis, of the *Action Française* newspaper, who believed racial survival depended on dominating nonwhites and occupying their lands. The West was "spiritually undone" by the Reformation and physically broken by the Great War, Massis wrote, but still contained its essence: "Personality, unity, stability, authority, continuity—these are the root ideas of the West." Works by Muret and Massis were translated into English and American white-supremacist writings were translated into French—a transatlantic counter-Enlightenment that reached consensus on the Yellow Peril. Asia's teeming millions threatened Western dominance, and Bolshevism was "Asiatic," spreading the idea of racial equality to Asia and fomenting race treason among European workers. Massis wrote that Asia "is not seeking merely to arouse its native peoples to revolt in order to deprive our impoverished continent of the immense resources Asia holds. It is the soul of the West that the East wishes to attack."[30]

Lyautey convinced Muret and Massis to exempt Morocco from this synecdochical racial schema. In writing *Defense de l'Occident*, Massis sought out the *maréchal* in retirement and spent weeks in consultation with him. For the moment, the writer agreed that Morocco was the exception to global race war and the inferiority of the nonwhite world. But Lyautey had subordinated Berber policy to corporate economic penetration, and his noble ideal, observed the antiimperialist Ignace Lepp, became a squalid, Machiavellian tactic of divide-and-rule well before settler encroachments united Arabs and Berbers to resist the Berber dahir of 1930. Berbers became more Arabized and Islamicized in the struggle to shake off French rule. By 1935, LeGlay himself was disillusioned, and in *L'Afrique française*, the journal of the colonial party, he wrote the Berber policy's epitaph. Nostalgic loss thus echoes through *Itto*, relieved only by Epstein's feminist hope that mother love would reconcile the races.[31]

Harbingers of the Yellow Peril appeared in France before the Great War. For example, in *L'Invasion jaune* (1909), a fantastic, paranoid, three-volume espionage novel, Britain aids an Asian invasion of Europe to protect its empire. English spies and Asian human-wave tactics almost overrun the French, weakened by antimilitarism and poor eugenics, but submarines finally overcome British naval superiority.[32] The Russian Revolution and the Rif War prompted purveyors of this Great Fear to replace perfidious Albion with Bolshevism as puppetmaster of the Yellow Peril. "Beyond the pale of Western Civilization . . . displacing ideological debates onto racial ground . . . the Red threat in Asia on the plane of an eternal conflict between East and West . . . one more Oriental assault upon Europe . . . one more race war."[33] Serge de Chessin called the 1917 revolution a "renewal of the Mongol invasion on a spiritual plane . . . an apocalyptic raid from bolshevized Asia." Paul Morand commented in his account of his Inner Asian travels that going to "Asia via Russia the transition is imperceptible." He joined the staff of *1933*, a magazine edited by Henri Massis as a cultural counterpoint to the Left's *Marianne*; he was also a high-level *fonctionnaire* of the Foreign Ministry and a chief screenwriter for Paramount's Paris-Joinville Studios.[34]

By the time Lyautey died in July 1934, six months before *Itto* premiered, racialism had softened anti-Germanism within the French Right. If Nazism evoked the nightmare of German revanche, it also awakened the dream of a vigorous ally in the global race war, holding back Bolshevized "lesser breeds" battering Europe's eastern gates. Pudovkin's *Storm over Asia* arrived in Paris movie theaters in 1929's racially charged atmosphere. An ode to the Soviet revolution in Asia that celebrated the Buryat Mongols as agents of their own history, it incited right-wing fears that Bolshevism would goad Asiatic hordes into overrunning the West, and since it portrayed the British as a murderous occupation force, it was banned by the British Board of Film Censors and shown outside the USSR over British protests. A German distributor, PAX-Film, edited the film, changed the title from *The Heir of Genghis Khan,* renamed the lead character with the more Mongol-sounding Timour, and rewrote the intertitles to identify the occupying army as White Russian, led by a general named Petroff, whose manner remained, nonetheless, unmistakably English.[35]

This cinematic palimpsest superimposed Mongolian events on the Buryat Soviet Republic, born after the Red Army had defeated Admiral Aleksandr Kolchak's army and executed him on 7 February 1920. The British had indeed tried and failed to hold this army ("more Tatar horde than modern force") together. They used not only advisers but eighty freighters of war materiel, shipping 2,000 machine guns, 600,000 rifles, and 350 million rounds of ammunition from Vladivostok along two thousand miles of the trans-Siberian railroad. Remnants of the army retreated into Mongolia proper and captured Urga (Ulan Bator) from the Chinese. Backed by Japan, with its sights set on Manchuria, a White general, Baron von Ungern-Sternberg, and a sadistic aide, Colonel Sepailov, built a murderous warlord regime in a reign of torture and terror against pro-Soviet Mongols, Jewish merchants, and pro-Chinese lamas. Red Army and Mongol forces crushed the baron's last offensive in May 1921, occupied Urga in June, and ended his deranged dream of carving an anti-Soviet Central Asian empire out of this crossroads of Mongol, Siberian, Tibetan, Turkic, and Chinese peoples.[36]

Storm premiered in Paris after the rightist government elected in 1928 had imposed a total ban on Soviet films, as much to restrict foreign competition as to censor the Left. Public distribution of Pudovkin's *Mother,* Eisenstein's *Battleship Potemkin,* and six other films was halted, but a network of *ciné-clubs* sprang up to screen them privately. The Communists' Amis de Spartacus grew fivefold in 1928, to fifty thousand members, and celebrated the Bolshevik Revolution's tenth anniversary by showing Eisenstein's *October* to packed halls. A "German" film, *Storm* escaped the ban, but not the political controversy. The Soviet writer Ilya Ehrenburg, living in Paris, summed up the Right's response to *Storm over Asia* as: "Mongols chasing white men? . . . Where's the justice in that?"[37]

To Paul Morand, the film reflected Asia's "ingratitude" to the West for Alexander the Great, the Venetian ambassadors, the Jesuit missionaries, and the modern imperialists who had abolished torture, conferred healing arts, and imparted technology. And poison gas and coolie labor, Ehrenberg sarcastically added. Ehrenberg pointed out that in League of Nations commissions, France piously condemned Chinese opium addiction and white slavery in Shanghai while collecting revenues from Indochina's opium monopoly and justifying a network of state-sanctioned brothels in Vietnam as essential to army morale. Ehrenberg did forego mentioning that this *maison close* (residential brothel) system had prevailed in France itself until 1914; and he also did not acknowledge Asia's contributions to the West.[38]

A Bolshevist Yellow Peril resurfaced in popular fiction in *The Lead Idol* (1935). This lurid spy novel featured Mâh le Sinistre, a fanatical Mongol Comintern agent, who posed as an innocuous, inscrutable exporter by day and disemboweled his enemies in seedy Paris hotel rooms by night. A brilliant chemist, he creates a poison gas to wipe out Paris and an aphrodisiac to make women his sexual slaves. Bram Stoker's Dracula evoked no greater racial-sexual fear-fascination and paranoia. Author Charles Robert-Dumas poured out the 1930s' most fearful images: Red infiltration, Asiatic barbarity, poison gas.[39] Algerian pieds noirs played on these fears; they, like the Germans, manned the front lines of the global race war.

Doctors and Diseases: Civilizing Mission and Great Fear

A sturdy triad—technology, science, and medicine—supported French notions of racial superiority. This threesome accompanied the Croisière Jaune of 1931–32 on a trek across inner Asia. As did Citroen's Croisière Noire expedition, Haardt and Audoin-Dubreuil crossed the Pamir Mountains filming their journey, and also as with the Citroen crew the scenes unintentionally revealed their equipment's dependence on local labor. Bearers—stereotypically called Sherpa bearers—hacked away stone outcroppings where roads became too narrow for the half-track *autochenilles* and disassembled them to carry the pieces across river gorges, which finally defeated the cars. A westbound team crossing the Gobi picked up the stranded party and whisked them to Hong Kong, where Haardt, like Berriau, contracted a fatal case of influenza.[40]

By 1900, Western medicine had triumphed over malaria, typhus, typhoid, and yellow fever, diseases that previously had carried off whole garrisons of French and British troops in Africa. The imperial myth made the toubib, or Western doctor, a powerful symbol of improvement through basic hygiene. Ideologists of race war also valued medical science, since it stopped barbarian diseases at Europe's gates and prevented contamination of blood and body by a "rising tide of color."

But the Great War shook Europe's faith in technological progress and showed that medical advances were neither exclusively benign nor omnipotent. The conquest of infectious disease had allowed the massing of troops in permanent positions and hence the wholesale slaughter of trench warfare on the Western Front. And medicine had proved helpless to prevent the influenza pandemic of 1918. The deadly virus, which seemed always to come from "elsewhere," had mutated from endemic, less-virulent strains brought together from four continents by wartime recruitment. Carried by demobilized soldiers and migrant workers, it spread rapidly, killing 20 million worldwide. French death rates were comparable to those of other industrial countries, but the virus struck down twice as many women as men. Displaying extraordinary resignation, Catholics said God had sent *la grippe* to restore the balance of the sexes. The French press promised cures were imminent, but viruses were still unknown, and news accounts, still blanketed in wartime censorship, were epidemiological *bourrages de crâne,* fraudulent attempts to allay public fears.[41]

Lying and self-deception carried over from war propaganda to film. In *Itto,* Western science conquers colonial disease and wins the war against "superstition," an anachronistic prewar optimism growing out of Marie Epstein's unconventional views of gender. The Berber women assimilate Cartesian norms despite the menfolk's irrational loyalty to the old ways. Diphtheria strikes Itto's newborn son and she carries him over a snowbound mountain pass to the French medical station. The toubib cures the baby, which sets up the chain of events that lead her to defy her father. To prevent an epidemic, she brings the doctor to the *souk,* the market, to inoculate Chleuh children. Outraged by the infidel's interloping, local sorcerers start a riot. In the melée, Hamou's men steal the medicines; the medicines are packed in wooden cartridge cases and the thieves think they contain bullets. At the fortress, they open the boxes, realize the mistake, and, in an attempt to imbibe the *baraka* of the toubib, a sorcerer swallows some of each serum and pill; he is left writhing and moaning in pain. Hamou orders the thieves to sell the drugs to buy ammunition, but when they return to the market, the women surround them and force them to relinquish the medicines. Itto leads a band of women and children through the mountains to the medical station. Half-dead from exposure, they arrive with the precious vaccines in time for the doctor to save his own baby, whom he inoculates before their children.[42]

Itto's actions drive the plot, both here and elsewhere. The film, which opens with Hamou on horseback, the absolute center of attention of the crowd around him and of the camera's focus, ends with Itto and Hamou standing side by side on the ramparts of Tidikelt, where they are cut down by the attacking French forces. Throughout the film, the story revolves more and more around Itto and her alter-ego, the toubib's wife. In the penultimate scene, before she goes to die by her father's side, Itto entrusts her infant to the doctor's wife, whose own infant Itto has saved. Reluctantly at first, the European woman accepts the baby, and in response to its hungry cries, she suckles it at her breast alongside her own. The film bends gender norms in other ways. Instead of the obligatory spectacle of the 1920s, the big battle scene, *Itto* concentrates on the aftermath, the bodies strewn across the field and the wounded in hospital. The bawdy café owner is transformed into a nurse, and when one soldier tries to grab her, the others warn him off. As one lies dying, she cradles him in her arms and sings him a lullaby, as if he were a child. The sanctification of the nurse recalls attitudes toward women's roles in war that arose in the 1914–1918 conflict.[43]

Itto's scenes of sorcerers and stomach ache stereotyped a non-Western healing system as ineffectual; the film portrayed such practitioners as ignorant opportunists preying on superstition. Thanks to the women, "science" wins, but a film made the same year as *Itto*, *L'Aventurier,* holds out no such hope. When Arabs attack a mine in Tunisia, the young French engineer in charge arms his men and beats back the raid. But the wanton assault destroys the mine. The engineer returns to France, where he faces a strike in which his miners attack their boss's home. Agreeing to hear their demands, the hero calms them down, suggesting that French workers can be swayed by reason, whereas Arabs respond only to force. Director Marcel L'Herbier remade his film from a 1923 original; but whereas in the silent-era version the hero became rich from the colonial venture, in the the 1934 sound version of *L'Aventurier* he is ruined. And although the new lead-in scarcely changed the plot, it indicated an altered mindset toward the potential of the colonies and natives for rational development.[44]

L'Homme du Niger, one of the last films to be made before World War II, echoed not only *Itto*'s themes of combating diseases and backwardness but also the ominous outlook seen in *L'Aventurier*. Filmed on location in the French Sudan in April 1939 as war clouds gathered over Europe, *L'Homme du Niger* acknowledged in its credits the Office of Niger's cooperation. One of a series of films promoting official policy in favor of the military defense of the empire, its narrative alluded to the ongoing work of this colonial authority. It featured a military doctor and engineer, favorite sons of the "mission civilisatrice."[45] Aided by *les petites soeurs,* the nurses, the two professional men battle native passivity and superstition through science and technology. The captain of the engineers is building a dam to bring prosperity and progress, but he contracts leprosy. The doctor tries to convince the captain that with rest he can be cured, but the engineer knows his fate is sealed, and he sacrifices himself to finish the dam. Spurning his fiancée, the daughter of a cabinet minister who has supported his plans, he urges his lieutenant to marry her in his stead. In the climax, an African sorcerer, "un nègre fanatique" who holds the tribe under his spell, incites his followers to burn the clinic and damage the dam. While his minions gesticulate wildly and yell inarticulate cries, the sorcerer grabs a gun and shoots the doctor through the heart.

Whereas *Itto* asserted faith in the rationality of the Berber women in adopting Western medicine, *L'Homme du Niger* reflected a deep pessimism accompanied by undertones of disingenuous vexation with the scrofulous, passive race squandering its own resources. Though France's heroic, selfless devotion to duty might be in vain, it had to take the ungrateful savages in hand. Publicity photos taken on location show cast and crew lounging on a veranda attended by a retinue of African servants. The picture suggests that colon attitudes of overlordship rubbed off on director, writers, and actors. Leprosy, loathsome companion of medieval and equatorial backwardness, represented a rot eating away at the Third Republic. *L'Homme du Niger* premiered two months after the Nazi attack on Poland and seven months before the fall of Paris. In a mode similar to *Heart of Darkness*, where a tale of the Congo is told from a vessel that was in fact anchored in the Thames, in *L'Homme du Niger* the Seine doubles for the Niger.[46]

Concern over the spread of infectious disease also figured in Jean Renoir's *La Vie est à nous*. Immigration from North Africa had stimulated French fears of moral decay and infection, conjuring up repellent images of vice, disease, and rape. The prefect of the Loire had urged the government to expel foreigners in 1925, saying they carried tuberculosis and syphilis and contributed nothing to France. On the Left, these migrants aroused pity without evoking a challenge to the stereotype or the cause of the wretchedness. Renoir's movie, filmed for the Communists' 1936 election campaign, contains a scene of an Algerian washing cars in a garage. The unemployed worker who is the central character hears the Algerian's hacking tubercular cough and asks if he feels well. "Mohammed" tells him things are better here than at home. Renoir's vision was broad enough to see the Arab as part of the Popular Front, but Mohammed, with only one line to tell his story, is a half-visible wraith, like the ghostly figures who roam the jungle around the camp of Joseph Conrad's Kurtz.[47]

In Paris, municipal councillor Pierre Godin warned that North Africans in Paris were spreading syphilis and other diseases. His alarms promoted and financed a Hôpital Franco-Musulman to serve and control the new arrivals. His son, André, became head of the Service des Affaires Indigènes Nord-Africains (SAINA) in 1932. A forty-man police unit created to keep North Africans in Paris under surveillance during the Rif War, SAINA provided employment, health, and welfare services to migrants and weeded out and deported "undesirables." Maghrebins in Paris hated SAINA, and Etoile Nord Africain militants roundly condemned it. During the Colonial Exposition of 1931, Pierre's wife, Huguette, organized a women's conference that held aloft the maternalist ideal of white women as enlightened bearers of civilization to colonial peoples—saviors who would abolish "barbaric" customs and improve the treatment of Arab women. As settler power grew, the Godins reproduced a miniature Lyauteyisme in Paris, while films made during the Popular Front era transformed white women into agents of the white man's destruction.[48]

Aside from two noteworthy exceptions, Julien Duvivier's internationally acclaimed *Pépé le Moko* (1937) and Pierre Chenal's *Maison du*

Maltais (1938), the scope of colonial film narrowed in the late 1930s to a subgenre, the Foreign Legion movie. Nearly a dozen such films were made. Typical of them is one based on a novel by a favorite writer of the Legion high command, André Armandy, that had won an Académie française prize: *Les Reprouvés* (The outcasts). Séverac, whose Moroccan trilogy had fared so badly, adapted Armandy's novel in 1936.

The "outcasts" of the disciplinary Bataillons d'Afrique were not Legionnaires per se, but soldiers convicted of crimes while in military service. Ironically nicknamed Les Joyeux, they were the dregs of the dregs. In Séverac's scenario, a handsome nobleman, deceived in love, volunteers to take command of a unit of Joyeux in the Sahara. A former mistress joins him at the fort, just before unnamed insurgents attack and surround it. The officer tries all the tricks and ruses of war to lift the siege, but his ingenuity cannot overcome the weight of numbers of the invisible, off-camera attackers. About to be overrun, he poisons his mistress so she will not fall into the rebels' hands, then blows up the fort. Reinforcements arrive too late to save the last stand, but they defeat the Arabs. A parade in honor of the fallen sings the outcasts' anthem.

In this second foray into the colonial genre, Séverac took his cameras to Bou Sâada, 175 miles south of Algiers. The fort at the outskirts of the town, half-destroyed in an uprising fifty years before, was a symbol-laden landmark featured in films, travel posters, and guided tours. In its shadow, Séverac adopted the settler stereotypes: cunning but unintelligent, Arabs lusted after white women and understood only force; anonymous and invisible, they win through numbers and cruelty, not strategy. The relief column's technological superiority and discipline sweeps them away, and with them Lyauteyisme and *Itto*. There was no room for the Berber myth in the settler worldview, no political legacy for the Berber policy in Algeria.[49]

Foreign Legion films with a penchant for military action came to dominate colonial cinema at a stage when the issues of colonial rule had become more intractable and less amenable to simplistic solutions. Location shooting shifted from Morocco to Algeria where, in a climate of military censorship, authorities subsidized celebratory, unimaginative films that presented a self-sacrificing, tough, disciplined colonial army, a public face the Legion command most desired. *Itto* and the Moroccan-based output of the silent era had portrayed a polychromatic, nuanced Maghreb. In contrast, even the best Legion films, such as *Le Grand jeu* (1934), made North Africa a place where white males fought an invisible, anonymous alterity, described only as *les salopards,* or *l'ennemi.* Hackneyed scripts revolved around lovelorn white men who had committed crimes and sought redemption in the desert. Giving their lives for comrades, regiment, and corps, they held the "thin white line" defending the West against the colored hordes of the earth. *Pour Vous*'s readers attest to *Itto*'s discourse pre-dating and contesting these films.

Itto also reflected the strains of its creators' disparate points of view. Strange bedfellows, they made common cause. Lyautey's mythologizing protégés and heirs gave voice to a paternalistic colonialism consistent with Benoît-Lévy's idea of the Berber as overgrown child. Benoît-Lévy's perception of the Chleuh derived from their Berber myth, which blinded him to the proletarianization and other intrusions of the capitalist market that were changing their way of life. The contradiction of hiring the Chleuh and paying them to "act natural" escaped him. Marie Epstein infused the film with feminist hope and power. She holds the best claim to having made it a democratic, anti–white supremacist vision of the future.

But Epstein's was a voice crying out in the wilderness. Cinéma colonial found new sponsors among the military defenders of the settler regime in Algeria. Dark and ominous visions of the West menaced by fearsome African hordes, ghastly tropical diseases, and Asiatic Bolshevism took hold of filmmakers as they revamped images and scenarios to project the face of race war.

7 | The Thin White Line of Western Civilization

Foreign Legion Movies, Masculinity, and Family Life

In Barika, Algeria, a small town on the edge of the Sahara, two hundred miles south of Constantine, the settler-controlled town council *(commune mixte)* acquired film projectors and ran an outdoor cinema that attracted large native audiences to every screening. It showed *Fils du Soleil* in September 1926, and the Algerians "applauded and stamped their feet" when the "dissidents" temporarily put the Legion to rout. In true Lyauteyiste spirit, *Ciné-Miroir* admired the film as a "new means of persuasion that will help us improve understanding and love for French civilization."[1] Thus even in the 1920s, when 90 percent of rural Algerians spoke no French, cinema reached into the bled. The number of *cinémathèques* rose from 150 in 1933 to 300 in 1954, although, predictably, they catered to European audiences concentrated in Algiers, Oran, Constantine, and Bône, and one can imagine that the reaction of Barika's natives left local Foreign Legion posts uneasy. Legion commanders were as aware of film's power as Lyautey had ever been, and they energetically suppressed film that sullied the corps' "honor" or suggested a lack of fighting will that might agitate the natives and stir up disorders.

Film production in Morocco had dwindled as the cities became more volatile and settler agriculture drew rural labor away from short-term projects like movie-extra work. The shift to Algeria meant an end to the silent era's battle-spectacles. Hundreds of natives massed in military formations made the army nervous, and the Code de l'Indigénat curtailed the customary horsemanship-and-gunfire fantaisie displays. In 1937, Henri Fescourt's Algerian-made version of *L'Occident* left to the audience's imagination the elaborate battle employing hundreds of Chleuh extras that he had filmed in Morocco in 1927. In contrast to the Moroccan-made spectacle of 1922, Marcel L'Herbier's Algerian version of *Les*

Hommes nouveaux (1936) avoided native extras by cleverly shooting the climactic confrontation between French and "dissidents" with the camera pointing toward the French command post. The officers scan the horizon with binoculars, their lenses and those of the cameras facing one another. The forgoing of big battles simplified logistics, cut the expenses of location shooting, and offset spiraling costs and technical complexities imposed by sound equipment. It also removed a source of contention with the army, which exercised wide censorship powers.[2]

A protracted public-relations war conducted against Hollywood film producers and Anglophone writers intensified pressure on French directors. Legion headquarters, incensed by treatments that belittled the corps and undermined morale, fought back by sponsoring sympathetic French portrayals and by achieving a symbiosis with the settlers. While the army protected pied-noir dominance, colon political clout ensured generous budgetary support for Algerian-based units. The bonds grew so strong during the last phase of the Algerian War that Legion regiments conspired with pied-noir ultras in a coup to prevent Algerian independence by overthrowing the Fifth Republic.[3]

The Legion, 1914–1962: Recruitment, Training, Politics

Filmmakers and Legion officers alike treated the unit's headquarters, Sidi Bel Abbès, as both Mecca and Jerusalem. Located near the Saharan-Moroccan border, the Legion's main theater of operations, it was named for a local marabout whose tomb was the oldest structure in the vicinity. The French-built town combined features of a movie lot, Potemkin village, and slum. The main street looked like a French provincial town. Behind this façade stretched squalid Berber, Arab, and Jewish quarters, formally termed *faubourgs Bugeaud* but popularly called *villages nègres*. The Legion had tried to move its headquarters from Sidi Bel Abbès to Morocco in the early 1920s to gain greater autonomy from the Nineteenth Army Corps, but the army command had blocked the transfer. With the Rif War's end and Lyautey's departure, Algeria became the "Legion's temple and its prison." Born on the same day as French Algeria, 10 March 1831, the Legion renewed this historic tie at Algeria's centennial. The dedication of the Colonial Exposition in Paris coincided with the publication of the Legion's commissioned history, written in "heroic mode." As ties to Morocco unraveled, the Legion's bonds to the settler regime's policy of white-supremacist rule tightened.[4]

Within the framework of direct rule in Algeria in the 1920s, the Legion Command had had to recruit and train new troops without exacerbating the underlying contradictions in its structure and mission. Heavy losses on the Western Front in 1914–18 led to problems of assimilating new recruits. Rising desertion rates compromised Spartan discipline, and *"avâchissement"* (slackness) risked breeding native restiveness and settler anxiety. French opinion accepted the draft to protect the nation's borders, but using conscripts, ill-adapted to the rigors and isolation of colonial service, invited public disapproval and government scrutiny. Therefore France, like other colonial powers, adopted a "two-army system." Conscripts guarded the home front, while European professionals were sent overseas and incorporated with local native units. Poorly paid mercenaries consigned mainly to garrison duty, the Legion was an anachronism that persisted because Algeria's anomalous status required such a force.[5]

Native units became a source of anxiety after 1921; Abd el-Krim's Rif Republic inflicted military disaster on Spain, and the army uncovered a rash of desertion plots. It disbanded its Tunisian Spahi regiments and worried that the Legion had been contaminated, since after 1918 40 to 50 percent of its ranks were German mercenaries and only 25 percent of the privates were French. Before the Great War, patriotic Alsatians eager to acquire military skills to reclaim France's lost territories had stiffened the ranks. The command esteemed the loyalty of postwar French recruits, but found them "worthless" as soldiers. Those who proved tough, however, made up one-half of the Legion's sergeants and corporals, the corps' backbone.[6]

Legion intelligence reports alleged that German deserters under Sergeant Klems were serving the Riffians as artillerymen and machine-gunners. While a leaflet in German was discovered that invited Legionnaires to join Abd el-Krim's crusade against France or be repatriated through Tangier, faulty assumptions that the Riffians could defeat a European army, even one as poorly trained as Spain's, only with the technical help of Europeans may have clouded judgments. Recent monographs on the Rif War, using Berber as well as French sources, confirm that desertions rose well before hostilities erupted with the Rif Republic in April 1925, and as Abd el-Krim himself sensibly pointed out to a French reporter, deserters "could turn on us as easily as they did on you."[7]

Postwar recruiting methods designed to recoup the losses of 1914–18 offer a nonconspiratorial explanation for desertions. Before 1914, enlistees had to sign up in France, where recruiting sergeants explained the harsh realities of Legion life and gave applicants twenty-four hours to rethink their decision. After 1918, the Legion lifted restrictions and waiting periods and authorized recruitment by French military attachés and consuls abroad. New men, often young and rash, had no chance to reconsider before being transported across the Mediterranean, debarked at Oran, and herded onto the train to Sidi Bel Abbès. Foreigners arrested in Paris were often offered a choice between a trial or the Legion. But impressed men invited trouble. The Great War's sacrifices had bled the Legion of those who could train and discipline newcomers, so raw recruits could threaten the cohesion of what was a heterogeneous, polyglot force. In the absence of patriotism, the interwar Legion's "architect and impresario," General Paul Rollet, instilled loyalty to regiment and corps. Emblazoning *Legio Patria Nostra* (The Legion is our fatherland) on monuments and training manuals, he invented a tradition. And since this brotherhood was all the family a ranker was supposed to have, the motto could as easily have read *Legio Familia Nostra*.

The Legion's officers, recruiting sergeants, and drillmasters approved film and print portrayals that helped their work, and the Legion banned specific films they felt hindered them, leaving to others the larger questions of the legitimacy of French rule. Anglophone film, fiction, or retired-Legionnaire memoirs aroused suspicion: they were often critical, in part because English or American enlistees tended to be better off than those from the Continent, and such recruits had to make a double adjustment from civilian to military life and from a middle-class to a working-class standard of living. What, to English or American petits bourgeois, seemed a coarse, brutal existence was security to an unemployed German or Belgian worker—a fate better than begging or sleeping under bridges. As was testified to by the ragged recruits arriving each week at Sidi Bel Abbès and Saida, Legion ranks were a working-class milieu. The ranks swelled to thirty-three thousand as the Great Depression deepened: 80 percent were driven in by hunger, homelessness, and misery. The twenty-four-hour cooling-off period was reinstated, but many men refused to accept the offer or the warnings of recruiting sergeants. After seven thousand joined in 1931, Paris cut back enlistments as an economy measure; with war on the horizon in 1938, it started recruiting again.

A romantic, mysterious image attracted foreign Beau Gestes bored with modern society, disappointed in love, infatuated with masochistic notions of self-abnegation and sacrifice. But they were rare. Fond of asking what men had done "before," Rollet heard few replies such as the White Russian emigré's "J'étais un colonel, mon colonel." Such exceptions attained the proper rigid Spartan discipline and self-sacrifice. But the Legion rarely lived up to expectations, and disappointment bred resentment and recalcitrance that hindered training.

Language barriers and working-class backgrounds imposed restrictions on officers and sergeants in what they could employ as training methods and military style. A minimum of spoken instruction or military theory, short commands—often no more than *"faites comme moi"* (do like me)—meant that officers led from the front, by example, and won the respect of the troops in that way. More than most units, the Legion emphasized imagery, symbolism, and ritual—an example of Benedict Anderson's "imagined community." Rollet and Colonel Jean-Jacques Azam, his successor, created a cult of the Legion. They dedicated a monument to the Legion's dead in Sidi Bel-Abbès and honored the fallen in an annual memorial ceremony called the Camerone, after a minor battle in the Mexican campaign of 1863 in which a company of Legionnaires made a last stand. To tighten loyalty among men beyond the bounds of nationality, the Legion promoted a cult of sacrifice and heroic death, assuring them it never abandoned its own, even risking lives to recover the corpses of comrades. The signature white hat *(kepi blanc)*, epaulets, sash, and distinctive march cadence catered to the cult members' need to feel special, and Rollet insisted on them despite opposition from the high command as well as a disproportionate number of head wounds from snipers aiming at the bright caps.

After the Nazi regime took power in Germany in 1933, German nationalism intensified among German Legionnaires and conflict arose with a new influx of leftist and Jewish refugees from Eastern Europe's fascist and military regimes. In 1936, "communist" demonstrations in the First Regiment supported the Popular Front, and in February 1937 the Legion created an internal surveillance unit, imposed postal censorship, and infiltrated "grasses" *(mouchards)* into the ranks. In 1938, Azam produced a sixty-page pamphlet, *Memento du Légionnaire*, a kind of military Benedictine rule, to reinforce loyalty. Rollet had balanced the Legion between refuge for misfit losers and military environment that transformed by harsh, even brutal discipline the flotsam of Europe into soldiers. The *anonymat*, a regulation permitting enlistment under a false name, promoted the idea that men could escape their former lives. The appeal to Legionnaires to sacrifice for the good of humanity, to become missionaries of Western civilization, helped motivate them to risk their lives in combat and also legitimated them as defenders of the white race. Friction occasionally erupted with settlers at the local level, but overall the Legion's objectives dovetailed with the colon agenda of preserving white rule.[8]

The metropole's attempts at reform strengthened ties between settlers and army. Their formidable lobby encouraged the myth of "the three *départements*," an indissoluble bond with the Hexagon, which impelled the Fourth Republic from 1952 to 1962 to send half a million draftees per year, three million in all, to occupy and pacify the Algerian bled. A third generation of war veterans *(génération de feu)*, the *djebel* generation, took its place in the ranks. This cohort, like that in the United States during and after the Vietnam War, indicted their country for indifference to them and for fighting an unjust war.[9]

During the Algerian War, the Legion committed itself totally to Algérie française. On the outer wall of Fort Bou Sâada, in three-foot-high white letters, Legionnaires painted "Ici c'est la France à tout jamais" (This is France for all time). The Première Régiment Etrangère des Parachutistes (the First REP) carried out the infamous *ratonnades* (rat-catchings) in the Battle of Algiers in 1957, and its ranks were peppered with German SS men who had taken advantage of the *anonymat* to escape justice in Europe. Zéralda, its headquarters, was "in permanent contact with the overheated political climate of . . . [Algiers]. Legionnaires and their officers fraternized in the cafés of the Rue Michelet with pied-noir militants, inhaling the city's atmosphere, . . . thick with revolutionary defiance."[10] With the pied-noir ultras, they mounted a coup on 22 April 1961 to stop de Gaulle from abandoning the settlers. But conscripts in other units went on strike, refusing to leave their barracks, and this foiled the coup. Zéralda was surrounded, and after five days the First REP's officers and men were conducted from the base under arrest. Passing through Algiers in their trucks, they sang "Je ne regrette rien," Edith Piaf's hymn to the Resistance. Pieds noirs lined the streets and wept openly as the last hope of preserving white rule was carried off in disgrace to France, where it was disbanded.[11]

The Legion's Cultural Politics and Audience Reactions

Authenticity demanded that filmmakers go into the outback, which required the army's permission and cooperation and thus implicitly constrained them. The Legion's censors wanted movies to show men hardened by military discipline laying down their lives to atone for past misdeeds. According to Richard Abel, this myth of redemption "achieves its apotheosis" in Jacques Feyder's *Le Grand jeu* (1934) and Julien Duvivier's *La Bandera* (1935).[12] The action in both films takes place during the Rif War, but renders the Berbers invisible, effacing even their name by referring to them only as *salopards* (bastards) or *l'ennemi*.

In Lyauteyiste films of the 1920s, the Legion participated in a civilizing mission. But the logic of race war dictated that Muslims understood only force, and since this logic redefined the mission as military, and hence male, the North African bled was no place for white women. The Legion buried a man's past so that he could redeem himself, so the Legionnaire must foresake family, which was viable only in the metropole or in settler enclaves. Subplots warned of interracial love's tragic consequences, and ironically this negative attention to family gave these "men's stories" an appeal to women. The Legion film "served as backdrop for somber dramas or sentimental adventures intended to make young working girls *[midinettes]* cry and dream on Saturday evenings."[13]

"Virile" films appealed to women but also left them feeling excluded. Eavesdropping on an audience that had just seen *La Bandera,* Blanche Vogt, a reporter for the film magazine *Pour Vous,* overheard comments on the film's assumptions about sex roles. Two women in their thirties lamented that a man could erase his past and redeem himself, whereas a woman needed a birth certificate or nursing diploma to enter a convent, become a Carmelite, or even to care for lepers. A husband and wife agreed that seeing *Bandera*'s professional soldiers die was "less intolerable" than seeing the deaths of poor draftees in the Great War, but the wife was appalled that the Legion captain volunteered for a suicide mission when he had a wife and children. A Legion officer ought to be celibate, she thought, like a medieval Knight Templar, or form a liaison with a native woman. "You believe a Moorish dancer has no heart? That she cannot suffer like you?" her husband asked. "A bit wounded," wrote the reporter, Madame cut off the discussion. Two young women found actor Jean Gabin attractive even though the character he played had killed and expressed no remorse. Swept up in the idea of living dangerously, they envied men's prerogative to take up such a life. One mentioned that the Ministry of War had banned the use of soldiers as movie extras; her friend suggested that the unemployed "could make up entire regiments." The first thought that such deployments might not be as realistic, to which her friend replied, "Oh, all men are good at playing soldiers!"[14]

Since "it was rare to count fewer women than men in the theaters," this hybrid genre—action mixed with melodrama—served French cinema well, attracting both sexes. Attendance, which had reached 220 million admissions a year with the advent of sound in 1930, remained a concern: American and British totals, both in proportion to total population and in number of visits per year, still dwarfed French figures. The publicity resources of the French *ateliers* paled compared with the public-relations machines of the giant American studios, and French film magazines sought to help boost ticket sales by piquing expectations of genre and stars. So the contradiction that Miriam Hansen finds at the heart of American silent film applied to French cinema as well: a "massive catering to women viewers in a medium that increasingly depended, for the kinds of pleasure it offered the viewer, on a patriarchal organization of vision."[15]

Supplanting Lyauteyisme

Legion films took over the colonial genre because they were the most suitable vehicle for the racially polarized worldview that lent credence to the policies of white rule. In 1928 and 1931, four films were released, two still bearing the signature elements of Lyautey's touch and two promoting the Legion's peculiar male code of honor and family life. In John Waters's *The Spahi* (1928), an officer's European lover arouses the covetous desire of a q'aid, who demands her as a condition of a treaty of alliance. A man of honor, will the Spahi abandon the woman to serve his country? A deus ex machina resolves his dilemma. The q'aid is attacked by a traitorous subordinate, and the Spahi metes out justice to this wretch, and a fellow officer saves the life of the q'aid, who gratefully signs the treaty without condition. Duty and love reconciled, the Spahi returns to his garrison. This was vintage Lyautey: pacification by a treaty of submission to French authority and persuasion of the q'aid by noble example rather than by force. But the audience also saw a lascivious Arab and a woman who would have avoided trouble by staying at home. In Rex Ingram's *Baroud* (The last stand), two sergeants of the Spahis, André Duval and Si Ahmed, are friends, but when André seduces Si Ahmed's sister, the Moroccan wants to avenge his family's honor. When bandit-rebels attack Si Ahmed's father's *q'asbah* (citadel) and André saves the family, Si Ahmed forgives him. One of Lyauteyisme's "last stands," this 1931 film synecdochically appointed the French army defender of the Arab family and interracial cooperation, but clearly disapproved of sexual liaisons. Later films jealously reserved protection for European women.[16]

In contrast, a 1928 film, *La Pente* (The slope), told a tale of a Montmartre mechanic, Lucien, accused of a crime. His boss, who can prove Lucien's innocence, is himself imprisoned, so Lucien enlists in the Legion for five years. In the Rif, he saves his captain's life, wins the confidence of his superiors, and returns to Paris with his courage and character remolded by the Legion. He hopes his mother and fiancée, whom he has treated badly, will forgive him. They welcome him home, and the young couple look bravely to the future. *La Pente*—a recruiting poster of a film—projected the Legion not only as redeeming the man, but also as teaching him to respect the women in his life.[17]

Russian emigré director Vladimir Strijewski and actor Ivan Mosjoukine (formerly with Films Albatros) paid homage to the Legion and its values in *Sergent X* (1931). Legionnaires, Spahis, and camel cavalry *(méharistes)* occupy a world apart from the civilian universe of affection and friendship; they are isolated mercenaries, whose sexual needs are filled by traveling bordellos that follow the troops. Tchernoff (Mosjoukine) enters this world. A White Army officer swept away by the Russian Revolution and presumed dead, he goes to Paris in search of wife and son, who have emigrated to France. Olga has married a rich captain. Penniless and emphatically denying his past as an officer, Tchernoff joins the Legion and finds himself in the unit commanded by his wife's new husband. She does not recognize him and, seeing his son happy and secure, Tchernoff stands aside. He goes on a dangerous mission, is again given up for dead, and the captain discovers Olga's photo among his effects. Once again Tchernoff survives, and when he returns he asks the captain to keep his secret. Better that his wife and son not know of him; his destiny as a Legionnaire is never again to know hearth, home, and family. Thus Olga's fate is decided by two men of the officer caste and their "gentlemen's agreement": Thou shalt not lower thy wife's class status.[18]

On a lighter note, in *Un de la Légion* (1936), the comedian Fernandel plays a stereotypical henpecked husband who is robbed and knocked out by a brigand while on the road. He awakes to find himself on a boat with his assailant's enlistment papers in hand, bound for Sidi Bel Abbès and five years in the Legion. The comedy derives from his attempts to navigate this unfamiliar world, but having escaped his banal, empty life and shrewish wife, he reenlists under his real name. As in the dramas, the Legion makes him a better man. Fernandel's talents won praise for the film, but *Ciné Liberté*, the Communist film monthly, took it to task for adding to an "epidemic of films on the Legion." Bemused critic Gaston Modot, himself a well-known actor, wondered what title would come next, "Four of the Fire Department" or "Sixteen of the Funeral Parlor"? The film had stock characters: the cheeky Paris boulevard youth *(le Titi parisien)*, the comic with a foreign accent, the bad-tempered *râleur,* or grumbler (critic Modot had himself played one in *La Bandera*). These were tied to a predictable, hackneyed plot that included the inevitable brawl in the Arab café, the desert attack, and the apotheosis, a demobilized soldier who reenlists on the spot. Even so, Modot admitted, director Christian-Jaque had filmed a well-staged, exciting spectacle, and entirely on location in Marseille and Sidi Bel Abbès. Christian-Jaque had served eighteen months in the military in southern Morocco, which smoothed the way for help from the Legion, and the film clearly proclaimed the Legion's message. It built character, and the Legionnaire had no family but the Legion.[19]

Fernandel's comedic foray and the drama *Les Réprouvés* (1936) (see chapter 6) expressed the Legion's line in its purest form. Subsequent dramas invented few variations on the Legion myths of honor and family. *Les Hommes sans nom* (1937) is a fictional biography of Colonel de Joyeuse, who was in fact Henri de Corta, brother-in-law of Jean Desvallières, the author of the film's screenplay. De Corta saw action in the Zaian war; and Hamou, Itto's father (see chapter 6), figures in the film cast of characters.

The colonel, devoted to his regiment, refuses promotion to general and dies in battle. His widow tells his officers, "My family reproached me for allowing my husband to remain in the Legion. I have no regrets." He had turned to her for a loan when the Colonial Affairs office was late in making a payment to a q'aid who submitted to France on condition he receive a subvention of 500,000 francs. She had given him her entire dowry. Recidivist traces of Lyauteyisme and maternalism deviate from the Legion line here, but the idealized colonel's wife creates an impossible standard for Frenchwomen's participation in the colonial mission. *Légions d'honneur* (1938), subsidized by the War Ministry and the Algerian governor's office, lent official sanction to the Legion code

of French family and womanhood. A grueling tour in the Sahara bonds
Captain Dabrau and Lieutenant Vallin, who falls in love with Dabrau's
wife but does not violate his trust. Dabrau thinks he is betrayed and
shoots Vallin, who is court-martialed for "self-mutilation." Vallin keeps
silent rather than dishonor the lady or accuse his friend, is stripped of
his commission, enlists in the Legion, and goes to a glorious death. The
film's male bonding is so strong it is tinged with homoeroticism, and it
implies that white women can be protected only if confined to France.
In the bled, they risk a "fate worse than death" such as that which, filmgoers were asked to believe, awaited the loyal mistress in *Les Réprouvés* if her officer-lover's poison had not allowed her to escape the clutches
of the "salopards."[20]

Defending the Legion against Hollywood's Imagery

The romantic fascination the Legion held for Europeans and Americans
complicated its efforts to maintain control over its image. Hollywood,
encouraged by thematic similarities to the western, the success of *The
Sheik* (1921), and the proximity of desert locales to Los Angeles studios, quickly grasped the potential to exploit the Legion's mystique.
Christopher Wren's *Beau Geste* and its two sequels endlessly fascinated
Anglo-America and went through a dozen editions in Britain and the
United States before 1950. The original film starring Ronald Coleman
brought the novel to the screen just two years after it was published
in London in 1924, and it was remade three times. But in France, the
works of Major Wren, as he was known, held little interest. *Beau Geste*
was translated into French in 1931, but only one of the two sequels,
Beau Sabreur, was translated and saw print (in 1936). Since all sixteen
books of the Tarzan series were translated and published from 1937
to 1940, this indifference to Wren is curious. The Anglophone racial
mythmaking of Edgar Rice Burroughs never strained Franco-American
relations the way *Beau Geste* did.[21]

The film premiered in France in the wake of the nasty colonial war
that destroyed the Rif Republic, and in one scene a sergeant strips the
personal effects from the bodies of his dead soldiers. It prompted widespread protests in the French press. With the U.S. Congress and the press
pointedly contrasting France's bullying of the Rif with its support for
the American underdog in 1776, the film appeared to be part of an orchestrated anti-French campaign. It was banned in France and Algeria,

and the French ambassador in Berlin won assent to deny it a license for presentation in Germany, too, where before and during the war anti-Legion propaganda had been virulent. For its 1939 remake, Paramount Studios issued a disclaimer in the credits, saying the story was fictional and not intended to slander the Legion, but the remake was banned in France until 1977, along with Ronald Coleman's *Condemned* (1934). Both films touched on mutiny or desertion in ways the French army found intolerable.[22]

Algiers censors banned *Morocco* (1930), Josef von Sternberg's adaptation of Benno Vigny's 1927 novel *Amy Jolly* that was written in 1917 in Ain-Guettara, Morocco. Released in France in 1931 as *Coeurs Brûlés*, it starred Marlene Dietrich as Amy, the Woman-with-a-Past, Gary Cooper as Legionnaire Brown, whom she loves, and Adolphe Menjou as the sophisticated millionaire (so suave, said one wag, that he wore triple-breasted suits) who falls for Amy but whom she rejects. Dietrich's sensual glances could not rescue the silly dialogue ("There is a Foreign Legion of women, who wear no uniform and no medals, but we have the wounds.") or the plot. When Sergeant-Major Césaire discovers Brown dallying with his wife, as well as Amy, he orders him on a suicide reconnaissance mission. Amy urges Brown to desert, but Brown refuses and reports for duty. Césaire volunteers to join him and dies saving him. In the last scene, Amy abandons Menjou beside his limousine. As Brown's unit marches off into the desert, kicking off her high heels she rushes to join a contingent of camp followers, helping the other women tug at donkey and goat halters, struggling to catch up with the men. Anglophone audiences may have found such sentimentality acceptable, a French critic wrote, but French audiences, cynical about women's motives and too calloused by the trench warfare of 1914–18 to suspend disbelief at the "terrible, desperate love" of Jolly and Brown, found it absurd. Since they "habitually put their feelings in the service of general ideas" like *le patrie en danger* or noble sacrifice to save another, and Césaire embodied that ideal, he was more credible than Jolly or Brown.[23]

The Legion command hated this movie. General Paul Rollet, architect of the Legion's reorganization and refurbisher of its image, explaining to journalist Paul Safar why the Algiers censor stopped its distribution, called it "an abracadabran fantasy with unveiled, seminude native women jumping around in the streets." The "form of dress of the men," Rollet went on, is not accurate for Morocco. As for the Legion, it was depicted as a pack of brutes, out of uniform, carrying their rifles like broomsticks, dragging themselves in a disorderly line behind a miserable bugler and a "German" drummer. In the evening, one sees the Legionnaires making an uproar in a nightclub [a *dancing*] in Mogador [Rollet places a question mark against *Mogador,* which is the name of an Atlantic coastal town far from the Legion's zone of military responsibility], drinking with prostitutes beside their sergeants for whom they demonstrate no respect. There is also a troop muster in the middle of the street, while women dressed in gypsy costumes follow their men to the city gates as they depart for the desert. . . . The unit goes to meet the enemy (from Mogador, as usual). Voilà la Legion "made in Hollywood"![24]

Since the film upheld Rollet's duty-above-love code of honor, his nitpicking seems overblown. But Legion command found *Morocco*'s sins unforgivable. Going where no white woman should, Amy Jolly arrives in Morocco without male escort, urges Brown to desert, mixes with native camp followers, and traipses into the bled. From the Legion's perspective the film treated Cesaire's fate too lightly. Attempts to reconcile family ties with duty to the corps inevitably led to tragedy, and although Brown ends his affair with the sergeant major's wife, Brown is hardly blameless in his self-destruction.

Civic Heroism and Colonial Hegemony

Film derived its "tropes of empire"[25] from an array of pre–World War I sources that had immersed the childhood years of interwar adult moviegoers in a cult of "civic heroism." Film traced its media origins to the nineteenth century—to orientalist painting, postcards, and expositions—but its discourse came mainly from the classroom. Both Lyauteyiste paternalism and settler militarism originated in the early Third Republic's school curriculum. When it was found that one-quarter of the army's recruits of 1903–7 had never heard of Joan of Arc and that two-thirds did not recognize the name of Napoleon, the state deployed a new "pedagogical strategy" to overcome this appalling "patriotic ignorance." War memorials, schoolbooks, and *Almanachs de Drapeau,* yearly records of heroic exploits of soldiers and policemen, inculcated a cult of courage to combat pacifism, antimilitarism, and a sense of decline. The Great War's arbitrary mass death shattered this plan. Veterans' novels made "war . . . the enemy, its human instruments its victims." Sympathy for the simple soldier as "heroic victim," who killed to survive, ran high. But one venue reconstituted the prewar culture, the colonies. Fulfilling longings to escape the war's horrors and the humdrum of civilian life, they evoked a male fantasy world where human will and courage could change the course of history.[26]

The celebrity of T. E. Lawrence ("Lawrence of Arabia"), for example, was a product of such desires, as well as of the newsreel camera and closer economic ties to the colonies. However, imperial unity proved as illusory as the myth of Europeans heroically initiating the history of "timeless" Asia and Africa. As Raymond Betts says, "If empire ever had a heroic phase, which is doubtful, it was gone by the twentieth century. The *Lives of a Bengal Lancer* and *Beau Geste* were now filmed, not lived." But the persistence of myth was revealed in a 1962 survey of thirteen hundred former colonial civil servants that summed up why they had chosen their careers. Inspired by visits to the Exposition of 1931 and the novels of Jules Verne, Pierre Loti, Rudyard Kipling, and Daniel DeFoe, they wanted to see exotic places, escape French social restrictions, take command, and "change the world." Films such as *Lawrence of Arabia* and *Fort Saganne* testify to the colonial myth's staying power.[27]

The oldest Third Republic schoolbooks, which blended secular Republic and Roman Catholic values and addressed girls and boys of every region and class, proved remarkably durable, and Second Empire Education Minister Ernest Lavisse's history primers went through dozens of editions. They were still in use after 1945. Thirty grade-school histories circulated before 1914; all, except socialist Gustave Hervé's anti-imperialist text, which was deemed subversive, celebrated the heroic deeds of France's mission, emphasizing paternalism and conquest to varying degrees depending on the author's politics. Lavisse introduced Pierre de Brazza with a simple story: "One day when our flag was hoisted near a village in the Congo, a troop of slaves passed. Brazza stopped it and said 'Wherever the French flag flies there should be no slaves.' And he saw that the collars were taken off. . . . This again proves that France is good and generous to peoples that submit to it."[28]

The benevolent imperial face shining on French pupils dimly reflected on colonial children. In 1935, Brévié, governor of French West Africa, made clear that assimilation meant relinquishing African culture. Education would "develop a potential governing class. . . . Wholehearted acceptance of the African by the French" would bring Africans into "wider contact with French life and institutions through the diffusion of the French language." By building schools and teaching practical skills in French, "the school is working its way into native life . . . to bring it into conformity with a French pattern."[29]

From Brévié's remarks, British observers concluded that the French had overcome backward thinking on race. Former labor and education commissioners of Tanganyika, on a fact-finding tour of Brévié's domain in 1935, said, "Association of mental capacity with colour of skin would be placed by France in the same category as character-judging by cranial bumps." To the British, skin color was the only marker of race, and they admiringly noted that French and African children attended school together. But the substance of cultural dominance escaped their eye; their book was revealingly entitled *Africans Learn to Be French*.[30] A British missionary who studied French education of Algeria's Kabyles firsthand concluded the Berber "belongs to the white stock: his stature, features, hair and colour are Caucasian." Incorporating the Berber myth into his own racial phenotypology, he implied that the Kabyles, who had resisted French compulsory education before 1914, now "clamour for schools" because they were white. But he also pointed out that "all teachers in government elementary schools . . . are required to use the French language exclusively." Kabyle and French teachers received equal pay, including an overseas incentive bonus of 25 percent, but Kabyles had to become citizens and renounce their personal religious status. Such ambiguities allowed the French to assert the superiority of their colonial rule over Britain's and to couch their stories of conquest in paternal ideals.[31]

Masculinity and Family Life à la Foreign Legion

Just as Hollywood westerns inverted the role of the invader, whites defending forts and wagon trains from Indian assault, the French posed as victims of unprovoked attacks. French stories, like Hollywood's, upheld masculine ideals and edified boys and girls with heroic deeds and inspiring words. Nonwhite rulers insulted France's honor; "her" soldiers defended it, a folklore resting on bedrock myths of the Algerian conquest that launched the "second French empire." The fly whisk flicked in the French ambassador's face by Hussein, the dey of Algiers— a suggestively effeminate gesture—was "an affront that our country could not let pass. . . . [T]he insolent monarch [paid dearly for his] moment of anger." Overlooked was the fact that three years passed between incident and invasion, that Marseille grain merchants had refused to pay a large debt to the dey, and that King Charles was anxious to curry their favor. Other "insults" were repaid in kind. Dahomey's King Behanzin, "without respect for our treaties[,] attacked our possessions of Porto Novo and Wydah . . . [and] was put to flight with his battalions of Amazons in 1892. . . . Abomey, the capital . . . was soon in our power." The Siamese king "ignored our rights and insulted our colors, so a French fleet appeared before Bangkok." Madagascar's Queen Renavalo "no longer respecting our treaties . . . an expedition sent in 1895 . . . entered Tananarive."[32] Such leaders were synecdoches for entire peoples, who paid dearly for their "crimes and sins." Their names and that of Abd el-Qadr, the leader of Algeria's war of resistance against the French (1830–47) were the only non-European ones that French schoolchildren learned.

In the schoolbooks, courage in the face of overwhelming odds proved French mettle, heroes faced death stoically, and dying words were carefully recorded. There are many examples of their Spartan cadences and self-effacing, laconic language in the textbooks—words that later found their way into film dialogue. Repulsed from the Constantine escarpment in 1836, Colonel Changarnier took charge of the rearguard, ordering the men to form a square and hold fast: "See these natives [gens] facing you; they are six thousand, you are three hundred, the match is equal." When the French took the city in 1837, Colonel Combes's dying words to General Valée were, "Those who so happily returned to this assault can say they have seen a beautiful and glorious day."[33]

Captain Lelièvre's 123 men held off Abd el-Qadir's 12,000 at Mazagran in 1840 in four days of fighting so fierce that the smoke and powder, said one Arab, "shut out the rays of the sun." In 1842, Sergeant Blandin, his 16 men surrounded by 300 Arabs, urged them to show "these people that we do not know the meaning of surrender; above all don't hurry, aim true, and swear that none of us will give ground." He died the next day, but they had saved the secret dispatches they carried. In 1874, Tonkin pirates in the pay of the mandarins surprised 117 French marines and cut their throats. Commander Berthe de Villiers vowed to "put an end to the disloyal maneuvers of the court in Hué" and died reopening Haiphong and Hanoi to French trade. In 1884, 400 Legionnaires and 200 Tonkinese tirailleurs held off a siege of 15,000 Black Flag pirates. Sergeant Bobillot and eight other engineers fortified

the ramparts that repelled the enemy.[34] He died of his wounds, joining
Blandin and other noncommissioned heroes in the empire's pantheon.
The Third Republic encouraged children of the *petits gens* to identify
with the empire and defend it as their own.

A few schoolbooks compiled thumbnail biographies of France's military heroines, but the obligation to defend France's honor remained a
masculine virtue and male monopoly, accommodating an occasional
Joan of Arc but in the main excluding the female sex from the "War
Myth." Born of defeat at the hands of Prussia, the Third Republic
"couched national revival in terms of virility and rampant male honor."
The War Myth became the "signature tune" of the Right in the 1890s
and "played across the whole political spectrum" in the next decade, as
did male anxiety over feminism. Emile Zola agreed with men of the
Right such as Maurice Barrès as to its dangers. By 1914, masculinity
was as closely identified with war as femininity was with childbirth.
"The only relationship the War Myth admitted between women and
war was a hostile one . . . [women were seen as] opponents, antimili-
tarists, pacifists, and spies." The discourse on women's motives expressed suspicion, either trivializing or denigrating their participation.
Men made sacrifices, while women who worked in munitions plants or
in nursing or volunteer charity work were relieving boredom, profiteer-
ing from high wages, or seeking sexual liaisons with soldiers. The per-
vasive unease of associating women and the war is highlighted in the
way nurses and their advocates deliberately subordinated their experience to that of the wounded soldier: she was the "disciple" of the *poilu;*
his suffering was hers. And her experience barely survived the war. Even
nurses who wrote memoirs "did not reshape the War Myth to include
women . . . [but] commemorated World War I as the trench-fighters'
war and the confirmed essence of the war experience as masculinity."[35]

The end of the war constricted women's place in the public sphere
once again. The French equivalent of the flapper, *la garçonne,* tried once
more in the mid 1920s to expand women's role at least in terms of leisure
and the social sphere. But antifeminists denounced what she represented
to them, egoism and unwillingness to live up to civic duty to provide
sons to fight a revanchist Germany. In the face of that backlash, maternal feminists turned to the colonies as an arena where women could act
autonomously in economic and social realms. *Toubibas* (nurses) and missionary nuns who ministered to soldiers and natives contradicted the
exclusively male view of the frontier. Their "mothering" image helped

feminist moderates assert a role for women in the civilizing mission. Indeed, Roman Catholic missions noted that whites in Africa needed spiritual guidance as much as the natives. But French religious orders were shorthanded, and it was only reluctantly that they supplied nuns for Africa, delaying departures for years. The length of time that it took for medical and language training led Cardinal Lavigerie to found the Soeurs Blanches as a complement to the Pères Blancs missionaries. Only those ready to dedicate their lives to Africa were selected. A government-sponsored film, *The Dancer and the Dagger,* featured a Soeur Blanc hospital where the motto on the crucifix above each bed read, "God sends the little sisters for those who, alas! no longer have a mother!" As *Pour Vous* reporter Blanche Vogt wrote, the sisters and nurses were often upper-class women, as two examples illustrate. After years of preparing for her vocation at her family's expense, Lavigerie's protégé Marie Louise de l'Eprevier became White Sister Mary Claver. And Comtesse Septans of Vannes, Brittany, a Dame de France nurse, aimed a temperance campaign at Legionnaire Adolphe Cooper while he recuperated at a military hospital in Ain Sefra; fellow intellectuals, they became friends, despite her ban on alcohol.[36]

Imperial "mothering" in Lyauteyiste films coincided with the interwar feminist discourse that claimed a place in the colonies on the basis of women's innate traits. The director of a leper hospital in Madagascar with fourteen hundred beds was touted as both a nurturer and a heroine: "All the lepers are her children. She loves them with great tenderness." A missionary teacher who ran a boarding school for orphaned girls had to be "doubly well educated because she entirely molds these primitive creatures . . . who arrive among us *en sauvages.*" Warmhearted and loving, she taught them to be mothers of intelligent families, knowing their duties and rights as wives; thus, men treated them as equals and did not crush them. Madame A. Querillac, professor at the Colonial Institute of Bordeaux and correspondent for *La Depêche coloniale,* held a three-day conference in 1932 to prepare European women for colonial life. She focused on women doctors, whose "prudence and tact" could improve conditions for native women. "Penetrating the lives of the natives . . . [in family matters] her intervention confers considerable influence . . . [providing] the best object lesson on European civilization." In 1967, Franz Fanon indicted such efforts as subverting the Arab family to neutralize Algerian resistance in the 1950s.[37]

Le Grand jeu: The Grand Synthesis

Feyder's film *Le Grand jeu* rejected the women-as-civilizers myth while affording film critics an opportunity to tout the superiority of French over American film production. The star of the movie was Pierre Richard-Willm, and a 1934 article in *Pour Vous* compared his portrayals of men in uniform with those of Gary Cooper. Both men had played a variety of military types—officers, mercenaries, and enlisted men—but Cooper's celebrated role in *Morocco* had been less than convincing (Cooper had learned to ride as a boy in Montana; Richard-Willm had served in the war). Although *Le Grand jeu* contained scenes of drunken Legionnaires and native troops brawling in the street, demoralizing bouts of le cafard—the infamous homesickness—and manslaughter, Richard-Willm's realistic portrayal of an effete, refined Parisian hardened by the Legion vindicated and reinforced its invented traditions.[38] A letter by a film fan who signed off as Spectator echoed the views of the article and surely warmed the hearts of Colonels Rollet and Azam: "*Grand jeu* shows the snobs and foreigners that French cinema is not trailing in the wake of American and German film. The Legion has been battered by so much scorn by American films that a Frenchman was obliged to rehabilitate it."[39]

Feyder had set the precedent for shooting colonial films on location with his sensational 1921 *L'Atlantide*. By the time he arrived in Sidi Bel Abbès to make *Le Grand jeu*, however, Legion Command was so disgusted with the "disfigurement" of the Legion by Hollywood it issued orders banning aid to filmmakers. Feyder showed his script to some of the officers to convince them that he had not set out to vilify the Legion. They were sorry, they said, but they could no longer "allow our men to participate in films because the Americans have too often shown a fantastical deformed Legion. If you have need of them, however, tell us where you want to film, exteriors only, and we will send the troops."

They were as good as their word. For one important scene, the reentry of the regiment into Sidi Bel Abbès, officers of the regiment actually stationed there provided crucial support. They showed Feyder the route of the march and at his request loaned him a trooper who played the fife to give him its cadence. With stopwatch and clipboard, Feyder planned the shot, placed his cameras, and filmed the scene in one take. He then intercut closeups of the two stars and several extras to look as if they were part of the march. "One sees there an authentic image of the Foreign Legion, with all its strict bearing, rhythm, and force." The image, evoking audacity, decisiveness, and disciplined military comportment, was worth a thousand words of mushy dialogue of the type in *Coeurs Brûlés.*[40]

Film historian Pierre Boulanger claims the authorities made Feyder strike one sentence: "The Riffians defend their land." Feyder himself never said publicly that *Le Grand jeu* was censored. In a February 1935 speech on censorship, reprinted in *Comoedia,* Feyder argued that censorship did more harm "by the fear it inspires at the moment of choosing a subject than by the cuts that it demands after the film is made." Anticipating trouble with the authorities, filmmakers avoided the great issues of the day—class conflict, unemployment, politics, religion, the military—in favor of another "little love story or marshmallow operetta." To combat this graver threat, he called for a revival of cinema clubs to stimulate a demand for better-quality films and appealed to his audience to judge works like *Le Grand jeu* on artistic merit, not literal accuracy of correct buttons on a uniform or regimental insignia on a képi.

Controversy around the film continued when the jury of the Grand Prix du Cinéma Français passed over *Le Grand jeu* in favor of Julien Duvivier's more edifying *Marie Chapdelaine.* Critics protested and unanimously accorded Feyder the laurels. The jury may have had grounds for trepidation. Racial xenophobes of the Ligue des Patriotes and the Ligue Antisémitique had rioted against Luis Buñuel's *L'Age d'or* in 1931, forcing the police to ban the film to stave off further violence. However, *Le Grand jeu* was a box-office success throughout Europe, and French audiences praised its artistic achievement as a revival of French cinema as well as Feyder's career. Yet the film never identified the Riffians by name; it distilled the story to a metaphysical interweaving of characters devoid of history and politics.[41]

Le Grand jeu served as a standard to judge later Legion-movie fare. Its protagonist, Pierre Martel, a brilliant, cynical young lawyer infatuated with a shallow, venal woman, Florence, satisfies her expensive tastes by overdrawing his firm's accounts and is forced to leave Paris to avoid scandal and arrest. After Florence refuses to accompany him, he enlists in the Legion. Building roads in Morocco, Pierre spends furloughs in Sidi Bel Abbès with Nicolas, a Russian comrade with a murky past. They frequent a seedy cabaret and brothel run by Clément, an unsavory lecher, and his wife, Blanche, who reads fortunes in tarot cards—

The poster for *Le Grand jeu* shows a pastiche of scenes from the film, with little emphasis on its Foreign Legion theme. The eyes and intense gazes of the main characters dominate the poster. At bottom left, the cafe owner's wife studies the double nines of "the Great Game," predicting death. The inset harem scene is an invention of the poster artist; it is not a scene from the film. *Credit:* copyright Galerie Cine-Images, Paris the *grand jeu,* or great game. Pierre, she predicts, will meet a brunette, and Clément, who draws two nines, will die.

The next time the two friends have leave, Nicolas introduces Pierre to Irma, a prostitute who caters to customers in Blanche's bar; she is a dark look-alike of Florence. Marie Bell played both parts, with Feyder dubbing a deeper, throaty voice for Irma. In France, dubbing was unpopular because it was thought to alter an actor's personality. Here it works well to do just that: Irma is Florence's opposite. Amnesia and a recent scar on her temple she thinks are the result of a suicide attempt, and her clouded memory justifies Pierre's conviction that she *is* Florence. He persuades Blanche to let her tend bar to extricate her from "the life." Behind the counter, Irma stares past the camera at off-screen customers, an imitation in celluloid of Manet's "Bar at the Folies Bergères." She arouses the seedy Clément, who forces her into a back room. Pierre discovers them and kills Clément in a terrible fight, thus fulfilling the tarot's prediction that he would die. The police arrive, and Blanche covers up the crime as an accident.

Nicolas volunteers for a mission, but Pierre refuses to go out of concern for Irma. Nicolas is killed, and Pierre, in agony over abandoning his friend, destroys the room they shared. With Blanche, he burns Nicolas's letters, granting him the anonymity he earned by his sacrifice for the Legion. Pierre then comes into a legacy, which allows him to pay back the money he embezzled and clear his name. He decides to return to France with Irma, and he is buying steamship tickets when the real Florence appears, escorted by the city's pasha in his open touring car. Supercilious as ever, she rejects him again. Pierre realizes that he never loved Irma for herself, gives her all his remaining cash, and puts her on the ship to France, promising to follow in a few days. After she sails, he reenlists for another five years.

Before reporting for duty, Pierre gets drunk with Blanche in her cabaret. On impulse, he asks her to read the cards. Double nines appear. He says goodbye, knowing he is going on his last mission. The camera pans in on the two nines, still on the table, then on Blanche, who scatters the cards, kneels, sobbing, and picks them up one by one; the camera then precipitously backs away and up, as if recoiling from her despair, from being "infected by her angst."[42]

The American treatments of the Legion produced an action-adventure and a sentimental romance, but French filmgoers preferred *Le Grand jeu*'s exploration of the dark side of the human psyche. Heat dominates the street scenes in Casablanca and Sidi Bel Abbès; the bar and back room are settings for irrational impulse and fate. Irma stands on a table hanging strips of flypaper in the heat, obvious sexual metaphors. Clément, eyes glued to Irma, sweats profusely as his menacing seduction begins. Fatefully, Pierre discovers them and falls on Clément in a murderous rage. The film's sweaty, gritty realism and the performances of Pierre Richard-Willm and Françoise Rosay, Feyder's wife, who played Blanche, were unanimously applauded by the critics. But the doppelgänger device troubled them. They found the effect overly subtle and confusing, since Feyder obscured whether Irma's fantastic resemblance to Florence was "real" or in Pierre's mind. They were also unimpressed with Bell's acting. At one point, Irma (Bell) asks Blanche's advice: should she humor Pierre or force him to face the reality that she is not Florence? Blanche (Rosay) tells her to play the part and let Pierre think what he wants. It is as if Rosay is advising audiences to do the same. For Rosay, there was a clear explanation for why Pierre Martel reenlists: "He realizes that he can never live in France with the girl of the low-class cabaret [beuglant]." It was a straightforward matter of class.[43]

Rosay's offhand remark belies the subtleties in Le Grand jeu's doubling. Irma first appears on screen surreptitiously talking with two Arab men at a table in the bar. The implication that she sells her sexuality to Arabs as well as whites hangs in the air, and immersion in North Africa "nativizes" Irma, opposing her darkness to blonde, pale-skinned Florence. Irma plays the same role as native lovers such as Tanit-Zerga in L'Atlantide. Feyder uses her as a literary foil, self-effacingly highlighting the venal, destructive, selfish Florence's effect on Pierre. Yet Florence's arrival as the pasha's companion mimics Irma's racial trespasses, casting doubt on her racial identity. So both women undergo figurative racial slippage.

Whether or not Irma is Florence, the Legion has declassed and proletarianized Pierre, redefining his male identity as it transformed him from effete bourgeois into hardened ranker. He "can't go home again" and reproduces with Irma in Africa a union libre, a working-class marriage unsanctioned by church or state but legitimated by a proletarian community, the bar. Pierre protects Irma from male predation by the brutal means instilled by his Legion training. But this "family" violates his duty to comrades and corps. Male and Legion codes converge and he reenlists, perhaps even before Florence's arrival shatters his illusions about Irma, to recoup his male identity and give Irma a new life in

France. Only Blanche remains. In her café, cold sober and utterly displaced, she burns Pierre's letters and belongings as he had burned Nicolas's possessions. A new recruit looking on asks what she will do. She shrugs, "They have the Riffians' bullets, these two. Me, I don't even have that."[44] *Le Grand jeu* thus voiced the Legion-sponsored message relentlessly: the bled is no place for a white women.

La Bandera: Redemption in the Spanish Legion

Duvivier's *La Bandera*, made the year after *Le Grand jeu*, begins its "apotheosis" of redemption in lower criminal depths than its forerunner.[45] Pierre Gilieth (Jean Gabin), its protagonist, is no respectable bourgeois gone wrong; he is a remorseless, brutal, working-class murderer. From its grisly opening scene, Duvivier conjured images of "criminal man," the fin de siècle view of the criminal as extension of the "laboring and dangerous classes . . . a separate race, primitive, animal-like and threatening."[46] Cesare Lombroso, founder of the "science" of criminology, and his disciples claimed criminals were savage atavisms unleashed on civilization, a species apart, marked by hereditary traits, "stigmata" such as physiognomy, toe spacing, shape of the head, insensitivity to pain, and, notably, tattooing, which is a leitmotif of *La Bandera* (The flag). Lombroso's ideas resonated with Paul Broca's racial hierarchy of human evolution, Gustave Le Bon's crowd psychology, and Cyril Burt's heritability of intelligence. Social deviance, whether criminality, homosexuality, or "excessive" sexuality, of any type, excited suspicions of racial otherness—suspicions that George Mosse aptly described as "the alliance between racism and respectability."[47]

Press reports, detective novels, and commissions expressed this discourse on crime, and the organizations of the respectable proletariat joined in the "consensual we"—a "public united in its need for protection from criminal deviance." To isolate the criminal "residuum," this consensus supported the creation of police forces authorized to protect bourgeois property and repress organized protest, thus shedding their own image as part of the "dangerous class." They purchased the removal of the barriers to full citizenship for workers by contributing to the construction of a class-transcendent, democratized, white racial identity. In this context, *La Bandera*, like *Sarati le Terrible*, presented deviance as a useful social atavism to be enlisted by a Europe grown too soft to hold back barbarians at the gates. The criminal assumed the cen-

The first of these two *La Bandera* posters is divided into two scenes from the film. Gabin is shown facing the ominous blockhouse where his company of Spanish Legionnaires make their last stand. Anabella's face has customary Berber tattooing on forehead and chin; she looks out over the Moorish cafe that caters to the troops and is her home as prostitute/waitress. The figures on both halves of the poster are enveloped by night. The second poster, showing the lovers embracing, presents the blockhouse from the defenders' viewpoint, with a bomb exploding outside its walls. *Credit:* copyright Galerie Cine-Images, Paris

SOCIÉTÉ NOUVELLE DE CINÉMATOGRAPHIE PRÉSENTE :
ANNABELLA
JEAN GABIN
DANS UN FILM DE
JULIEN DUVIVIER
LA BANDÉRA
SCÉNARIO de JULIEN DUVIVIER et CHARLES SPAAK
INSPIRÉ du ROMAN de PIERRE MAC ORLAN (Editions N.R.F.)
avec
AIMOS
PIERRE RENOIR
GASTON MODOT
et MARGO LION et CHARLES GRANVAL
SNC

turion's post, subdued the nonwhite savage, and, through a suicidal act of redemption, reclaimed his white identity and entered the realm of True France.[48]

The Popular Front movement was under way when *La Bandera* premiered, and its cultural organ, *Commune,* criticized the film's sympathetic portrayal of military adventure, since "we know how well it has served Hitlerian fascism." Another leftist critic, unconvinced by the film's "self-satisfied camaraderie," judged *La Bandera* "a very mediocre film," compared with *Le Grand jeu.* The critiques tentatively tied the violence of colonial rule to political violence at home, but tacitly accepted the civilizing myth and ignored the Rif War—also mistakenly identifying Riffians as Arabs, not Berbers. The true import of the film, the inclusion of the criminal in the white race, escaped these critics, who also failed to explain why the film linked a proletarian protagonist with a theme of regeneration through violence.[49]

As *La Bandera* opens, a tipsy *fille de noces* (lady of the night) kisses a stranger under a dim street lamp in Rouen. He pushes past her, and in the light she realizes he has covered her with blood; she screams. The stabbing victim is never seen, and Gilieth, the murderer, flees to Barcelona, where he is robbed by a gang of thugs. With the police closing in, he joins the Spanish Foreign Legion, the Tercio Extranjero, sailing the Gibraltar strait in a small *barca* with other recruits bound for the Spanish colony in northern Morocco. Lucas (Robert LeVigan), an undercover police detective in hot pursuit, enlists and follows his quarry into the same *bandera* (brigade). Only if Gilieth commits a new crime in the Tercio, however, can Lucas extradite him. Each aware of the other's identity, they begin a tense game of cat and mouse. In the garrison town's café-bordello, Gilieth falls in love with Aicha (Anabella) la Slaoui, a Berber dancer and prostitute from Sla (Salé, near Rabat), who promises to help Gilieth escape south to the French zone. They marry, but before they can leave, a revolt breaks out in the Rif. "Rebels" besiege a Tercio outpost, and the captain calls for volunteers to form a relief column. To a man, the soldiers step forward. They retake the blockhouse, but the unseen enemy has poisoned their water barrels and lays siege. Bullets and thirst whittle their number. Gilieth shows leadership and courage under fire, and the fatally wounded captain promotes him to corporal. Before he dies, the captain makes Lucas swear to return to France and forget about Gilieth. Mulot (Raymond Aimos) tries to reach a well and is wounded. In the end, only the cop and the killer remain. Facing death, they bury their enmity and clasp hands. Gilieth orders Lucas to hold the fort while he tries to save Mulot, but snipers pin him down; a bullet finds him just as the relief column arrives, trumpets blaring. Lucas returns to the garrison, breaks the news to Aicha, and recounts Gilieth's last words. "He told me: If you can see Aicha tell her that Pierre Gilieth begs her pardon. He cannot go live with her in the south. But he died thinking of her as he promised." Aicha's face is "*catastrophée.*" Head bowed, she silently weeps.[50]

Pierre MacOrlan, the author of *La Bandera*, became enamored of the Tercio while on assignment as a reporter. He toured Barcelona, Madrid, Tangier, Ceuta, Tetouan, and Sidi Bel Abbès in 1930 and wrote *Légionnaires,* a documentary account of life in the Legion and the Tercio, filled with details of the daily life of the troops. The novel followed in 1931. MacOrlan derived the plot from real events that took place in the Dutch Foreign Legion in Indonesia, grafting onto the story line his own precise descriptions of life in the Spanish legion. The plot fails to clarify why the police would send a secret agent in pursuit of a common criminal, and so strained credulity. But MacOrlan's own past drew him to the world of soldiers for hire. His father had been a papal Zouave who had abandoned his sons in 1870; his older brother had raised him, then joined the French Legion. He died in the service in 1900. Haunted by his brother's memory, Pierre enlisted in 1909, but never began his tour of duty. A letter from his brother, which he kept all his life, described Legion life as daily misery and boredom punctuated by episodes of terror, and the characters of his novels are preoccupied with banal routines and survival, not adventure. MacOrlan admired the Tercio commander Francisco Franco, who filled a void left by the deaths of his father and brother, and Gilieth's Nietzschean amorality may reflect his view of Franco. He persuaded Duvivier to dedicate the film to Franco to thank him for his cooperation, and during the Spanish Civil War the writer attended pro-Franco rallies in Paris.[51]

La Bandera's inverted history of the Rif War turned Spanish invaders who had bombed, burned, and pillaged thousands of farms and homes into purveyors of civilization. The aroused Berbers drove its army back to the coast and nearly into the sea. Madrid then created the Tercio to avoid using draftees for the bloodiest fighting. Under Franco's command, it led the reconquest of the Rif. Ten years later, and a year after the film's release, Franco led the revolt that plunged Spain into a three-year civil war.[52] To the great landowners who financed the military uprising after tens of thousands of landless peasants occupied their vast estates in southern Spain, Franco was a savior. His Tercio and "Moorish" Regulares, recruited mainly from the same Riffian clans he had defeated in 1926, crossed the straits to Spain in the first wave on 18 July 1936. Their first mission was to destroy the peasant movement. Executing thousands of leaders and militants, they deprived the republic of its base of support in one-third of Spain and earned a terrifying reputation as death squads and shock troops. Since the Left had ignored Riffian anticolonial aspirations, it lost the chance to win them as allies. Thus the Republic bore partial responsibility for the disaster that befell it.[53]

The Popular Front and Colonial Cultural Politics

The Popular Front, which united the Left in 1935, fell into step with the racial consciousness of the time. And despite its efforts to address the "woman question" and mobilize female support, the French Left defined the proletariat and all political life as male-centered; it remained profoundly uneasy about feminism. The Rif War had thickened the atmosphere of racial superiority, exacerbating tensions between Socialists, who had demonized the Berber republic, and Communists, who had romanticized, Westernized, and laicized it. As the Communist Left's commitment to solidarity with the Riffians evaporated, the way was opened to cooperation in the Popular Front. Predicated on opposition to fascism and big business, the alliance also subordinated the rights of women and colonial peoples to this goal. In effect, it achieved an exclusive solidarity between middle- and working-class European men.[54]

Duvivier anticipated this discourse in *La Bandera*.[55] Subsequent films, *Pépé le Moko* (1937) and *La Belle équipe* (1938), legitimated *fraternité*'s racial and gender exclusivity. His nuanced, fluid directorial style was well suited to pick up and reflect such shifts in public mood. André Lang, who wrote the dialogue for *La Bandera*, said, "Duvivier thinks . . . it must be the work that imposes its style on the director, not the other way round." Combining music, sound, lighting, and camera technique to evoke an atmosphere and a "look," Duvivier's films were part of a body of work that evolved into the poetic realist "optique." G. W. Pabst's remake of Feyder's *L'Atlantide* demonstrated how effectively a Legion film could carry a racialized message. *La Bandera* bathed the Tercio in the same sympathetic light that *Le Grand jeu* had played on the French Legion. It conveyed the idea that all the Legions of the world redeemed the dregs of Europe to defend its civilization against the darkling hordes. Capitaine Weller (Pierre Renoir) calls for volunteers for the relief mission by invoking the duty to fulfill their contract:

> Legionnaires! You are men without a country. Spain has hired you to serve her, has need of you. She asks you bluntly to die for a cause she defends and by virtue of a contract you have signed. At the moment you go off to your death, she gives you no other explanation. An entire region of the Riff is in revolt. For several days and nights a post in the mountains a hundred kilometers from here has held the enemy back. While the resistance is being organized it is necessary for me to have twenty-four men to occupy this post. [He turns to the sergeant] I have every right to designate these twenty-four men. But I want volunteers. I want volunteers to die. This post where I send you is one where none of your comrades has returned alive. It is necessary for me to have twenty-four men to defend it. Those who are ready to die, step forward. [Camera shot of the soldiers' legs. The entire company steps forward. The captain asks the sergeant to pick twenty-four men.][56]

The captain voices the inverted logic of the time. Riffian resistance to an invasion is a revolt; the Spanish punitive expedition is resistance. The image of the ranks stepping forward to plug the breach in the West's defenses sums up the film's theme. But *La Bandera* went a step further than previous Legion films by linking this racial vision to the Popular Front's outlook. As we saw above, later in the film the dying captain makes Lucas promise to return to France without Gilieth and to forget him. Lucas vows to Gilieth that "it is over." "Class" enemies reconcile in the face of a common racial enemy. Gilieth says, "It's just us two. Who gives a fuck what the world thinks. OK . . . since we're going to die [pause], let's die like men. [He puts out his hand] Allez!"[57] Men without a country but not without a race, eye to eye, arm muscles flexed, they shake hands. In an earlier scene, as the men pack gear, a veteran cuts short their banter about a "vacation in the mountains" with a stock cliché of "war without mercy,"[58] a psychological projection of European fears of savage revenge: "Always have a cartridge in reserve to blow your brains out. If these bastards take you alive, they cut off your head, give the rest to their *mouquères* (women), who open your belly, fill it with stones, and make a fire inside it."[59]

In the Spanish Civil War, Franco's officers incited Moorish troops to such savagery that the terrorized republicans believed this myth. The

Left fell victim to its own selective memory. Few remembered the Spanish army's savagery during the Rif War; fewer still had protested. General Sanjurjo's attempted coup in 1932 and the use of the Tercio and Moorish Regulares in 1934 to crush the Oviedo uprising should have set off alarm bells. A cauldron was brewing in the colony. "Africanista" officers in collusion with the Spanish Right were bent on destroying the republic. What eluded the Spanish Left, close as it was to events, escaped the French Left's notice entirely. Legion films encouraged amnesia and historical inversions.[60]

In *Le Grande jeu* and *La Bandera,* the Legionnaires build a road, a great icon of "civilization," while natives specialize in random, senseless, violent opposition to progress. A. R. Cooper thought "[we were] opening up a new country by the sweat of our brows. . . . [W]e wondered if history would record the fact that the Legion had tamed a savage land."[61] In both films, invisible snipers shoot men on road crews. European *mentalités* then could not see what is apparent today—that snipers were resisting an occupying army that used the roads to insure colonial dominance, and roads permitted wheeled vehicles to displace the camel and undermine the nomads' way of life.

Shrouding the Riffians in anonymity and obscuring their motives, *La Bandera* applied the symbolic power of names to define the Westerner as subject of history.[62] Prompted by the Tercio recruiting sergeant, Pierre Gilieth enlists under his real name. This second baptism enables Lucas to track him, but the naming also makes it possible to record his deeds. In the film's penultimate scene, after the relief column has routed the besiegers and reassembled, Lucas stands rigidly at attention as a voice calls his unit's role. The sole survivor, he replies after each name "[Mort] à l'ennemi!" ("Killed by the enemy"). At Gilieth's name, he gives a terse speech reminiscent of the history primers: "Promoted to corporal on the field of honor. Mort à l'ennemi."[63]

Aicha, the only native granted a name and personal history, embodies the tattered remnants of the Berber myth. Her marriage with Gilieth forms the only bridge across the racial divide, sanctioned in a ceremony that is a scene of surpassing ethnographic surrealism. The bordello owner, Plânche-pain, mingles their blood and tatoos their names on each other's arms as they make the sign of the cross. Neither French nor Berber culture accommodated this liaison; Aicha was without a family, and hence as far beyond normal social bounds as Gilieth. In Moroccan marriages, a couple had little to say about their choice of mate, which

was arranged by the men of both families. In a ceremony before an official, women signed a legally binding document setting down the dowry
(sdaq), which was returned to the woman if the husband divorced her.
Since the bride went to live with the groom's family, women of his household, had closer daily contact with her than would her husband and
hence exercised a de facto veto over the choice. All women agreed that
marriages should never be left entirely to the men, so the bride's female
relations also participated in the decision.[64]

The Aichas of the real world reflected a breakdown of the Muslim
family, but the Legion film romanticized them and bestowed on them
redemptive powers. Nevertheless, the conventions of the genre dictated
that Gilieth's union with Aicha, both a racial transgression and an attachment outside the Legion, inevitably meet with tragedy.

Even so, this unique "family" bond prompted a unique authentica-
tion. Tattooing, reminiscent of Lombroso's criminology, was a custom
that Legionnaires shared with the natives, and MacOrlan probably
drew the film's bizarre rituals from real experience. Berbers applied
henna to their skin as a semipermanent dye; Legionnaires, according to
A. R. Cooper, used almost anything for ink, and over the years, out of
sheer boredom, decorated their entire bodies. Some tattooed obsceni-
ties on their palm, visible to those they had to salute. "Those who tattooed their faces . . . have given up all hope" of returning to "civilization." In *La Bandera* a soldier is adding more designs to his face, already
decorated as elaborately as a Maori warrior's. "Ah, I want to see the
civilian dunghill *[fumier de civil]* again," he explains to Gilieth's buddy
Mulot, "This will take away the longing to go home if le cafard strikes
me one day." "What a world!" the bemused Mulot exclaims.[65]

Le Cafard: The "Tragic Flaw" of French Colonialism

Homesickness, le cafard, permeated French colonial film. It evoked the
audience's sympathy for the European invaders and occupiers, provided
a stock alibi for their excesses, and unintentionally exposed the "ner-
vousness" that Chinua Achebe perceived, a fear of engulfment and need
for constant affirmation of white racial superiority.[66] Africa swallows
Conrad's Kurtz, unleashing the heart of darkness within him, and Kurtz-
like characters in the novels and films of the Legion convey the feeling
of evil lurking in the bush, obliquely recalling the rampage through the
Sudan by Captain Voulet and Lieutenant Chanoine. Sergeant Lejaune in

Beau Geste, who in the remakes of the film is called Markoff to assuage French outrage, has a counterpart in French writer André Armandy's Deucalion, a psychotic former officer who, in the novel *Le Renégat*, escapes into the Legion. Both men surrender to the "savage" world, disturbing Western order and morality even after their deaths.[67] *Le Grand jeu* depicts le cafard in Nicolas's drunken outbursts, Pierre's episode of furniture smashing, and a street scene of Legionnaires, Spahis, and native troops drinking, fighting, carrying off shrieking women. In *La Bandera*, Aicha first meets Gilieth after his friends restrain him from a barroom brawl. She is afraid of him, she explains, because she has seen French soldiers go into fits of rage, smashing everything in a room. He assures her that he is calm. But the murder he committed in Rouen drove him south to elude his pursuers, first to Barcelona and then further south to Ceuta. Aicha's plan is to escape still further south into the mountains of French Morocco. The film implies that Gilieth's bloodstained soul belongs in Africa. And in the novel, Lucas is affected as well. He can neither exorcise the Maghreb nor readjust to civilian life, and he reenlists.[68]

Le Grand jeu and *La Bandera* were the last two films of note to expound the great colonial themes in contemporary settings. Later Legion films by lesser directors more dependent on the military adjusted their art to the hackneyed formulas that encouraged social order and military discipline. Léon Poirier's film biographies of Captain Charles de Foucauld, *L'Appel du silence* (1937) and *Brazza, ou l'Epopée du Congo* (1939), were exceptions, but they paid homage to nostalgia-drenched figures from French colonialism's heroic, and largely imagined, past.[69]

Colonial films of the Popular Front era drifted away from grand themes of male sacrifice. The new narratives were personal tales that reintegrated natives into the story line and explored the racial boundaries of working-class solidarity. Yet a common thread of pessimism runs through the colonial films, a sense that despite repeated displays of power the European presence in Africa was tentative and its colonial ventures fleeting. At the end of *L'Homme du Niger* (1939), the young hero is shown dedicating himself to rebuilding the dam destroyed by natives who also murdered his friend the doctor. A sense of futility belies his words. Seven of the twelve classic colonial films resolve the plot with the hero's death and the European woman's return to the metropole. In French-made Foreign Legion films, the ride to the rescue, a classic device of Hollywood westerns, arrives too late. Protagonists, including the real-life Foucauld, seem to invite martyrdom. On heroes' quests, they break all ties with home. Pale, female specters of Europe drive them away, dark-skinned girls lure them, and the obsession to complete their journey draws them inexorably south.[70]

8 | Poetic Realism's *Cinéma Colonial*
Native Sons of the Popular Front?

As the French public's growing familiarity with North Africa dispelled illusions about the empire, *la plus grande France,* colonial cinema dispensed with the grand myths of Legion films, grown formulaic and stale, and reduced the scale of its stories. Tales of putting down rebellions gave way to domestic melodramas about identity crises and love affairs.[1] Poetic realism, a distinctly French cinematic style associated with the cultural flowering that accompanied the Popular Front, framed the exotic within the mundane, giving the personal a new importance as the vessel through which cinema revealed the stresses of the transition to modernity. It introduced working-class heroes buffeted by forces beyond their control and elegized a fraternité that transcended the social barriers between middle- and working-class males. In poetic realism's imaginary Maghreb, orientalism mingled with paternalism toward the metropolitan working class and paralleled efforts during the years of the Popular Front (1936–38) to transform Algerian politics from above. But the settlers prevailed, excluded the natives from the polity, and prolonged the white-supremacist regime's life for two more decades, while in France, fear of Muslim immigrants and of changing gender roles confounded working-class solidarity and clouded the Popular Front's vision of social justice.[2]

A rich cinematic vein that juxtaposed life on the screen with the era's social conflicts, poetic realism achieved critical acclaim along with box-office success. Three films among the ten most popular of the three hundred films made during the Popular Front had colonial themes. Ticket sales reported by theater managers suggest an audience of more than two million,[3] and although this era preceded the advent of opinion polls, audience reception hints at the ways these films expressed a new sensibility and deflected racial and gender conflict.[4]

172

In *Pépé le Moko* (Julien Duvivier, 1937) and *Maison du Maltais* (Pierre Chenal, 1938), an uprooted exile enmeshed in a self-destructive love affair finds his sense of self dissolving in a strange milieu. Both die by their own hands, Pépé because he cannot remain a free white male, Matteo because he cannot become one. Barred from home, yet subliminally drawn back, the heroes evoke a magical sense of dread and nostalgic chords of longing. In *Gueule d'Amour* (Jean Grémillon, 1937), an array of male fantasies, misogynist fears, and oedipal dilemmas overwhelms a possessive, working-class man carrying on an affair with a woman who is kept by a wealthy man. Above his status and station, she controls his destiny even after she rejects him, and he strangles her. The murder forces him to flee to the colonies.[5]

Graham Greene's review of *Pépé le Moko* described it as a tale of "the freedom-loving human spirit trapped and pulling at the chain." The film's subtle ambiguities provide what Umberto Eco termed an "open text." Appropriately for a time of social upheaval, it invited audiences to make interpretive choices and democratic decisions "from below."[6] Jean Gabin, leading man of this film and other memorable poetic-realist films, honed an image of a working-class outsider, a man apart from True France. Wearing a *casquette*, the worker's cloth cap, and talking the slang of the slums, Gabin was accepted by audiences as authentically working-class despite the widely known fact that he had been a famous music-hall singer before becoming a film star. His screen persona—struggling to gain admission to bourgeois society yet striking out in new directions—was itself an open text. It typified the internal conflict the working-class parties faced in that era.

Whereas classic Hollywood cinema put women on display, with the audience looking on through the male character's gaze, French directors displayed Gabin as the object of a female gaze, a feminized "spectacle of masculinity." In an assortment of roles as a worker, a petty criminal, and a soldier, he strained against a web of circumstances with violent but futile outbursts of energy. His portrayals elicited sympathy for working-class heroes but implied that the proletariat's destiny was beyond its collective control. Directors thus subjected working-class men to the paternalism ordinarily reserved for women and colonials.[7]

Pépé le Moko: Pépé is shown with three members of his gang, one of them the hapless Arab informer who will be murdered. Behind them is a street scene from the Algiers Casbah, which plays a major part in the film. The credits list Lucas Gridoux in smaller letters and among the supporting cast, despite the centrality of his role as the Arab police inspector Slimane. This poster—one of three known to have advertised this film—emphasizes Pépé's role; another poster, which focused on the story's love triangle, featured Slimane's voyeuristic gaze. *Credit:* copyright Galerie Cine-Images, Paris

Pépé le Moko: Labyrinths of Algiers and Paris

Duvivier once said that his films were "men's stories." In fact, they celebrated male bonding by excluding and brutalizing women. *Pépé le Moko,* one of the most successful French films of the 1930s,[8] reinforced the male bond with racial exclusivity, as it blended elements of the American gangster movie, detective film *(policier),* and cinéma colonial.

Pépé, a notorious Parisian jewel thief, and his gang have gone to ground in the Casbah, the "native quarter" of Algiers. Confined to the Casbah because he is the object of a massive manhunt directed from Paris and will be arrested at once if he leaves, Pépé is sheltered by the locals and beyond the reach of the law. His haven becoming a prison, Pépé restlessly longs to return to Paris, deriving little comfort from his "gypsy" paramour Inès. Inspector Slimane, an Arab who moves freely between the Casbah and the police commissariat, resolves to break the stalemate between the criminals and police. Pépé nimbly avoids Slimane's traps until a chance encounter with a beautiful, kept Parisienne, Gaby, throws him off balance. Early in the film, she and her champagne-magnate *protecteur* are tourists visiting the Casbah and are separated by a chaotic gun battle between the police and Pépé's gang. Pépé takes her to cover and, covetously attracted to the jewelry dripping from her neck, wrists, and ears, invites her to return. The next night, with Slimane in tow, she and her rich friends "go slumming" to a Casbah nightclub. Gaby's and Pépé's repartee reveals streetwise kindred spirits.

> Pépé: "What did you do before?"
> Gaby: "Before what?"
> Pépé: "Before the jewels."
> Gaby: "I wanted them."

They recite the stations on one line of the Paris Métro, drawing closer with each stop and coming together at "Place Blanche," where working-class Montmartre met the Pigalle underworld. Although he at first saw her jewels as his ticket out of the Casbah, Pépé now falls in love with her.[9]

But the police use women as traps. After eavesdropping on Pépé's affairs, Slimane warns him that women will be his downfall. The youngest gang member and Pépé's favorite, Pierrot, dies in a shootout with the police when a letter from his mother, forged by a spy in the gang's midst, lures him from the Casbah. Pépé ferrets out the spy, Régis, and the gang wreaks deadly vengeance on him. Later, Slimane convinces Gaby that Pépé was killed in a shootout, confines her to her hotel room, and dispatches a second informer to tell Pépé where to find her. Wily Pépé again flushes out the spy and forces him to reveal the plan. As he leaves to book passage and slip aboard the ship taking Gaby back to France, his paramour Inès complains: "Why are you leaving? What have I done to you? You have nothing to reproach me for." "Listen Inès," he replies, "You're a good kid. I like you a lot and I don't blame you. All this, it's the fault of the Casbah."

He heads for the ticket office, while the anguished Inès goes to the hotel where Slimane is lying in wait; she offers up her lover. With Inès, now remorseful, in tow, Slimane and his men dash to the ship and capture Pépé before he can reach Gaby. Handcuffed, Pépé stands gazing through the bars of the quay's iron gate. He asks Slimane for a moment alone. As the ship sails, he cries out Gaby's name, but a long, mournful blast of the ship's horn drowns out his voice. He slips a knife from his sleeve and plunges it into his chest.[10]

At the core of the film's ambiguities stands the liminal figure of Slimane. Obsequious yet ubiquitous, he controls the plot. But Duvivier's camera denies the audience Slimane's point of view, refuses to adopt his gaze. Wearing a chéchia (fez) and a European suit and tie, he occupies both white and nonwhite social space. His police colleagues treat him with contempt, yet his authority derives from the French state. Slimane, committed to Pépé's capture yet distressed by his suicide, is a double who mirrors Pépé and understands him better than Pépé understands himself. His opaque persona is a paradigm of hybridity, a mix of dispassionate professionalism, superior intellect, and "Indian scout" loyalty to the police hierarchy.

Disturbingly ambiguous in gender traits and sexual orientation, lascivious yet sexless, Slimane bears a name that is an Arabic version of Solomon yet sounds like the hiss of a snake. He drops suggestive innuendoes to women yet he also seems to be flirting with Pépé. Eavesdropper and voyeur, he plays on Pépé's desires for Gaby and Paris to ensnare him. His sly glances and hooded eyes are a stereotypical display of Arab cunning and feminine wiles. Lighting cigarettes for both, he "triangulates" or brokers the affair as *meneur-du-jeu* (manipulator) and universal outsider, stereotypical traits of "Jewishness" that could serve as a scapegoat for the failure of the Popular Front or as model for its tentative gestures toward interracial solidarity. The actor who played the role, Lucas Gridoux, was a Romanian Jewish emigré, as was Alexandre Stavisky, the financial manipulator who had provoked the right-wing riots of February 1934 that in reaction prompted the Left to unite in the Popular Front. *Les Misérables* had premiered two days before the unrest erupted and had stirred deep emotions that spilled into the streets, indirectly catapulting film into the political arena.[11]

The Casbah plays a key role in *Pépé le Moko,* like the desert sand in *L'Atlantide,* and like le cafard in Legion films, its atmosphere excuses Pépé's violence and his abandonment of Inès. Identified with its women, it envelopes Pépé like a protective womb or a prison. Its chaotic twisting streets and alleys evoke a spatial arena of "oriental" anarchy beyond the reach of French law and rationality.[12] Screenwriter Charles Spaak described this human environment and its inhabitants' activities in terms associated with insects and vermin. Reviews, including those in *Commune* and the PCF's *L'Humanité,* uncritically reflected in print what Duvivier and Spaak projected on the screen.[13] In an early scene, a police inspector lectures his Paris colleagues on the difficulties of dislodging Pépé from the Casbah. He stands before a map of the quarter, pointer in hand, as the scene fades to rapid cuts of winding stairs, twisting alleys, and heterogeneous population. His narrative voice-over is couched in the discourse of orientalist pseudo-anthropology.

> From a bird's eye view, . . . the Casbah, deep as a forest and teeming like an anthill, is a vast stair, each terrace a step that descends to the sea. In its reaches, tortuous dark alleys, alleys like traps . . . alleys that cross, overlap, lace, and unlace in a jumble of labyrinths. Some narrow, others vaulted like caves. From all sides, in all directions, stairs that go up abruptly like ladders, that descend to dark smelly pits or doorways oozing slime. . . . Dark cafés, jammed with people at all hours, silent streets with odd names [a montage of street signs appears: Rue de l'Impuissance, Rue de la Ville de Soum Soum, Rue de l'Hotel à la Miel, Rue de l'Homme à la Perl].
>
> There are forty thousand people where there should be ten. Forty thousand come from everywhere, those from before the conquest, those of barbaric past and their descendants, simple, traditional, and for us mysterious: Kabyles, Chinese, Gypsies, Heimatlos, Slavs, Maltese, Blacks, Sicilians, Spaniards, and women *[filles]* of every country, every shape. Big ones, fat ones, little ones. Ageless and shapeless ones, so fat no one would touch them. Houses with inner courtyards, without ceilings, echoing like wells, intercommunicating by means of terraces controlled by

the women and descending to the sea. Colorful, vibrant, there is not one Casbah, there are a hundred. A thousand. In this labyrinth *[dédale]*, in this vermin's nest *[grouillement]*, Pépé is at home, well protected by his gang and the local grapevine. News travels fast; there are spies on every roof who pass the word. Doors open, you don't know why. Revolvers appear, shots are fired. There le Moko has only friends; we have only enemies.[14]

In fact, although it offended the obsessive Cartesianism of France's colonizers, the Casbah, the center of old Algiers, typified precolonial cities of the Arab world and adhered to a rational environmental design. Narrow, winding streets adhered to the contours of the land, provided shade and shelter from hot winds, and permitted greater population density. Large cities were accessible to pedestrians, facilitating social relations, albeit encouraging the spread of disease. Small perimeters allowed easy defense, and the windowless exterior walls and courtyards made for efficient regulation of water consumption. Far from turning people inward to "amoral familism," as Edward Banfield called it, such urban arrangements turned streets and intersections into centers, rather than boundaries, serving quarters and neighborhoods. Islamic urban concentrations, linked by camel caravans and dhow fleets, became the hub of world trade and culture after the decline of Rome. Europe's cities overtook them scarcely three hundred years ago. Before Western cities could assume their modern role as world centers, wheeled transport required them to invest vast technical and financial resources to widen and pave streets: they had to allow passage of vehicles and pedestrians, clear corners for wide cart axels, eliminate stairs, steep grades, and dead ends, and remove encroachments on the public way such as buildings and merchants' stalls.[15]

French-built Algiers enveloped the old *q'asbah,* and isolated it from the bled. Maps of the city starkly reveal the contrast between its rectilinear geometry and the old quarter's winding streets. After 1918, rural peonage spread, and coastal cities, where 90 percent of the Europeans lived, began filling with dispossessed Muslim peasants. Shantytown bidonvilles ringed the cities, and migrants embarked for France to work in the factories or on the streets. Meanwhile emigrants from Spain, Italy, and Malta remained in Algiers in poverty.[16] The pied-noir patois *(pataouète)* gave way to French, and intermarriage reinforced white, Algérien exclusivity vis à vis the indigenous population. The European population proportionally declined from 14 to 10 percent between 1930 and 1954, and French-educated Muslims, mainly Kabyles, began occupying clerical and lower administrative posts once reserved for whites. In the face of tentative efforts by the moderate Left to proffer citizenship to the natives, the pied noir blocked all reforms and strengthened the rigid social barriers erected since the 1870s to exclude Jews and Muslims from their society. In this atmosphere, impulses toward interracial working-class solidarity evaporated.[17]

Europeans freely circulated in the Casbah, but Muslim access to the European quarters was restricted. Working-class pied-noir Algerines were habitués of the Casbah, not inhabitants. In the manner of picaresque literary creations Pépète and Cagayous, they went there to play cards, frequent prostitutes, eat *cous-cous,* or bash the heads of a few "bicots." Filmmakers, moviegoers, and tourists found this setting exotic, but despite its poverty, the real Casbah was law-abiding: "Most Algiers *commissaires de police* agreed that in the time of *Pépé le Moko* the Casbah was one of the most tranquil sectors of the city."[18]

In Duvivier's imaginary Casbah, Pépé is deprived of freedom of movement, a key privilege of Europeans in the real Algiers. Restricted to "native" space, he faces social death. His urge to reclaim his status as a white male, to separate himself from subordinated, ghettoized, dark-skinned members of his own class, impels his final descent down the Casbah steps as strongly as his desire for Gaby or freedom. Graham Greene pointed out this universal impulse but ignored the equally strong but opposite dimension, the urge to subjugate the Other. Duvivier and his French audience shared Greene's blind spot.

Paris/Casbah: North African Slums and Race in the Metropole

Pépé's contradictory identity is imprinted on Paris, the city he claims, and Algiers, the city that claims him. The thief, supremely individualistic and covetous, inhabits the same persona as the "proletarian" gang leader. The two women, the dark savior and the white destroyer, embody the two locations that pull him apart. His fatal nostalgia for Paris recalls the Legionaire's homesickness, le cafard, but his pungent name evokes Algiers. His name is significant; it is after all both the name of the lead character and the title of the film, and the film critics have puzzled over its meaning. One critic associated his nickname, le moko, with the Arab port of Moka. But the entire name is redolent with the odors of the

European working-class districts of Algiers that surround the Casbah. In French, *le moco* is maritime argot for *marin toulonais,* a sailor from Toulon, a port in Provence, original home of many French pied noir, and the novel begins in Marseille with a member of the gang hiding in Pépé's mother's house. In Spanish, Pépé, a diminutive of José, and *el moco,* mucous, yields "snotnosed little José," as picaresque a name as ever there was. Spanish immigrants settled Bab el-Oued, the working-class quarter abutting the Casbah, where Louis Bertrand set the stories of his picaresque and homonymic character Pépète. Bertrand's prolific work popularized the idea of a New Latin race whose amalgamation would protect Europe from impending race war with Islam.[19]

Other elements of the film besides Pépé's name and persona intertwine Paris and Algiers. The movie set designed by Jacques Kraus and built in a Paris studio marked a departure from the standard practice of shooting colonial scenes on location. Krauss and Duvivier invented this Casbah and shot most of the film in it to create "an illusion of authenticity while paying minimal attention to documentation. The Casbah of *Pépé le Moko* is a miracle of studio design, with streets and alleyways forming a thematically pertinent and visually exotic labyrinth."[20] The set was an invention and a reaction to the North African micro-ghettoes that began appearing in the 1920s in French cities. As North Africans flowed into France to fill shortages of labor, fears arose that the so-called *sidis* would turn poor neighborhoods into mini-Casbahs, as if the Colonial Exposition of 1931 had come "unwrapped" and its "exhibits" had escaped to infest surrounding areas. The right-wing, pro-settler press manipulated this fear and revulsion, as did Duvivier.

Parisian workers were particularly susceptible to racially inspired fears about their living conditions. Unions offered some protection from bosses who undermined wages, skills, and job security by hiring foreign migrants, and the privileges of French citizenship gave added advantages, but housing was another story. Workers' housing had been in perpetual crisis since Baron Haussmann's day. The baron's renovation of the city under the Second Empire and subsequent urban renewals had forced workers into dense slums east and north of Paris, where two-thirds of the residents lived in overcrowded conditions, four times the city average. Rent controls during the 1914–18 war had exacerbated housing shortages, as real-estate investment shifted to more profitable sectors. Reluctant to tamper further with the market, postwar ministries took over mass transit instead, extending lines to the industrial centers

on the outskirts of the city. Workers bought vacant lots from speculators and built homes in this suburban ring. Inadequate roads, sewers,
and services such as garbage collection persisted for decades, conditions
that fostered the rise of a "Red Belt" of Communist-led municipalities.[21]

Meanwhile, nearly four hundred thousand inhabitants of the Paris region, the poorest 10 percent, lived in furnished single rooms, or *garnis.*
Hôteliers crowded entire French families into garnis; the most unscrupulous evicted families to extract more rent from single, male migrants,
four or five to a room. These hôtels-garnis in the worst areas housed
many of the sixty thousand North Africans; shantytowns devoured
the rest. Concentrated in Paris's Fifteenth Arrondissement, near a Citroen plant where four thousand of them were employed, the migrants
avoided contact with Europeans. Their experience with settlers at home
made them distrustful of all Europeans. The stress of isolation led to
violence. On 7 November 1925, an unemployed, mentally ill Kabyle,
Khemilé Ousliman, stabbed to death two Frenchwomen in the Rue
Fondary, a neighborhood street, and wounded two others. Rumors flew.
Primed by right-wing, colonialist press campaigns that had intensified
in response to the Rif War, a mob of locals lynched a bystander, Belkacem Lladi Mohammed, in the adjacent Rue Frémicourt, and attacked
Muslims at random. The press sensationalized the murders and linked
them with other crimes by Maghrebins in several cities. Officials in
charge of migrant control, led by Octave DePont, Pierre Godin, and
Adolphe Gérolami, took advantage of the publicity to win support for
a special police unit, the Service des Affaires Indigènes Nord-Africain
(SAINA). Funded in 1927 by parliament and the Paris city council on
the pretext of helping migrants adjust to French urban life, SAINA en-
ticed North Africans with jobs and welfare and indexed them on the
infamous police *fichier,* the catalog of people suspected of criminal and
radical activity. Thus disguised, it carried out its main goal of suppressing the influence of the nationalist, Communist-backed Etoile Nord-
Africain (ENA).[22]

The murders helped the right-wing press keep alive fears of infesta-
tion by primitive, violent, knife-wielding rapists, child molesters, and
cannibals. Socialists sympathized with the plight of the migrants, but
concurred with police bureaucrats that their infantile behavior, primitive psychology, religious fanaticism, and uncouth manners were to
blame. Even readers of the Communist paper *L'Humanité* harbored the
prevailing view. A January 1925 letter complained that "people write

fine things about the wogs *(khouia)*, but as for the Parisian he hasn't a place to live, no work, only poverty. . . . Build houses for the large families, we'll take care of the sidis later." The ENA protested in 1933 that the press, "in the pay of the colonizers, has hounded us with such rage that European public opinion is out of control . . . diseases, theft, debauchery, and immoral values are the terrible accusations with which we are freely credited." In 1931, shopkeepers in Paris's Fourteenth and Fifteenth Arrondissements had opposed building hostels and a police-authorized, segregated brothel for North Africans. In the Fifth, plans for hostels in the Rues Monge and Mouffetard were blocked. Hostels had also aroused Gennevilliers, a Red Belt suburb northwest of Paris; in 1924, the town council, reacting to public protests, criticized the Seine Prefecture for conferring special treatment on the migrants, while at the same time illogically arguing that the Maghrebins were being exploited because landlords were lodging them five and six to a room.[23]

Fear of disease went hand in hand with fear of crime, and SAINA's chiefs decided to found a Muslim hospital in Paris. ENA and the Communists denounced the facility as an instrument of imperial control and propaganda. In retaliation, the General Council of the Seine shrewdly took advantage of the conflict between the PCF's internationalism and its constituents' growing hostility to Arab incursions to "decant . . . the social problems and costs of the North Africans into the left-wing suburbs." The département council forced the smallest and weakest Red Belt suburb, Bobigny, to cede land for the hospital and a cemetery. Despite five years of protests by Bobigny's town council, in March 1935 both institutions opened their gates.[24]

Masculinity and the Female Space

Pépé le Moko's female characters form another link between the workers' districts of Paris and Algiers, and they diverge from colonial film archetypes to do so. One of them is played by Fréhel, the *chanteuse réaliste*; in the role of an aging, sexless "mammy," she uses her powerful voice and nostalgic songs to evoke an overwhelming longing for Paris. The bejeweled Gaby is available to Pépé in the Casbah, but she herself becomes an unattainable jewel, becomes Paris, once she leaves. Inès, the "gypsy," saves Pépé from his drunken dash down the Casbah steps, then surprises even Slimane by betraying him. She eschews the expressions of devotion by nonwhite women that were typical in film. She neither betrays her people, stands nobly aside for the white woman, nor sacrifices her life for the white man. But neither does she exhibit any cultural distinctiveness whatsoever, and Duvivier offered no roles to Algerian actors. In that sense, no "natives" inhabit Duvivier's Casbah.[25]

If women characters link the Casbah to Paris, they also embody it, while the men, particularly the men of Pépé's gang, occupy its space. And Pépé, as the fulcrum of their masculinity, occupies the pivot point, ground zero, balancing the shortcomings of the rest of the gang, who are too brutish or dull or immature to seduce women or lead men. They are caricatures who reduce proletarian solidarity to two imperatives: do not trust the state and do not "rat." The Arab hangers-on, Régis and Larbi, are informers. The gang holds Régis liable for Pierrot's death and in a grim scene murders him. The film inverts reality. Europeans, not Arabs, betrayed solidarity.

The blind spot in this racialized male gaze produced other inversions. Cinematic portrayals of erotic relationships between mature men and young women, narratives that inverted Hollywood standards of virility, had been a feature of 1920s silent film. The Great War had taken a vast toll of young men, and older actors held on to the leading roles, besting younger rivals on and off screen, by virtue of experience and overawing the *jeune fille*, like the colonial woman, with their status and power. By the mid 1930s, the older man had turned loathsome and sinister, a potentate of Victorian orientalist painting whose favorite prey for his harem was Circassian white slaves. Irma, in *Le Grand jeu* (1934), and Saffia, of *Maison du Maltais* (1938), were transposed from older mediums. Exotically attractive to European men yet tainted by implications of sexual contact with Muslims, they stimulated rescue fantasies, helplessness heightening the erotic appeal. M. Batalà, the cynical exploiter and predatory publisher in Jean Renoir's *Le Crime de M. Lange* (1936), locks the ingenue in his office, rapes her, and abandons her with child. M. Lange murders him, then is acquitted by a "jury" of farmers on the Swiss border, who hear his story and allow him to escape. Marcel Carné's *Quai des brumes* (Quay of frogs) (1938) featured a theme of sexual abuse by a guardian, which reappeared in his *Le Jour se lève* (Daybreak, 1939). The younger men kill these villains. In contrast, a settler impelled to incest is pardoned, his impulse ascribed to *le simoun*, the Saharan wind that drove men mad. *Le Simoun* (1933) and *Sarati le terrible* (1928 and 1937) implied that such men could not be judged by standards set in Europe. On the frontier, facing the barbarians, the films seem to suggest, incest was preferable to miscegenation.[26]

Poetic realism expressed class conflict by stereotyping the sexes. It inverted oedipal narratives, sympathizing with younger, working-class men drawn down a path to self-destruction trying to rescue women from older, wealthy, despicable *protecteurs*. Women act as agents of the hero's downfall, passively in the case of the ingenues, actively if they display "mannish" independence. As lightning rods for the political turmoil of the times, they recall the male anxieties of German *freikorps* men after 1918, anticipate American film noir, and reveal an acute "crisis of masculinity" accompanying the decline of the Popular Front. In the face of fascist neighbors with virile aggressive leaders, the Third Republic was cast as a doddering cuckold of a maliciously emasculating Marianne. Duvivier's *La Belle équipe* (1937), an allegory of the Popular Front, again placed Gabin at the fulcrum of masculinity in a story of five unemployed friends who win a lottery and invest in a café. Their venture collapses through "bad luck" and the failings of the men.

In the end, only Charles, husband of Gina, a femme fatale, and Jean (Jean Gabin) remain of the "splendid team." Gina wants Jean and sows jealousy, which in Duvivier's climax ends with Jean strangling Charles and being led away by the police. The film's producers, sensing financial disaster, forced Duvivier to rewrite this gloomy ending: the friends close ranks against the conniving female and expel her from their lives. The two versions played simultaneously for a few months. Box office preferences proved the producers right, and they withdrew the "director's cut." Jean Grémillon's *Gueule d'Amour* (1938), like *La Belle équipe*, epitomized misogynous retribution against a woman who undermined the solidarity of an all-male "team" or challenged a sympathetic male's manhood.[27]

Gueule d'Amour: The Kept Woman and Internalized Oppression

Grémillon reunited Jean Gabin and Mireille Balin for a reprise of their roles in *Pépé le Moko*. After a tour of duty in Algeria, a Spahi cavalry regiment is garrisoned at Orange in the south of France; its quartermaster sergeant, Lucien Bourrache (Gabin), is so attractive to women he is nicknamed *gueule d'amour*, or Loverboy. In Cannes on leave, he enters the casino in his dashing Spahi uniform and turns every woman's head. Madeleine (Balin) catches his eye. Elegant, frivolous, and vain, a "reversed, deformed" Lucien, Mady brings doom, not salvation. Lucien follows her to Paris and takes up his trade as a printer. Demobilized, horse and uniform gone, he rides a bicycle, works in a printer's apron and casquette, the emblematic flat cap, and seems shorn of his power over women. His *amour fou* will not give up the comfortable apartment and fashionable gowns that her well-heeled businessman-*protecteur* provides for her and her mother. Like Gaby's champagne magnate, Mady's *protecteur* remains in the background until Lucien confronts him at her apartment, demanding that Mady choose between love and money. She chooses money, and the rich man retakes possession of her. Herself a kept woman, she later offers to keep Lucien, crushing his sense of manhood. He returns to Orange a beaten man. A renewed friendship with the regimental medical officer, René (René Lefèvre), now in private practice, revives his spirits. Then Mady arrives in Orange and rejects him again. His verbal abuse goads her to reveal she has seduced René; her spiteful gloating throws him into a rage, and he strangles her. Stumbling blindly to René's home, he confesses. René puts him on a train to Marseille and books him passage to North Africa, telling the nearly catatonic Lucien to enlist in the Legion, where the *anonymat* will cover his tracks. As the train pulls away, René kisses Lucien's cheeks and seals their bond with a passionate embrace.[28]

A popular success, the film won critical esteem for its intense yet unsentimental treatment of the recurring theme of heterosexual passion versus male friendship. Shooting on location in Paris and Orange, Grémillon captured the warm sun and dusty roads of Provence and the wet, somber streets of Paris. But for some filmgoers, his documentary-style shots of workers changing shift at Paris factory gates was a difficult mix of genres. Even more troubling to conservative viewers was Lucien's escape from the police. It disturbed the social order. Whereas Duvivier had begun *La Bandera* with the evasion of the law's retribution, this film cut short the atonement, expiation, and redemption. René, like the laborers in the café on the Swiss border in *Le Crime de M. Lange,* "acquits" Lucien. The tour-de-force performance wedded Gabin's persona to the Popular Front myth of interclass *fraternité.*

If poetic-realist films demonized some women as enemies of male solidarity, it treated the colonies as a "marginally visible presence," as Edward Said wrote of the empire's presence in the Victorian novel, "a literary equivalent of Eric Wolf's . . . people without history."[29] Lucien

Guele d'Amour: Gabin was such a big star by the time this film was made that his name, topping the credits, appears "above the title." He is dressed in the striking, colorful uniform of a Zouave of the colonial Algerian regiments. His leading lady, the same Mireille Balin who played opposite him in *Pépé,* wears a cynical expression and strikes a predatory pose. The action takes place entirely in France, but the poster suggests the colonial backdrop's importance to the storyline. It frames the film fore and aft, like bookends. *Credit:* copyright Galerie Cine-Images, Paris emerges from Algeria a heroic Spahi; his crime of passion plunges him back into the colonial lower depths. Thus Grémillon encased his French story inside colonial bookends. This colonial frame also enclosed Marcel Carné's *Quai des brumes*, in which the doomed hero (Gabin) is a deserter haunted by the memory of his part in a terrible massacre in Indochina.

Prostitution also hovered just within poetic realism's peripheral vision, and the Third Republic's political discourse associated sex-commerce with the colonies. Given a situation in which there was the seclusion of "respectable" women in the Maghreb and state-sponsored brothels in Indochina, tourists, soldiers, and colonists encountered mainly marginal native women. This fertile ground for the imagination afforded ample opportunity for orientalist projections of French conditions. And the republic's atavistic subordination of women undergirded a discourse on prostitution that was as hypocritical as it was misogynist. Women could not vote or control property; wages of working-class women were half those of men; wives could be divorced and prosecuted for adultery, but not husbands. Both popular and medical discourse legitimated male extramarital sex as arising from urges that respectable women did not share. It branded prostitutes as morally defective and justified the degradation and exploitation of working-class women as prostitutes as the only means to preserve the virtue of middle-class young ladies. State-licensed *maisons tolérées* legitimated the brothel keeper.

Although all but 30 live-in brothels, *maisons closes*, shut their doors after 1918 due to economic pressures, 270 *maisons de rendez-vous*, where women came to work as they would to a factory, replaced them. The new casual, day-labor system employed 20,000 women; they served several million customers a year. From 1871 to 1903, Paris's *police des moeurs*, the vice (morals) police, which kept track of the trade, had registered 155,000 professionals and arrested 725,000 other women on suspicion. In 1924, two-thirds of those arrested were unregistered. Since police assumed any unescorted woman was soliciting, prostitution haunted women of a wide social spectrum, undermining the presumption of innocence, freedom of movement, and other basic rights for all women. Working-class women were most likely to have tasted "the life." Personal misfortune or hard times often forced the urban poor—factory girls, barmaids, waitresses, entertainers, household servants—to sell themselves in lieu of other resources. But the sex industry drew in women of all backgrounds: the social structure created enormous demand and profits.[30]

Women in the sex trade aroused both sympathy and hostility among leftists. Women who were kept by wealthy men, which was seen as prostitution by choice, were put at one end of the moral spectrum; working-class women who sold their bodies out of desperation were perceived as victims of class oppression and social injustice. Socialists and labor unions took a protective view of "their" women, calling for programs that would keep women off the street by providing male workers with the wages to sustain their families and enable their wives to stay at home. They condemned factory owners and managers in the same terms as maternal feminists used against Muslim men: just as the imagined oriental potentate preyed upon vulnerable women, so did the bourgeois, and in both cases women were deemed to need protection.

The Marxian socialist critique of misogyny originated with August Bebel, leader of the German Socialist Party, whose book *Women and Socialism* appeared in French in 1891. Bebel viewed prostitution as part of the chattelization of women in class society; he saw capitalism's tendency to reduce social relations to a "nexus of cash payments" as breeding especially pernicious forms of sexual exploitation. The French labor movement concurred with Bebel, but tended to exclude women from politics. Although one-third of working-class women worked, unions defined the factory as a male sphere of activity and stymied women's participation. Indifferent to women's demands for reproductive rights or the vote, they called for strengthening the moral purity of working-class families. Socialist and trade-union congresses at the turn of the century heard regular denunciations of the prostitution of working women. Rank-and-file men condemned factory owners who preyed upon their sisters, daughters, and wives as "minotaurs of modern times." Unions justified demands for raises and an eight-hour day as enabling working men to provide for their families and thus shield working-class wives and daughters from sexual subornation.[31]

Postwar natalist policies of the employers and the state co-opted this demand for a "family wage." To protect the women in their lives, workingmen turned to simple and direct solutions, such as excluding women from the shops and above all abolishing night work (a measure enacted by the Paris Commune of 1871). Demands for equal pay were often raised in hopes that employers would cease hiring women if they had to pay them the same wage as men. After 1918, urban proletarian life became more family-centered as rural migrants settled in. As the hôtels-garnis filled with foreign, and especially North African, migrants, overwhelmingly single men, they seemed less tolerable as fit homes for French families. Housing concerns enlarged the new and mostly imagined threat of predation, fueling xenophobia, racial tension, and, ironically, the urge to sequester Frenchwomen.[32]

While anarcho-syndicalists advocated equality in the workplace, the PCF, the Communist party, deepened the masculinist bias of the socialist Left by idealizing the image of the "militarized male revolutionary, weapon in hand, trampling the ruins of capitalism."[33] From fewer than 2 percent in 1926, the proportion of women PCF members grew to a little more than 11 percent in 1946, but the Popular Front had seen a tenfold increase in party membership, from thirty thousand to three hundred thousand. In its efforts to rally wide sectors of French citizens to the Popular Front against the "two hundred families" of the ruling class and the threat of fascism at home and abroad, the PCF worked "laboriously to construct a natalist common front." It echoed prewar denunciations of "sexual commerce" and of bosses exacting sexual favors from women employees, but it ignored organizing women workers so that they could protect themselves from unwanted advances as a solution to sexual harassment. Within the PCF's sphere of influence, its weekly mass-circulation photo-magazine *Regards* shaped opinion on the role of women, sexuality, and social life and honed the image of the proletarian family man paternally providing for and protecting wife and children.[34]

The Popular Front gave the organized working class wider hearing and greater voice than ever before, yet the PCF's line on issues involving the sexes followed they mores of the still-dominant rural, provincial, and small shop society. It did so "spontaneously, . . . without even knowing where these [attitudes] came from." Yet a protrayal such as Grémillon's Gaby reflected a view of morality seen through the prism of class, a sign of the PCF's success in convincing the middle classes of the elite's immorality. *Regards* described women in bathing suits on the Riviera as "*putains [whores] de luxe* tanning their haunches on the beach," whereas its photos of vacationing workers playing volleyball in the sun gave the impression that they were healthy and natural when they shed their clothes. Its opprobrium for *poules de luxe* and procurers, camp followers of the rich, contrasted with sympathy for poor prostitutes driven into the profession by dire straits.[35]

An autonomous discourse on sexuality and gender, a "room of its own," eluded the PCF. It discontinued the weekly *l'Ouvrière*, devoted to women factory workers' shop-floor issues, inaugurating in July 1935 a women's page in *Regards* that reshaped the image of the working-class woman as attractive, fashionable helpmate. It described woman strikers and picketers as charming—*charmentes* became a watchword—and included helpful domestic hints for homemakers. By 1937, *Regards* was unconsciously imitating fan magazines, adorning its pages with movie actresses modeling fashions and makeup. Diminishing women in this way aroused unreasonable expectations of men to defend hearth, home, and civilization.

Heroes in poetic-realist films try to live up to this role and fail. They are the antinomies of *Regards'* stalwart males. Acting out puerile displays of virility, they run away from responsibility, regress to a state of permanent adolescence, and recoil from true intimacy with either women or other men. They cannot overthrow the "symbolic order of the father" to become fathers themselves. The films blame their failures and downfalls on an egoistic woman, who usurps the dominant role like a whore in mercenary sex. The screen thus offered an imaginary and nostalgic retreat from maturity: men "joined the Foreign Legion"—literally—to escape the realities of class struggle. Films that did not "provide consolation and therapeutic release" for male anxieties provoked stridently defensive reactions that attest to the persistence of accepted images of masculinity. Such was the case with Jean Renoir's *Règle du jeu* (1939), which "showed how male posturing brings destruction on those who engage in it," and Henri-Georges Clouzot's *Le Courbeau* (1943), which shattered assumptions about gender-stereotyped behavior.[36]

The working-class men of these films are violent, oversexed, impulsive, irresponsible. Such infantilization was so familiar when applied to people of color that it was able to hybridize characters who were clearly European. The same could be said of the bourgeois Minotaur, who bore striking resemblance to the orientalist's oriental potentate, and his prey the factory girl, who could double as Circassian white slave. Her miscegenational contact with Arab men, captivity, and self-sacrificing behavior hybridize Irma in *Le Grand jeu*. In failing to save Pierre, she is saved by him, his money enabling her to erase her past and reassimilate in France, while her double, the venal Florence, a poule de luxe, acts as the direct agent of Pierre's destruction. The actress Anabella, who played Aicha the Berber of *La Bandera,* was so well known that her stardom disrupted the suspension of disbelief, her hybridity thus transcending the screen. *Maison du Maltais* used hybridity to achieve an even more sweeping effect: it allegorically sensitized audiences to the effects of racial oppression, male dominance, and anti-Semitism.

Chenal's Allegorical *Maison du Maltais*

An astute agent brought Pierre Chenal the rights to Jean Vignaud's novel *Maison du Maltais,* also acquiring, for the film that ensued, the services of the star, Vivian Romance. The novel, as well as Henri Fescourt's silent film adaptation of 1927, which inveighed against miscegenation and justified patriarchal authority, bored Chenal. Scrapping Vignaud's themes, in the 1938 screenplay Chenal and writer Jacques Companeez explored *depaysement,* the exile's loss of identity, the sisterhood of women, and interracial working-class solidarity. Consciously or in reflexive reaction to the climate of the times, Chenal, born Philippe Cohen, to a Jewish family, in Brussels, 1904, created a film that covertly challenged anti-Semitism through a sympathetic portrayal of a Muslim man. Julien Duvivier, a close friend whose wife was Jewish, convinced Chenal to go ahead with the project, primarily to remain in the public eye. Chenal cast Marcel Dalio, also Jewish, "against type" *(contre-emploi),* as the leading man. No he-man, Dalio exuded an ethereal, diasporan quality that colored his rendition of the character. Honorable and self-sacrificing, his Matteo challenged stereotypes of Jews and Arabs as egoistical, greedy, and underhanded. Chenal followed Duvivier's precedent in *Pépé le Moko,* building an elaborate set at the Paramount de Saint-Maurice studios, a replica of the market quarter of the Tunisian port of Sfax, peopled with a host of exotic types. His studio footage he then mixed with location shots filmed on a brief excursion to the town with the cast.[37]

Hostility to Jews in the film industry surfaced repeatedly in the late 1930s, and events in Algeria suggest that Chenal was drawing connections between anti-Arabism and anti-Judaism, which the Great Depression had reawakened after thirty years. Settlers resurrected the demand to abrogate the sixty-year-old Crémieux decree, narrowing the boundaries of whiteness to exclude Jews. As had occurred during the Dreyfus Affair, Jewishness became contested racial terrain, and Jew baiting shifted the electorate to the right. The 1924 election was the last in which Algerian leftists won seats in parliament. Preaching "neo-Latin unity"

As Saffia, the prostitute who makes good, Viviane Romance, the most popular film actress of the decade, dominates this poster for *Maison du Maltais* (1938). Her opposite in the film, Dalio, is given only fourth billing for his role as Matteo, an Arab. Saffia's black, curly hair offsets her face, which is colored distinctly light-skinned flesh tones. The poster reveals that, in contrast to the novel and the 1928 silent-film version, this Saffia is European, not Arab. At lower right in this night scene, the glow of a lantern highlights the Sfax docks. *Credit:* copyright Galerie Cine-Images, Paris against "les métiques, les Juifs et l'International bolchevique" a Latin League formed in Oran. The irony of calling others *métiques* ("half-breeds"), when their New Latin Race had such a motley birthright, was lost on these proponents of Mediterranean Aryanism. The masthead of the movement's Oran daily called on readers to apply "sulphur, pitch, and the fire of Hell to the synagogues and Jewish schools, to destroy the houses of Jews, take their capital, and chase them into the open country like mad dogs." When authorities censored the paper, it replaced its words with a swastika. Pied-noir mayors openly espoused anti-Semitism, urging the abrogation of the Crémieux decree that in 1870 had conferred French citizenship on Algerian Jews. While French metropolitan fascists rejected Nazism, the Algérien fascists, even in the same parties, often embraced it. Anti-Jews adopted the anticapitalist rhetoric that Max Régis had used in 1898 to capture and channel the energies of the poorest settlers. Latin Leagues spread from Oran to Sidi Bel Abbès and from Constantine to Algiers, using "proletarian" slogans such as "Worker, your enemy is the Jew: he exploits and steals from you; Jews cause inflation; buying from Jews ruins French commerce."[38]

The anti-Semitic riot in Constantine from 3 to 6 August 1934 was a classic case of Jews being caught in the middle. A Jewish drunk profaned a mosque, urinating on praying Muslims and touching off attacks on the Jewish quarter. Local government, in the hands of European anti-Semites, allowed the Muslim reaction to boil out of control. European expropriations had forced Muslim peasants who had lost their land into town to look for work, while Jews had improved their status by foreclosing Muslim properties. Virulent European anti-Semitism had prompted Jews to buy firearms, which were used against Muslim looters. Twenty-eight Jews were killed, and about thirty-five from each community were wounded. The army killed more than a hundred Muslims in the ensuing repression, but Muslim notables called for calm and placed Jews under their protection. Algerian Jewish community leaders, maintaining ties to the moderate Left, reached out to the Muslim religious community. While condemning irresponsible Arab nationalists for the riot, they emphasized that Muslim elected officials had condemned it. They infuriated the colons by adding that "Jews do not find it normal that the natives are held as subjects."[39]

Fascist movements grew rapidly in this anti-Semitic climate. The Algerian Croix de Feu had six thousand members in January 1934, twenty thousand when the Popular Front outlawed it in June 1936, and (as the

Parti social français, or PSF) it grew to twenty-six thousand by 1939. Jacques Doriot's PPF, the Naziphile Parti populaire français, grew from four thousand settlers in December 1936 to twenty thousand in August 1937. Algerian Communists numbered fifty-one hundred at the time. Even in the election of 1936, the Algerian Right increased its popular vote. The only Radicals elected were those who professed anti-Semitism, opposed the Crémieux decree, and won support from the Latin Leagues and the Algerian sections of the metropole's far Right, the Croix de Feu, the Faisceau, and the Action Française. The Popular Front campaigned against the "fifty feudal families of Algeria who ruin the people and maintain five million natives in slavery"—an ambiguous linguistic distinction that left unresolved the matter of interracial solidarity and attracted few pied-noir voters. As assaults on Popular Frontists grew bolder, leftists protested harassment by thugs protected by local officials. In Sidi Bel Abbès on 26 February 1937, two days before municipal elections, two thousand leftists marched on city hall. Fascist ligueurs shouting "Vive Doriot, à bas les Juifs" fired on the march, leaving one dead and ten wounded. Police then protected the attackers from the wrath of the crowd by breaking up the demonstration.[40]

Although scholars disagree on which groups in the Right's spectrum were fascist, settler attachment to racial dominance certainly reinforced fascist sympathies. Groups that ranged from the Parti social français-Croix de Feu, arguably not fascist, to Doriot's unquestionably fascist Parti populaire français closed ranks on racial matters. In Algeria, anti-Semitism was an essential ingredient of their electoral platforms, as was the obsessive focus on the repeal of the Crémieux decree. Oran's Anti-Semites were particularly violent, even appealing to Muslims to side with the colons against the Jews. But few native nationalists succumbed to anti-Jewish impulses, despite infusions of German money, and rapprochement between Jews and Muslims expanded after the Constantine riots, even at a time when Zionism was growing. The career of George Valois, the Faisceau's founder, illustrates how fascist and racist ideology intermingled. Going to Singapore in 1895 an anarchist, he abandoned republicanism after confronting the "savagery and barbarism of Asia," where, he thought, the mixing of the races threatened European world supremacy. This epiphany led him to reject Enlightenment values of the fraternity of peoples that Chenal's *Maison du Maltais* upheld.[41]

Chenal's film begins in the market of Sfax, in Tunisia. Matteo is the feckless son of a Maltese immigrant, a bitter, reclusive sponge fisherman who married a Bedouin Arab girl and allowed her to raise his only son as a Muslim. Matteo lives hand-to-mouth by reciting stories to merchants and laborers, bartering his tales in return for necessities. When he returns to his father's house—a stark-white, traditional structure at desert's edge that is the maison du Maltais of the title—the old man rebukes him as ne'er-do-well and locks him out. Why should I work, Matteo retorts; working is for people who have nothing better to do. I must listen to the birds' songs and await what Allah wills for me.

Matteo's destiny appears in the form of a European prostitute, Saffia (played by Viviane Romance). He falls in love with her and follows her everywhere. She finds him an absurdly amusing contrast with the grim world she inhabits. Saffia's consumptive friend Greta (Jany Holt), who has an alarming cough, is scaring away customers. Rosina, the landlady, played by Fréhel (the chanteuse réaliste of *Pépé*), throws her out: "Pas sou, pas clé." But Saffia is fiercely loyal. After stormy recriminations with Rosina, she shares her room and bed with Greta, tenderly caring for her waif-like friend. To pay for a doctor, she picks a customer's pocket, handing off the wallet to Matteo; she avoids arrest because he stands up to the police and covers up the theft. His daring impresses her and softens her tough exterior.

Saffia gives herself to Matteo, and in a reversal of roles he takes a job working on the docks while she refuses customers. They move to his father's house to live together. At night he holds her in his arms and tells her stories, especially a tale of two pearls. One day she tells him she is going to have his child. Matteo is ecstatic, and he blesses her with a prayer to Allah. But to get money for the baby, he joins fellow dockers in a risky smuggling and gun-running excursion, telling Saffia that he has gone sponge fishing and will return in a few days.

Weeks pass. The old man and Saffia fight. He accuses her of leading Matteo astray, blames her for his son's disappearance, and throws her out. As she wanders alone in the night, a sandstorm engulfs her and she is nearly struck by a car. An archaeologist, Chervin (Pierre Renoir), returning to the site of an ancient ruin in the desert, rescues her, and she spends the next weeks with him at the dig. He falls in love with her and asks her to return with him to Paris. Back in Sfax, about to board ship for Marseilles, she wavers, but her friend Greta, with her dying breath, urges Saffia to go. Saffia debarks for France, reaching the ship only moments before Matteo returns.

Chervin installs Saffia in his large Paris house. His wealth and position allow her to rapidly acquire education and refinement. He marries her, and she convinces him the child she is carrying is his. Matteo returns to the docks; for years he can think of nothing but his lost lover and child. His pal *(copain)* Gégène convinces him to leave Sfax and join Gégène's old gang of thieves in Paris. Matteo becomes the despised servant of the gang, addressed only by the vilest white racist epithet in French, *krouyah*, which ironically derives from the Arabic word for brother.

In a park one day, Matteo tells a group of small children his tale of the pearls. An English nanny pulls one child away; it is Saffia's daughter, who repeats the tale at home. Saffia, now an elegant society woman, thinks Matteo has turned up to blackmail her. She hires a detective to find him and arranges a meeting in a seedy hotel. Dressed as a prostitute, she convinces him that she lost the child and returned to "the life." She propositions him. Appalled, he flees back to the gang's hideout. The gang boss orders him to bring whisky. Crossing the room with the glass, Matteo pours it over the boss's head, then knocks him out. He confronts the gang, finds no challengers, pours a glass of whisky and swallows it in one long draught. With this symbolic act, he rejects his faith, takes over the gang, and becomes a wealthy, successful underworld boss and cynical alcoholic.

Saffia, meanwhile, falls prey to blackmail at the hands of the detective she had hired to elude Matteo. As the price of his silence, the detective forces her to sell an expensive necklace that Chervin had given her. Chervin discovers the jewels are missing and, when she refuses to explain why, he throws her out. She returns to the hotel that is Matteo's gang's headquarters, arriving while he is holding a drunken, boisterous party. Believing Matteo the author of the blackmail, Saffia reveals the whole story in an outburst of recriminations. Matteo is stunned, dismisses the gang, and with Gégène by his side goes to Chervin's house. Pistol in hand, he forces his way into the study. He convinces Chervin that he extorted the jewels from Saffia because she left him, that Saffia loves Chervin, and that Chervin is the father of her child. With a longing glance at a photo of his daughter, Matteo returns to the hideout, takes off his European clothes that symbolize his assimilation, dons his old white *gondoura* (a wool poncho) from the inlaid wooden chest he had brought from Sfax, begs Allah's forgiveness, and shoots himself. Hearing the shot, Gégène bursts into the room. In a tone of shock, pity, and reproach, he exclaims "khouyah!" and takes Matteo in his arms. Matteo makes Gégène swear to keep his secret and protect Saffia and his daughter. The two friends bid each other "salaam."

Assimilation and Hidden Children

In consoling Matteo, Gégène restores the corrupted Arabic. *Sidi,* an Arabic honorific, also was used as a racial epithet; *bled,* countryside, or outback, came to mean a dive, or hole, and the term for a notable, *q'aid,* became slang for gang leader.[42] French slang's ironic inversions captured the negative feelings toward North Africans that the film seems to counteract. Gégène (played by Aimos) and another French docker (Gaston Modot) work alongside Matteo in Sfax and carry out a dangerous smuggling excursion together. Chervin wins out in the end, possessing and assimilating Saffia and the child she bore Matteo (replete with English nanny), but this film conceives of his triumph as a reconciliation of races, a far cry from Vignaud's original intent. The unscrupulous pearl merchant of the novel is transformed into a scholar with a deep respect for North Africa's ancient cultures. Viviane Romance received top billing, which made box-office sense since she was the most popular female star of the late 1930s. Dalio was not even on the top ten list.[43] As much the focus of the film as Matteo, she is a hybrid whose name suggests the Bedouin original in Vignaud's novel (Saffiyah). And her sisterly solidarity, her ability to transform herself from working-class prostitute to bourgeois intellectual's wife, her defense of her child, match Matteo's nobility of soul.

Maison du Maltais sympathizes with subaltern cultures more than any film with the possible exception of *Itto,* yet French culture remains a one-way street; assimilation is the road to emancipation for people of color, the working class, and women. And the subtext on anti-Semitism casts a prophetic, eerie shadow, a foreshadowing of a haunting consequence of the Holocaust, the hidden children of the Jews whom Vichy and the Germans sent via Drancy to their deaths in the concentration camps. Most of the French who hid Jewish children urged them to assimilate, to forget their Jewishness. Survival, well-meaning liberalism, and a sense of superiority over *shtetl* Jews prompted "conversions," which left older children confused and estranged while younger ones were lost to, or stolen from, their cultural community. Jewish survivors reclaiming relatives' children after the war were forced into custody battles; the most notorious, the Finaly affair, ended after a four-month trial in 1953 and illustrates the "Vichy Syndrome." A film of the Vichy era, *La Voile bleue* (The Blue Veil, 1942, Jean Stelli & François Campaux), stars the "Pétainist muse" Gaby Morlay as a dedicated nanny who raises children of distant or preoccupied parents into ethical adults who pay homage to her and by implication to Vichy's Catholic New Order. Overwhelmingly popular in the provinces, the film is a paradigm of willful ignorance of the Jewish experience of Vichy. It "produced the symbolic denial of Jewish reality on the screen" and facilitated the erasure of Jewish life from French society. Its silence speaks volumes and captures on film an essential blind spot in the eye of France.[44]

Conclusion
Political Consequences of Blind Spots and Privilege

Maurice Thorez, who had been general secretary of the PCF, the French Communist party, since 1934, visited Algiers in February 1939 and proclaimed: "There is an Algerian nation that is constituting itself in the mix of twenty races . . . all brothers, if not by blood then at least by the heart of the Great Revolution, which made no distinction between races and religions when it affirmed that the French Republic was one and indivisible."[1]

Thorez's elegy to assimilation as the road to unity against fascism committed the PCF to protecting the empire. He had come a long way from the position he had taken when he assumed the chair of the party's national action committee against the Rif War in July 1925. At that time he called for "a united front between metropolitan workers and colonial slaves" to overthrow French rule in North Africa and set the stage for an assault on capitalism at home.[2] In a sense, his 1939 speech reflected the PCF's own assimilation, for the Popular Front and later the Resistance absorbed Communists into the political mainstream. Assimilationism disguised the privileged position of metropolitan working-class men under the assumption that they were the proletarian norm, much as colonialism made Frenchness the norm to which the colonized must conform. Colonial cinema helped conceal the reality that French civilization imposed an inferior status on women and people of color, a status they resented and fought to overthrow. Once this resistance surfaced, the PCF, as well as most socialists, defined class solidarity in terms that protected privilege and enabled the Left to reject demands for equality as diversions from the class struggle. At three critical junctures—the struggle over Popular Front colonial policy; the early stage of armed struggle in Algeria; and the women's movement's assertion of reproductive rights—the French Left revealed its blindness to solidarity.

The Popular Front and the Blum-Violette Bill

Under the Popular Front, relations between the Algerian and metropolitan Left deteriorated. French socialists had helped to form native trade unions, but they spurned "bourgeois nationalists," whom they saw as native exploiters replacing imperialists and offering workers nothing. After adhering to the Popular Front, the PCF backed away from solidarity with the colonized. Its constituents and middle-class allies sympathized with the pied noir, and they in turn propped up the boss rule of colon-elected officials and business interests. The Blum-Violette bill granted native veterans, elected officials, and graduates of French high schools *(lycées)* full voting rights. Although adding only twenty-six thousand new citizens, it incorporated them into a single electorate without relinquishing their personal status as Muslims and threatened the pied noir with a step toward majority rule: one man, one vote. Wholeheartedly supported by the Muslim Congress, it was denounced by 302 of Algeria's 304 European mayors. In the parliamentary debate that began in December 1936, deputies of the parti colonial aimed at preserving the Jonnart formula, repudiation of Muslim personal status as a condition for citizenship. In one breath they criticized Islam because, they argued, it denied the principle of equality before the law; in the next breath they defended the two-tiered electoral system through which the European minority of 10 percent effectively thwarted the native majority.

Before the Popular Front, the PCF had condemned the Violette reform as giving native intellectuals and bourgeois the right to vote while excluding native workers and peasants. Once Blum took power, the Communists accepted Maurice Violette's rationale for limiting the reform to évolués:

> It seems impossible to call on the general native population to exercise political rights immediately since the immense majority of them do not at all yet wish to exercise these rights, and in any case they do not appear to be capable of doing so in a normal and intelligent manner . . . [but it is no longer possible to] continue to treat as subjects deprived of essential rights French natives [sic] who have completely assimilated the French manner of thinking and who, however, for family reasons or religious motives, cannot abandon their personal status.[3]

Algerian Communists had dissented from the unity agreements with the socialists in June and October 1934. The "circulaire Barthel," an internal document leaked to the press in September 1935, criticized the Popular Front in Algeria as exclusively European, giving the impression of "a Franco-Jewish front against the Arab people." Barthel (the name was an alias for party theoretician Jean Chaintron) told his comrades that to conquer power they had to create "an essentially native party" with an "Arab imprint." At this juncture, the PCF changed course. It withdrew from circulation a thoroughly researched book that advocated Maoist-style agrarian revolution, and in March 1936 it expelled the author, Nachman List. It disbanded the Ligue contre l'impérialisme, replaced it with a group with a moderate program, and in April reconstituted its Algerian sections into the PCA, or Algerian Communist party. The PCA allied with the Muslim Congress in support of the Violette bill and refrained from attacking Muslim reformists as traitors. Scrapping demands for independence and a parliament elected by universal suffrage, it preached a "free union of the Algerian people with the great fraternal people of France." By October 1936, the number of Muslims in the PCA grew to 750, and in early 1937, to 1,100, more than one-fifth of the total membership; but after the Violette bill failed in 1938, the number plummeted to 100.[4]

For the PCF, the accommodation to European racial loyalty and superiority was an unconscious part of the party's efforts to win acceptance within the Popular Front and redefine the Third Republic's body politic to include the metropole's working class in "True France." The party had helped Messali Hadj, the leading Algerian separatist, found Etoile Nord-Africain (ENA) in 1927, but had treated him as a protégé. When the ENA refused to subordinate independence to the Popular Front's program, the PCF accused Messali of "playing the game of international fascism" and in 1936 tacitly supported Blum's arrest of Messali and the outlawing of ENA. At the PCF's ninth congress in Arles, December 1937, PCA secretary Quaddour Belkacim stated, "The Muslims do not want, with the achievements they have obtained, to divorce from France . . . the union of the people of Algeria and France is necessary and will always be." Tailing after native assimilationists, the PCF denied the ENA's characterization of Algeria as a nation in its own right. But the Blum-Violette reform failed in 1938, and the moderates turned to the ENA. As native nationalism's conflicts with white-settler supremacism grew irreconcilable, the PCF became irrelevant; its numbers in Algeria dwindled to a few dissident colons. The stereotype of the Communists as Machiavellian manipulators of their united-front partners is far from reality. Having chosen the French middle-class parties and socialists as its primary allies over the "colonial slaves," the French Communists abandoned their unique role in return for mainstream acceptance and evanescent gains in membership.[5]

The failure of Violette's Algeria bill dashed the hopes of Muslim reformists such as Ferhat Abbas, and the defeat of other colonial reforms strengthened the ENA's case for independence. The Chamber of Deputies rejected a plan for self-rule in Syria, despite its inclusion of a military alliance with France. The Senate defeated proposals to eliminate forced labor in Vietnam and Senegal. Amnestied colonial political prisoners were rejailed when they tried to exercise their political rights, and the PCF accepted the repression without protest. Blum's minister of colonies, Marius Moutet, intended to preserve colonialism: he "was merely offering a more flexible and intelligent colonialism than that of his conservative predecessors: the objectives were similar." He justified budgeting funds to alleviate a severe agricultural crisis in Vietnam, precipitated in the first place by colonial practices, by arguing that "our army will find healthy recruits only from a reinvigorated indigenous peasantry." Blum's secretary for foreign affairs, Pierre Viénot, startled Robert-Jean Longuet, one of the few anticolonial socialists, by touting to him the benefits of the French civilizing mission, and Moutet claimed that if the French colonial presence suddenly disappeared it "would at the present bring more dangers than advantages."[6]

Algerian workers' organizations were swept up in the same racial currents. Construction and dockworkers strikes in 1927–29 led by the Communist-affiliated CGTU unions called for equal pay for equal work and an end to "special" wages for Muslims, demands motivated more from a desire to exclude than include. As in France when male workers demanded equal pay for women, whites in Algeria expected that employers would prefer to hire whites over natives if pay rates were equal. In Algeria, the CGTU avoided all mention of colonial self-determination, while in the metropole, where the demand for equal pay could have educated workers in the habit of solidarity, it mouthed empty phrases of solidarity with colonial nationalism and kept silent on wages. Since it was illegal to meet in Algeria, socialists held their 1928 congress in France; loyally defending the interests of their constituents, lower- and mid-level civil servants, they resolved that "colonization is in itself legitimate."[7]

The railway workers' newspaper printed a statement in 1928 that "the native belongs to an inferior race . . . and cannot raise himself through his own efforts to the level of the European. . . . The native is a cheat, dirty, thieving, sly, ungrateful. To do him good is like giving jam to pigs. To injure him is to teach him to become submissive and civilized."[8] The Popular Front victory touched off a wave of strikes in Algeria that involved ten thousand native agricultural workers, but neither European "wet coopers" (barrelmakers), key workers in the wine industry, nor CGTU dockers, fishermen, railroaders, and factory hands would cooperate across racial lines. In March 1937, native copper miners in Constantine struck and clashed with European workers. Several were killed on both sides, and expressions, much less acts, of solidarity vanished.[9]

Using their clout within the Radical party, settler deputies killed the Violette bill by inches, dragging out the debate from December 1936 to the summer. By then a financial crisis had forced Blum to resign, and his cabinet was replaced by a more conservative one. As the Violette bill was about to be tabled, three thousand Muslim elected officials in Algeria resigned in protest. The action convinced Albert Sarraut, leader of the colonial lobby, that settler intransigence was setting the stage for a native revolt. But in early 1938, he failed to broker a Jonnart-style compromise; settler deputies blocked his move in committee and hamstrung it with unfriendly amendments, while European mayors held a second antireform conference in Algiers, and 225 of them resigned. The cabinet wilted under this combined assault, and the settlers again prevailed.[10]

The Antipodes of Anti-Semitism

When all was said and done, settler power rested on the metropole's deference to the colons' monomaniacal defense of privilege, white racial solidarity, and the overweening urge to circle the wagons against the indigenous. The settler mayors who resigned en masse and the deputies who sabotaged the Violette bill were reelected. With the ENA outlawed and the reformist road barred, the imprisoned Messali founded the Parti Populaire Algérien (PPA). Although bitterly disappointed by the defeat of reform, Ferhat Abbas, the Fédération des Elus Indigènes, and other évolués who represented the gallicized Muslim elite still refused to abandon France. In 1939, Abbas declared that "I will not die for the Algerian nation, because it does not exist." His view coincided with Thorez's proclamation of Algeria as a "nation in formation" and a melting pot of twenty Mediterranean "races."[11] But both views were becoming irrelevant.

After the fall of France to Germany, the Vichy regime fulfilled the heart's desire of the colons; it repealed the Crémieux decree and revoked the citizenship of Algerian Jews. Messali, who refused to collaborate with the collaborators, was sentenced in March 1941 to sixteen more years. As a result, Algerian Muslims and Jews drew closer. Doctor Mohammed Loufrani, a key proponent of Jewish-Muslim entente, received support from Mohammed Ali Boumendjel, a respected *maître avocat* (lawyer) elected in November 1938 to the Algiers municipal council as a representative of Messali's PPA. He joined Sheikh el-Okbi, a member of the ulaama, the scholars under Sheikh Ali Ben Badis who preached Islamic reformation *(salifiyah)*, in writing an open letter to Loufrani:

> By putting down the Jew, one only brings him even closer together with the Muslim. It was thought that Muslims would rejoice at the abrogation of the Crémieux decree; but they can easily see the dubious worth of a citizenship that the granting authority can take away after seventy years' employment. If the antagonism between Jews and Muslims had existed, it would not have failed to show itself during the events of recent years. Nothing has been spared to set the Muslim and Israelite communities against each other.[12]

During the Vichy years, Muslims resisted anti-Judaism and risked prison to sell Jews necessities from the black market, to protect Jewish property by putting it in their name, and to hide Jews threatened with deportation. The Palestine crisis and the Arab-Israeli war soured Muslims, but many Jewish leftists supported the FLN. Good relations ruptured only after most Jews sided with France in the war of independence.

Sétif: Historic Blind Spots and Constructions of Memory

With the Allied landings in North Africa in early 1943, Algerians began to press for application of the Atlantic Charter. Abbas issued the Manifeste du Peuple Algérienne in February 1943, calling for self-determination within a French federation and electoral reform: one person, one vote. To avoid United Nations trusteeship, the Gaullists in January-February 1944 convened the Brazzaville Conference, which abolished corvée labor and l'indigénat, the Black Code, planned elections, and invited native participation in local affairs. Still reflecting the opinions of moderates, Abbas revived hopes that had been dashed by the Popular Front's failures. France's Liberation would liberate the Maghreb: "The Resistance was not going to desert us . . . it was unthinkable that the French people, which had been subjected to four long years of Hitlerian domination, would not recognize our legitimate aspirations."[13]

Yet the events that followed demolished Abbas's last hopes and opened a breach with the French Left. Abbas and the moderates founded the Association des Amis du Manifeste et de la Liberté (AML); the PCA condemned the AML's nationalism, but the ulaama joined, and Messali's PPA controlled the base. Before the war's end, AML had attracted one hundred thousand members, and under its cover, the PPA began forming paramilitary cells in the Constantinois and the Kabyle, areas remote from French military control. On 23 April 1945, de Gaulle's regime deported Messali to Brazzaville, giving the PPA an issue to rally their forces. A bad fall harvest, a bitter winter, and spring famine heightened tensions, and farmers crowded into urban slums, bidonvilles, ripe for agitation.

May Day demonstrations in Oran and Algiers turned violent and left dead in the streets. Then on VE Day, 8 May 1945, the Gaullist authorities gave permission for parades celebrating victory, and the AML seized the chance to demonstrate for their rights. The storm broke at Sétif, ninety miles west of Constantine. Sétif was Abbas's home town and the place where the AML had been founded. It was a market day, and the PPA led farmers from the surrounding rural areas into town. They clashed with the police, shots rang out, and the famine-stricken farmers went on a rampage. They killed twenty-one Europeans and some Muslims they accused of collaborating with the French authorities. Violence spread to the bled, and isolated pied-noir farmers were killed, often by their own workers and at times by Algerians with whom they had grown up. Army units arrived on 11 May. Planes strafed native villages. Naval units bombarded towns with long-range guns. Joined in its ratonnades, or rat-catching expeditions, by settler militia, the army hunted down suspects, shooting hundreds out of hand. Thousands were rounded up and interned in camps. A pied-noir newspaper, L'Echo d'Alger, summed up its alarm in dramatic terms: "When the house is on fire . . . when the ship is about to sink . . . it's the hour of the fireman . . . the lifeboat. For North Africa, c'est l'heure du gendarme."[14]

The French government declared the toll as fifteen hundred dead;

later (after 1962) Algerian officials claimed forty thousand; a reliable American reporter estimated between seven thousand and eighteen thousand. Charles André Julien, the preeminent historian of the Maghreb, saw documents in the governor-general's office and calculated that there were from six thousand to eight thousand dead in the immediate aftermath of Sétif, but the killings went on for months. The settlers' nightmare, servile insurrection, had prompted the greatest violence since 1871. The state-sanctioned terrorism was utterly invisible in France. Only Albert Camus protested; the PCF and the PCA denounced the AML as foreign-controlled and condemned the uprising as a Nazi plot—offering this explanation even though it was after the German surrender. VE Day, etched in French memory as the euphoric close of the heroic chapter of French Résistance, marked Algerian memory indelibly in blood and terror and mourning and spawned the Algerian Résistance.[15]

French blindness opened an unbridgeable gap; Sétif awakened a generation of Algerians to the necessity for armed struggle. Abbas gave up on France: the French Resistance movement—the Résistants, the "best" of France—had failed to "recognize our legitimate aspirations" despite having endured occupation themselves. Whether Brazzaville represented an opportunity manqué remains an ongoing debate, but Sétif was the point of no return for Algeria. Admittedly, the PPA had set out in May 1945 to wreck AML's attempts to compromise, yet unrestrained settler violence forced the PPA deep underground and provided skilled recruits for armed struggle as demobilized Algerian servicemen came home from fighting Nazism to find their families massacred and villages destroyed. News of French atrocities made antiimperialists of those not touched directly. In 1947, the pied-noir-dominated Algerian Assembly rejected a charter of rights drawn up by Paris. It was one more nail in the coffin.

The PPA destroyed itself in factionalism by 1947, but its remnants founded the FLN. In 1954, they embarked on a military phase of struggle on All Saints Day (1 November), coordinating attacks on cities throughout Algeria. In Paris ten days later, the socialist premier, Pierre Mendès-France, barely won a vote of confidence; he was saved only by a score of votes controlled by the pied-noir lobby. Committed to Algerian reform yet captive to the forces intransigently arrayed against it, Mendès-France was trapped. "If he were to start implementing the 1947 statute and honest elections . . . let alone negotiating with any Algerian nationalists, then the pied-noir lobby would cause his government to fall overnight." The Algerian War brought down his government, and within four years the entire regime was gone. Abbas joined the FLN in 1955 and became the first president of the Algerian Provisional Government (GPRA). The settlers' virtual veto over negotiations with the GPRA prolonged the fighting for eight years, at a toll of a million dead.[16]

A repetition of Sétif swept Algeria on 20 August 1955. In Philippeville, on the coast, one hundred miles from the Tunisian border, an uprising of FLN-led peasants hacked to death seventy-one settlers and fifty-two Algerian collaborators. At El Halia, Algerian miners slaughtered overseers, their families, and collaborators. The atrocities traumatized the socialist governor-general, Jacques Soustelle, and pushed him into the camp of the pied-noir ultras, the vigilante groups, inflicting indiscriminate collective reprisals on villagers. The words uttered by Thorez in 1939, quoted at this chapter's opening, rang hollow; the PCA's base was reduced to a tiny fraction of the settler working class. Soustelle's military adviser resurrected the images of race war invoked by rightists since the days of the Rif War: "Now the breach is yawning, the two communities are drawn up against each other, race war, unaccountable and merciless, is at our doors."[17]

War without mercy ensued. The distinguished lawyer Ali Boumendjel was arrested and tortured by the "paras" (Foreign Legion paratroops) in early 1957 and "fell" out of a six-story window in an Algiers prison. The verdict was suicide. Francis Jeanson, a Communist intellectual and close friend of Boumendjel, declared that active resistance was the only course open to those of good conscience. In a reference to Vichy, he asked, "For the second time in fifteen years, will official France condemn Frenchmen to betrayal?"[18] Jeanson organized his pied noir and French students as *porteurs de valises,* couriers to carry money to Switzerland from migrant workers in Paris to pay for arms. They were accused of carrying explosives as well. In the absence of a mass movement, such as only the PCF could have organized, the choices for Europeans of conscience were helplessness or treason.

The isolation of such Europeans grew as Euro-Algerian workers increasingly subordinated their interests to those of the colon elite to defend their privileges as whites. Colon bosses could appeal to white solidarity to enlist the poor whites in the domination of native labor and resources. The arrangement gave the settlers inordinate power to block a mass movement against the war. They controlled the colonial bureaucracy and access to information about Algeria, and hence influenced elite and mass opinion in the metropole. France had become increasingly dependent on colonial markets for goods and capital, sources of military recruits, raw materials, and labor reserves; political and economic leaders in Paris were thus reluctant to tamper with this consolidation of settler rule, and instead they reinforced it.[19]

Gender Blindness: Abortion and Birth Control

French socialism had encoded the working class first of all as essentially male, then as essentially European. Racial blind spots reinforced male bias and gender bias as the two forms of prejudice went hand in hand into the twentieth century. The Socialist-affiliated CGT's congress of 1898 accepted equal pay for widows and spinsters, but as a rule declared that otherwise "man must feed woman." The Third Republic fell, then Vichy, without altering the Left's perception that race and gender oppression were exceptional circumstances to be addressed after socialism had been achieved. The Resistance regime, with the Communists playing a central role, granted women the right to vote, but state-sanctioned brothels, *maisons tolerées,* remained open for three more years. Bowing to Catholic and pronatalist opinion, however, the leftist government did nothing to insure women's control over their bodies. Abortion remained illegal, and the anticontraception law of 1920 remained on the books until 1969.[20]

What amounted to a ban on all forms of birth control deprived women of the basic human right to autonomy of person. Every year in the late 1940s, more than half a million backstreet abortions were performed, a figure slightly larger than the number of live births. One-half of these abortions were self-induced, involving the use of household disinfectants or probes, and a virtual holocaust ensued; twenty thousand women died each year. As postwar recovery and economic growth took hold in the 1950s, the number of abortions doubled, while deaths from complications declined to ten thousand a year—still a staggering toll of women's lives.[21]

Statistics on illegal abortions are by definition hard to come by, but a wealth of evidence in the form of interviews with hospitalized women compiled by doctors and lawyers revealed a horrifying mosaic that converted many of the researchers into militant activists. Half of all visits by women to an emergency room were to treat septic shock and hemorrhage, the complications of abortions. And of course, it was "the poor who fill the casualty wards" as Communist reporter Jacques Derogy pointed out. Women flooded the clinics on Saturday nights because Sunday gave them a day to recover from an abortion without missing work. "I am treated like an animal" and "I live like an animal" were often-heard responses of women about their reproductive lives.[22]

The Mouvement Français pour le Planning Familial (MFPF) opened its first clinic, in Grenoble, in 1961. It was led by a Jewish woman doctor, Marie-Andrée Weill-Hallé, and Dr. Pierre Simon. But by and large, doctors hid behind the 1920 laws and refused to help women to prevent or terminate unwanted pregnancies. At the end of the decade, only 4 percent of France's forty thousand doctors were cooperating with the MFPF. Only after 1965 did "the national conspiracy of silence on birth control" break down. François Mitterand made repeal of the 1920 law part of the platform of his unsuccessful 1966 presidential campaign. In 1971, 343 prominent women, including Simone de Beauvoir, Catherine Deneuve, and Marguerite Duras, published a "confession" that they had had abortions and called for the abrogation of the 1920 law.[23] The PCF, however, proved more hostile to this campaign than progressive Roman Catholic groups, and the party resisted setting up birth-control clinics in the Paris Red Belt towns and other localities it controlled. In response to Jacques Derogy's 1956 book on abortion, Thorez argued that family planning was an "illusion" that diverted the proletariat from political struggle: "The path for women's liberation is through social reforms, through social revolution, and not through abortion clinics."[24]

Coda

Heart of darkness, heart of light: Mediterranean Africa's hypnotic light, the Sahara's deadly sun, serve as metaphor for the fate of the struggle for social equity in France. There is "no man so blind as he that will not see, nor so dull as he that will not understand." Transfixed by exotic images and blind to colonial and sexual realities, the Left proved incapable of assessing the interests of the "class-as-a-whole" or mapping a line of march. Its cadres took on tasks that called for the longest and broadest vision with sight clouded by avoidance, willful ignorance, cultural superiority, and denial. Lacking insight into the totality of class conflict, they shouldered an unbalanced load. The burden slipped from their grasp, blocking the way to just solutions to the needs of women and to the racial troubles that beset France.[25]

Ye are the salt of the earth: but if the salt have lost his savour, wherewith shall it be salted? It is thenceforth good for nothing, but to be cast out, and to be trodden under foot of man.[26]

Notes

In the notes, full citations are not given for all works: readers are directed to the bibliography for details. In some notes a "see also" list, giving names of authors whose works appear in the bibliography, suggests further reading. Some titles have been abbreviated, as listed below.

Au miroir	Abdelghani Megherbi, *Les Algériens au miroir du cinéma colonial*
AHR	*American Historical Review*
AN	Archives Nationales
C-M	*Ciné-Miroir*
FFL	Douglas Porch, *The French Foreign Legion*
FHS	*French Historical Studies*
First Wave	Richard Abel, *French Cinema: The First Wave, 1915–1929*
Générique	Michéle Lagny, Marie-Claire Ropars, and Pierre Sorlin, *Générique des années 30*
HAC	Charles-Robert Ageron, *Histoire de l'Algérie contemporaine*
JCH	*Journal of Contemporary History*
JOC	France, *Journal Officiel des Chambre des Députés*
Mists	Dudley Andrew, *Mists of Regret*
RASJEP	*Revue algérienne des sciences juridiques, économiques, et politiques*
T&C	Richard Abel, *French Film: Theory and Criticism*

1. Cultural Hegemony in French-Algerian History

1. Hervé Hamon and Patrick Rotman, *Les Porteurs des valises*, 371; Anne Tristan et al., *Le Silence du Fleuve*, 120–34.

2. Hamon and Rotman, *Les Porteurs*, 375 (quotes), 372–75, 378, 414; Jean-Luc Einaudi, *La Bataille de Paris;* Anne Tristan, "France admette massacre sécrète en Paris," *Le Monde* (1991; trans. in *Manchester Guardian Weekly*);

Tristan et al., *Le Silence,* 129–30; Benjamin Stora, *La Gangrène et l'oubli,* 46–74, 121–80; Ali Haroun, *La Septième Wilaya,* 419–29.

3. Einaudi, *La Bataille,* 276 (quote, and Saddok's remark to Georges Mattei at the funeral); Tristan et al., *Le Silence,* 120–34, 135 (on Saddok); Kathryn Amdur, *Syndicalist Legacy,* xiii (on CFTC); Alistair Horne, *A Savage War of Peace,* 500–504.

4. Henry Rousso, *Vichy Syndrome,* 71–86; Alain Finkielkraut, *Remembering in Vain,* 25–32; Richard J. Golsan, ed., *Memory, the Holocaust, and French Justice,* 17–22, 184–95; Henry Rousso and Eric Conan, *Vichy: Un passé qui ne passe pas;* Pierre Truche (chief prosecutor at the trial of Paul Touvier), "Que faire Vichy?" special issue of *Esprit* (1992) on France's crimes-against-humanity statute.

5. Mireille Rosello, *Declining the Stereotype,* 18–20.

6. See also Weber, Nord, Zdatny, Soucy, Gallissot; William B. Cohen, "The Colonial Policy of the Popular Front," *FHS:* 368–93.

7. See also Lustick, Prochaska, Lebovics, Clancy-Smith, Gouda; also Kedward and Wood, Dina Sherzer, Jonathan G. Katz.

8. Antonio Gramsci, *Selections from the Prison Notebooks,* 326–27, 333; T. J. Jackson-Lears, "The Concept of Cultural Hegemony: Problems and Possiblities," *AHR* (1985): 567–93; see also Adamson, Anderson, Cammett, Femia, Fiori, Mannheim, Marzani, Bellamy and Schecter, and Karabel.

9. Quoted from Theodore William Allen, "Summary of the Argument," in *Cultural Logic* (1998): 13; idem, *The Invention of the White Race,* 2:253–59; Leften S. Stavrianos, *Global Rift,* 570–72; George M. Frederickson, *White Supremacy,* 232; Leonard Thompson, *A History of South Africa,* 159–60; see also Ignatiev, Bernstein, Saxton.

10. Antonio Gramsci, "The Southern Question," in *The Modern Prince and Other Writings,* 31–32; Eugene Genovese, "On Antonio Gramsci," *Studies on the Left* (1967): 83–108; Jackson-Lears "Concept," 590; see also Lustick, *Unsettled States;* Lebovics, *True France.* The Hexagon refers to the roughly six-sided boundaries of modern European France.

11. Mahfoud Bennoune, *The Making of Contemporary Algeria,* 40–42; idem, "Socio-economic Changes in Rural Algeria," *Peasant Studies Newsletter* (1973): 12; Charles-André Julien, *L'Histoire de l'Algérie contemporaine,* 1:316; de Tocqueville quote, "Deux Lettres sur l'Algérie" (1837), is in *Oeuvres complètes* 3, pt. 1, 129–53; V. G. Kiernan, *From Conquest to Collapse,* 71–77, 146; B. H. Liddell Hart, "Armies," in *New Cambridge Modern History,* 10:320–21; Domingo F. Sarmiento, *Viajes, 1845–1847: Collected Works,* 5:218–19; Louis Bertrand, *Un grand Africain: Le maréchal de Saint-Anaud,* 44–45; Raphael Danziger, *Abd al-Qadir and the Algerians,* 6–21.

12. Bennoune, *Contemporary Algeria,* 54–57; Pierre Gaffarel, *L'Algérie: Histoire, conquête, et colonisation,* 48; Ageron, *Les Algériens musulmans et*

la France, 1:548; Philippe Lucas and Jean-Claude Vatin, eds., *L'Algérie des anthropologues*, 179–89; Augustin Bernard, *Enquête sur l'habitation rurale des indigènes de l'Algérie*, 123–24.

13. *HAC*, 11–13, cites Warnier's speeches in the Chamber of Deputies.

14. Ibid., 23–26, 189, 251; Ageron, *Les Algériens musulmans*, 1:173–76; Vincent Confer, *France and Algeria*, 14, 29–31; David Prochaska, *Making Algeria French*, 232; James J. Cooke, "The Magrhib through French Eyes, 1880–1929," in James J. Cooke and Alf A. Heggoy, eds., *Through Foreign Eyes*, 66–67.

15. Jules Cambon, *Le Gouvernement général de l'Algérie*, 59–60 (my trans.); Roger Murray, "The Algerian Revolution," *New Left Review* (1963): 14–65, viz. 29.

16. Jules Ferry, *Le Gouvernement de l'Algérie*; Edward Behr, *The Algerian Problem*, 31; see also Ian Lustick, *State-Building Failure*, 63; see also Betts, *Assimilation*.

17. Charles-Robert Ageron, *L'Anticolonialism en France de 1871 à 1914*, 38–41; Confer, *France and Algeria*, 14, 37; Jonnart and Bourde, *Le Temps*, 12 May 1912.

18. Stuart M. Persell, *The French Colonial Lobby*, 39–40; Lebovics, *The Alliance of Iron and Wheat*, 157–58; Raoul Girardet, *L'Idée coloniale en France de 1871 à 1962*, 13–14; J. M. Mayeur, *Les Débuts de la Troisième République, 1871–1898*, 133–53, 135–36; Charles Alfred Perkins, "French Catholic Opinion and Imperial Expansion, 1880–1886," Ph.D. diss., Harvard University, 1964, 172–246; Walter D. Gray, "French Algerian Policy during the Second Empire," *Proceedings of the Western Society for French History* (1976): 477–89; Rand Edwards, "Cardinal Lavigerie and the Imperialism of the Third Republic," *Proceedings of the French Historical Society* (1977): 174–87; Joseph Dean O'Donnell, *Lavigerie in Tunisia*, 17, 149, 158, 169, 182–83, 195, 201–3; William Burridge, *Destiny Africa*, 105–10, 187–88; Bernard Arens, *Manuel des Missions Catholiques*, 86–89.

19. Patricia Lorcin, *Imperial Identities*, 153, 183–86, 198–211; Lucas and Vatin, *L'Algérie des anthropologues*, 130–34, 161–67, 195–96; Auguste Pomel, *Des races indigènes de l'Algérie et du rôle que leur réservent leurs aptitudes*, 5–7, 56–60; Louis Bertrand, *Le Sang des races*, 8–13; Girardet, *L'idée coloniale*, 244–45; Jules Harmand, *Domination et colonisation*, 171; Confer, *France and Algeria*, 19–20, 73; Raymond Betts, *Uncertain Dimensions*, 52–54; Jean Cazeneuve, *Lucien Lévy-Bruhl et son oeuvre*, 20.

20. *HAC*, 344.

21. Prochaska, *Making Algeria French*, 189–90; Stephen Wilson, *Ideology and Experience*, 230–33; *HAC*, 366; Richard S. Levy, *Antisemitism*, 115–25; see also Geehr, Mendelsohn, Lichten, Heller, Levin, Klier and Lambroza, Arendt; Richard Abel, "The 'Blank Screen of Reception' in Early French Cin-

ema," *IRIS* (1990): 40–41; on "cementing," see Emile Durkheim, *Les Règles de la méthode sociologique.*

22. Michel Ansky, *Les Juifs d'Algérie du Décret Crémieux à la Libération,* 38–40; André Chouraqui, *Histoire de Juifs d'Afrique du Nord,* 289–95; Geneviève Dermenjian, *La Crise anti-juive oranaise,* 53–54; on AIU, see Chouraqui, Laskier, Abitbol, Rodrigue.

23. Edward W. Said, "Orientalism Reconsidered," *Race and Class* (1985): 1–15; see also Sadik Jalal al-'Azm, Barsamian, and articles by Daniel Singer, *Nation,* 1 Aug. 1987, 18 June 1988, 20 Apr. 1992, 25 May 1992, 19 July 1993, 5 Sept. 1994; Finkielkraut, *Remembering,* 25–37.

2. The Form of Rule in Cultural Context

1. Marcia Landy, *Film, Politics, and Gramsci,* 99 (quote), 100, 157; Marcia Landy, *Cinematic Uses of the Past,* esp. chap. 2, "Which Way Is West? Americanism, History, and the Italian Western," 67–106.

2. Landy, *Film, Politics, and Gramsci,* 99–100.

3. Chinua Achebe, "An Image of Africa: Racism in Conrad's *Heart of Darkness,*" in *Heart of Darkness* (1988), 251–52, 261 (quote); Vanessa Schwartz, *Spectacular Realities,* 134–37, 149–50, 177–99.

4. Martine Astier Loutfi, *Littérature et colonialisme,* 24–27; Alec G. Hargreaves, *The Colonial Experience in French Fiction,* 41–45; Pierre Loti, *Le Roman d'un spahi,* 18, 115, 117, 158, 179, 253; Pierre Loti, *Romance of a Spahi,* 15, 36–37, 43, 202, 211–16, 222, 236, 252–64, 270–76; Léon Fanoudh-Siefer, *Le mythe du nègre et de l'Afrique noire dans la littérature française,* 12–14, 104–9, 187; Jan Nederveen Pieterse, *White on Black,* 13, 57–63, 177–83; Paul Morand, *Paris-Tombouctou,* 267–70.

5. Bibliothèque Forney, 1, rue du Figuier, Paris 75004, Fonds Iconographique, Cartes Postales, "Scènes et types du Maroc par Marcellin Flandin, artiste photographe, Editions "MARS," 20 cartes de luxe en héliogravure"": Forney holds several hundred cards from the Maghreb; Adonis Kyrou, *L'Age d'or de la carte postale,* 10–16; Madeleine Rebérioux, "La carte postale de grève: Propos sur une collection et une exposition," *Movement Sociale* (1984): 141–44; David Prochaska, "The Archive of *Algérie Imaginaire,*" *History and Anthropology* (1990): 375–76; Aline Ripert and Claude Frère, *La Carte Postale, son histoire, sa fonction sociale,* 35, 94–95; also on postcards: David H. Slavin, "Anticolonialism and the French Left," 82–83.

6. Malek Alloula, *The Colonial Harem,* 11–18, 26–35, 72–83, 98–105; Elizabeth Anne McCauley, *Industrial Madness,* 149–94; Kyrou, *L'Age d'or,* 106–40; Annie Stora-Lamarre, *L'Enfer de la IIIè République,* 202–12; Mieke Bal, "The Politics of Citation," *Diacritics* (1991): 25–45; Sarah Graham-

Brown, *Images of Women*, 134–39; see also Catherine A. Lutz and Jane L. Collins, *Reading National Geographic*.

7. Prochaska, "Archive," 373–75.

8. Ada Martinkus-Zemp, "Européocentrisme et exotisme: L'Homme blanc et la femme noire dans la littérature française de l'entre-deux-guerres," *Cahiers d'Etudes Africains* (1973): 61.

9. Karen Offen, "Liberty, Equality, and Justice for Women: The Theory and Practice of Feminism in 19th Century Europe," in Bridenthal, Koonz, and Stuard, eds., *Becoming Visible;* Bonnie Anderson and Judith Zinsser, *A History of Their Own*, 2:367–70.

10. Grace Corneau, *La femme aux colonies*, 47, 49–56, 73–74; Hubertine Auclert, *Les Femmes arabes en Algérie*, 49; Wil Swearingen, *Moroccan Mirages*, 15–35; Graham-Brown, *Images of Women*, 17–19, 21–23; Steven C. Hause, with Anne R. Kenney, *Women's Suffrage and Social Politics in the French Third Republic*, 46; Steven C. Hause, *Hubertine Auclert*, chap. 7; Julia Clancy-Smith, "Islam, Gender, and Identities in the Making of French Algeria, 1830–1962," in Clancy-Smith and Gouda, eds., *Domesticating the Empire*, 154–74; Rana Kabbani, intro. to Eberhardt, *Passionate Nomad*, vii–x, and Eberhardt, ibid., 100; Julia Clancy-Smith, "The 'Passionate Nomad' Reconsidered," in Nupur Chaudhuri and Margaret Strobel, eds., *Western Women and Imperialism*, 62–67, 70, 73; see also Annette Kobak, *Isabelle*.

11. Mary Louise Roberts, "Samson and Delilah Revisited: The Politics of Women's Fashion in 1920s France," *AHR* (1993): 662, 683; Elizabeth Ezra, "Colonialism Exposed: Miss France d'Outre-Mer, 1937," in Ungar and Conley, eds., *Identity Papers*, 50–62; Alice Y. Kaplan, *Reproductions of Banality*, 101–6; Sandy Flitterman-Lewis, *To Desire Differently*, 184–85; William Schneider, *Quality and Quantity;* Offen, "Liberty, Equality, and Justice," 359–62; see also Gwendolyn Mink, *The Wages of Motherhood*.

12. Irene L. Szyliowicz, *Pierre Loti and the Oriental Woman*, 92–93, 118–19; Rana Kabbani, *Europe's Myths of Orient*, 50–51; Mary Ann Doane, "The Clinical Eye: Medical Discourses in the 'Woman's Film,'" in Susan Rubin Suleiman, ed., *The Female Body in Western Culture*, 152–74, on "hysterical" narrative; *Mists*, 222–31, 378 n. 71; Claude Gauteur and Ginette Vincendeau, *Jean Gabin: Anatomie d'un mythe*, 147: In the director's version, Viviane Romance's perfume drives Gabin to shoot her husband, his closest friend and rival, wrecking their dream. The producers changed the ending to a scene where the men reject her and celebrate, dancing through the night.

13. Martinkus-Zemp, "Européocentrisme et exotisme": 60–81; Fatima Mernissi, *Beyond the Veil;* Fatna Sabbah, *Women in the Muslim Unconscious;* Barbara Stowasser, "Women's Issues in Modern Islamic Thought," in Judith E. Tucker, ed., *Arab Women*, 3–28; Judith E. Tucker, "The Arab Family in

History: 'Otherness' and the Study of the Family," ibid., 195–207. esp. 195–97 and intro., x.

14. Victoria de Grazia, "Mass Culture and Sovereignty: The American Challenge to European Cinemas, 1920–1960," *Journal of Modern History* (1989): 53–87, 70 (quote).

15. Jacqueline Lenoir, "Les grandes enquêtes de *Ciné-Miroir:* Blonde ou Brune?" *C-M* (1928): 403; "*La Femme idéale,*" *PV* (1935); "La Vie du cinéma," *PV* (1937); Gisèle de Biezville, "Tailleurs de sport," *PV* (1938); from the 1920s, see also *C-M,* "Attitudes" (1929); see also "Un original concours au studio" (1925), esp. the photo; see also "*L'art de séduire*" (1928); "*Mon idéal masculin*" (1929); see also Ella Shohat, "Gender and the Culture of Empire: Toward a Feminist Ethnography of the Cinema," *Quarterly Review of Film and Video* (1991): 45–84; Ella Shohat and Robert Stam, *Unthinking Eurocentrism,* 164; Richard Dyer, *White,* 42–43; see also Gladwell, McCracken.

16. Gisèle de Biezville, "Teints Pales ou Brulés," *PV* (1937). De Biezville wrote: "Rochelle Hudson, son teint de brune se pare sous l'effet des rayons solaires, d'une belle teint cuivrée dont maintes jeunes femmes sont jalouses. Mais sa coquetterie lui défend de rester longtemps au soleil, car si on recherche ce ton chaud, on n'aime plus, par contre, les tons qui nous font ressembler aux métisses."

17. David Lloyd George, *Memoirs of the Peace Conference,* 1:362 (Clemenceau quote); W. P. Crozier, "France and her 'Black Empire,'" *New Republic* 37, 23 Jan. 1924, 222–24; Ezra, "Colonialism Exposed," 50–51, 61.

18. Steven Ungar, "*La Maison du Maltais* as Text and Document," in Sherzer, ed., *Cinema, Colonialism, Postcolonialism,* 42–46; Jean Vignaud, *La Maison du Maltais,* 78–80; Lorcin, *Imperial Identities,* 218–21; Charles Géniaux, *Le Choc des races;* Ferdinand Duchêne, *Kamir: Roman d'une femme arabe,* in *Le Petite Illustration* (1926); *Au Miroir,* 79; "*L'Esclave blanche,*" *C-M* (1927); "La Symphonie pathétique," *C-M* (1929); Girardet, *L'Idée coloniale,* 422, cites three French Indochinese novels about the perils of race mixing: Jean d'Esme, *Thi-Ba, Fille d'Annam,* Jean Casseville, *Sao, L'amoureuse tranquille,* and Jean Marquet, *Le Jaune et le blanc;* d'Esme was also a documentary filmmaker who worked in French Sudan, viz. Pierre Leprohon, *L'Exotisme et le cinéma,* 216–21.

19. On the silent version of *Sarati le Terrible,* see *C-M* (1 Sept. 1923); on the remake, see *PV* (13 May 1937): 10; *PV* (5 Aug. 1937): 5–6.

20. Jean Vignaud, *Sarati le Terrible,* 202, 246.

21. Ibid., 189–90.

22. "*Sarati,*" *C-M* (1923); J.-M. Huard, "*Sarati,*" *PV* (1937).

23. Ginette Vincendeau, "Daddy's Girls," *IRIS* 5 (1988): 74; Theodore Zeldin, *France, 1848–1945,* 285–314; James McMillan, *Housewife or Harlot.*

24. Pierre Bourdieu, *The Algerians*, 96–98, 102; Fuad Khuri, "Parallel Cousin Marriage Reconsidered," *Man* (1970). Qur'anic law entitles daughters to one-half the sons' share of an estate, making cousin marriage more complex: Robert Cresswell, "Lineage Endogamy among Maronite Mountaineers," and Ian Whitaker, "Familial Roles in the Extended Patrilineal Kingroup in Northern Albania," in J. G. Peristiany, ed., *Mediterranean Family Structures*, 101–14, 195–203, and intro., 7–12; cousin marriage is discussed also by Banfield, Braudel, Goody, Schilcher, and Tillion.

25. Jean Vignaud, *Notre enfant, l'Algérie*, 81–82 (quote), 238–39.

26. Ibid., 11, 55–65, 94–95, 102–13, 150–65, 200 (quote), 201.

27. *Générique*, 133–35, 152–54, 158–60 for *Bourrasque;* René Lehmann, "*Bourrasque*," *PV*, no. 345 (27 June 1935): 7.

28. *Bourrasque* (1935) dir: Pierre Billon, story: Léopold Gomez; Lehmann, "*Bourrasque*"; *Au Miroir*, 145–48; *Générique*, 135, 152–54, 158–60.

29. André Gide, *The Immoralist*, 169–70; Justin O'Brien, intro. to *The Journals of André Gide*, 1:vi–xi, 35–36; Antony Copley, *Sexual Moralities in France, 1780–1980*, 159–70.

30. Henry Bataille, *Maman Colibri* (four-act comedy that premiered 8 Nov. 1904), 40–41, 46–47, 62–64; *Au Miroir*, 179–81; Raymond Chirat, *Julien Duvivier*, 6, 98–99.

31. Francis Jennings, "The Indians' Revolution," in Alfred Young, ed., *The American Revolution*, 75; Sorlin, "The Fanciful Empire," *French Cultural Studies* 2, no. 5 (1991): 150.

32. See Jeanne Bowlan, "Polygamists Need Not Apply: Becoming a French Citizen in Colonial Algeria, 1918–1939," paper presented at the Western Society for French History Conference, 31 Oct. 1996; Bowlan cites *Journal Officiel: Débats—Sénat*, 21 Mar. 1935, 347–57.

33. Robin D. G. Kelley, "Notes on Deconstructing 'The Folk,'" *AHR* (1992): 1405.

34. A. S. Kanya-Forstner, *Conquest of the Western Sudan*, 257–64; Michel Pierre, "L'affaire Voulet-Chanoine," *L'Histoire* (1984): 67–71.

35. Sarah Maza, "Stories in History: Cultural Narratives in Recent Works in European History," *AHR* (1996): 1493–515.

3. Heart of Darkness, Heart of Light

1. Léon Fanoudh-Sieter, *Le mythe du nègre et de l'Afrique noire dans la littérature française de 1800 à la 2e guerre mondiale;* Pieterse, *White on Black*, 159; William H. McNeill, "Mythistory, or Truth, Myth, History, and Historians," *AHR* (1985); see also Lebovics, *True France;* Fernand Braudel, *The Identity of France;* Edward Said, *Orientalism;* Kabbani, *Europe's Myths.*

2. Achebe, "Image of Africa"—a supplementary reading in the 1988 Norton edition of Conrad's *Heart of Darkness,* 251–52, 261.

3. Abel, Boulanger, and Megherbi focus on the 1921 film but also refer to the talkie and the novel; Pabst made French, German, and English versions in 1932; I watched a video of "The Mistress of Atlantis" (in English) held by the UCLA Film Archive. The sound quality is poor. See also Martine Astier Loutfi, "North Africa in the French Movies," in Cooke and Heggoy, eds., *Proceedings,* 136; Karl Sierek ("The Primal Scene of the Cinema: Four Fragments from *The Mistress of Atlantis,*" in Eric Rentschler, ed., *The Films of G. W. Pabst*). Sierek saw the German-language *Die Herrin von Atlantis,* and there are some discrepancies between English and German versions. To maintain narrative flow, I refer to specific versions only when it affects the argument.

4. Louis Delluc, "Notes," *Cinéa* (1921), and "Quelques films français," *Cinéa* (1921), cited in *First Wave,* 154–56; Boulanger, *Cinéma colonial,* 42; *Au Miroir,* 85; George Root, "Sur la piste du Hoggar" (interview with Pabst), *PV* (1932).

5. John H. Galey, "Bridegrooms of Death," *JCH* (1969).

6. Sierek, "Primal Scene," 126, 128, 133.

7. Ibid., 128–29, 134, 139, 144–45; *Générique,* 169, 172–73.

8. Quote from René Lehmann's summary, *"L'Atlantide,"* *PV* (1932); on the "Aryan model," see Martin Bernal, *Black Athena,* vol. 1; Molly M. Levine and Robert Pounder review of Bernal, *AHR* (1992): 440–64.

9. Charles-Robert Jouvé, *Leçons d'histoire et de civilisation,* 8–10; Emmanuel Sivan, "Colonialism and Popular Culture in Algeria," *JCH* 14 (Jan. 1979): 26; Fanny Colonna, *Instituteurs Algériens, 1883–1939,* 163–65, 172 (on report cards); Albert Memmi, *The Colonizer and the Colonised,* 104–5; John Ruedy, *Modern Algeria,* 119–21.

10. Glenn D. Kittler, *The White Fathers,* 100–105; O'Donnell, *Lavigerie;* Loutfi, *Littérature et colonialisme,* 52–55; Louis Noir (nom de plume of Lt. Col. Salman, author of more than a hundred "dime novels" published by Bibliothèque universelle de poche) wrote a 3-vol. account of Flatters's mission.

11. Porch, *Conquest of the Sahara,* 115–24, 136–46, 156–57, 211.

12. The term *housebreaking* is used by Lyautey, writing to Poincaré, 19 Feb. 1924, in Pierre Lyautey, ed., *Lyautey l'Africain: Textes et lettres,* 4:245–50.

13. Lebovics, *True France,* 52, 81; Michèle Salinas, *Voyages et voyageurs en Algérie, 1830–1930,* 69–71, 77, 79, 99; France, *Annuaire statistique (AS)* (1930), 313; *AS* (1935), 298; *AS* (1936), 303; The *AS* chart "Mouvement des voyageurs entre l'Algérie et l'extérieur" showed an average of ca. 180,000 per year; on postcards, Prochaska, "Archive," 414–16; Alloula, *Colonial Harem,* 3–7.

14. Edmund Burke III, "The Image of the Moroccan State," in Micaud and

Gellner, eds., *Arabs and Berbers;* Ageron, *Les Algériens musulmans,* 1:268–83, 2:873; Lebovics, *True France,* 135–49.

15. Loti, *Roman d'un spahi,* 115, 117, 179, 253; Hargreaves, *Colonial Experience,* 41–45; Loutfi, *Littérature et colonialisme,* 24–26; Fanoudh-Siefer, *Le Mythe du nègre,* 13, 107, 187; Ada Martinkus-Zemp, *Le Blanc et le Noir.*

16. Pierre Loti, *Vers Ispahan,* 294, cited in Hargreaves, *Colonial Experience,* 37; Basil Davidson, *Lost Cities of Africa,* 9–14; J. H. Greenberg, *Studies in African Linguistic Classification,* the first study of African language origins to counter the "Hamitic hypothesis."

17. Ruedy, *Modern Algeria,* 9; Robin Bidwell, *Morocco under Colonial Rule,* 48–49, quoting General Brémond, Professor Bernard, Mostafa Bechir, and Mehdi Ben Barka; Philip E. Ross, "Hard Words: Trends in Linguistics," *Scientific American* (1991): 136–47; Luigi Luca Cavalli-Sforza, "Genes, Peoples, and Languages," *Scientific American* (1991): 107–8; Basil Davidson, "The Ancient World and Africa: Whose Roots?" *Race and Class* (1987): 8–11; Michael Brett and Elizabeth Fentress, *The Berbers,* 1995; see also Asante, Diop.

18. Kiernan, *Conquest to Collapse,* 71–76; Liddell-Hart, "Armies," 320–21; Dennis Mack Smith, *Mussolini's Roman Empire,* viii, 32, 42–43, 84; Prochaska, *Making Algeria French;* Swearingen, *Moroccan Mirages,* 28–35.

19. Alali al-Fasi, *The Independence Movements of Muslim North Africa,* 118–19; Porch, *Conquest,* 65.

20. Davidson, *Lost Cities,* 97 (Ibn Khaldun); Richard Bulliet, *The Camel and the Wheel,* 216–36; William H. McNeill, "The Eccentricity of Wheels," *AHR* (1987): 111–26.

21. Alan K. Smith, *Creating a World Economy,* 142–50; Porch, *Conquest,* 67–75; Eric Hobsbawm, *Primitive Rebels;* see also Anstey, Cooper, Curtin, Inikori, Wolf.

22. Porch, *Conquest,* 236–39, 259, 262, 271–72.

23. Duse, *African Times and Orient Review,* quoted in Immanuel Geiss, *The Pan African Movement,* 229–30 and 222–28 (Duse as colleague to W. E. B. DuBois and mentor to Marcus Garvey); Immanuel Geiss, *War and Empire in the Twentieth Century,* 43.

24. Edmund Burke III, "Moroccan Resistance, Pan-Islam, and German War Strategy, 1914 to 1918," *Francia* (1975): 434–64; Charles de Foucauld, *Reconnaissance au Maroc;* Porch, *Conquest,* 299–301; al-Fasi, *Independence Movements,* 50–51, 118.

25. Jacques Delmas, *Mes hommes au feu;* Porch, *Conquest,* 278–86; al-Fasi, *Independence Movements,* 118.

26. Ginette Vincendeau, "French Cinema of the 1930s: Social Text and Context," 173. The three top films were *César* (Marcel Pagnol), an oedipal

drama set in a Marseilles café; *Le Roi* (Pierre Colombier), about the love affairs of a Ruritanian king; and *Mayerling* (Anatole Litwak). During the Popular Front, escapism and Roman Catholic edification filled the screen. In 1938, the most popular film in France was Disney's *Snow White and the Seven Dwarfs*.

27. Lucien Wahl, "*L'Appel du silence,*" *PV* (1936); J.-M. Huard, "Léon Poirier nous parle de Charles de Foucauld," *PV* (1936); review of *L'Appel du silence* in *l'Ami du Peuple* (11 Oct. 1936). The film has become a cult classic for contemporary France's racist Right; Raymond Chirat, ed., *Catalogue des films françaises,* 1929–39; Ernst Gellner, *Muslim Society,* 155–65; Fanny Colonna, "Cultural Resistance and Religious Legitimacy in Colonial Algeria," *Economy and Society* 3 (1974): 233–52; Porch, *Conquest,* 284–86.

28. Porch, *Conquest,* 287–89; François Dessommes, *Notes sur l'histoire des Kabyles:* the Algerians allowed the Pères Blancs to stay after 1962.

29. Louis-Marie Clénet, "Benoit et le mouvement intellectuel français de l'entre-deux-guerres," in Edmond Jouve, Gilbert Pilleul, and Charles Saint-Prot, eds., *Pierre Benoit, témoin de son temps,* 178, 185.

30. Louis Chaigne, *Vies et oeuvres d'écrivains,* 237–40, 249–52; Jouve, Pilleul, and Saint-Prot, *Pierre Benoit,* 19, 54–57, 64, 127, 135–37; Sanford Elwitt, *The Third Republic Defended,* 293; Benjamin Martin, *Hypocrisy of Justice in the Belle Epoque;* Roberts, "Samson and Delilah Revisited": 657–84, esp. 668–74 on conservative, Catholic, and natalist criticism of the *femme moderne;* see Victor Margueritte, *La Garçonne.*

31. Chirat, ed., *Catalogue,* 1919–29 and 1929–39; Sorlin, "Fanciful Empire": 143–44 (on *l'Argent*).

Films from works by Emile Zola: *Le Rêve* (1930, Jacques de Baroncelli); *L'Assomoir* (1933, Gaston Roudès); *L'Argent* (1936, Pierre Billon); *La Bête humain* (1938, Jean Renoir).

Films from works by Pierre Loti: *Pêcheur d'Islande* (1915, Henri Pouctal; 1924, J. de Baroncelli; 1933, Pierre Guerlais); *Le Roman d'un spahi* (1914, H. Pouctal; 1936, Michel Bernheim); and *Ramuntcho* (1918 and 1937, both by de Baroncelli). *Pêcheur* is set on the Côtes-du-Nord, *Ramuntcho* on the Basque coast; only *Le Roman d'un spahi,* set in the Basque region and West Africa, qualifies as colonial cinema.

Films from works by Pierre Benoit include *L'Atlantide* (1921, Feyder; 1932, Pabst); *Koenigsmark* (1923, Léonce Perret; 1935 and 1952, Maurice Tourneur); *La Ronde de nuit* (1925, Marcel Silver, screenplay by Benoit); *Le Puits de Jacob* (1925, Edward José); *Chatelaine du Liban* (1926, Marco de Gastyne; 1933, Jean Epstein; 1956, Richard Pottier); *Princesse Mandane* (Benoit's *l'Oublié*; 1928, Germain Dulac); *Les nuits moscovites* (1934, Alexandre Grandowsky); *Boissière* (1937, Fernand Rivers, screenplay by Benoit); *Angelica* (1939, Jean Choux).

Films from Jean Vignaud's novels: *La Maison du Maltais, Sarati le Terrible,* and *Vénus.* The first two were remade in the 1930s.

32. Pierre Benoit, *L'Atlantide;* Chaigne, *Vies,* 240; Eberhard Zangger, *The Flood from Heaven: Deciphering the Atlantis Legend.*

33. Lehmann, *"L'Atlantide."*

34. *Cinémagazine* (17 June 1921).

35. "In the mountains of the Hoggar / A queen with an evil gaze / Reigns, it is said / Antinéa is her name"; quoted in Boulanger, *Cinéma Colonial,* 132; *Au Miroir,* 85–87.

36. "Extraits du carnet d'un filmeur, par Jacques Feyder," doss., *L'Atlantide,* 1st folder, Bibliothèque de l'IDHEC, Palais de Chaillot, Avenue Albert de Mun, Paris; letter from Jacques Feyder, *PV* (1929) on the rerelease of *L'Atlantide;* Boulanger, *Cinéma colonial,* 38: 131–41 (Feyder's 1921 version). Frédérique Moreau, "Le cinéma colonial: Un sous-genre, le film légionnaire dans les années 30," *L'Avant-scène* (1982) lists eight remakes besides *L'Atlantide: Les Cinq Gentlemen maudits* (Luitz-Morat, 1919; J. Duvivier, 1931); *Sarati le Terrible* (L. Mercanton, 1922; A. Hugon, 1937); *Les Hommes nouveaux* (L. Donatien, 1922; M. l'Herbier, 1936); *Le Prince Jean* (R. Hervil, 1927; J. de Marguenat, 1934); *Le Maison du Maltais* (H. Fescourt, 1927; P. Chenal, 1938); *Feu!* (J. de Baroncelli, 1927; J. de Baroncelli, 1937); *L'Occident* (H. Fescourt, 1928; H. Fescourt, 1938); and *Le Roman d'un spahi* (H. Pouctal, 1914; J. Gremillon, 1936).

37. *C-M,* no. 1 (1922), sixteen tabloid pages, is devoted entirely to text and photos of Feyder's film; *L'Atlantide* script and program (8 pp.), Cinémathèque français, no. 664 A-B-C, Bibliothèque de l'IDHEC.

38. Jean Angelo, "Au hasard de mes souvenirs," *C-M* (1928); Stacia Napierkowska, "Mes souvenirs," *C-M* (1923); Yves Dartois and Marcel Carné, "Les Deux Atlantide," *PV* (1932); Root, "Sur la piste du Hoggar"; Lehmann, "*L'Atlantide*"; *Au Miroir,* 85–87; Jacques Feyder and Françoise Rosay, *Le cinéma, notre métier,* 14, 21–22, 50; de Grazia, "Mass Culture and Sovereignty," 53–87, esp. 57–58, 61–65, 70; Douglas Gomery, "Europe Converts to Sound," and Dudley Andrew, "Sound in France: The Origins of a Native School," *Yale French Studies* (1980): 80–93, 94–114.

39. Freud, *Civilization and Its Discontents,* 44, 50–51, 61, 69; Marianna Torgovnick, *Gone Primitive,* 198–204, 215–16; Uli Linke, "Formation of White Space"; Betts, *Uncertain Dimensions,* 49–53; Lucien Lévy-Bruhl, *La Mentalité primitive,* preface; idem, *Les Fonctions mentales dans les sociétés inférieurs.*

40. Salinas, *Voyages et voyageurs,* 54–56, 70, 82.

41. André Gide, *The Journals,* 1:36; Gareth Stanton, "The Oriental City: A North African Itinerary," in *Third Text,* 3–38, 21; Wyndham Lewis, *Journey into Barbary,* 25.

42. Napierkowska, "Mes souvenirs": 157; Angelo, "Au hasard de mes souvenirs": 742; Root, "Sur la piste du Hoggar."

43. Jean Benoît-Lévy, *The Art of the Motion Picture,* 167, 214–16; Timothy Mitchell, *Colonising Egypt,* 4–5 (on "Beaudrillard moments"); Boulanger, *Cinéma Colonial,* 117–18.

44. Kiernan, *Conquest to Collapse,* 127, 130.

45. Porch, *Conquest,* 195–97.

46. Ibid., 183; Kanya-Forstner, *Conquest of Western Sudan,* 263–74; *FFL,* 249–50.

47. Achebe, "Image of Africa," 261.

4. French Cinema's Other First Wave

1. T. J. Clark, *The Painting of Modern Life,* 205–58; Noel Burch, *Life to Those Shadows,* 43–49, 55–71, 73–75; Noel Burch, ed., *In and Out of Synch;* Henri Fescourt, *La Foi et les montagnes,* 47; Jean-Paul Sartre, *The Words,* 118; Abel, "Blank Screen": 28, 32, 40–41; Richard Abel, *The Ciné Goes to Town,* 3–10, 58, 286–89; Donald Crafton, *Emile Cohl, Caricature, and Film,* 60–63; Lenard Berlanstein, *The Working People of Paris,* 122–27 (on leisure); Tyler Stovall, *The Rise of the Paris Red Belt,* 148; see also August, Miller, Nord, Schneider *(Empire),* and Weber.

2. Narrowly defined, 46 feature films out of the 1,055 made in the 1920s and 85 out of the 1,305 made in the 1930s were colonial. Sorlin, "Fanciful Empire": 150–51, lists 62 colonial films: 13 made in Morocco, 14 in the Sahara, 5 in Algeria, 4 in Tunisia, 9 in Africa, 7 in the Near East, 8 in the Far East; Geneviève Nestorenko, "L'Afrique de l'autre," in *Générique;* François Chevaldonné, "Notes sur le cinéma colonial en Afrique du Nord: Naissance et fonctionnement d'un code," in Sylvie Dallet, ed., *Guerres révolutionnaires: Histoire et cinéma;* Christian Jouhaud, "L'Afrique noire au cinéma," *Mouvement social* (1984): 83–89; Leprohon, *L'Exotisme et le cinéma,* 203–48.

3. François Laurent, *Le Cinéma,* 24 May 1912, quoted in Burch, *Life to Those Shadows,* 52–54.

4. *Au Miroir,* 13–38; "Discours prononcés au banquet de la chambre syndicale française de cinématographie et des industries s'y rattachant," 29 Mar. 1914—speech by M. Demaria, repr. in *Le Film* and cited by Marcel l'Herbier, *Intelligence du cinématographe,* 97–100.

5. Albert Sarraut, quoted in Jacques Marseille, *L'Age d'or de la France coloniale,* 5.

6. A. S. [Albert Sarraut], "Ciné-Miroir aux colonies: En Indo-Chine," *C-M* (1922); Thomas G. August, *The Selling of the Empire,* 101–4, 103; Ilya Ehrenburg, *Usines de rêves,* 179–80.

7. AN, Papiers Albert Thomas, 94 AP, carton 394, Thomas to Alexandre

Varenne, 2 Aug., 6 Oct. and 20 Oct. 1927; AN 94 AP 380 for Thomas's aid to Gance; see also Oved, Sivan, and both titles by Cohen.

8. *C-M* (15 June 1923): 183, 186–87; James Clifford, *The Predicament of Culture*, 136–37, cites Barthes; Michael B. Miller, *Shanghai on the Métro*, 394–95 n. 89: Plon printed 57,000 copies of Georges-Marie Haardt and Louis Audoin-Dubreuil, *La Croisière noire*, double the usual run; on La Croisière jaune, see also Miller, *Shanghai*, 280–304.

9. Salinas, *Voyages et voyageurs*, 70; Marc Allégret, *Carnets du Congo: Voyage avec Gide*, 53: Allégret's colonial films were *En Tripolitaine* (1927), *L'Île de Djerba* (1928), and *Papoul* (1928); Jouhaud, "L'Afrique noire au cinéma": 83–89; Mary Louise Pratt, *Imperial Eyes*, 155–71; see also Enloe, Gide *(Voyage)*, Leiris.

10. Léon Poirier, "Le cinéma exotique," *C-M* (1926); Raymond de Nys, "Comment fut tournée La Croisière noire" (interview with Poirier), *C-M* (1926); *First Wave*, 152 (on Poirier).

11. Napierkowska, "Mes souvenirs"; "Amours Exotiques," *C-M* (1928); "Siliva le Zoulou," *C-M* (1928).

12. "Un voyage chez les Pygmées," *C-M* (1929); "Une grande chasse aux gorilles," (1927); Jacques Bernier, "Cimbo," *C-M* (1930); "Face aux fauves" [on Mr. and Mrs. Martin Johnson in Central Africa], *C-M* (1924): 346–47; "Vers le Tchad," *C-M* (1925); "*Chang*" [docudrama on Indian tiger hunt], *C-M* (1927).

13. Ehrenburg, *Usine des rêves*, 171–77, on the lion attack; "Africa Speaks! First African Sound Film," *New York Times* (1930): on the day of the New York premiere, no audience reaction was reported; Georges-Henri Rivière, "L'Afrique vous parle," *PV* (1931): Rivière, assistant director of the Trocadero Museum, hints that scenes of a Massai lion hunt included some "anguishing" footage; Lebovics, *True France*, 149–56, 164–71, 176–83; Pierre Assouline, *Gaston Gallimard*, 172 (Simenon quote); Fenton Bresler, *The Mystery of Georges Simenon*.

14. McNeill, "Mythistory."

15. Police reports titled "Jean," no. A500, 9 June 1925, AN F-7 12953; *JOC*, 9 June 1925, 2612–13; Henri Barbé, "Souvenirs d'un dirigeant et militant communiste" (MS, Hoover Institution, Stanford, CA, n.d.), 82; *L'Humanité*, 10 June 1925; Robert Charvin, "Le PCF face à la guerre du Rif," *Abd el-Krim et la République du Rif, colloque*, 218–36.

16. *JOC*, 9 June 1925: 2612–13; *L'Humanité*, 10 June 1925; *L'Etincelle socialiste*, 19 June 1925: 20; on the "conspiracy," see Georges Oved, *La Gauche française et le nationalisme marocain*, 1:147–97, chap. 4, "Le 'complot bolchevique'"; Slavin, "Anticolonialism," 135–36, 164.

17. Luitz-Morat's, *Au Seuil du Harem* (1922), Viollet et Donatien's *Les Hommes nouveaux* (1922), and Le Somptier's *Les Fils du Soleil* (1924–25);

René Jeanne, "Le Maroc a l'écran," *Cinémagazine* (1922): 259–63; for a photo and the quote re. "*Les Fils du Soleil*," see Marcel Oms, "Un Cinéaste des années vingt: René le Somptier," *Cahiers de la cinémathèque* (1981): 211–12; "Le Visage de l'Islam fidèlement refleté par le cinéma français," *PV* (1938); V. Guillaume Danvers, "Au Seuil du Harem," *C-M* (1925).

18. All quotes are from Jeanne, "Le Maroc à l'écran," 262–63; Fescourt, *La Foi*, 347; Leprohon, *L'Exotisme*, 215.

19. Jeanne, "Le Maroc à l'écran," 259–62; "Les Hommes nouveaux," *C-M* (1923); Chirat, *Catalogue*, 1919–29.

20. Emile Mauchamp, *La Sorcellerie au Maroc*, 27–29, 41; Edmund Burke III, *Prelude to Protectorate, 1860–1912*, 95–97; Daniel Rivet, "Mines et politique au Maroc, 1907–1914," *Revue d'histoire moderne et contemporaine* (1979) 558–59; Magali Chappert, "Le Projet français de banque d'Etat du Maroc," *Revue français d'histoire d'outre-mer* (1975); see also Vandevoort, Katz.

21. Rom Landau, *Moroccan Drama*, 65; Burke, *Prelude*, 95–97, 106–25, esp. 117–18; Jean-Claude Allain, *Agadir, 1911*, 316–24, 339–40, 349–68; Slavin, "Anticolonialism," 11, 15, 17, 23. Standard texts—for example, William L. Langer, *Encyclopedia of World History*, 4th ed. (1968), 877, and Christopher M. Andrew and A. S. Kanya-Forstner, *The Climax of French Imperial Expansion, 1914–1924*, 37—ignore the Fulani, Sanga, Fang, and Baya inhabitants of the French Congo and German Cameroons.

22. "*C'était écrit*" (dir: Jules Pinchon and Daniel Quintin); "*In'ch'Allah!*" *C-M* (1923); interview with Stacia Napierkowski, *C-M* (1923); Oms, "*Un Cinéaste*": 208–10, on "*La Sultane d'Amour*" (Louis Nalpas, 1918).

23. The phrase *widowed land* is from Francis Jennings, *The Invasion of America*, 146–70.

24. Oms, "*Un Cinéaste*": 211–12.

25. Boulanger, *Cinéma Colonial*, 85, 92; Pierre Mercourt, "*Fils du Soleil*," review, *C-M* (1925); V. Guillaume Danvers, "Les films tournées au Maroc" (excerpts from Le Somptier's travel log), *C-M* (1925).

26. Slavin, "Anticolonialism," 58, 92, 146–48; in *L'Humanité*, 10 June, 1925, and *JOC*, 9 June, 1925, 2612–13; Berthon, in *L'Humanité*, 12 May 1925, cites articles in *L'Echo de Paris* and the *Star* (London); AN, ser. F-7, carton 13413, police report, 14 May 1925, no. F9869 (15 pp.).

27. David Woolman, *Rebels in the Rif*, 143; Vincent Sheean, *Personal History*, 85–86; Webb Miller, *I Found No Peace*, 159–60; Shannon Earl Fleming and Ann Fleming, "Primo de Rivera and Spain's Moroccan Problem," *JCH* (1977): 85–99; James A. Chandler, "Spain and Her Moroccan Protectorate, 1898–1927," *JCH* (1975); see also Boyd, Payne.

28. Gael Faim, "Une industrie-clé intellectuelle" and "Pour une politique française du Cinéma," in l'Herbier, *Intelligence*, 441–55; R. Ducasable, "Aug-

mentation des exportations," *Film-Revue* (1914); Colin Crisp, *The Classic French Cinema*, 1–42.

29. Crisp, *Classic French Cinema*, 37–42; Gael Faim and R. Ducasable, "Augmentation des Exportations," in l'Herbier, *Intelligence*, 427–28, 441–45; August, *Selling of the Empire*, 101 (on the 1927 law); Raymonde Borde, "The Golden Age: French Cinema of the 30s," in Mary Lea Bandy, ed., *Rediscovering French Film*, 67–70; Flitterman-Lewis, *To Desire Differently*, 169–87; *Mists*, 93–95; François Chevaldonné, "Fonctionnement d'une institution idéologique coloniale: La diffusion de cinéma dans les zones rurales d'Algérie avant la deuxième guerre mondiale," *RASJEP* (1975): 531–48; see also de Grazia, Moussinac, Sadoul.

30. [René Jeanne], "Nègres et peaux-rouges au cinéma," *C-M* (1922): 139.

31. "*L'Atlantide*," *C-M* (1922); *L'Atlantide* script and program (8 pp.), Cinémathèque français, no. 664 A-B-C, Bibliothèque de l'IDHEC, Palais de Chaillot, Paris.

32. Edith M. Hull, *The Sheik*, 122; Irving Shulman, *Valentino*, 128–29; Shohat and Stam, *Unthinking Eurocentrism*, 156–70.

33. *C-M*, no. 218 (7 June 1929); Gaylyn Studlar, *Mad Masquerade*, 150–98; *Variety Film Reviews, 1907–1980*; René Prédal (with Robert Florey, Valentino's cameraman), *Rudolph Valentino, 1895–1926* (supplement to *L'Avant-scène du cinéma*, May 1969): 219, 229, 241–45.

34. Shulman, *Valentino*, 252 (quote), 253, 262; Cecil B. DeMille, *Autobiography*; "*Le Fils du Cheik*," *C-M*, nos. 110–17 (15 Nov. 1926 to 1 Mar. 1927); "*La Glorieuse Reine de Saba*" (Fox Film), *C-M* (1922); "*Les Dernières Aventures de Tarzan*" (director Elmo Lincoln), *C-M* (1922); "*Robinson Crusoe*" (O.-J. Monat), *C-M* (1922); "*Le Voleur de Bagdad*" (Raoul Walsh), *C-M* (1924).

35. "*L'Arabe*," *C-M* (1925); "*Le Spahi*," *C-M* (1928): 276; Boulanger, *Cinéma Colonial*, 92; Leprohon, *Exotisme*, 206.

36. Harry Waldman, *Paramount in Paris*, vii–xix, 23; the following are quoted in *Mists*, 93–95: articles in *Film Mercury* (1930), *Variety* (1930), and *Fortune* (1947), on Paris Paramount and Western Electric, German GE competition over sound projection and recording equipment. In *T&C* 2:150 ff., Georges Altman, "Esprit du Film," *La Revue des vivants* (1931): 529–38; ibid., *La Revue des vivants* 2:80–86, esp. 85 on "Jewish imperialism"; see also Ezra *(Colonial Unconscious)*, Hayward.

37. De Grazia, "Mass Culture and Sovereignty," 85; Walt Disney, "*Blanche-Neige, ma dernière fille*" ("Snow White, my latest daughter"), *PV* (1938); Vincendeau, "French Cinema," 173–75.

38. Crisp, *Classic French Cinema*, 20 ("color cinematography [was] already well advanced in America by the end of the thirties"); "*Jardin d'Allah*," *PV* (1938): 8; "*Garden of Allah*" (Rex Ingram version 1927; remake 1936;

French release 1938). The director was Richard Boleslawski, producer, David O. Selznick; in color, with Marlene Dietrich, Charles Boyer, and Basil Rathbone. A Trappist monastery in North Africa whose monks have sworn a vow of silence makes a superior brandy. Brother Antoine (having been taught the formula by an elderly brother who has just died) loses his faith and flees into the world, leaving the monastery without a winemaker. He meets Dominie, a devout Catholic on a trip to North Africa to get over the death of her mother, and they fall in love. She rekindles his faith but loses him because he must return to the monastery; see my chap. 7 for the *Beau Geste* affaire.

39. "Le visage de l'Islam fidèlement réfleté par le cinéma français . . . mais travesti par Hollywood," *PV* (1938).

40. See the poll results in chap. 8, n. 43.

41. Joseph Boskin, *Sambo,* 137, illustrated advertisement of lynching with the motto "Hang 'em!/And Keep 'em Straight"; Michael Rogin, "'The Sword Became a Flashing Vision': D. W. Griffith's *The Birth of a Nation,*" *Representations* 151 (1985), on private screening for President Wilson; Robert Stam and Louise Spence, "Colonialism, Racism, and Representation," *Screen* (1983): 2–20; see also Bataille and Silet *(Pretend Indian Images),* Friar, Kabbani, Gilman, Alloula, Graham-Brown; *Générique,* 127.

42. Torgovnick, *Gone Primitive,* chap. 2, "Taking Tarzan Seriously," 42–72; John Newsinger, "Lord Greystoke and Darkest Africa: The Politics of the Tarzan Stories," *Race and Class* 28, no. 2 (1986): 59–71; Eric Cheyfitz, *The Poetics of Imperialism; La Librairie française* lists fifteen Tarzan novels printed from 1934 to 1940: four in 1937, four in 1938 and three in 1939; Henry Hardy Heins, *A Golden Anniversary Bibliography of Edgar Rice Burroughs,* 203–5 lists eight Tarzan books published by Librairie Hachette, 1937–39; Mansell's *National Union Catalogue* lists twenty-two Tarzan books first published between 1914 and 1932; fifteen were translated and published in France, 1934–41. The French did not translate Burroughs's many westerns, such as *Apache Devil* (1933), or his dozen books in the "Men from Mars" series or *Cave Girl* (1925) and *Jungle Girl* (1931).

43. "*Bouboule 1er, roi nègre,*" *PV,* no. 284 (1934); *[Bouboule]:* "Le parole est aux spectateurs," *PV,* no. 309 (1934); quote from Guy Hennebelle's preface to Boulanger, *Cinéma Colonial,* 7.

44. J.-K. Raymond-Millet, "Les nègres sont-ils photogéniques?" *C-M* (1929)—an example of the generic use of "Sénégalaises"; Claude Farèrre, *Quatorze histoire de soldats,* 195–204; idem, *Les Hommes nouveaux;* Myron Echenberg, *Colonial Conscripts,* chap. 3; Marc Michel, *L'Appel à l'Afrique,* 379–97.

45. Boskin, *Sambo,* 139; Pieterse, *White on Black,* 84–85; Claudie Roger, "Il était une fois . . . Banania," in Anne-Claude Lelieur and Bernard Mirabel, eds., *Négripub: L'image des Noirs dans la publicité depuis un siècle,* 144–52,

and plates #55, #77, #125; Ungar, *"La Maison du Maltais,"* 30–50; Jean Garrigues, *Banania;* John Mendenhall, *French Trademarks;* N. Robert Short, *Dada and Surrealism;* Helena Lewis, *The Politics of Surrealism;* Léopold Sédar Senghor, *Poèmes,* 55; Rosello, *Declining the Stereotype,* 4–5; see also Hergé, *Les aventures de Tintin au Congo;* Marie-Rose Maurin Abomo, "Tintin au Congo ou la Négrerie mise en clichés," in P. Halen and János Riesz, *Images d'Afrique et du Congo/Zaire dans les lettres Belges de langue française et alentours,* 151–62.

46. "Le visage de l'Islam," *PV,* no. 494 (1938): 8–9; de Grazia, "Mass Culture and Sovereignty," 60–64, 70; travel poster collection in the Bibliothèque Forney, 1 rue du Figuier 75004, Paris: *affiches* nos. 197632 (Tayler "Messageries Maritimes"), 1970019 (Hohlwein "Mittelmeer-Fahrten"), 172720 (Dorival "Casablanca" 1917).

47. William Hoisington, *The Casablanca Connection,* 44–48, 110, 158–62; Burke, *Prelude,* 197–99.

48. Jean Marguet, "Sidi Mohammed à Paris," *C-M* (1929).

5. Tourists, Rebels, and Settlers

1. *Dans l'ombre du Harem:* director, Léon Mathot and André Liabel; play and scenario by Lucien Besnard; made in Morocco and France, released 6 July 1928. *La Comtesse Marie:* director, Bonito Perojo; scenarist, Luca de Tena; made in 1927 in Spain, released 31 Aug. 1928. *L'Occident:* director, Henri Fescourt; play and scenario by Henri Kistemaekers; Franco-German production, made in Morocco, released 26 Sept. 1928. *L'Esclave blanche:* director, Augusto Genina; scenarist, Norbert Falk; made 1927, released 4 Nov. 1927. *La Symphonie pathétique:* director: Henri Etievant and Mario Nalpas; scenario based on novel by Léo Duran; made 1928, released 9 Oct. 1928.

2. In Morocco, 1929–31, Jacques Séverac made three other films but they received little publicity or distribution; see my chaps. 6 and 7; Said, *Orientalism,* 55, 167, 231, 234; and Edward Said, *Culture and Imperialism,* 63, 169–85.

3. Persell, *French Colonial Lobby,* 150.

4. Ibid., 152–55; Melvin Knight, *Morocco as a French Economic Venure,* 92–93, 186; Alan Scham, *Lyautey in Morocco,* 92; Hoisington, *Casablanca Connection,* 7–12, 30, 106–9 (on land sold in Morocco by 1935); *HAC,* 2: 287–88; Confer, *France and Algeria,* 65, 99, 111; Gwendolyn Wright, *The Politics of Design in French Colonial Urbanism,* 143; Prochaska, *Making Algeria French,* 208–23; Swearingen, *Moroccan Mirages,* 20, 27–35 (on "granary of Rome"), 51–55, 62–63; René Gallissot, *Le Patronat européen au Maroc,* 122–25.

5. "Sommaire: *La Comtess Marie,*" blue folder, 6 pp., filmscript: 125 pp., doss. 3: expenses, docs. SM 26898 and SM 26900: agreement between Albatros and César in carton "Albatros F 67," Cinémathèque française, Bibliothèque Musée, Grande Palais (Trocadero), 75008 Paris; "*La Comtesse Marie,*" C-M (1928); on Films Albatros, founded by Russian emigrés in 1920, see Crisp, *Classic French Cinema,* 167–69.

6. Shlomo Ben-Ami, *Fascism from Above,* 207; Carolyn P. Boyd, *Praetorian Politics in Liberal Spain,* 239–41, 258–61; Stanley Payne, *Politics and the Military in Modern Spain,* 201–55; Shannon Earl Fleming, "Primo de Rivera and Abd el-Krim: The Struggle in Spanish Morocco, 1923–1927," 82–84; Thomas Granville Trice, "Spanish Liberalism in Crisis, 1913–1923"; Carlos Martinez de Campos y Serrano, *España Bellica: El siglo XX, Marruecos,* 141, 277–80 (on the 4.2 million peseta ransom of prisoners); the literary Marqués Juan Ignacio Luca de Tena would have known the tradition of colonial love stories in Spanish literature, e.g., Cervantes' *La fuerza de la sangre* and *El amante liberal;* see also Juan Antonio Gaya Nuño, *Historia del cautivo: Episodios nacionales,* an autobiographical novel of the Rif War by a Spanish historian, writer, and critic. Its title is taken from a section of *Don Quixote* in which Cervantes recounts in fictional form his ten-year captivity among the Moors.

7. U.S. Department of State (USDOS) 852.00B/9 no. 186 (embassy, Madrid), 29 Dec. 1923; *ABC,* 26 Dec. 1923; USDOS 852.00B/10 no. 204 (embassy, Madrid), 14 Jan. 1924; USDOS 852.00B/11 no. 2144 (legation, Riga Latvia), 22 May 1924, and no. 2677, 22 January 1925, on alleged Comintern involvement in plots; USDOS 852.00/1322 (consulate, Barcelona), 15 Nov. 1924.

8. Maria Rosa de Madariaga, "L'image et le retour du Maure," *L'Homme et la Société* (1988): 71–74; idem, "The Intervention of Moroccan Troops in the Spanish Civil War: A Reconsideration," *European History Quarterly* (1992): 67–97; idem, *L'Espagne et le Rif: Pénétration coloniale et résistances locales, 1909–1926;* Andrée Bachoud, *Los españoles ante las campañas de Marruecos,* 191–212 (for more on the debate over the role of Islamic civilization in Spain, see also Américo Castro and Claudio Sanchez-Albernoz); James T. Monroe, "The Hispanic-Arabic World," in José Rubia Barcia, ed., *Américo Castro and the Meaning of Spanish Civilization,* 69–90, esp. 70–72.

9. Henriette Celarié, *L'épopée Marocaine,* 7–9; Celarié's work, one of the few contemporary military histories of the Rif War, makes no mention of Lyautey and is prefaced by Pétain; Judith Hughes, *To the Maginot Line,* 45–47, 167, 217–19; William L. Shirer, *The Collapse of the Third Republic,* 158, 172–74, 177–79.

10. Robert Paxton, *Vichy France,* 35, 210–11, 222; Shannon Earl Fleming, "Spanish Morocco and the *Alzamiento Nacional,* 1936–1939," *JCH*

(1983): 27–42; idem, "'A Firm Bulwark for the Defense of Western Civiliza-tion': The Nationalists' Uses of the Moroccan Protectorate during the Span-ish Civil War"; on Luca de Tena, see Hugh Thomas, *The Spanish Civil War,* 203–4.

11. *"Dans l'Ombre du Harem,"* C-M (1928): 740–41; the film *Dans l'Ombre du Harem* is directed by Léon Mathot and André Linbel; Lucien Besnard (author of the play), *"Dans l'Ombre du Harem,"* La Petite Illustra-tion (1927) (Théâtre): 1–26. In the film, the female lead is named Simone, in the play, Isabelle, but the plots are identical; *Au Miroir,* 133–35.

12. Robert de Beauplan review of Besnard's play in *La Petite Illustration* (1927); *Comoedia* (May 1927); see also Muret, Massis.

13. Besnard, *"Dans l'Ombre du Harem."*

14. *La Petite Illustration* (11 June 1927): 6, 8–9.

15. *"L'Esclave Blanche,"* C-M (1927). In the film, Warner is renamed Varnier.

16. *"Dans l'Ombre du Harem,"* C-M (1928); *Au Miroir,* 133–35; *Koran Interpreted,* 100.

17. Hause, *Women's Suffrage,* 46–47; Auclert, *Les femmes arabes,* 42–52; Hause, *Hubertine Auclert,* 132–48; Julia Clancy-Smith, "Islam, Gender, and Identities," 167–72; Henriette Célarié, *Behind Moroccan Walls,* 77–85; idem, *Nos soeurs musulmanes: Scènes du désert;* idem, *Du sang et de l'amour dans l'harem.*

18. On the imprisoned moukère, see Alloula, *Colonial Harem,* 17–25; quote from Zora Neale Hurston, *Mules and Men:* "We gointer lie up a nation . . . lie above suspicion. . . . We never run outer lies and lovin"—cited in Trinh T. Minh-ha, *Woman, Native, Other,* 119–50; Jean Barreyre, *"Sirocco,"* PV, no. 162 (1931); *Sirocco,* 1930, was directed by Jacques Séverac; Flitterman-Lewis, *To Desire Differently,* 161–62; *Itto* (1934) was directed by Marie Epstein and Jean Benoit-Lévy; Franz Fanon, *A Dying Colonialism,* 37–39.

19. *C-M* (1 Mar. 1929): 132–33.

20. *C-M* (14 Sept. 1928): 600–601; *First Wave,* 157.

21. J. Roger-Mathieu, "Au Maroc, avec les interprètes de *L'Occident,"* C-M (1928); C-M (27 July 1928) 490; C-M (3 Aug. 1928) 501; Fescourt, *La Foi,* 348 (my trans.).

22. Roger-Mathieu, "Au Maroc," *C-M* (1928); C-M (27 July 1928) 490; C-M (3 Aug. 1928): 501; the French actors' union, *Chambre syndicale,* founded in 1890, included film personnel in 1917 and changed its name to the Union des artistes. See Crisp, *Classic French Cinema,* 198.

23. Fescourt, *La Foi,* 348 (my trans.); *First Wave,* 157, 159 cites A. Colom-bat, *"L'Occident,"* On Tourne (Oct. 1928): "The fundamental banality of *L'Occident* . . . the characters confirm our hypocrisy."

24. Betts, *Uncertain Dimensions,* 76. Betts's source is *Life,* 10 Jan. 1937.

25. Fescourt, *La Foi,* 347; *First Wave,* 157; the case of Claudia Victrix is one of life imitating art: in the film *Le Lion des Mongols,* the star is the producer's mistress.

26. *PV* (8 Dec. 1937): 6; *C-M* (16 Feb. 1938): 5 (quote); *First Wave,* 157; *Au Miroir,* 148–53, 156–57; Robert Roy, "Rama Tahé jouera Zouzour dans 'Cain,'" *PV* (1929); cited in Dudley Andrew, "Preying Mantis," in Matthew Bernstein and Gaylyn Studlar, eds., *Visions of the East: Orientalism in Film,* 241.

27. Alain Ripert and Claude Frère, *La Carte Postale, son histoire, sa fonction social,* 35, 87, 90–95, 106; Elizabeth Ezra, "The Colonial Look: Exhibiting Empire in the 1930s," *Contemporary French Civilization* (1995): 39–44; Alloula, *Colonial Harem,* 14–21; Sylviane Leprun, *Le Théâtre des colonies,* 181–92; Prochaska, "Archive," 375–76; Catherine Hodeir and Michel Pierre, *L'exposition coloniale;* Charles Rearick, *Pleasures of the Belle Epoque,* section on the expositions; William H. Schneider, *An Empire for the Masses,* 168–72; *First Wave,* 151; see also Lutz and Collins, *Reading National Geographic;* Martine Astier Loutfi, "Imperial Frame: Film Industry and Colonial Representations," in Sherzer, ed., *Cinema, Colonialism, Postcolonialism,* 20–21; Boulanger, *Cinéma colonial,* 21; Félix Mesguich, *Tours de manivelle: Souvenirs d'un chasseur d'images.*

28. Raymond-Millet, "Les nègres," *C-M* (1929). The same photo illustrated the article "Siliva le Zoulou," *C-M* (1928); on "moral economy," see Peter Linebaugh, *The London Hanged,* and E. P. Thompson, *Customs in Common.*

29. Wright, *The Politics of Design,* 85, 130–31, 134, 137, 141–54; Betts, *Uncertain Dimensions,* 125–27, 138–39.

30. Wright, *Politics of Design,* 146–48, 154; Betts, *Uncertain Dimensions,* 145; Janet Abu-Lughod, *Rabat.*

31. Speech to Université des Annales, président Jean Gallotti, inspecteur-général des Beaux-Arts, Paris, 10 Dec. 1926, in Louis-Hubert Lyautey, *Paroles de'action,* 455; André Le Révérend, *Lyautey,* 431–32; Wright, *Politics of Design,* 87–88, 342.

32. France, *AS* (1930), 313 ("Mouvement des voyageurs entre l'Algérie et l'extérieur"); *AS* (1935), 298; *AS* (1936), 303; Wright, *Politics of Design,* 134, 137; Lelieur and Mirabel, *Négripub;* Archives des affiches, Bibliothèque Forney, 1 rue de Figuier, Paris 75004: posters 197632, 197019, 172720.

33. Bidwell, *Morocco,* 202, 274; Hoisington, *Casablanca Connection,* 30, 106; idem, "Cities in Revolt: The Berber Dahir (1930) and France's Urban Strategy in Morocco," *JCH* 13 (1978): 435.

34. Roger Gaudefroy-Demombynes, *L'oeuvre française en matière d'enseignement au Maroc,* 119.

35. Maurice Le Glay, "Ecoles pour les Berbères," *l'Afrique française,* Mar.

1921; idem, *Chronique*; Paul Marty, *Le maroc de demain*, 241–52, 251; al-Fasi, *Independence Movements*, 120.

36. John P. Halstead, *Rebirth of a Nation*, 60–63, 65, 72–75, 98–110; Burke, "Image," 195; Hoisington, "Cities in Revolt," 435, 437–42; Bidwell, *Morocco*, 52–53, 249–50; Scham, *Lyautey in Morocco*, 144–61.

37. Hoisington, *Casablanca Connection*, 10–12, 30, 36, 39; idem, "Cities in Revolt," 433, 434–36, 440–43; Charles-André Julien, *Maroc face aux imperialisme*, 117; Bidwell, *Morocco*, 274.

38. Hoisington, "Cities in Revolt," 433–48; idem. *The Casablanca Connection*; al-Fasi, *Independence Movements*, 118–24; Halstead, *Rebirth*, 64, 73–75, 178–79.

39. Halstead, *Rebirth*, 180; al-Fasi, *Independence Movements*, 124; Hoisington, "Cities in Revolt," 442, 445.

40. Halstead, *Rebirth*, 113–14.

41. Jacques Berque, *French North Africa between the Wars*, 328–30; Oved, *La Gauche française*, 1:336–42.

42. This summary is based on several screenings by Dudley Andrew and Steven Ungar, University of Iowa, of an uncut, 16mm print of the film.

43. Lebovics, *True France*, 57; Fredric Jameson, *The Politics of Post-Modernity*, 101–29.

44. "*Cinq Gentlemen maudits*" (1931), *PV* (18 Feb. 1932); *Générique*, 150–53; Chirat, *Julien Duvivier*, 8–9, 40–41; the Moroccan actors were Aicha Mabrouka as "la marchande d'amulettes" and Ahmed ben Abdallah as her father; Julian Jackson, *The Politics of Depression in France, 1932–1936*, 11–16; Shirer, *Collapse*, 164–66; Stephen A. Schuker, *The End of French Predominance in Europe*, 383–93; *Mists*, 255, 381, citing *Excelsior*, 26 June 1935 for remarks on Franco by Mac Orlan, author of *La Bandera*; Goffredo Fofi, "The Cinema of the Popular Front in France, 1934–1938," *Screen* 13 (winter 1972/73): 40.

45. Mock-up books were used as stage props to avoid possible copyright infringement; the prop in this production looks like Mauchamp's *La Sorcellerie au Maroc* with the author's name removed from the cover.

46. Hoisington, *Casablanca Connection*, 117–18, cites Lucien Paye, a Rabat college professor who conducted a survey, "L'Agriculture dans la Région de Fès," that was presented at a conference, 2 June 1937, Centre des Hautes Etudes sur l'Afrique et l'Asie Moderne (CHEAM) Paris.

47. Hoisington, *Casablanca Connection*, 110–11, 245–47.

48. Charles O'Brien, "The *Cinéma Colonial* of the 1930s: Film Narration as Spatial Practice," in Bernstein and Studlar, *Visions of the East*, 223.

49. Jackson, *Politics of Depression*, 12; *Mists*, 59, 61, 62, 99, 368; René Clair, *Entr'acte and A nous la liberté*, preface.

6. French Colonial Film before and after *Itto*

1. Maurice Bardèche and Robert Brasillach, *Histoire du cinéma*, 199, 320–21: "unfortunately this documentary is mixed with a ridiculous . . . story, a bog of offensive silliness"; Boulanger, *Cinéma colonial*, 117–18: "a haven . . . in the midst of the colonial productions"; Sorlin, "Fanciful Empire": 142–44: "There is only one film which does not follow the pattern (of colonial stereotyping)"; Flitterman-Lewis, *To Desire Differently*, 161–62, challenges this consensus.

2. Edmund Burke III, "A Comparative View of French Native Policy in Morocco and Syria, 1912–1925," *Middle Eastern Studies* (1973): 178.

3. Ageron, *Les Algériens musulmans*, 1:268–83, 2:873, 890; Bidwell, *Morocco*, 51, cites Bernard-Georges Gaulis, *Lyautey intime*, 209 (quote of Lyautey).

4. Burke, "Image," 175–79, 193–94: Lyautey's adjutants, Colonels Henrys, Simon, and Maurice LeGlay, and Berriau's widow, were associated with filming *Itto*; Didier Lazard, *Max Lazard, ses frères et Lyautey. Lettres, 1894–1933*; René Gallissot, *Le Patronat européen au Maroc*; see also Porch, Rivet.

5. Burke, "Image," 194–95: unpublished reports by Colonels M. LeGlay, W. Berriau, and H. Bruno, in Ministry of War Archives, series E-2; William Hoisington Jr., *Lyautey and the French Conquest of Morocco*, 41–53.

6. Burke, "Image," 191, 195–99: the decree of 1914 led to the Berber Dahir of 1930: Hoisington, "Cities in Revolt: The Berber Dahir of 1930 and France's Urban Strategy in Morocco," *JCH* (1978): 433–48.

7. Le Glay's other works include *Récits Morocains de la plaine et des monts; Badda: Fille Berbère; Le Chat aux oreilles percées: Histoire Marocaine; Itto* (1923); *La mort du Rogui* (1926); *Les sentiers de la guerre et de l'amour* (1930); *Nouveaux récits marocains* (1932); *Chronique marocaine* (1933). Cie. Berger-Levrault published eight of his books and those of other Lyauteyistes. Plon published two. Germaine Ayache, "Societé rifaine et pouvoir central marocaine," *Revue historique* (1975) 345–70.

8. Gaulis, *Lyautey intime*, 209 (quote); Germaine Ayache, *Les origines de la guerre du rif*, 25–31, on Le Glay's "two Moroccos"; Maurice Le Glay in *l'Afrique française* (1935); Le Glay, "Ecoles françaises pour les berbères"; al-Fasi, *Independence Movements*, 120; Paul Marty, *Le Maroc de demain*, 241–52, on *écoles franco-berbères*.

9. Opening credits *(générique)* of *Itto* are given in *PV* (20 Dec. 1934): 7.

10. *Itto* (1934), videotape from Dudley Andrew; Boulanger, *Cinéma colonial*, 112–15 (plot summary).

11. Maurice Le Glay, *Itto: Récit Marocain d'amour et de bataille*, 32, 37, 61, 94–98, 126–27, 234–37; Daniel Rivet, *Lyautey et l'Institution du Pro-*

tectorat Français au Maroc 1912–1925, 2:121, 137, 168, 188, 196–99; Hoisington, *Lyautey,* 63.

12. Hoisington, *Casablanca Connection,* 7; Burke, *Prelude,* 197–99.

13. Hoisington, *Lyautey,* 65–78, 89–92; Rivet, *Lyautey,* 1:188–200; Ross Dunn, *Resistance in the Desert,* 26, 166–67, 181, 221; Burke, "Moroccan Resistance," 434–64; idem, *Prelude,* 9, 110, 112, 118, 122, 203, 455; Pierre Lyautey, *Lyautey l'Africain,* 1:23, 27, 253, 2:197, 203–10, 275, 300–301, 314–15; *Larousse du XXe siècle,* 2:229 (Chleuh), 6:1120 (Zaian); al-Fasi, *Independence Movements,* 49–52, 92–94, 118–19; Douglas Porch, *Conquest,* 278–89.

14. Bidwell, *Morocco,* 181, for Berriau's remarks; "Conférence de Meknès," Rabat 1918, text reprinted in *l'Afrique française* (Nov. 1920); Scham, *Lyautey in Morocco,* 92; Centre de Haute Etude Administratif sur l'Afrique et l'Asie Moderne, Rue du Four, 75006 Paris (CHEAM) contains an archive housing 4,495 of these theses in 257 volumes.

15. Henry Malherbe, *"Itto," PV* (1935); Boulanger, *Cinéma Colonial,* 118; Papiers Lyautey, Archives Nationales (AN 475 AP), folder 610, Personnel du Maroc (thanks to William Hoisington Jr. for bringing this document to my attention); Lyautey's eulogy to Berriau in *l'Afrique Française* (1918) 417–19; Rivet, *Lyautey,* 1:61, 196–99, 2:29, 194–200, 215–16, 3:191–92; Etienne Rey, *La Renaissance de l'orgueil français.*

16. Bidwell, *Morocco,* 258–61; René Cruchet, *La conquête pacifique du Maroc;* Pierre Delatère, "Dans l'Atlas marocain avec Jean Benoît-Lévy, Marie Epstein, et la troup de *Itto," PV* (1934).

17. Benoît-Lévy, *Art of Motion Picture,* 167; Leprohon, *L'Exotisme,* 209.

18. Benoît-Lévy, *Art of Motion Picture,* 212–13; Roger-Mathieu, "Au Maroc," *C-M* (1928); *C-M* (27 July 1928): 490; *C-M* (3 Aug. 1928): 501; Fescourt, *La Foi,* 347; Boulanger, *Cinéma colonial,* 117; besides *Itto,* the three by Sévérac, and *L'Occident,* the Chleuh acted in Violet and Donatien's *Les Hommes nouveaux* (1924), René Le Somptier's *Les Fils du soleil* (1924), two films by Luitz-Morat—*Le Sang d'Allah* (1922) and *Au Seuil du harem* (1921)—and other, minor films; see David H. Slavin, "French Cinema's Other First Wave," *Cinema Journal* (1997); Betts, *Uncertain Dimensions,* 49–53; Lévy-Bruhl, *La Mentalité primitive,* i; Cazeneuve, *Lévy-Bruhl,* 20; Robert Briffaut, *The Making of Humanity,* 73.

19. Richard Abel, "Booming the Film Business: The Historical Specificity of Early French Cinema," in Abel, *Silent Film,* 116–19; *First Wave,* 326–27, 500–501; *T&C* 2:106–10, 212–15; Léon Moussinac, "Etat du cinéma international" (1933), in *L'Age ingrat du cinéma,* 331–54; Jean Epstein, *Ecrits sur le cinéma,* 1:191–93; Jacques Aumont, *Montage Eisenstein,* 179; Constantine Dorokhine, "Les Emigrés russes à Paris et les films Albatros," in Pierre Guibert, ed., *Le Cinéma français muet dans le monde, influences réciproques,* 127–

37; Robert Sklar, *Film,* 151–53; Robert Stam, Robert Burgoyne, and Sandy Flitterman-Lewis, *New Vocabularies in Film Semiotics,* 9–15.

20. Vsevolod I. Pudovkin, "Types Instead of Actors" (speech to London Film Society, 3 Feb. 1929), *Cinema* (6 Feb. 1929), in V. I. Pudovkin, *Film Technique and Film Acting,* 140–42; I. Rostovtsev, "Pudovkin on His Early Films," in Jay Leyda, *KINO: A History of Russian and Soviet Film,* 51–66, 248–49; A. Mariamov, *Vsevolod Pudovkin;* Luda and Jean Schnitzer, *Vsevolod Pudovkin;* "*Le Lion des Mongols,*" *C-M* (1924).

21. In *C-M* (14 Dec. 1924): 379–80, the photo captions give a sense of the film: "In the fabled kingdom of the Mongols, the bloody and cruel Great Khan shows himself at the palace gate once a year to his prostrated people." The film's costumes and bizarre mix of cultures illustrate ethnographic surrealism: Clifford, *Predicament of Culture,* 135–36, on Musée Trocadéro.

22. Clifford, *Predicament of Culture,* 122, 132; "ethnographic surrealism" crops up in *La Sirène des Tropiques* (1927), Josephine Baker's first film, directed by Henri Etievant and Mario Nalpas, with Luis Buñuel as assistant director—see *C-M* (15 Mar. 1928): 184–85; Paul Gilroy, *The Black Atlantic,* 1–40; Phyllis Rose, *Jazz Cleopatra,* 5, 6, 8, 28, 31, 119–21, 163; Bryan Hammond and Patrick O'Connor, *Josephine Baker,* 43–44, 47–49, 72–73; Denise Tual, *Le Temps dévoré,* 60; Luis Buñuel, *My Last Breath,* 90–91; Jean Mitry, *Ivan Mosjoukine* (supplement to *L'Avant-scène du cinéma,* no. 96 (Oct. 1969): 441–42.

23. Peter Bishop, *The Myth of Shangri-la,* 8–19, 173–74, 216–18; E. Chandler, *The Unveiling of Lhasa;* James Hilton, *Lost Horizon,* 211; Peter H. Hansen, "The Dancing Lamas of Everest," *AHR* (1996): 712–45; Pudovkin, *Film Technique and Film Acting,* 143.

24. Pudovkin, *Film Technique and Film Acting,* 143; Jay Leyda, *Kino,* 249; N. Yezuitov, *Pudovkin, Creative Paths;* Peter Dart, *Pudovkin's Films and Film Theory,* 19–20, 47–48.

25. Vladimir N. Brovkin, *Behind the Front Lines of the Civil War,* 403–22; Leyda, *Kino,* 248–49; Dart, *Pudovkin's Films,* 19–21, 47–48; "*Tempête sur l'Asie,*" *C-M,* no. 235 (1929): 635.

26. Dart, *Pudovkin's Films,* 19–23, 47–48; Jay Leyda, *Kino,* 248–50.

27. Jean Barreyre, "*Sirocco,*" *PV* (1931).

28. Sorlin, "Fanciful Empire": 142; Crisp, *Classic French Cinema,* 123–25.

29. *PV* (27 June and 11 July 1935): letters published in the column "La parole est aux spectateurs." Seven letters are from Paris, with one each from Joigny (a Paris suburb), Var, Cannes (from a former colon), Casablanca (Georgette Benneville), Algiers (Robert L.), and Fez ("Lectrice"). Parisienne (a former colon?) writes that it is "hypocrisy to disguise conquest as philanthropy." Of fourteen commentators, six are women. There are only two examples of calling the Chleuh Arabs, not Berbers (the film titles use both). On *Lives of a*

Bengal Lancer, directed by Henry Hathaway, with Franchot Tone and Gary Cooper (not to be confused with *Gunga Din,* a later film with Cary Grant, Douglas Fairbanks, Victor McLaughlin), see the following reviews: Otis Ferguson, *New Republic,* 23 Jan. 1935: 305; William Troy, "Blood and Glory," *Nation,* 30 Jan. 1935, 139–40; "Pierette, Paris," *PV* (1935).

30. Michael B. Miller, *Shanghai,* 267, 393; Lebovics, *True France,* 16–19, 49–50 (on Louis Marin); William Irvine, *French Conservatism in Crisis,* 6–7, 34–38, 81–82; Jean-Noel Jeanneney, *François de Wendel,* 621–22; Jacques Decornoy, *Péril Jaune, Peur Blanche,* 191–95; Claude Bellanger, Jacques Godechot, Pierre Guiral, and Fernand Terrou, eds., *Histoire général de la presse française,* 3:393, 529, 532, 557, 591, 596; Maurice Muret, reviews of *Le Crépuscule des nations blanches, (Twilight of the White Races): Nation,* 18 Sept. 1926; *Saturday Review,* 23 Oct. 1926; *Literary Review,* 4 Dec. 1926; Lothrop Stoddard, *The Rising Tide of Color;* Henri Massis, *Défense de l'occident,* 14–16; idem, *Defense of the West,* 26–28.

31. Ignace Lepp, *Midi sonne au Maroc,* 66 (also cited in Bidwell, *Morocco,* 60, and Halstead, *Rebirth,* 61, 293); Halstead, *Rebirth,* 68–75, 178–90; Scham, *Lyautey in Morocco,* 45–47.

32. Capitaine Danrit [Emile Augustin Cyprien Driant], *La guerre au vingtième siécle;* Miller, *Shanghai,* 26–28, 411.

33. Miller, *Shanghai,* 27.

34. Ibid., 268, cites Morand's *Rien que la terre,* 23, and Serge de Chessin, *La nuit qui vient de l'Orient,* 5–6, 243; Capitaine Danrit's *L'Invasion jaune,* luridly illustrated by Paul de Sémant, remained in print (1913 and 1920 editions): *La Librairie française Catalogue général des ouvrages parus du 1930;* Jacques Decornoy, *Péril Jaune, Peur Blanche;* Daniel Segal "The European: Allegories of racial purity," *Anthropology Today* (Oct. 1991): 7–9.

35. Dart, *Pudovkin's Films,* 19–23, 47–48; Jay Leyda, *Kino* 249–50; Pudovkin, *Film Technique and Film Acting,* vii, 142–43, 194–95; *C-M* (4 Oct. 1929): 635.

36. G. Patrick March, *Eastern Destiny,* 190–200, 205–10; Alan J. K. Sanders, *Mongolia,* 16–19; William B. Ballis and Robert A, Rupen, *Mongolian People's Republic,* 2:462–507; George G. S. Murphy, *Soviet Mongolia,* 4–28; Richard Ullman, *Anglo-Soviet Relations, 1917–1921:* vol. 2, *Britain and the Russian Civil War,* 183–85, 252–53, and vol. 3, *The Anglo-Soviet Accord,* ix, 5; Evan Mawdsley, *The Russian Civil War,* 143–44 (on British supplies from Vladivostok), 153–55, and 238 (on Kolchak's "horde"); Peter Kenez, *Cinema and Soviet Society,* 62–64; Miller, *Shanghai,* 279–84.

37. Ehrenburg, *Usine des rêves,* 181; *T&C* 2:29; Robert Sklar, *Film,* 164–65, 171.

38. Ehrenburg, *Usine de rêves,* 180–81; Joseph Needham's works among others for Chinese science and technology; Hugh Tinker, *A New System of*

Slavery; V. G. Kiernan, *The Lords of Humankind; First Wave,* 40, 264–66; Leprohon, *L'Exotisme,* 259–62.

39. Charles Robert-Dumas, "Ceux de S.R." (the Deuxième Bureau's "section de renseignement"), series of seven novels (Paris: Fayard, 1934–39); *L'idole de plomb* (1935) sold 27,500 copies, cited by Miller, *Shanghai,* 179; for a contemporary comparison, see Luise White, "Alien Nation: The Hidden Obsession of UFO Literature: Race in Space," *Transition* (1994): 24–33.

40. Miller, *Shanghai,* 276–305, on the Croisière Jaune and other scientific expeditions; Ferdinand Ossendowski, *Beasts, Men, and Gods.* Ossendowski, a geologist and aide to Kolchak, escaped from Central Asia through Mongolia; a French translation by Robert Renard sold 40,000 copies: Miller, 279–81.

41. William H. McNeill, *Plagues and Peoples;* Philip D. Curtin, *Death by Migration,* 28–39; Alfred W. Crosby, *Ecological Imperialism,* 294–308; idem, *The Columbian Exchange,* 1972; idem, *Epidemic and Peace, 1918;* Richard Collier, *The Plague of the Spanish Lady;* H. Phillips, *"Black October";* Michael Adas, *Machines as a Measure of Men,* 345–401; David H. Slavin, "Social History of the Influenza Pandemic in France" (unpub.), includes survey of press accounts from ten Paris newspapers during the two most virulent outbreaks, Nov. 1918 and Feb. 1919; Ministère de la Guerre, *Statistique médicale part IIIe: Pandémie de grippe du 1ère mai 1918 au 30 avril 1919;* Michel Corday, *The Paris Front,* 382.

42. Boulanger, *Cinéma colonial,* 112–15, does not discuss this theme or mention the sorcerer scenes in his four-page summary of the film.

43. Margaret H. Darrow, "French Volunteer Nursing and the Myth of War Experience in World War I," *AHR* (1996): 80–106.

44. Boulanger, *Cinéma colonial,* 116–17; Sorlin, "Fanciful Empire": 144; *L'Aventurier* (Maurice Mariaud, 1923).

45. O'Brien, "Cinéma Colonial," 213–14.

46. *L'Homme du Niger* (1939), dir. Jacques de Baroncelli; review in *Débats* (1940); M. Doringe, "Jacques de Baroncelli, Harry Baur, Victor Francen . . . sont partis pour le Niger," *PV* (1939); photos, *PV* (1939); Kira Appel, "Ce que sera *'l'Homme du Niger,'*" *PV* (1939); review by M.B., *PV* (1939); *Générique,* 140–44.

47. Ralph Schor, *L'opinion française et l'étrangères,* 166–67; *La Vie est à nous* (1936) (director, Jean Renoir); Jonathan Buchsbaum, *Cinéma Engagé,* 130, 224–25, 229–30, 286; Benjamin Stora, "Les Algeriens dans le Paris de l'entre-deux-guerres," in André Kaspi and Antoine Marès, *Paris des étrangères,* 154; *Mists,* 213–20; Jean-Pierre Jeancolas, "French Cinema of the 1930s and Its Social Handicaps," in Ginette Vincendeau and Keith Reader, eds., *La Vie est à nous,* 61–71, and Ginette Vincendeau, "The Popular Cinema of the Popular Front," ibid., 73–101; Fofi, "Cinema of the Popular Front."

48. Huguette Godin, "Le mouvement féministe," *Le Quotidien* (29 Dec.

1930); Octave DePont, *Les Berbères en France;* on L'Etoile Nord Africain, Archives de la Prefecture de Police, Paris (APP), carton B/A 56, 57.

49. Lorcin, *Imperial Identities,* 225; *Au Miroir,* 192–95; *FFL,* 59, 202, 293–94; *Firmin, Le Muet de St. Pataclet* (1938), directed by Séverac, about a veteran who suffers through a terrible bombardment during the Great War and returns home to Provence a shell-shocked, tragic hero, having lost the power of speech. Years later, the powder magazine of a nearby arsenal blows up as he is walking by. He regains his speech and enlists in the Legion.

7. The Thin White Line of Western Civilization

1. Report on Barika in *C-M* (1 Oct. 1926): 300.

2. *Au Miroir,* 26–28 (number of theaters); "*Les Hommes nouveaux,*" *C-M* (1923): 20 (photo "Les rebelles surgirent, en armes, sur leurs petits chevaux vifs"); Pierre Boyer (archiviste en chef du Départment d'Alger) *Cohabitation en Algérie,* 59–60; *Générique,* 133, 142; Ruedy, *Modern Algeria,* 89 (on the Code de l'Indigénat); Chevaldonné, "Fonctionnement": 529–48, and "La Cinéma colonial en Afrique du Nord," *RASJEP* (1977); August, *Selling of the Empire,* (on the Cinematographic Protection Act of 1927), 101–4; Rosaleen Smyth, "The Development of British Colonial Film Policy, 1927–1939," *Journal of African History* (1979): 437–50.

3. *FFL,* 598–616.

4. Ibid., 410–13, 423, 567; Lebovics, *True France,* 51–97.

5. *FFL,* xix; Hoisington, *Lyautey,* 14–20; Louis-Hubert Gonzalve Lyautey, "Du Rôle colonial de l'armée," *Revue des Deux Mondes* (1900): 308–18; idem, *Paroles d'action,* 5.

6. *FFL,* xviii–xxi, 183–84, 385, 437.

7. J. Roger-Mathieu, ed., *Mémoires d'Abd el-Krim,* 146–47 (Abd el-Krim quote); *FFL,* 385, 395: cites Service d'Histoire de l'Armée de la Terre (Vincennes/SHAT) 3H 697, 1924 Legion report, "Questions relatives à la Légion étrangère"; SHAT 3H 259 23 Feb. 1920, 12 Feb. 1921; Rudyers Pryne, *War in Morocco,* 217; Oved, *La Gauche française,* 1:147, 186–95; Ayache, *Les origines,* 331–40; C. Richard Pennell, *A Country with a Government and a Flag,* 130–31; Adolphe R. Cooper, *Twelve Years with the Legion,* 223, says many deserters in the Atlas Mountains during the 1920s had been there a long time.

8. *FFL,* 172, 384, 394–95, 412, 423, 436–38; Eric Hobsbawm and Terence Ranger, eds., *The Invention of Tradition,* 1–14; Benedict Anderson, *Imagined Communities.*

9. Philip Dine, *Images of the Algerian War,* 8–9, 109–11; Emmanuel Mounier, "Impossibilités algériennes," *Esprit* (1947); Bruce Marshall, *The French Colonial Myth,* 2–4; Maurice Kahler, *Decolonization in Britain and*

France, 367–68; Martin Evans, "Rehabilitating the Traumatized War Veteran," in Evans and Ken Lunn, eds., *War and Memory in the Twentieth Century,* 73–85; see also Lustick, Evans, Peyrefitte.

10. *FFL,* 605.

11. Horne, *Savage War,* 98–99, 432, 434–58, 459–60, 545–48; *FFL,* 566–69, 602–5, 613–14; Mort Rosenblum, *Mission to Civilize,* 260; David H. Slavin, "Race Traitors in France?" *Race Traitor* (1995): 117–21.

12. *First Wave,* 160; Boulanger, *Cinéma Colonial,* 8; Peter Christensen, "Feyder's *Le Grand jeu," Film Criticism* (1988): 11, 13–14.

13. René Prédal, *La société française, 1914–1945 à travers le cinéma,* 181–82.

14. *PV* (1929): 1, for statistics; Crisp, *Classic French Cinema,* 213–61; Blanche Vogt, "Les Femmes et *La Bandera," PV* (1935).

15. Miriam Hansen, *Babel and Babylon,* 18, 249–50; Laura Mulvey, "Visual Pleasure and Narrative Cinema," *Screen* 18 (1977): 6–18.

16. Boulanger, *Cinéma colonial,* 92, claims *Ombres sur le Rif,* by director J. de Kuharsky, is the only film on the Rif War. A fire destroyed the print and negative and it was never shown in public. In fact, *La Pente* (1928) and *La Comtesse Marie* (1927) deal with the Rif War; *FFL,* 428, 430, 432; Chirat, *Catalogue,* no. 122, 1928.

17. "*La Pente," C-M* (1928).

18. "*Le Sgt. X," PV* (1932); Chirat, *Catalogue,* no. 1113, 1932; Boulanger, *Cinéma colonial,* 90; *Au Miroir,* 184–89.

19. Francia-Rohl, "A Marseille . . . sur les traces du Légionnaire Fernandel," *PV* (1936); "Ou l'on Termine *Un de la Légion," PV* (1936); *PV* (24 Sept. 1936): 5; Gaston Modot, "*Un de la Légion," Ciné Liberté* (1936); Modot was a well-known actor and member of the Communist party, viz. *Mists,* 217–19; *Un de la Légion:* dir. by Christian-Jaque, from a novel by J. D. Newson.

20. Lucien Wahl, "Les Hommes sans nom," *PV* (1937); *FFL,* 428–30; *Générique,* 174; George Mosse, *Nationalism and Sexuality,* 36, 128–29, 175–76.

21. *Catalogue général des ouvrages en langue française,* vols. 1926–1929, 1930–1933: 2979; *Catalogue général des ouvrages parus du 1 janvier 1933 au 1 janvier 1946:* 305.

22. Boulanger, *Cinéma Colonial,* 84–85; David Strauss, "The Rise of Anti-Americanism in France: French Intellectuals and the American Film Industry, 1927–1932," *Journal of Popular Culture* (1977); Carlton J. H. Hayes, *France: A Nation of Patriots* 186; *FFL,* 429–32.

23. Jean George Auriol, "Revue: *Coéurs Brûlés [Morocco]," La Revue du Cinéma* (1931); *FFL,* 432; *Morocco,* director, Josef von Sternberg, adaptation by Jules Furthman; Benno Vigny, *Amy Jolly,* 245.

24. Quoted in Maurice-Robert Bataille and Claude Veillot, *Caméras sous*

le soleil, and Boulanger, 84–85; Rollet was describing *Morocco,* not *Beau Geste. FFL,* 682 n. 77 corrects Boulanger.

25. Hayden White, *Tropics of Discourse,* 58; Shohat and Stam, *Unthinking Eurocentrism,* 101–3.

26. Quote from Omer Bartov, *Murder in Our Midst,* 40–47 (on Ernst Junger, Henri Barbusse, Erich Maria Remarque, and Louis-Ferdinand Céline); Robert A. Nye, *Masculinity and Male Codes of Honor in Modern France,* 218–19, 226–27; Paul Gerbod, "L'Ethique héroïque en France 1870–1914," *Revue historique* 268, no. 2 (1983): 409–12; Gerbod cites Louis Huot and Paul Voivenel, *Le Courage;* Marc Bloch, *Memoirs of War,* 166.

27. Quote from Betts, *Uncertain Dimensions,* 76; *FFL,* 171; on T. E. Lawrence, see Christopher Caudwell, *Studies and Further Studies in a Dying Culture,* 20–43; see also Turner, Silverman; Peggy Sabatier, "Charles Béart," in Cooke and Heggoy, eds., *Proceedings,* 141–56; Raymond Betts, "Sources of French Imperialist Ideology before WWI," ibid., 165–73: Betts cites Jules Verne, *The Mysterious Island,* 80; Arthur B. Evans and Ron Miller, "Jules Verne, Misunderstood Visionary," *Scientific American* (1997): 92–97; *Fort Saganne* (1984)—a recent example of the Foreign Legion genre, based on a novel by Louis Gardel—was directed by Alain Corneau, with screenplay by Henry de Turenne, Alain Corneau, and Louis Gardel and starring Gerard Depardieu, Catherine Deneuve, Phillippe Noiret, and Sophie Marceau; William B. Cohen, "The Lure of Empire," *JCH* (1969): 103–16.

28. Ernest Lavisse, *Histoire de France,* 169 (Bibliothèque Nationale textbook series L32–L42).

29. M. Brévié (governor-general of French West Africa), "The Present Position of Education in French West Africa," Dec. 1930 and Dec. 1935, in W. Bryant Mumford, with Major G. St. J. Orde-Brown, *Africans Learn to Be French,* 89, 95–96. Mumford and Orde-Brown's work is a review of educational activities in the seven federated colonies of French West Africa, based on a tour of the region (and Algiers) in 1935. Mumford, a former superintendent of education, Tanganyika Territory, headed the colonial department of the University of London's Institute of Education; Orde-Brown, a member of the ILO's Committee on Native Labour, was formerly Tanganyika's labor commissioner; Jacques and Mona Ozouf, "Le thème du patriotisme dans les manuels primaires," *Le Mouvement social* (1964): 5–31, 22–25.

30. Mumford and Orde-Browne, *Africans Learn to Be French,* iv.

31. J. T. C. Blackmore, "The Educational Work of the French Government in Algeria," *International Review of Missions* 19 (1930) 266–76, 267, 271; compare Gail Paradise Kelly, "Colonialism, Indigenous Society, and School Practices: French West Africa and Indochina, 1918–1938," in Philip G. Altbach and Gail Paradise Kelly, eds., *Education and the Colonial Experience,* 9–23; Manuela Semidei, "De l'Empire à la décolonisation à travers les manuels

scolaires français," *Revue française des sciences politiques* (1966): 56–86, 75, 85; Said, *Culture and Imperialism,* 180.

32. On the dey's fly whisk, see Gauthier and Deschamps (with the collaboration of teachers and historians), *Cours . . . d'histoire de France* (1916) 58 (the myth is challenged by Yves Lacoste, André Nouschi, and André Prenant, *L'Algérie passé et présent,* 233–46); on Dahomey, see J. Renaudin and Charpentier, *Petite histoire de France du jeune âge,* 116, 126–27.

33. George Duruy, *Petite histoire populaire de la France depuis les origines jusqu'à la constitution de 1875,* 209–10.

34. Gustave Ducoudray, *Leçons moyennes d'histoire de France à l'usage des écoles primières,* 360 (Bobillot), 326 (Blandin); George Duruy, *Pour la France,* 130–33; on de Villiers, see Réunion des professeurs, *Chronologie de l'histoire de France à l'usage des écoles primaires,* 105, 110. This text is the Roman Catholic *école libre* primer. Bibliothèque Nationale's archivist M. Christian Amalvi guided me to representative texts.

35. Quotes from Margaret H. Darrow, "French Volunteer Nursing and the Myth of War Experience in World War I," *AHR* (1996): 81, 82, 106; Gerbod, "L'Ethique héroique," 421, 424; Michelle Perrot, "The New Eve and the Old Adam," in Margaret Higonnet et al., eds., *Behind the Lines,* 53–60; Steven C. Hause, "More Minerva than Mars," ibid., 99–113; Michelle Perrot, "L'Eloge de la Menagère dans le discours des ouvriers française," *Romantisme* (1976): 105–21; Judith Coffin, "Social Science Meets Sweated Labor," *Journal of Modern History* (1991): 230–70, 269–70.

36. Yvonne Turin, *Femmes et religieuses au XIXe siècle: le féminisme en religion,* 209–10; JoAnn Kay McNamara, *Sisters in Arms,* 583–92; see also Arens *(Manuel),* Burridge, Gibson.

37. R. Dogimont, "Les Femmes missionaires aux colonies," *La Française* (1931); A. Querillac, "Le rôle de la femme médecin aux colonies," *Depêche coloniale* (1932); Hélène Gosset, "Les Toubibas, ou l'oeuvre des femmes françaises au Maroc," *L'Intransigeant* (1932); Franz Fanon, "Beyond the Veil," in *A Dying Colonialism,* 35–67, 162–76; Kittler, *White Fathers,* 218–19; Ilya Ehrenbourg, *Usines de rêves,* 177–78 ("Dieu a envoyé les petites soeurs pour ceux qui, hélas, n'ont plus de maman!"); Adolph R. Cooper, *Born to Fight,* 180, 194, and idem, *Twelve Years with the Legion,* 202–6.

38. J. G. Auriol, "Sous l'uniform: Gary Cooper et Pierre Richard-Willm, officiers, soldats, et mercenaires," *PV* (1935).

39. "La Parole est aux spectateurs," *PV* (1934) (a letter signed Etienne Begramian—xenophobic despite his Armenian-sounding last name).

40. Quotes from Rosay, *La Traversée,* 190–92 (Rosay's information was secondhand, from the producer; she paraphrases the officers); Charles Ford, *Jacques Feyder,* 52–57; Victor Bachy, *Jacques Feyder,* 121–22; Feyder and Rosay, *Le cinéma, notre métier,* 38–39; Boulanger, *Cinéma colonial,* 110.

41. Jacques Feyder, "La censure cinématographique," *Comoedia* (10 Feb. 1935): 1; Bachy, *Jacques Feyder*, 122; Georges Altman, "La Censure en France," cited in *T&C* 2:71–73; "La Parole est aux spectateurs," *PV* (1934); Boulanger, *Cinéma colonial*, 110.

42. *Mists*, 247 (quote); Roger Régent, "Le Grand jeu," *PV* (31 May 1934); "Le Grand jeu," *PV* (3 May 1934); "Le Grand jeu," *PV* (14 Sept. 1933): 7.

43. Rosay, *La Traversée*, 190; reviews by Maurice Bardèche and Alfred Savoir, *Marianne* (9 May 1934): 23–24; Raoul d'Ast, review, *Liberté*, 21 Apr. 1934; see also Albert Cervoni's review of a revival of *Grand jeu* in *l'Humanité*, 10 Mar. 1971, for an amnesiac leftist view; "La Parole est aux spectateurs," *PV* (1934); *PV* (11 Oct. 1934): 2.

44. Régent, "Grand jeu," *PV* (31 May 1934).

45. Peter Christensen, "Feyder's *Le Grand Jeu*," *Film Criticism* (1987–88): 11, 13–14; *First Wave*, 160; Boulanger, *Cinéma Colonial*, 8.

46. Marie-Christine Leps, *Apprehending the Criminal*, 4–7.

47. George Mosse, *Towards the Final Solution*, xiv, xv–xvi; idem, *Nationalism and Sexuality*; Leps, *Apprehending the Criminal*, 1–12, 130–34; Susanna Barrows, *Distorting Mirrors*, 125–44; Gustave Le Bon, *The Crowd*, 160–65; also, ibid., intro. by Robert K. Merton, xxxvii–xxxix; Stephen Jay Gould, *The Mismeasure of Man*, chaps. 5 and 6 (on Cyril Burt), and 104–5, 122–45; Cesare Lombroso, *Criminal Man*; A. Bordier, "Etude anthropologique sur une série de crânes d'assassins," *Revue d'Anthropologie* 2nd ser., 2 (1879): 265–300; Deborah Thom, "Wishes, Anxieties, Play, and Gestures: Child Guidance in Inter-war England," in Roger Cooter, ed., *In the Name of the Child*, 200–219; see also Goldstein, Bederman.

48. Lebovics, *True France* 162–88, 193–203; Leps, *Apprehending the Criminal*, 132–33.

49. Roger Leenhardt, "Encore *Le Mouchard* et *La Bandera*," *Esprit* (1935): 331–32, in *T&C* 2:193–94; André-René Zart, "*La Bandera*," *Commune* (1936): 652–53; on the regeneration-through-violence theme, see Richard Slotkin, *Gunfighter Nation*, 642–43, and his two previous works, *Regeneration through Violence* and *The Fatal Environment*.

50. *L'Avant-scène* (1–15 Apr. 1982): 70; Bernard Baritaud, "El Christo y la Virgen," ibid.: 13–14.

51. *Mists*, 255, 361, cites *Excelsior* 26 June 1935; Fofi, "Cinema of the Popular Front": 40; Nino Frank, "Le soleil noir de *La Bandera*," *L'Avant-scène* (1982): 10–12; Baritaud, "El Christo," ibid.: 13–14; the dedication is quoted ibid., 31: "au Colonel Franco et aux soldats qui ont donné leur temps dans les montagnes arides d'Haff al Ouest."

52. On the Rif War, 1921–26, see monographs by Woolman, Ayache, Bachoud, Chandler, Shannon Earl Fleming, de Madariaga, and Pennell; David

H. Slavin, "The French Left and the Rif War," *JCH* (1991): 5–32; Oved, *La Gauche française,* 1:207.

53. Galey, "Bridegrooms": 47–64; Charles R. Halstead, "A 'Somewhat Machiavellian' Face: Colonel Juan Beigbeder as High Commissioner in Spanish Morocco, 1937–1939," *History Journal* (1974): 46–66; Fleming, "Firm Bulwark," and David H. Slavin, "The Achilles Heel: The Republican Response to Morocco's Role in the Spanish Civil War," paper read at AHA Convention, Dec. 1986; Fleming, "Spanish Morocco": 27–42; Martin Blinkhorn, "Spain: The 'Spanish Problem' and the Imperial Myth," *JCH* (1980): 5–25; Victor Morales-Lezcano, "Marruecos en la guerra civil," *Historia* 16 (1986): 104–30; Maria Rosa de Madariaga, "The Intervention of Moroccan Troops in the Spanish Civil War: A Reconsideration," *European History Quarterly* (1992): 67–97.

54. Siân Reynolds, *France between the Wars;* Eric D. Weitz, "The Heroic Man and the Ever-Changing Woman: Gender and Politics in European Communism, 1917–1950," in Laura L. Frader and Sonya O. Rose, eds., *Gender and Class in Modern Europe;* Carol G. Cox, "The 'Real' vs. the 'Ideal': Leftist Representations of Women in the Era of the Popular Front," unpub., Emory University, Dept. of History, Apr. 1999.

55. André Lang, "*La Bandera,*" *PV* (1935); *Mists,* 19, 262, 299.

56. "*La Bandera,*" *l'Avant-scène* (15 Apr. 1982): 65.

57. Ibid., 70.

58. John W. Dower, *War without Mercy,* 3–14; this psychological projection has been noted since first contact: see Michel de Montaigne, "Of the Cannibals," (1590); Moshe W. Arens, *The Man-Eating Myth,* 49; Cheyfitz, *Poetics;* Peter Hulme, *Colonial Encounters;* Shohat and Stam, *Unthinking Eurocentrism,* 307–12, 347–59; James Baldwin, *The Devil Finds Work,* 62; Stephen Steinberg, "The Politics of Memory," *New Politics* (1991): 64–70; Malcolm X, *The Autobiography of Malcolm X,* 204: "Do you know why the white man really hates you? It's because every time he sees your face, he sees a mirror of his crime—and his guilty conscience can't bear to face it."

59. "*La Bandera,*" *L'Avant-scène* (1982): 60–61.

60. "Jose Canel" [Jose Diaz Fernandez], *Octubre Rojo en Asturias,* 119–205; Gabriel Jackson, *The Spanish Republic and the Civil War,* 232; Julio Alvarez del Vayo, *Freedom's Battle,* 124, and, idem, *The Last Optimist,* 32–33.

61. Cooper, *Born to Fight,* 146; Jose Diaz Fernandez, *The Blockhouse,* 83; Arturo Barea, *The Track.*

62. On the power to name, see Ethiopian filmmaker Haile Gerima, "Triangular Cinema, Breaking Toys, and Dinknesh versus Lucy," cited in Jim Pines and Paul Willeman, eds., *Questions of Third Cinema,* 67–80; see also Athol Fugar, *Sizwe Banzi Is Dead.*

63. *L'Avant-scène* (15 Apr. 1982): 70.

64. Clifford Geertz, Hildred Geertz, and Lawrence Rosen, *Meaning and Order in Moroccan Society,* 363–69; "*La Bandera,*" *L'Avant-scène* (15 Apr. 1982): 56–57; Clifford, *Predicament of Culture,* 120–44.

65. *L'Avant-scène* (15 Apr. 1982): 56, 57; Baritaud, "El Christo," ibid., 14; Cooper, *Twelve Years in the Legion,* 84, 96–97.

66. Kimbrough, ed., *Heart of Darkness* by Conrad, 261.

67. *FFL,* 428–32.

68. Porch, *Conquest,* 195–97; Warwick Anderson, "The Trespass Speaks: White Masculinity and Colonial Breakdown," *AHR* (1997): 1343–70 (on American officers in the Philippines contracting "tropical neurasthenia"); Waltraud Ernst, "European Madness and Gender in Nineteenth-Century British India," *Social History of Medicine* (1996): 357–82; Ashis Nandy, "The Savage Freud: The First Non-Western Psychoanalyst and the Politics of Secret Selves in Colonial India," in Nandy, *The Savage Freud,* 81–144; see also Bederman, Ernst.

69. Review of *Brazza* in *Le Figaro,* 24 Jan. 1940.

70. *Générique,* 154; Rogin, "Sword," 157, 164, 178–79, 187, esp. 178 on Griffith's use of the device: "The ride of the Klan reenacts and reverses Civil War battles"; Joseph Campbell, *The Hero with a Thousand Faces;* Robin Morgan, *The Demon Lover,* 54–68, esp. 58–63 (feminist critique of Campbell's hero myth).

8. Poetic Realism's *Cinéma Colonial*

1. Salinas, *Voyages et voyageurs,* 69–71, 77, 79, 99; France, *Annuaire Statistique,* 1930: 313, 1935: 298, 1936: 303 ("Mouvement des voyageurs entre l'Algérie et l'extérieur" averaged about 180,000 per year); on postcards: Prochaska, "Archive," 414–16; Alloula, *Colonial Harem,* 3–7; Lyautey to Poincaré, 19 Feb. 1924, in Pierre Lyautey, *Lyautey l'Africain,* 4:245–50.

2. Said, *Orientalism,* 205; Julian Jackson, *The Popular Front in France,* 149–58; Schor, *L'Opinion,* 166–68, lists films.

3. Vincendeau, "French Cinema," 173–75; Flitterman-Lewis, *To Desire Differently,* 169–87; see Stroebel, *French Social Cinema.*

4. Joseph Conrad, *Heart of Darkness,* 251; Leprohon, *L'Exotisme,* 206; Loutfi, "North Africa in French Movies," in Cooke and Heggoy, *Proceedings,* 134–36; Loutfi, *Littérature et Colonialisme;* Betts, *Uncertain Dimensions,* 5–8, and *Tricouleur,* chap. 7; Paul Rabinow, *French Modern,* 12–13; Tyler Stovall, "The Color Line behind the Lines: Racial Violence in France during the Great War," *AHR* (1998): 737–69; see also Braudel, Loutfi *(Littérature),* Wolf.

5. *Mists,* 259–60, connects the three films.

6. Umberto Eco, *The Role of the Reader,* 4, 9–10, 22–23; Graham Greene review in the *Spectator,* 23 Apr. 1937, 759.

7. Ginette Vincendeau, "Community, Nostalgia, and the Spectacle of Masculinity," *Screen* (1985): 31; Laura Mulvey, "Visual Pleasure and Narrative Cinema," in *Visual and Other Pleasures,* 19–21.

8. Janice Morgan, "In the Labyrinth: Masculine Subjectivity, Expatriation, and Colonialism in *Pépé le Moko,*" *French Review* (1994) 1–16; Jacques DuPont, "*Pépé le Moko,*" *Fiche Filmographique* (1987): 7. Hollywood bought the rights and remade it as *Algiers* (director, John Cromwell, 1938), starring Charles Boyer. It did not do as well as the orginal: Boyer was too refined for the role.

9. Vincendeau, "Community, Nostalgia, Masculinity": 21.

10. "*Pépé le Moko,*" *L'Avant-scène* (1981): 17–18, 24–26, 42–46.

11. *Générique,* 137, 161–67, 175; *Mists,* 212–13.

12. Vincendeau, "Community, Nostalgia, Masculinity": 24; Gauteur and Vincendeau, *Jean Gabin,* 147, 162; Henry A. Garrity, "Narrative Space in Julien Duvivier's *Pépé le Moko,*" *French Review* (1992): 623–28; Deborah Linderman, "*Pépé le Moko* and Orientalism," unpub., SCS, May 1992; *Mists,* 225–27, 255–60; Janice Morgan, "In the Labyrinth: Masculine Subjectivity, Expatriation, and Colonialism in *Pépé le Moko,*" in Bernstein and Studlar, *Visions of the East,* 253–68 (repr. from *French Review,* Mar. 1994).

13. Pierre Robin, review, *Commune* (Mar. 1937): 89–90; A.-A. Joulty, review, *L'Humanité,* 26 Feb. 1937, 5.

14. "*Pépé le Moko,*" *l'Avant-scène* (1981) 10. My trans.: the subtitles do not fully translate the script.

15. Prochaska, *Making Algeria French,* maps of Bône/Annaba before and after French colonial development: 37 (fig. 2.3), 158 (fig. 5.10); Prochaska cites Glanville Downey, *Ancient Antioch,* plates 4 and 5, and Marcel Clerget, *Le Caire,* 1:289; Bulliet, *Camel and Wheel,* 219–21, 224–27; Roger le Tourneau, *Fès avant le Protectorat,* 229; Warren Johnson, "Keeping Cool," *Aramco World* (1995): 10–17; see also Daniel, Johnson, Said.

16. Sivan, "Colonialism and Popular Culture": 37; René Gallissot, "Emigration coloniale, immigration post-coloniale," in Larbi Talha, ed., "Maghrébins en France: émigrés ou immigrés?" *Annuaire de l'Afrique du Nord* 20 (1981): 30–41; René Lespes, *Alger* (Paris: Alcan, 1930) (Lespes, a pied noir, had access to raw census data on the two cities); see also Djaffar Lesbet, Abu-Lugod, Wright.

17. Wilson, *Ideology and Experience,* 231; *HAC,* 366; Sivan, "Colonialism and Popular Culture": 24, 29, 41–43, 44; *Le Cheminot algérien,* 1 Apr. 1928; Prochaska, *Making Algeria French,* 237; Boulanger, *Cinéma colonial,* 7 (Hennebelle preface); Berque, *French North Africa,* 383; Benjamin Stora, *Histoire d'Algérie coloniale,* 98–100; Jacques Jurquet, *La Révolution nation-*

ale algérienne et le PCF, 1:58–60; Albert Lefevre, "Observations on the French Left During the Algerian War," *Revolution* (1984): 54–63; see also Rioux and Sirinelli, Schalk.

18. Quote on Casbah from Bataille and Veillot, *Caméras sous le soleil,* 63; Chevaldonné, "Cinéma colonial": 510. Pépète and Cagayous are the central characters of a series of novels authored by Louis Bertrand (Pépète) and Auguste Robinet (pseud. Musette) (Cagayous)—see Sivan, "Colonialism and Popular Culture": 29; Prochaska, *Making Algeria French,* 223–26.

19. Lorcin, *Imperial Identities,* 153, 183–86, 198–211; Lucas and Vatin, *L'Algérie des anthropologues,* 130–34, 161–67, 195–96; Bertrand, *Le Sang des races,* preface to new ed. and 8–13; on Bertrand, see Girardet, *L'idée colonial,* 244–45; Confer, *France and Algeria,* 19–20, 73; Betts, *Uncertain Dimensions,* 52–54; "*Pépé le Moko,*" *L'Avant-scène* (1981): 3 (on Moka); Rutgers students Juan Carlos Baltodano and Paula Popowski, native speakers of Puerto Rico and Argentina, pointed out the Spanish translation; for the French *le moco,* see *Petit Robert:* "(1854 origine inconnue) argot maritime, marin toulonais, un provençale"; Prochaska, *Making Algeria French,* 190, 237; idem, "History as Literature, Literature as History: Cagayous of Algiers," *AHR* 101 (June 1996): 695; André Sarrouy, "Julien Duvivier est passé à Alger pour repérer les exterieurs de *Pépé le Moko,*" *PV* (1936); Ginette Vincendeau, *Pépé le Moko,* 11, 63, 73; Henri La Barthe (detective Ashelbé), *Pépé le Moko.*

20. *Mists,* 186–87.

21. Neil MacMaster, *Colonial Migrants and Racism,* 118–33; Stovall, *Paris Red Belt,* 31–40; Berlanstein, *Working People,* 70–121; Gérard Noiriel, *Les Ouvriers dans la société française,* 120–52.

22. MacMaster, *Colonial Migrants,* 126–27; DePont, *Les Berbères,* 46–47. DePont says the Rue Fondary crime took place in 1925; MacMaster's date is 1923. Given the time frame for founding SAINA, DePont's date seems more likely; Depont, ibid., 43–52.

23. Article in SFIO's *Le Peuple,* by "RA," 17 Jan. 1931, cited by Schor, *L'Opinion,* 165; *L'Humanité,* 10 Jan. 1925; Neil MacMaster, *Migrants,* 257 n. 53; also in C. Ben Fredj, "Aux origines de l'émigration nord-africaine en France," doctoral diss., Univ. Paris 7, 1990, 665; *El Ouma* (the ENA's paper), Dec. 1933, in Benjamin Stora, *Ils Venaient d'Algérie,* 132; on the use of *sidi,* see DePont, *Les Berbères,* 46.

24. MacMaster, *Colonia Migrants,* 106, 126–27, 130–31 (quote), 166, 253; Stora, *Ils Venaient d'Algérie,* 35–36; DePont, *Les Berbères;* Ahmed Boukhelloua, *L'Hôpital Franco-Musulman de Paris;* Joany Ray, *Les Marocains en France;* Pierre Godin, *Note sur le fonctionnement des Services de Surveillance, Protection, et Assistance des Indigènes Nord-Africains,* 42–72; Céline (Pierre Destouches, M.D.) worked at the hospital in its early years.

25. Vincendeau, *Pépé le Moko*, 21–26; compare Josephine Baker's roles in Marc Allégret's *Zouzou* (1934) and in *Princesse Tam-Tam* (1937): Bryan Hammon and Patrick O'Connor, *Josephine Baker*, 93–98; Phyllis Rose, *Jazz Cleopatra*, 162–63; Denise Tual, *Le Temps Dévoré*, 60.

26. Vincendeau, "Daddy's Girls"; Kabbani, *Europe's Myths*, 10, 67–85; Jean Barreyre, "*Sirocco*," *PV* (1931); *Sirocco* 1930, director Jacques Séverac; *Le Simoun* (1933), director Firmin Gémier played the lead; see also Alloula, Enloe, Julian.

27. Kaplan, *Reproductions of Banality*, 12–19; Robin Bates, "Audiences on the Verge of a Fascist Breakdown: Male Anxieties and Late 1930s French Film," *Cinema Journal* (1997): 25–27; *Mists*, 222–31; Gauteur and Vincendeau, *Jean Gabin*, 147, 162; Vincendeau, "Community, Nostalgia, Masculinity": 18–38, 35–38; Klaus Theweleit, *Male Fantasies*.

28. Richard Roud, "Jean Grémillon and *Gueule d'Amour*," in Mary Lea Bandy, ed., *Rediscovering French Film*, 121–23; *Gueule d'Amour* (1937): scenario by Charles Spaak from a novel by André Beucler (in the 1950s, the film was revived almost every summer in Paris cinemas); *Mists*, 229–31; on gueules cassées, see Antoine Prost, *In the Wake of War: 'Les Anciens Combattants' and French Society, 1914–1939*, 39.

29. Said, *Culture and Imperialism*, 62–64, and 80–97 (on Jane Austen's *Mansfield Park*).

30. Jill Harsin, *Policing Prostitution in Nineteenth Century Paris*, 319–22, 323–57; McMillan, *Housewife or Harlot*, 13–16, 21–23, 106–8, 175–78; Charles Bernheimer, *Figures of Ill Repute*; Zeldin, *France*, chaps. 11 and 13, 309, 346; Alain Corbin, *Women for Hire*, 53, 188–89, 235–40.

31. Michelle Perrot, "L'éloge de la ménagère," *Romantisme* (1976): 105–21 (also in Perrot, *Mythes et représentations de la femme français au XIXe siècle*, 110); Gary Cross, "*Les Trois Huits*: Labor Movements, International Reform, and the Origins of the Eight-Hour Day, 1919–1924," *FHS* (1985): 263–64.

32. *Die Frau und der socialismus*, trans. as *La femme dans le passé, le présent et l'avenir*; Laura Frader, "Engendering Work and Wages: The French Labor Movement and the Family Wage," in Frader and Sonya O. Rose, *Gender and Class in Modern Europe*, 142–45, 159–64; and ibid., 14–26.

33. Weitz, "Heroic Man and Ever-changing Woman," 313.

34. François Delpla, "Les communistes français et la sexualité, 1932–1938," *Le Mouvement social* (1975): 121–52, esp. 125, 127, 133 (quote), 143; Annie Kriegel, *Les communistes français dans leur premier demi-siècle, 1920–1970*, 76–78.

35. Delpla, "Les communistes français et la sexualité," 151–52.

36. Ibid., 124, 127, 130; on 137 Delpla cites articles in *Regards*: (28 July 1935), (4 June 1936—a film review by Georges Sadoul), and (10 Mar. 1938—

article by François Drujon); Kathryn Norbert, "The Libertine Whore in French Pornography from Margot to Juliette," in Lynn Hunt, ed., *The Invention of Pornography,* 239; Vincendeau, "Community, Nostalgia, Masculinity": 34–37; Ginette Vincendeau, "Melodramatic Realism: On Some French Women's Films in the 1930s," *Screen* (1989): 51–69; Bates, "Audiences," 41–50, with the *Règle du Jeu* quote at 40; *Le Courbeau* script in *Avant-scène* (15 Apr. 1977) ; Richard Roud, intro. to Mary Lea Bandy, ed., *Rediscovering French Film,* 29–31; Evelyn Erlich, *Cinema of Paradox,* 122–23; Alan Williams, *Republic of Images,* 254–64.

37. Pierre Chenal, *Souvenirs du cinéaste,* 115–21; Lucie Derain, "*Maison du Maltais,*" *La Cinématographie française* (1938); Alan Williams, *Republic of Images,* 240–42; *Mists,* 259; André Bazin, *French Cinema of the Occupation and the Resistance:* on the anti-Semitic climate, see intro. by François Truffaut, who quotes Lucien Rebatet, nom de plume of François Vinneuil, the film reviewer for the anti-Semitic *Je Suis Partout.*

38. Ansky, *Les Juifs d'Algérie,* 50–51; Claude Martin, *Les Israélites Algériens,* 368; Chouraqui, *Histoire de Juifs d'Afrique du Nord,* 289–95; Dermenjian, *La Crise,* 33–45, 53–54, 73–89; Prochaska, *Making Algeria French,* 207, 234; *HAC,* 363–65, 366–69, 374; Francis Koerner, "Répercussions de la guerre d'espagne en Oranie, 1936–1939," *Revue d'histoire moderne et contemporaine* (July-Sept. 1975): 476–84; Robert Soucy, *French Fascism: The First Wave, 1924–1933,* 78–80, 134–35, 214–15; Wilson, *Ideology and Experience,* 108, 111, 119–20, 212, 230–33.

39. *HAC,* 369, 372; Elizabeth Friedman, *Colonialism and After,* 83–84, 88–89, 100; al-Fasi, *Independence Movements,* 23–24, says that "several hundred Algerians and others lost their lives." Friedman gives an equally unlikely figure of three Muslim dead; Charles-Robert Ageron, "Une émeute antijuive à Constantine," *Revue de l'Occident Musulman et de la Mediterranée,* nos. 13–14: 23–40.

40. *HAC,* 363–68, 372–74; "La fusillade fasciste de Sidi-bel-Abbès," *L'Humanité,* 26 Feb. 1937, 2.

41. William Irvine, "Facism in France and the Strange Case of the Croix-de-Feu," *Journal of Modern History* (1991): 271–95, 288–91; *HAC,* 372; Georges Valois, *L'homme qui vient,* 74, 79, 85, 89, quoted by Soucy, *French Fascism,* 130–31, and see also 38–40, 44–47, 51–56, 61–64; Allen Douglas, *Georges Valois.*

42. See listings in *Grand Robert* for *sidi, bled, caid (q'aid),* and *crouyah.* The latter, "popular injurious French slang," from *khouyah,* the Arabic word for *brother*; MacMaster, *Migrants,* 257 n. 53, however, claims the word also may be a distortion of the name of the Berber people from the Aurès region, the Chaouia; Sivan, "Colonialism and Popular Culture": 29; Gellner, *Muslim Society,* 152.

43. The poll mentioned near the end of chapter 4 was published as "Quelles sont les vedettes qui font le plus d'argent?" ("Which stars make the most money?") in *PV* (19 Apr. 1939): 6. The following list, showing number of votes, gives the results.

Vivian Romance	1,524	Jean Gabin	1,840
Danielle Darrieux	1,194	Fernandel	1,258
Yvonne Printemps	554	Louis Jouvet	1,156
Michelle Morgan	525	Raimu	1,094
Corinne Lucaire	472	Pierre Fresnay	642
Annabella	279	Charles Boyer	527
Elvire Popesco	272	Sacha Guitry	448
Greta Garbo	253	Erich von Stroheim	413
Edwige Fuillère	240	Tino Rossi	359
Françoise Rosay	228	Michel Simon	308
Total votes (women)	5,441	Total votes (men)	7,735

44. The quote "symbolic denial" is from unpub. paper on *Le Voile bleu,* by Sandy Flitterman-Lewis, "Hidden Voices: Childhood, the Family, and Antisemitism in Occupation France," from a conference of the same title organized by Flitterman-Lewis, Columbia University, Apr. 1998; also see unpub. paper by Colin Crisp, "What Did Wartime Audiences Want to Watch?" from the conference organized by Alan Williams, "French Films under the Occupation," Rutgers University, Nov. 1996; Crisp, *Classic French Cinema;* Rousso, *Vichy Syndrome,* 54–59. The Finaly trial coincided with the trial of SS sergeants for the massacre of 642 men, women, and children of the village of Oradour-sur-Glane in Haute Vienne; André Kaspi, "L'Affaire des enfants Finaly," *L'Histoire* (1985); Jacques Adler, *The Jews of Paris and the Final Solution,* 49–50, 222, 253 n. 74: a Jewish Resistance veteran, Adler's work confirms that hidden children were raised as Christians and recounts parents' efforts to reclaim children from protectors who were often unwilling to give them up; Serge Klarsfeld, *French Children of the Holocaust: A Memorial;* Saul Friedlander, *When Memory Comes;* Claudine Vegh, *Je ne lui ai pas dit au revoir;* memoirs by those left behind by their families convey the depth of their feelings: Sara Kofman, *Rue Ordener/Rue Labat,* trans. Ann Smock; Frida Scheps Weinstein, *A Hidden Childhood;* Michel Goldberg, *Namesake* (trans. of *Ecorché Juif*); Renée Roth-Hano, *Touch Wood;* Georges Perec, *W, ou Souvenirs de l'enfance.*

Conclusion. Political Consequences of Blindspots and Privilege

1. Quoted in *HAC*, 2: 385.

2. Thorez's speech reproduced in a pamphlet edited by the Comité Central d'action, "Contre la guerre du Maroc," Paris, 1925, 15; Slavin, "Anticolonialism," 212.

3. Violette, cited in Jacques Jurquet, *La révolution nationale algérienne et le parti communiste français*, 2:345–46.

4. *HAC*, 2: 381–84; Michel Dreyfus, "La Ligue contre l'Impérialisme et l'Oppression coloniale," *Communisme* (1982): 49–55.

5. *HAC*, 2:385; Daniel Brower, *The New Jacobins*; Lebovics, *True France*, 138–40; see also the works of Annie Kriegel.

6. Jackson, *Popular Front*, 155, 157 (quote of Moutet), 149–58; Oved, *La Gauche français*, 2:198; D. Hémery, "Aux origines des guerres d'indépendence vietnamiennes," *Mouvement social* (1977): 3–35.

7. Quote from Berque, *French North Africa*, 269, 328–30; Gilbert Meynier, *L'Algérie Révélée*, 705–9; Harold Smith, "The Issue of Equal Pay for Equal Work in Great Britain, 1914–1919," *Societas* (1978); Omar Carlier, "Les traminots algérois des années 1930," *Le Mouvement social* (1989): 61–89.

8. *Le Cheminot Algérien*, 1 Apr. 1928, cited in Sivan, "Colonialism and Popular Culture": 44.

9. Al-Fasi, *Independence Movements*, 26–31.

10. Lustick, *State-Building Failure*, 75–76; *HAC*, 2: 358–60; Prochaska, *Making Algeria French*, 237; Berque, *French North Africa*, 383; Stora, *Histoire d'Algérie Coloniale*, 98–100.

11. According to the Wizard of Id cartoon, in a melting pot everything on the bottom gets burned while the scum rises to the top.

12. Quote from Paxton and Marris, *Vichy France and the Jews*, 194–95; Murray, "Algerian Revolution": 49, 51; Martin Evans, "Algeria and the Liberation: Hope and Betrayal," in Kedward and Wood, eds., *Liberation of France*, 255–67; Ansky, *Les Juifs d'Algérie*, 296–97.

13. Ferhat Abbas, *Guerre et révolution d'Algérie*, 151–52; Evans, "Algeria and the Liberation," 255–67.

14. Evans, "Algeria and the Liberation," 263; for details, see Radouane Ainad-Tabet, *Le mouvement du 8 mai 1945 en Algérie*, and the novels of Kateb Yacine, a participant in the events: *Nedjma* and *Le cadavre encerclé*; Horne, *Savage War*, 23–28, quotes *L'Echo d'Alger*, June 1945.

15. Boucif Mekhaled, *Chroniques d'un massacre, 8 mai 1945*, 204–9; Evans, "Algeria and the Liberation," 263; John Talbott, *The War without a Name*, 21–22; Horne, *Savage War*, 23–28; Behr, *Algerian Problem*, 45, 52–57. Similarly, in Dakar, 1 Dec. 1944, demobilized Senegalese veterans, after wait-

ing for months in Tiaroye barracks, demonstrated for their pay. The government, having brought up a tank squadron that fired on the barracks and killed thirty-five and wounded thirty-five, then charged the men with mutiny. The tanks were manned by Senegalese, a fact Ousmene Sembene's film *Camp de Thiaroye* (1988) ignores; Tony Chafer, "African Perspective: The Liberation of France and Its Impact on French West Africa," Kedward and Wood, *Liberation of France*, 244; "Sembene's *Ceddo*," *Quarterly Journal of Film and Video* (1991); "*Thiaroye*: Who's That Hiding in Those Tanks and How Come We Can't See Their Faces?" *IRIS*, no. 18 (1995): 147–52.

16. Horne, *Savage War*, 99.

17. Vincent Monteil [under pseud. François Sarrazin), cited in Talbott, *War without a Name*, 21–22, 50 (quote).

18. François Jeanson, "Para-Pacification," *Esprit* (1957): 817; Sarrazin, "L'Algérie, pays sans loi," *Esprit* (1955): 1664; David Schalk, *War and the Ivory Tower*, 58.

19. Lustick, *State-Building Failure*, 40–43, 63–69, 81–82; Ruedy, *Modern Algeria*, 95, 110–30; Andrew and Kanya-Forstner, *Climax*, 35; Prochaska, *Making Algeria French*, 190.

20. Zeldin, *France*, 346.

21. Maurice Larkin, *France since the Popular Front*, 179–80. John Ardagh, *The New French Revolution*, 253; Ménie Grégoire (a sociologist similar in outlook to Betty Friedan), *Le Metier de Femme;* Pierre Simon, *La Contrôle de Naissances.*

22. Jacques Derogy, *Des enfants malgré nous*, 40 (quote), 17–18, 24–45, 73, 95, 248–52, and articles in *Libération* (16 Oct. 1955); Anne-Marie Dourlen-Rollier (lawyer), *La vérité sur l'avortement*, 57–152; *France-Observateur*, 10 Nov. 1955; *L'Express*, 15 and 23 Feb. 1956; Claire Duchen, *Women's Rights and Women's Lives in France, 1944–1968*, 119–25, 179–89; Janine Mossuz-Lavau, *Les lois de l'amour: Les politiques de la sexualité en France de 1950 à nous jours*, 77–83; Chantal Horellous-Lafarque, "Une mutation dans les dispositifs de contrôle social: les cas de l'avortement," *Revue française de sociologie* (1982): 348; Mouvement français pour le planning familial, *D'une révolte à une lutte: 25 ans d'histoire du planning familial*, 75–90; "animal" quotes from Marie-Andrée Lagroua Weill-Hallé, *La grand'peur d'aimer*, 135–36; *3,000 foyers parlent* (*Clair foyer* [a Roman Catholic journal], 1966) (quoted in Duchen, *Women's Rights*, 120).

23. Ardagh, *New French Revolution*, 256; the "confession" appeared in *Le Nouvel Observateur*, 5 Apr. 1971.

24. Thorez, *L'Humanité*, 2 May 1956, cited in Duchen, *Women's Rights and Women's Lives*, 181; Marie-Claude Vaillant-Couturier, writing in *L'Humanité*, 9 Mar. 1956; Jean Freville, *L'épouvantail malthusien.*

25. The quote "There is no man so blind" is from Bishop Cranmer, "Answer

to Gardiner" (1551); c.f., J. Heywood, *Dialogue of Proverbs* (1546): "Who is so deaf and so blind that nother hear nor see"; P. Heylyn, *Examen Historicum* (1659): "but none so blind as will not see." All three quotes are cited in *Oxford Dictionary of Proverbs*.

26. From the Sermon on the Mount: Matthew 5: 13 (King James version).

Bibliography

The bibliography is divided into two sections. Primary-source periodicals and documentary sources are listed first; all books (both primary and secondary sources), as well as other articles from journals, are in the second section.

Documents and Newspaper/Magazine Articles

"Amours exotiques." *Ciné-Miroir*, no. 162 (11 May 1928): 314.

Angelo, Jean. "Au hasard de mes souvenirs." *Ciné-Miroir*, no. 189 (16 Nov. 1928): 742.

"*L'art de séduire*." *Ciné-Miroir*, no. 190 (23 Nov. 1928): 759.

Ast, Raoul d'. Review of *Le Grand jeu. Liberté* (21 Apr. 1934).

"Attitudes." *Ciné-Miroir*, no. 69 (1 Mar. 1935): 79.

Auriol, J[ean] G[eorges]. "Sous l'uniform: Gary Cooper et Pierre Richard-Willm, officiers, soldats, et mercenaires." *Pour Vous*, no. 346 (4 Jul. 1935): 8.

———. "Revue: *Coeurs Brûlés* [Morocco]." *La Revue du Cinéma* 3, no. 27 (1 Oct. 1931): 40–42.

La Bandera. Script. In *L'Avant-scène du cinéma*, nos. 285/286 (15 Apr. 1982).

Bardèche, Maurice, and Alfred Savoir. "Reviews: *Le Grand jeu.*" *Marianne* (9 May 1934): 23–24.

[Barika]. *Ciné-Miroir*, no. 107 (1 Oct. 1926): 300.

Baritaud, Bernard. "El Christo y la Virgen." *L'Avant-scène du cinéma*, nos. 285/286 (15 Apr. 1982).

Barreyre, Jean. "*Sirocco.*" *Pour Vous*, no. 162 (24 Dec. 1931).

Bernier, Jacques. "Cimbo." *Ciné-Miroir*, no. 249 (10 Jan. 1930): 19.

Besnard, Lucien. "Dans l'Ombre du Harem." *La Petite Illustration* (11 Jun. 1927).

Biezville, Gisèle de. "Teints Pâles ou Brûlés." *Pour Vous*, no. 347 (11 Jul. 1937): 13.

———. "Tailleurs de sport." *Pour Vous*, no. 485 (2 Mar. 1938).

Blackmore, J. T. C. "The Educational Work of the French Government in Algeria." *International Review of Missions*, no. 19 (1930): 260–76.

Bordier, A. "Etude anthropologique sur une série de crânes d'assassins." *Revue d'Anthropologie* 2d series, 2 (1879): 265–300.

"*Bouboule 1ère, roi negre.*" *Pour Vous*, no. 284 (26 Apr. 1934): 6.

[*Bouboule*]. "La Parole est aux spectateurs." *Pour Vous*, no. 309 (18 Oct. 1934): 13.

"*Chang.*" *Ciné-Miroir*, no. 130 (16 Sept. 1927).

Colombat, A. "*L'Occident.*" *On Tourne* (Oct. 1928).

Crozier, W. P. "France and Her 'Black Empire.'" *New Republic*, 23 Jan. 1924, 222–24.

Danvers, Guillaume V. "Au Seuil du Harem." *Ciné-Miroir*, no. 81 (1 Sept. 1925): 275–76.

Dartois, Yves, and Marcel Carné. "Les Deux Atlantides." *Pour Vous*, no. 188 (23 Jun. 1932).

Delatère, Pierre. "Dans l'Atlas marocain avec Jean Benoît-Lévy, Marie Epstein et la troupe de *Itto.*" *Pour Vous*, no. 283 (19 Apr. 1934): 14.

Delluc, Louis. "Notes." *Cinéa*, no. 6 (10 Jun. 1921).

———. "Quelques films français." *Cinéa*, no. 18 (9 Sept. 1921).

Derain, Lucie. "*Maison du Maltais.*" *La Cinématographie française*, no. 1020 (20 May 1938).

Disney, Walt. "Blanche-Neige, ma dernière fille." *Pour Vous*, no. 483 (16 Feb. 1938): 8–9.

Dogimont, R. "Les Femmes missionaires aux colonies." *La Française*, 18 Jul. 1931.

Ducasable, R. "Augmentation des exportations." *Film-Revue* (16 Mar. 1914): 427–28.

Ducoudray, Gustave. *Leçons moyennes d'histoire de France à l'usage des écoles primaires.* Paris: Hachette, 1880. [BN: L39 530.O]

DuPont, Jacques. "*Pépé le Moko.*" *Fiche Filmographique*, no. 101 (Jan. 1987): 7.

Duruy, Georges. *Petite histoire populaire de la France depuis les origines jusqu'à la constitution de 1875.* Paris: Hachette, 1881. [BN: L39 554]

———. *Pour la France: Patriotisme, esprit militaire.* 11th ed. Paris: Hachette, 1914 [1881]. [BN: L39 548I]

"*L'Esclave blanche.*" *Ciné-Miroir*, no. 125 (1 Jul. 1927): 208–9.

"*Face aux fauves.*" *Ciné-Miroir*, no. 61 (1 Nov. 1924): 346–47.

"*La Femme idéale.*" *Pour Vous*, no. 337 (2 May 1935): 13.

Ferguson, Otis. "Review of *Lives of a Bengal Lancer.*" *New Republic*, 23 Jan. 1935, 305.

Feyder, Jacques. "La censure cinématographique." Speech to Club cinématographique, 7 Feb. 1935. *Comoedia* (10 Feb. 1935): sec. Ciné-Comoedia, 1.

Francia-Rohl. "A Marseille . . . sur les traces du Légionnaire Fernandel." *Pour Vous*, no. 394 (4 June 1936): 11.

———. "Ou l'on Termine *Un de la Légion.*" *Pour Vous*, no. 402 (30 Jul. 1936): 11.

"La fusillade fasciste de Sidi-bel-Abbès." *L'Humanité*, 26 Feb. 1937, 1, 2.

Godin, Huguette. "Le mouvement féministe." *Le Quotidien*, 29 Dec. 1930.

Gosset, Hélène. "Les Toubibas, ou l'oeuvre des femmes françaises au Maroc." *L'Intransigeant*, 7 Mar. 1932.

[Le Grand jeu]. "La Parole est aux spectateurs." Letter by Etienne Begramian. *Pour Vous*, no. 307 (4 Oct. 1934): 3.

"Le Grand jeu." Pour Vous, no. 285 (3 May 1934): 4.

[Le Grand jeu]. Pour Vous, no. 252 (14 Sept. 1933): 7.

[Le Grand jeu]. "La Parole est aux spectateurs." *Pour Vous*, no. 307 (4 Oct. 1934): 3; and *Pour Vous*, no. 308 (11 Oct. 1934): 2.

Greene, Graham. Review of *Pépé le Moko. Spectator,* 23 Apr. 1937.

"Les Hommes nouveaux." Ciné-Miroir, no. 18 (15 Jan. 1923): 20.

Huard, J.-M. "Léon Poirier nous parle de Charles de Foucauld." *Pour Vous*, no. 390 (7 May 1936): 6.

Jeanne, René. "Le Maroc à l'écran." *Cinémagazine* 2 (1 Sept. 1922): 259–63.

[———]. "Nègres et peaux-rouges au cinéma." Author name given as R. J. *Ciné-Miroir*, no. 9 (1 Sept. 1922): 139.

———. "Para-Pacification." *Esprit* 25, no. 250 (May 1957).

Joulty, A. A. Review of *Pépé le Moko. L'Humanité*, 26 Feb. 1937, 5.

Journal Officiel-Sénat. 21 Mar. 1935: 347–57.

Jouvé, Charles-Robert. *Leçons d'histoire et de civilisation: Cours élémentaire des écoles indigènes et cours préparetoire des écoles françaises de l'Algérie et de l'Orient.* 12th ed. Paris: Belin frères, 1894.

Lang, André. *"La Bandera." Pour Vous*, no. 357 (19 Sept. 1935): 6.

Lehmann, René. *"Bourrasque." Pour Vous*, no 343 (27 Jun. 1935).

———. *"L'Atlantide." Pour Vous* (9 Jun. 1932): 9.

Lenoir, Jacqueline. "Les grandes enquêtes de *Ciné-Miroir:* Blonde ou Brune?" *Ciné-Miroir*, no. 168 (22 Jun. 1928): 6.

Malherbe, Henry. *"Itto." Pour Vous*, no. 331 (21 Mar. 1935): 4.

Mandouze, A. "Impossibilités algériennes ou le mythe des trois départments." *Esprit,* no. 5 (Jul. 1947): 10–30.

Marguet, Jean. "Sidi Mohammed à Paris." *Ciné-Miroir*, no. 229 (16 Aug. 1929): 523.

Ministère de la Guerre. *Statistique médicale part IIIe: Pandémie de grippe du 1ère mai 1918 au 30 avril 1919.* Paris: Imprimerie Nationale, 1922.

Modot, Gaston. *"Un de la Légion." Ciné Liberté*, no. 4 (1 Oct. 1936).

"*Mon idéal masculin.*" *Ciné-Miroir*, no. 226 (2 Aug. 1929): 491.

"Mussolini in Libya." *Life*, 10 Jan. 1937.

Napierkowska, Stacia. "Mes souvenirs." *Ciné-Miroir*, no. 24 (15 Apr. 1923): 125.

Nys, Raymond de. "Comment fut tournée La Croisière noire." Interview with Poirier. *Ciné-Miroir*, no. 106 (15 Sept. 1926): 285, and *Ciné-Miroir*, no. 107 (1 Oct. 1926): 298–99.

"Un original concours au studio." *Ciné-Miroir*, no. 72 (15 Apr. 1925): 141.

Poirier, Léon. "Le cinéma exotique." *Ciné-Miroir*, no. 101 (1 Jul. 1926): 195.

"*La Pente.*" *Ciné-Miroir* no. 173 (27 Jul. 1928): 491.

Querillac, A. "Le rôle de la femme médecin aux colonies." *Depêche coloniale*, 10 and 29 Apr. 1932.

Raymond-Millet, J.-K. "Les nègres, sont-ils photogéniques?" *Ciné-Miroir*, no. 227 (9 Aug. 1929): 503.

Régent, Roger. "*Le Grand jeu.*" *Pour Vous*, no. 289 (31 May 1934).

———. "12 spectateurs." *Pour Vous*, no. 307 (4 Oct. 1934).

Réunion des professeurs (deVilliers et al.). *Chronologie de l'histoire de France à l'usage des écoles primaires.* Tours: Mame, 1912. From 1887 to 1931 there were editions each year. [BN: L32 71 Aa]

Robin, Pierre. "*Pépé le Moko.*" *Commune*, no. 43 (Mar. 1937): 89–90.

Roger-Mathieu, J. "Au Maroc, avec les interprètes de *L'Occident.*" *Ciné-Miroir*, nos. 172, 173, 174 (20 Jul., 27 Jul., 3 Aug. 1928): resp., 471, 490, 501.

Root, George. "Sur la piste du Hoggar." *Pour Vous*, no. 182 (12 May 1932): 3.

Roy, Robert. "Rama Tahé jouera Zouzour dans 'Cain.'" *Pour Vous*, no. 27 (30 May 1929): 4.

[Sarraut, Albert]. "Ciné-Miroir aux colonies: En Indo-Chine." Author name given as A. S. *Ciné-Miroir*, no. 9 (1 Sept. 1922): 140.

Sarrazin, François [Vincent Monteil]. "L'Algerie, pays sans loi." *Esprit* 23, no. 230–31 (Sept.-Oct. 1955): 1621–31.

Sarrouy, André. "Julien Duvivier est passé à Alger pour repérer les exterieurs de *Pépé le Moko.*" *Pour Vous*, no. 198 (7 May 1936).

"*Le Sgt. X.*" *Pour Vous*, no. 177 (7 Apr. 1932): 6.

"*Siliva le Zoulou.*" *Ciné-Miroir*, no. 193 (14 Dec. 1928): 810.

"*La Symphonie pathétique.*" *Ciné-Miroir*, no. 198 (1 Mar. 1929): 132–33.

"*Tempête sur l'Asie.*" *Ciné-Miroir*, no. 235 (4 Oct. 1929): 635.

"*Vers le Tchad.*" *Ciné-Miroir*, no. 80 (15 Aug. 1925): 262.

"La Vie du cinéma." *Pour Vous*, no. 473 (8 Dec. 1937): 6.

"Le Visage d'Islam fidèlement reflété par le cinéma française." *Pour Vous*, no. 494 (4 May 1938): 8–9.

"*Voyage chez les Pygmées.*" *Ciné-Miroir*, no. 204 (1 Mar. 1929): 135.

Vogt, Blanche. "Les Femmes et *La Bandera.*" *Pour Vous,* no. 360 (10 Oct. 1935): 5.

Wahl, Lucien. "*L'Appel du silence.*" *Pour Vous,* no. 389 (30 Apr. 1936): 6.

————. "*Les Hommes sans nom.*" *Pour Vous,* no. 473 (8 Dec. 1937): 10.

Zart, André-René. "*La Bandera.*" *Commune,* no. 29 (Jan. 1936): 652–53.

Books, Monographs, and Journal Articles

Abbas, Ferhat. *Guerre et révolution d'Algérie: La nuit coloniale.* Paris: Julliard, 1962.

Abel, Richard. "Booming the Film Business: The Historical Specificity of Early French Cinema." In *Silent Film,* ed. Richard Abel. New Brunswick: Rutgers UP, 1996.

————. *The Ciné Goes to Town: French Cinema, 1896–1914.* Berkeley: U of California P, 1994.

————. *French Cinema: The First Wave, 1915–1929.* Princeton: Princeton UP, 1984.

————. *French Film Theory and Criticism: A History/Anthology.* 2 vols. Princeton: Princeton UP, 1988.

————. "The 'Blank Screen of Reception' in Early French Cinema." *IRIS* 6 (summer 1990).

Abitbol, Michel. *Les deux terres promises: Les juifs de France et le sionisme, 1897–1945.* Paris: Olivier Orban, 1989.

Abu-Lughod, Janet. *Rabat: Urban Apartheid in Morocco.* Princeton: Princeton UP, 1980.

Achebe, Chinua. "An Image of Africa: Racism in Conrad's *Heart of Darkness.*" *Massachusetts Review* 18 (1977): 782–94.

Adamson, Walter. *Hegemony and Revolution.* Berkeley: U of California P, 1980.

Adas, Michael. *Machines as a Measure of Men: Science, Technology and Ideologies of Western Dominance.* Ithaca: Cornell UP, 1989.

Adler, Jacques. *The Jews of Paris and the Final Solution: Communal Response and Internal Conflicts, 1940–1944.* Oxford: Oxford UP, 1987.

Ageron, Charles-Robert. *Histoire de l'Algérie contemporaine.* 2 vols. Paris: PUF, 1968.

————. *Les Algériens musulmans et la France, 1871–1919.* 2 vols. Paris: PUF, 1978.

————. *L'Anticolonialisme en France de 1871 à 1914.* Paris: PUF, 1973.

————. "Une émeute antijuive à Constantine," *Revue de l'Occident Musulman et de la Méditerranée,* nos. 13/14 (1977): 23–40.

Ainad-Tabet, Radouane. *Le mouvement du 8 mai 1945 en Algérie.* Algiers: Offices des Publications Universitaires, 1985.

al-'Azm, Sadik Jalal. "Orientalism and Orientalism in Reverse." *Khamsin* (1981): 5–26.

al-Fas, Alali. *The Independence Movements of Muslim North Africa.* New York: Octagon, 1970 [Washington: ACLS, 1953].

Allain, Jean-Claude. *Agadir, 1911: Une crise impérialiste en Europe pour la conquête du Maroc.* Paris: Panthéon-Sorbonne, 1976.

Allégret, Marc. *Carnets du Congo: Voyage avec Gide.* Paris: CNRS 1987.

Allen, Theodore William. "Summary of the Argument." *Cultural Logic* (spring 1998), http://eserver.org/clogic.

———. *The Invention of the White Race.* 2 vols. New York: Verso, 1994, 1997.

Alloula, Malek. *Le Harem colonial: images d'un sous-érotisme.* Paris: Garance, 1981.

———. *The Colonial Harem.* Minneapolis: U of Minnesota P, 1986.

Altman, Georges. "La Censure en France." In *Ça, c'est du cinéma,* 217–26. Paris: Les Revues, 1931.

Amdur, Kathryn. *Syndicalist Legacy.* Urbana: U of Illinois P, 1986.

Anderson, Benedict. *Imagined Communities.* London: Verso, 1983.

Anderson, Bonnie, and Judith Zinsser. *A History of Their Own: Women in Europe.* 2 vols. New York: Harper & Row, 1988.

Anderson, Perry. "The Antinomies of Antonio Gramsci." *New Left Review* 100 (1976–77): 5–78.

Anderson, Warwick. "The Trespass Speaks: White Masculinity and Colonial Breakdown." *American Historical Review* 102 (Dec. 1997): 1343–70.

Andrew, Christopher M., and A. S. Kanya-Forstner. *The Climax of French Imperial Expansion, 1914–1924.* Stanford: Stanford UP, 1981.

Andrew, Dudley. "Sound in France: The Origins of a Native School." *Yale French Studies,* no. 60 (winter 1980): 80–114.

———. "Preying Mantis." In *Visions of the East: Orientalism in Film,* ed. Matthew Bernstein and Gaylyn Studlar. New Brunswick: Rutgers UP, 1997.

———. *Mists of Regret: Culture and Sensibility in Classic French Film.* Princeton: Princeton UP, 1995.

Ansky, Michel. *Les Juifs d'Algérie du Décret Crémieux à la Libération.* Paris: Centre, 1950.

Anstey, Roger. *The Atlantic Slave Trade and the British Abolition.* Atlantic Highlands, NJ: Macmillan, 1975.

Ardagh, John. *The New French Revolution: A Social and Economic Study of France, 1945–1969.* New York: Harper & Row, 1969.

Arendt, Hannah. *The Origins of Totalitarianism.* New York: Meridian, 1958.

———. *Eichmann in Jerusalem.* New York: Penguin, 1977 [1963].

Arens, Bernard. *Manuel des Missions Catholiques.* Louvain: Museum Lessianum, 1925.

Arens, Moshe W. *The Man-Eating Myth: Anthropology and Anthropophagy.* New York: Oxford UP, 1979.

Asante, Molefi. *Kemet.* Philadelphia: Temple UP, 1989.

Assouline, Pierre. *Gaston Gallimard.* San Diego: Harcourt, Brace, Jovanovich, 1988.

Auclert, Hubertine. *Les femmes arabes en Algérie.* Paris: Littéraires, 1900.

August, Thomas, G. *The Selling of the Empire: British and French Imperialist Propaganda, 1890–1940.* Westport, CT: Greenwood, 1985.

Aumont, Jacques. *Montage Eisenstein.* Bloomington: Indiana UP, 1987.

Ayache, Germain. *Les origines de la guerre du rif.* Rabat: Morocco, 1990.

———. "Societé rifaine et pouvoir central marocaine." *Revue historique,* no. 516 (Oct.-Dec. 1975): 345–70.

Bachoud, Andrée. *Los españoles ante las campañas de Marruecos.* Madrid: Espasa Calpe, 1988.

Bachy, Victor. *Jacques Feyder: Artisan du Cinéma, 1885–1958.* Louvain: Librairie Universitaire, 1968.

Bal, Bal, Mika. "The Politics of Citation." *Diacritics* 21 (spring 1991): 25–45.

Baldwin, James. *The Devil Finds Work.* New York: Dial Press, 1976.

Ballis, William B., and Robert A. Rupen. *Mongolian People's Republic.* Human Relations Area Files no. 39. 3 vols. New Haven: Yale UP, 1956.

Banfield, Edward. *The Moral Basis of a Backward Society.* New York: Free Press, 1967 [1958].

Barbé, Henri. "Souvenirs d'un dirigeant et militant communiste." Unpub. MS, Hoover Institution, Stanford, CA, n.d.

Bardèche, Maurice, and Robert Brasillach. *Histoire du cinéma.* Paris: André Martel, 1948.

Barea, Arturo. *The Track.* Trans. Ilsa Barea. London: Faber, 1946.

Barrows, Susanna. *Distorting Mirrors: Visions of the Crowd in Late Nineteenth Century France.* New Haven: Yale UP, 1981.

Barsamian, David. "Edward W. Said: The Pen and the Sword: *Culture and Imperialism.*" *ZMagazine* (July/Aug. 1993): 63–71.

Bartov, Omer. *Murder in Our Midst: The Holocaust, Industrial Killing, and Representation.* New York: Oxford UP, 1996.

Bataille, Gretchen M., and Charles L. P. Silet, eds. *The Pretend Indians: Images of Native Americans in the Movies.* Ames: Iowa State UP, 1980.

Bataille, Henry. *Maman Colibri.* Paris: Série Modern-Théâtre, 1911.

Bataille, Maurice-Robert, and Claude Veillot. *Caméras sous le soleil.* Algiers: Heintz, 1956.

Bates, Robin. "Audiences on the Verge of a Facist Breakdown: Male Anxieties and Late 1930s French Film." *Cinema Journal* 36 (spring 1997): 25–55.

Bederman, Gail. *Manliness and Civilization: A Cultural History of Gender and Race in the United States, 1880–1917.* Chicago: U of Chicago P, 1995.

Behr, Edward. *The Algerian Problem.* London: Hodder & Stoughton, 1961.

Bellamy, Richard, and Darrow Schecter. *Gramsci and the Italian State.* New York: Manchester UP, 1993.

Bellanger, Claude, Jacques Godechot, Pierre Guiral, and Fernand Terrou, eds. *Histoire général de la presse française.* 3 vols. Paris: PUF, 1972.

Ben-Ami, Shlomo. *Fascism from Above: The Dictatorship of Primo de Rivera in Spain, 1923–1930.* Oxford: Oxford UP, 1983.

Bennoune, Mahfoud. *The Making of Contemporary Algeria.* Cambridge: Cambridge UP, 1988.

———. "Socio-economic Changes in Rural Algeria: 1830–1954." *Peasant Studies Newsletter* 2 (Apr. 1973).

Benoit, Pierre. *L'Atlantide.* Paris: Albin Michel, 1921.

Benoît-Lévy, Jean. *The Art of the Motion Picture.* New York: Arno, 1970 [New York: Coward McCann, 1946].

———. *Les Grandes missions du cinéma.* Paris: Parizeau, 1944.

Berlanstein, Lenard. *The Working People of Paris.* Baltimore: Johns Hopkins UP, 1984.

Bernal, Martin. *Black Athena: The Afroasiatic Roots of Classical Civilization.* 2 vols. New Brunswick: Rutgers UP, 1987.

Bernard, Augustin. *Enquête sur l'habitation rurale des indigènes de l'Algérie.* Algiers: Fontane, 1921.

Bernstein, Iver. *The New York City Draft Riots: Their Significance for American Society and Politics in the Age of the Civil War.* New York: Oxford UP, 1990.

Bernstein, Matthew, and Gaylyn Studlar, eds. *Visions of the East. Orientalism in Film.* New Brunswick: Rutgers UP, 1996.

Berque, Jacques. *French North Africa: The Maghreb between the Two World Wars.* New York: Praeger, 1967.

Bertrand, Louis. *Le Sang des races: Le cycle africain.* Paris: Albin Michel, 1930.

———. *Un grand Africain: Le maréchal de Saint-Anaud.* Paris: Fayard, 1930.

Betts, Raymond. *Assimilation and Association in French Colonial Theory, 1890–1914.* New York: Columbia UP, 1960.

———. *Tricouleur: The French Overseas Empire.* London: 1978.

———. *Uncertain Dimensions: Western Overseas Empire in the Twentieth Century.* Minneapolis: U of Minnesota P, 1985.

Bidwell, Robin. *Morocco under Colonial Rule.* London: Cass, 1973.

Bishop, Peter. *The Myth of Shangri-la: Tibet, Travel Writing, and the Western Creation of Sacred Landscapes.* Berkeley: U of California P, 1989.

Blinkhorn, Martin. "Spain: The 'Spanish Problem' and the Imperial Myth." *Journal of Contemporary History* 15 (1980): 5–25.

Bloch, Marc. *Memoirs of War.* Ithaca: Cornell UP, 1980.

Borde, Raymonde. "The Golden Age: French Cinema of the 30s." In *Rediscovering French Film,* ed. Raymonde Borde and Mary Lea Bandy, 67–70. New York: MOMA, 1993.

Boskin, Joseph. *Sambo: The Rise and Demise of an American Jester.* New York: Oxford, 1986.

Boukhelloua, Ahmed. *L'Hôpital Franco-Musulman de Paris.* Algiers: Imprimerie Nord-Africaine, 1934.

Boulanger, Pierre. *Le Cinéma colonial: de "L'Atlantide" à "Lawrence d'Arabie."* Paris: Seghers, 1975.

Bourdieu, Pierre. *The Algerians.* Trans. of *Sociologie de l'Algérie.* Boston: Beacon, 1962.

Bowlan, Jeanne. "Polygamists Need Not Apply: Becoming a French Citizen in Colonial Algeria, 1918–1939." Unpub. paper, Western Society for French History, 1997.

Boyd, Carolyn. *Praetorian Politics in Liberal Spain.* Chapel Hill: North Carolina UP, 1979.

Boyer, Pierre. *Cohabitation en Algérie.* Algiers: 1956.

Braudel, Fernand. *Civilization and Capitalism.* New York: Harper & Row, 1979.

———. *The Identity of France: History and Evironment.* Trans. Siân Reynolds. New York: Harper, 1988.

———. *The Mediterranean World in the Age of Philip II.* 2 vols. New York: Harper & Row, 1973.

Bresler, Fenton. *The Mystery of Georges Simenon.* London: Baufort, 1983.

Brett, Michael, and Elizabeth Fentress. *The Berbers.* London: Blackwell, 1995.

Briffaut, Robert. *The Making of Humanity.* London: Allen & Unwin, 1919.

Brovkin, Vladimir N. *Behind the Front Lines of the Civil War.* Princeton: Princeton UP, 1994.

Buchsbaum, Jonathan. *Cinéma Engagé: Film in the Popular Front.* Urbana: Illinois UP. 1988.

Bulliet, Richard W. *The Camel and the Wheel.* Cambridge: Harvard UP, 1975.

Buñuel, Louis. *My Last Breath.* London: Cape, 1984.

Burch, Noel. *Life to Those Shadows.* Berkeley: U of California P, 1990.

———, ed. *In and Out of Synch: The Awakening Cinedreamer.* Brookfield, VT: Wildwood House, 1990.

Burke, Edmund, III. "A Comparative View of French Native Policy in Morocco and Syria, 1912–1925." *Middle Eastern Studies* [UK] 9 (1973).

————. "The Image of the Moroccan State in French Ethnological Literature: A New Look at the Origin of Lyautey's Berber Policy." In *Berbers and Arabs*, ed. Ernest Gellner and Charles Micaud. London: Duckworth, 1972.

————. "Moroccan Resistance, Pan-Islam, and German War Strategy, 1914–1918." *Francia*, no. 3 (1975): 434–64.

————. *Prelude to Protectorate in Morocco: Precolonial Protest and Resistance, 1860–1912.* Chicago: U of Chicago P, 1976.

Burridge, William. *Destiny Africa: Cardinal Lavigerie and the Making of the White Fathers.* London: Chapman, 1966.

Cambon, Jules. *Le Gouvernement général de l'Algérie.* Paris: Champion, 1918.

Cammett, John M. *Antonio Gramsci and the Origins of Italian Communism.* Stanford: Stanford UP, 1967.

Campbell, Joseph. *The Hero with a Thousand Faces.* Princeton: Princeton UP, 1968.

Campos y Serrano, Carlos Martinez de. *España Bellica: El siglo XX, Marruecos.* Madrid: Aguilar, 1972.

"Canel, Jose" [Jose Diaz Fernandez]. *Octubre Rojo en Asturias.* Madrid: Librairía y Artes Gráficas, 1984 [1935].

Casseville, Jean. *Sao, L'amoureuse tranquille.* Paris: 1932.

Castro, Américo. *The Structure of Spanish History.* Princeton: Princeton UP, 1954.

————. *España en su historia: Cristianos, moros y judios.* Buenos Aires: Losada, 1948.

Caudwell, Christopher. *Studies and Further Studies in a Dying Culture.* New York: Dodd, Mead 1938.

Cavalli-Sforza, Luigi Luca. "Genes, Peoples, and Languages." *Scientific American* (Nov. 1991): 104–10.

Cazeneuve, Jean. *Lucien Lévy-Bruhl et son oeuvre.* Paris: PUF, 1977.

Célarié, Henriette. *Behind Moroccan Walls.* Trans. Constance Lily Morris. New York: Macmillan, 1931.

————. *Du sang et de l'amour dans l'harem.* Paris: Firmin Didet, 1930.

————. *L'épopée Marocaine.* Paris: Hachette, 1928.

————. *Nos soeurs musulmanes: Scènes du désert.* Paris: Hachette, 1925.

Chaigne, Louis. *Vies et ouevres d'écrivains.* Paris: Bossuet, 1933.

Chandler, E. *The Unveiling of Lhasa.* London: 1931 [1905].

Chandler, James A. "Spain and Her Moroccan Protectorate, 1898–1927." *Journal of Contemporary History* 10 (Apr. 1975): 301–22.

Chappert, Magali. "Le Projet français de banque d'Etat du Maroc." *Revue français d'histoire d'outre-mer* (1975).

Charvin, Robert. "Le PCF face à la guerre du Rif." In *Abd el-Krim et la République du Rif, colloque.* Paris: Maspero, 1976.

Chenal, Pierre. *Souvenirs du cinéaste: Filmographie, Témoignages, Documents*. Paris: Dujarric, 1987.

Chessin, Serge de. *La nuit qui vient de l'Orient*. Paris: Hachette, 1929.

Chevaldonné, François. "Notes sur le cinéma colonial en Afrique du Nord: Naissance et fonctionnement d'un code." In *Guerres révolutionnaires: Histoire et cinéma*, ed. François Chevaldonné and Sylvie Dallet. Paris: Sorbonne/L'Harmattan, 1984.

———. "Le Cinéma colonial en Afrique du Nord: Naissance et fonctionnement d'un code." *Revue algérienne des sciences juridiques, économiques, et politiques* 14 (Sept. 1977).

———. "Fonctionnement d'une institution idéologique coloniale: La diffusion de cinéma dans les zones rurales d'Algérie avant la deuxième Guerre Mondiale." *Revue algérienne des sciences juridiques, économiques, et politiques* 12 (Sept. 1975): 529–48.

Cheyfitz, Eric. *The Poetics of Imperialism: Translation and Colonization from "The Tempest" to Tarzan*. New York: Oxford UP, 1991.

Chirat, Raymond, ed. *Catalogue des films françaises, 1929–1939*. Bruxelles: Cinématheque Royale de Belgique, 1975.

———. *Catalogue des films, 1919–29*. Paris: Cinémathèque de Toulouse, 1984.

———. *Julien Duvivier*. Lyon: SERDOC, 1968.

Chouraqui, André. *Histoire de l'Alliance Israélite Universelle*. Paris: Hachette, 1985.

———. *Marche vers L'Occident: Histoire de Juifs d'Afrique du Nord*. Paris: PUF, 1952.

Christensen, Peter. "Feyder's *Le Grand Jeu*." *Film Criticism* 12 (winter 1987–88).

Clair, René. *"Entr'acte" and "A nous la liberté."* New York: Simon & Schuster, 1970.

Clancy-Smith, Julia. "Islam, Gender, and Identities in the Making of French Algeria, 1830–1962." In *Domesticating the Empire: Race, Gender, and Family Life in French and Dutch Colonialism*, ed. Julia Clancy-Smith and Frances Gouda, 154–74. Charlottesville: UP of Virginia, 1998.

———. "The 'Passionate Nomad' Reconsidered: A European Woman in *l'Algérie française* (Isabelle Eberhardt, 1877–1904)." In *Western Women and Imperialism: Complicity and Resistance*, ed. Nupur Chaudhuri and Margaret Strobel. Bloomington: Indiana UP, 1992.

Clark, T. J. *The Painting of Modern Life: Paris in the Art of Manet and His Followers*. Princeton: Princeton UP, 1984.

Clénet, Louis-Marie. "Benoit et le mouvement intellectuel français de l'entre-deux-guerres." In *Pierre Benoit, témoin de son temps*, ed. Louis-Marie Clénet. Paris: Albin Michel, 1991.

Clerget, Marcel. *Le Caire: Etude de géographie urbaine et d'histoire écono-mique*. 2 vols. Paris: Colin, 1934.

Clifford, James. *The Predicament of Culture*. Cambridge: Harvard UP, 1988.

Coffin, Judith. "Social Science Meets Sweated Labor: Reinterpreting Women's Work in Late Nineteenth Century France." *Journal of Modern History* 63 (Jun. 1991): 230–70.

Cohen, William B. "The Lure of Empire: Why Frenchmen Entered the Colonial Service." *Journal of Contemporary History* 4 (Jan. 1969): 103–16.

———. "The Colonial Policy of the Popular Front." *French Historical Studies* 1 (spring 1972): 368–93.

Collier, Richard. *The Plague of the Spanish Lady: The Influenza Pandemic of 1918–1919*. New York: Atheneum, 1974.

Colonna, Fanny. *Instituteurs Algériens, 1883–1939*. Paris: PFNSP, 1975.

———. "Cultural Resistance and Religious Legitimacy in Colonial Algeria." *Economy and Society* 3 (1974): 233–52.

Confer, Vincent. *France and Algeria: The Problem of Civil and Political Reform, 1870–1920*. Syracuse, NY: Syracuse UP, 1966.

Conrad, Joseph. *Heart of Darkness* [1902]. New York: Norton, 1988.

Cooke, James J., and Alf A. Heggoy, eds. *Proceedings of the Fourth Meeting of the French Colonial Historical Society, 6–8 April 1978*. Washington, DC: America, 1979.

———. *Through Foreign Eyes: Western Attitudes toward North Africa*. Washington, DC: UP of America, 1992.

Cooper, Adolph Richard. *Born to Fight*. London: Blackwood, 1967 [1936].

Cooper, Adolph Richard [with Sydney Tremayne]. *Twelve Years with the Legion*. Sydney, Aust. 1933.

Cooper, Frederick. "The Problem of Slavery in African Societies." *Journal of African History* 20 (1979).

Copley, Antony. *Seuxual Moralities in France, 1780–1980: New Ideas on the Family, Divorce, and Homosexuality*. London: Routledge, 1989.

Corbin, Alain. *Women for Hire: Prostitution and Sexuality in France after 1850*. Trans. Alan Sheridan. Cambridge: Harvard UP, 1990.

Corday, Michel. *The Paris Front: An Unpublished Diary, 1914–1918*. London: Gollancz, 1933.

Corneau, Grace. *La femme aux colonies*. Paris: Librairie Nilsson, 1900.

Cox, Carol G. "The 'Real' vs. the 'Ideal': Leftist Representations of Women in the Era of the Popular Front." Unpub. MS, Emory University, Department of History, 1999.

Crafton, Donald. *Emile Cohl, Caricature and Film*. Princeton: Princeton UP, 1990.

Cresswell, Robert. "Lineage Endogamy among Maronite Mountaineers." In

Mediterranean Family Structures, ed. J. G. Peristiany. Cambridge: Cambridge UP, 1976.

Crisp, Colin. *The Classic French Cinema, 1930–1960*. Bloomington: Indiana UP, 1993.

Crosby, Alfred W. *The Columbian Exchange*. Westport, CT: Westview, 1972.

———. *Ecological Imperialism: The Ecological Expansion of Europe, 900–1900*. Cambridge: Cambridge UP, 1986.

———. *Epidemic and Peace, 1918*. Westport CT: Westview, 1976.

Cross, Gary. "*Les Trois Huits*: Labor Movements, International Reform, and the Origins of the Eight-Hour Day, 1919–1924." *French Historical Studies* 14 (fall 1985).

Cruchet, René. *La conquête pacifique du Maroc*. Paris: Berger-Levrault, 1934.

Curtin, Philip D. *Death by Migration: Europe's Encounter with the Tropical World in the Nineteenth Century*. Cambridge: Cambridge UP, 1989.

———. *Economic Change in Precolonial Africa*. Madison: U of Wisconsin P, 1975.

Daniel, Norman. *Islam, Europe, and Empire*. Edinburgh: Edinburgh UP, 1966.

Danrit, Capitaine [Emile Augustin Cyprien Driant]. *La guerre au vingtième siécle: L'invasion jaune*. 3 vols. 2d ed. Paris: Flammarion, 1926 [1909].

———. *La Guerre au vingtième siècle: L'Invasion noire*. Paris: Flammarion, 1894.

Danziger, Raphael. *Abd al-Qadir and the Algerians: Resistance to the French and Internal Consolidation*. New York: Holmes & Meier, 1977.

Darrow, Margaret H. "French Volunteer Nursing and the Myth of War Experience in World War I." *American Historical Review* 101 (Feb. 1996).

Dart, Peter. *Pudovkin's Films and Film Theory*. New York: Arno, 1974.

Davidson, Basil. *Lost Cities of Africa*. Rev. ed. Boston: Little, Brown, 1970 [1959].

———. "The Ancient World and Africa: Whose Roots?" *Race and Class* 29 (fall 1987): 1–15.

Decornoy, Jacques. *Péril Jaune, Peur Blanche*. Paris: Grasset, 1970.

Delmas, Jacques. *Mes hommes au feu: Avec la division de Fer; à Morhange, sur l'Yser, en Artois, 1914–1915*. Paris: Payot, 1931.

Delpla, François. "Communistes français et la sexualité 1932–1938." *Le Mouvement social*, no.91 (1975): 121–52.

DeMille, Cecil B. *Autobiography*. New York: Prentice-Hall, 1959.

DePont, Octave. *Les Berbères en France: L'Hôpital Franco-Musulman de Paris et du Départment de la Seine*. Lille: Douriez-Bataille, 1937.

Dermenjian, Geneviève. *La Crise Anti-Juive Oranaise, 1895–1905: L'antisémitisme dans l'Algérie coloniale*. Paris: L'Harmattan, 1986.

Derogy, Jacques. *Des enfants malgré nous*. Paris: Minuit, 1956.

Dessommes, François P. B. *Notes sur l'histoire des Kabyles.* Fort National, Algeria: SNED, 1964.

Dine, Philip. *Images of the Algerian War: French Fiction and Film, 1954–1992.* Oxford: Clarendon, 1994.

Diop, Cheik Anta. *The African Origin of Civilization.* Chicago: Lawrence Hill, 1974.

Doane, Mary Ann. "The Clinical Eye: Medical Discourses in the 'Woman's Film.'" *The Female Body in Western Culture.* Ed. Susan Rubin Suleiman. Cambridge: Harvard UP, 1986: 152–74.

Dorokhine, Constantine. "Les Emigrés russes à Paris et les films Albatros." In *Le Cinéma français muet dans le monde, influences réciproques,* ed. Pierre Guibert, 127–37. Perpignan: Inst. Jean Vigo, 1989.

Douglas, Allen. *Georges Valois.* Berkeley: U of California P, 1993.

Dourlen-Rollier, Anne-Marie. *La vérité sur l'avortement.* Paris: Librairie Maloine, 1963.

Dower, John W. *War without Mercy: Race and Power in the Pacific War.* New York: Pantheon, 1986.

Downey, Glanville. *Ancient Antioch.* Princeton: Princeton UP, 1963.

Dreyfus, Michel. "La Ligue contre l'Impérialisme et l'Oppression coloniale." *Communisme,* no. 2 (1982): 49–55.

Ducasable, R. "Augmentations des exportations." Cited in *Intelligence du Cinématographe,* ed. Marcel l'Herbier. Paris: Corrêa, 1946. Originally published in *Film-Review* (1914).

Duchen, Claire. *Women's Rights and Women's Lives in France, 1944–1968.* London: Routledge, 1994.

Duchêne, Ferdinand. *Kamir: Roman d'un femme arabe. La Petite Illustration,* 27 Mar., 3 Apr., 10 Apr. 1926.

Dunn, Ross. *Resistance in the Desert.* Madison: U of Wisconsin P, 1977.

Durkheim, Emile. *Les Règles de la méthode sociologique.* Paris: Librairie Felix Alcan, 1927 [1895].

Dyer, Richard. *White.* New York: Routledge, 1997.

Eberhardt, Isabel. *Passionate Nomad: The Diary of Isabel Eberhardt.* Boston: Beacon, 1987.

Echenberg, Myron. *Colonial Conscripts: The Tirailleurs Sénégalais in French West Africa, 1857–1960.* Portsmouth, NH: Heinemann, 1991.

Eco, Umberto. *The Role of the Reader: Explorations in the Semiotics of Texts.* Bloomington: Indiana UP, 1979.

Edwards, Rand. "Cardinal Lavigerie and the Imperialism of the Third Republic." *Proceedings of the French Colonial Historical Society* 2 (1977): 174–87.

Ehrenburg, Ilya. *Usines de rêves* Paris: Gallimard, 1939 [1932].

Einaudi, Jean-Luc. *La Bataille de Paris: 17 October 1961.* Paris: Seuil, 1991.

Elwitt, Sanford. *The Third Republic Defended*. Baton Rouge: Lousiana State UP, 1986.

Enloe, Cynthia. *Bananas, Beaches, and Bases*. Berkeley: U of California P, 1990.

Epstein, Jean. *Ecrits sur le cinéma*. 2 vols. Paris: Seghers, 1974.

Erlich, Evelyn. *Cinema of Paradox: French Filmmaking under the German Occupation*. New York: Columbia UP, 1985.

Esme, Jean d'. *Thi-Ba, Fille d'Annam*. Paris: de France, 1920 [1932].

Evans, Arthur B., and Ron Miller. "Jules Verne, Misunderstood Visionary." *Scientific American* (Apr. 1997): 92–97.

Evans, Martin. *The Memory of Resistance: French Opposition to the Algerian War, 1954–1962*. Oxford: Berg, 1997.

———. "Algeria and the Liberation: Hope and Betrayal." In *The Liberation of France: Image and Event*, ed. H. Roderick Kedward and Nancy Wood, 255–67. Oxford: Berg, 1997.

Ezra, Elizabeth. "The Colonial Look: Exhibiting Empire in the 1930s." *Contemporary French Civilization* 19 (winter/spring 1995): 39–44.

———. "Colonialism Exposed: Miss France d'Outre-Mer 1937." In *Identity Papers*, ed. Steven Ungar and Tom Conley. Minneapolis: U of Minnesota P, 1996.

———. *The Colonial Unconscious: Race and Culture in Interwar France*. Ithaca: Cornell UP, 2000.

Faim, Gael. "Une industrie-clé intellectuelle" and "Pour une politique française du Cinéma" (Chambre syndicale française de la cinématogrphie, Paris 1928). [Speech material?] cited in *Intelligence du Cinématographe*, ed. Marcel l'Herbier. Paris: Corréa, 1946.

Fanon, Franz. *A Dying Colonialism*. New York: Grove, 1967.

Fanoudh-Siefer, Léon. *Le Mythe du nègre et de l'Afrique noire dans la littérature française*. Paris: Klincksieck, 1968.

Farèrre, Claude. *Les Hommes nouveaux*. Paris: Flammarion, 1922.

———. *Quatorze histoire de soldats*. Paris: Flammarion, 1916.

Femia, Joseph V. *Gramsci's Political Thought: Hegemony, Consciousness, and Revolutionary Process*. New York: Clarendon, 1981.

Fernandez, Jose Diaz. *The Blockhouse*. Trans. Helen B. Newsome. London: Hopkinson, 1930.

Ferry, Jules. *Le Gouvernement de l'Algérie*. Paris: A. Colin, 1892.

Fescourt, Henri. *La Foi et les montagnes*. Paris: Paul Montel, 1959.

Feyder, Jacques, and Françoise Rosay. *Le cinéma, notre métier*. Genève: Skira, 1944.

Finkielkraut, Alain. *Remembering in Vain: The Klaus Barbie Trial and Crimes against Humanity*. New York: Columbia UP, 1992.

Fiori, Giuseppe. *Antonio Gramsci: Life of a Revolutionary.* Trans. Tom Nairn. New York: Schocken, 1973.

Fleming, Shannon Earl. "Primo de Rivera and Abd el-Krim: The Struggle in Spanish Morocco, 1923–1927." Ph.D. diss., University of Wisconsin, 1974.

———. "'A Firm Bulwark for the Defense of Western Civilization': The Nationalists' Uses of the Moroccan Protectorate during the Spanish Civil War." Unpub. paper, AHA Convention, Dec. 1986.

———. "Spanish Morocco and the *Alzamiento Nacional,* 1936–1939: The Military, Economic and Political Mobilization of a Protectorate." *Journal of Contemporary History* 18 (Jan. 1983): 27–42.

Fleming, Shannon Earl, and Ann Fleming. "Primo de Rivera and Spain's Moroccan Problem." *Journal of Contemporary History* 12 (Jan. 1977): 85–99.

Flitterman-Lewis, Sandy. *To Desire Differently. Feminism and the French Cinema.* Urbana: Illinois UP, 1990.

Fofi, Goffredo. "The Cinema of the Popular Front in France, 1934–1938." *Screen* 13 (winter 1972–73).

Ford, Charles. *Jacques Feyder.* Paris: Seghers, 1973.

Foucauld, Charles de. *Reconnaissance au Maroc.* Paris: Challamel, 1887.

Fox, Elizabeth, and Eugene Genovese. *The Fruits of Merchant Capital.* New York: Oxford, 1983.

Frader, Laura. "Engendering Work and Wages: The French Labor Movement and the Family Wage." In *Gender and Class in Modern Europe,* ed. Laura Frader and Sonya O. Rose. Ithaca: Cornell, 1996.

Frank, Nino. "Le soleil noir de *La Bandera.*" *L'Avant-scène du cinéma,* nos. 285 and 286 (1 Apr., 15 Apr. 1982).

Frederickson, George M. *White Supremacy: A Comparative Study in American and South African History.* New York: Oxford, 1981.

Fredj, C. Ben. "Aux origines de l'émigration nord-africaine en France." Doctoral diss., Université de Paris 7, 1990.

Freud, Sigmund. *Civilization and Its Discontents.* Trans. and ed. James Strachey. New York: Norton, 1961.

Freville, Jean. *L'epouvantail malthusien.* Paris: Sociales, 1956.

Friar, Ralph, and Natasha Friar. *The Only Good Indian; The Hollywood Gospel.* New York: Drama Book Specialists, 1972.

Friedlander, Saul. *When Memory Comes.* Trans. Helen R. Lane. New York: Avon, 1980.

Friedman, Elizabeth. *Colonialism and After: An Algerian Jewish Community.* S. Hadley, MA: Bergen & Garvey, 1988.

Gaffarel, Pierre. *L'Algérie: Histoire, conquête, et colonisation.* Paris: 1933.

Galey, John H. "Bridegrooms of Death." *Journal of Contemporary History* 4 (Apr. 1969).

Gallissot, René. *Le Patronat européen au Maroc.* Rabat: Techniques Nord-Africains, 1964.

———. "Emigration coloniale, immigration post-coloniale: Maghrébins en France: émigrés ou immigrés?" *Annuaire de l'Afrique du Nord* [ed. Larbi Talha] 20 (1981): 30–41.

Garrigues, Jean. *Banania: Histoire d'une passion française.* Paris: May, 1991.

Garrity, Henry A. "Narrative Space in Julien Duvivier's *Pépé le Moko.*" *French Review* 65 (Mar. 1992): 623–28.

Gaudefroy-Demombynes, Roger. *L'oeuvre française en matière d'enseignement au Maroc.* Paris: Geuthner, 1928.

Gaulis, B.-G. *Lyautey intime.* Paris: 1938.

Gauteur, Claude, and Ginette Vincendeau. *Jean Gabin: Anatomie d'un mythe.* Paris: Nathan, 1993.

Gay, Peter. *Freud for Historians.* New York: Oxford UP, 1985.

Gaya Nuño, Juan Antonio. *Historia del Cautivo (Episodios Nacionales).* Mexico City: Imprenta Venicia, 1966.

Geehr, Richard. *Karl Lueger, Mayor of Fin de siècle Vienna.* Detroit: Wayne State UP, 1990.

Geertz, Clifford, Hildred Geertz, and Lawrence Rosen. *Meaning and Order in Moroccan Society: Three Essays in Cultural Analysis.* London: Cambridge UP, 1979.

Geiss, Immanuel. *War and Empire in the Twentieth Century.* Aberdeen: Abderdeen UP, 1983.

———. *The Pan-African Movement.* New York: Africana, 1974.

Gellner, Ernst, ed. *Muslim Society.* Cambridge: Cambridge UP, 1981.

Géniaux, Charles. *Le Choc des races.* Paris: Fayard, 1911.

Genovese, Eugene. "On Antonio Gramsci." *Studies on the Left* 7 (Mar.–Apr. 1967); repr. in *In Red and Black* (Knoxville: Tennessee, 1984).

George, David Lloyd. *Memoirs of the Peace Conference.* 2 vols. New Haven: Yale UP, 1939.

Gerbod, Paul. "L'Ethique héroique en France, 1870–1914." *Revue historique* 268, no. 2 (1983).

Gibson, Ralph. *A Social History of French Catholicism, 1789–1914.* New York: Routledge, 1989.

Gide, André. *The Immoralist.* New York: Knopf/Vintage, 1970.

———. *The Journals.* 4 vols. New York: Random House, 1955.

———. *Voyage au Congo: Journal.* Paris: Pléiade II, 1925.

Gilman, Sander L. *Difference and Pathology: Stereotypes of Sexuality, Race, and Madness.* Ithaca: Cornell UP, 1985.

Gilroy, Paul. *The Black Atlantic.* Cambridge: Harvard UP, 1993.

Girardet, Raoul. *L'Idée coloniale en France de 1871 à 1962.* Paris: Pluriel, 1972.

Gladwell, Malcolm. "True Colors: Hair Dye, and the Hidden History of Postwar America." *New Yorker,* 22 Mar. 1999, 70–81.

Godin, Pierre. *Note sur le fonctionnement des Services de Surveillance, Protection, et Assistance des Indigènes Nord-Africains.* Paris: Imprimerie Municipale, 1933.

Goldberg, Michel. *Ecorché Juif.* Paris: Hachette, 1980.

———. *Namesake.* New Haven: Yale UP, 1982.

Goldstein, Jan. *Console and Classify: The French Psychiatric Profession in the Nineteenth Century.* New York: Cambridge UP, 1990.

Golsan, Richard J., ed. *Memory, the Holocaust, and French Justice: The Bousquet and Touvier Affairs.* Hanover, NH: UP of New England, 1996.

Gomery, Douglas. "Economic Struggles and Hollywood Imperialism: Europe Converts to Sound." *Yale French Studies,* no. 60 (winter 1980): 84–114.

Goody, Jack. "The Evolution of the Family." In *Household and Family in Past Time,* ed. Peter Laslett and Richard Wall. Cambridge: Cambridge UP, 1972.

Gould, Stephen Jay. *The Mismeasure of Man.* New York: Norton, 1981.

Graham-Brown, Sarah. *Images of Women: The Portrayal of Women in the Photography of the Middle East, 1850–1960.* New York: Columbia, 1988.

Gramsci, Antonio. *The Modern Prince and Other Writings.* New York: International Publishers, 1957.

———. *Selections from the Prison Notebooks.* Trans. Quintin Hoare and Geoffrey Nowell Smith. New York: International Publishers, 1971.

Gray, Walter D. "French Algerian Policy during the Second Empire." *Proceedings of the Western Society for French History* 3 (1976): 477–89.

Grazia, Victoria de. "Mass Culture and Sovereignty: The American Challenge to European Cinemas, 1920–1960." *Journal of Modern History* 61 (Mar. 1989): 53–87.

Greenberg, J. H. *Studies in African Linguistic Classification.* New Haven: Yale UP, 1955.

Grégoire, Ménie. *Le Métier de Femme.* Paris: Plon, 1965.

Haardt, Georges-Marie, and Louis Audoin-Dubreuil. *La Croisière noire: Expédition Citroen centre-Afrique.* Paris: Plon, 1927.

Halen, P., and János Riesz. *Images d'Afrique et du Congo/Zaire dans les lettres Belges de langue française et alentour.* Brussels: Textyles, 1993.

Halstead, Charles R. "A 'Somewhat Machiavellian' Face: Colonel Juan Beigbeder as High Commissioner in Spanish Morocco, 1937–1939." *History Journal* 37 (Nov. 1974): 46–66.

Halstead, John P. *Rebirth of a Nation.* Cambridge: Harvard UP, 1967.

Hammon, Bryan, and Patrick O'Connor. *Josephine Baker.* Boston: Dodd Mead, 1988.

Hamon, Hervé, and Patrick Rotman. *Les Porteurs des valises: La résistance française à la guerre d'Algérie.* Paris: Albin Michel, 1979.

Hansen, Miriam. *Babel and Babylon: Spectatorship in American Silent Film.* Cambridge: Harvard UP, 1991.

Hansen, Peter H. "The Dancing Lamas of Everest: Cinema, Orientalism, and Anglo-Tibetan Relations in the 1920s." *American Historical Review* 101 (Jun. 1996): 712–45.

Hargreaves, Alec. *The Colonial Experience in French Fiction.* London: Macmillan, 1981.

Harmand, Jules. *Domination et colonisation.* Paris: Flammarion, 1910.

Haroun, Ali. *La Septième Wilaya: La guerre du FLN en France, 1954–1962.* Paris: Seuil, 1986.

Harsin, Jill. *Policing Prostitution in Nineteenth Century Paris.* Princeton: Princeton UP, 1985.

Hause, Steven C. *Hubertine Auclert: The French Suffragette.* New Haven: Yale UP, 1987.

Hause, Steven C., with Anne Kenny. *Women's Suffrage and Social Politics in the French Third Republic.* Princeton: Princeton UP, 1984.

Hayes, Carlton J. H. *France: A Nation of Patriots.* New York: Octagon, 1974 [1930].

Hayward, Susan. *French National Cinema.* New York: Routledge, 1993.

Heins, Henry Hardy. *A Golden Anniversary Bibliography of Edgar Rice Burroughs.* W. Kingston, RI: Grant, 1964.

Heller, Celia. *On the Edge of Destruction: Jews of Poland between the Two World Wars.* New York: Columbia UP, 1977.

Hémery, D. "Aux origines des guerres d'indépendance vietnamiennes: Pouvoir colonial et phenomène communiste en Indochine avant la Seconde Guerre Mondiale." *Mouvement Social,* no.101 (1977): 3–35.

Hergé. *Les aventures de Tintin au Congo.* Tournai: Casterman, 1974 [1946].

Hilton, James. *Lost Horizon.* New York: Grosset & Dunlap, 1933.

Hobsbawm, Eric. *Primitive Rebels.* New York: Norton, 1965.

Hobsbawm, Eric, and Terence Ranger, eds. *The Invention of Tradition.* Cambridge: Cambridge UP, 1983.

Hodeir, Catherine, and Michel Pierre. *L'exposition coloniale.* Brussels: Complexe, 1991.

Hoisington, William A., Jr. *The Casablanca Connection: French Colonial Policy, 1936–1943.* Chapel Hill: North Carolina UP, 1984.

———. "Cities in Revolt: The Berber Dahir of 1930 and France's Urban Strategy in Morocco." *Journal of Contemporary History* 13 (July 1978): 433–48.

———. *Lyautey and the French Conquest of Morocco.* New York: St. Martin's, 1995.

Horellous-Lafarque, Chantal. "Une mutation dans les dispositifs de contrôle social: Les cas de l'avortement." *Revue française de sociologie* 22 (Jul.-Sept. 1982).

Horne, Alistair. *A Savage War of Peace: Algeria, 1954–62.* New York: Penguin, 1979.

Hughes, Judith. *To the Maginot Line.* Cambridge: Harvard UP, 1971.

Hull, Edith M. *The Sheik.* New York: Burt, 1921.

Hulme, Peter. *Colonial Encounters: Europe and the Native Caribbean, 1492–1797.* London: Methuen, 1986.

Hurston, Zora Neale. *Mules and Men.* Bloomington: Indiana UP, 1989.

Ignatiev, Noel. *How the Irish Became White.* New York: Routledge, 1997.

———. *"The New York City Draft Riots."* Review of Iver Bernstein's book. *Journal of Social History* 26 (fall 1992): 163.

Inikori, J. E., ed. *Forced Migration: The Impact of the Export Slave Trade on African Societies.* New York: Africana, 1982.

Irvine, William. *French Conservatism in Crisis: The Republican Federation of France in the 1930s.* Baton Rouge: Louisiana State UP, 1979.

———. "Facism in France and the Strange Case of the Croix-de-Feu." *Journal of Modern History* 63 (Jun. 1991): 271–95.

Jackson, Gabriel. *The Spanish Republic and the Civil War.* Princeton: Princeton UP, 1966.

Jackson, Julian. *The Politics of Depression in France, 1932–1936.* Cambridge: Cambridge UP, 1985.

———. *The Popular Front in France: Defending Democracy, 1934–1938.* Cambridge: Cambridge UP, 1988.

Jackson-Lears, T. J. "The Concept of Cultural Hegemony: Problems and Possiblities." *American Historical Review* 90 (Jun. 1985): 567–93.

Jameson, Fredric. *The Politics of Post-Modernity; or, The Cultural Logic of Late Capitalism.* Durham: Duke UP, 1991.

Jeancolas, Jean-Pierre. "French Cinema of the 1930s and Its Social Handicaps." In *La Vie est à nous,* ed. Ginette Vincendeau and Keith Reader. London: British Film Institute, 1986.

Jeanneney, Jean-Noel. *François de Wendel en République: L'argent et le Pouvoir.* Paris: Seuil, 1976.

Jennings, Francis. "The Indians' Revolution." In *The American Revolution: Explorations in the History of American Radicalism,* ed. Alfred F. Young. DeKalb, IL: Northern Illinois UP, 1976.

———. *The Invasion of America: Indians, Colonialism, and the Cant of Conquest.* Chapel Hill: North Carolina UP, 1975.

Johnson, Warren. "Keeping Cool." *Aramco World* (May/June 1995): 10–17.

———. *Muddling toward Frugality: A Blueprint for Survival in the 1980s.* San Francisco: Sierra Club Books, 1978.

Jouhaud, Christian. "L'Afrique noire au cinéma." *Mouvement Social,* no. 126 (Jan.-Mar., 1984).

Jouve, Edmond, Gilbert Pilleul, and Charles Saint-Prot, eds. *Pierre Benoit, témoin de son temps.* Paris: Albin Michel, 1991.

Julien, Charles-André. *L'Histoire de l'Algérie contemporaine.* Paris: PUF, 1964.

Jullian, Philippe. *The Orientalists: European Painters of Eastern Scenes.* Oxford: Oxford UP, 1977.

Jurquet, Jacques. *La révolution nationale algérienne et le parti communiste français.* 4 vols. Paris: Centenaire, 1979–84.

Kabbani, Rana. *Europe's Myths of Orient.* Bloomington: Indiana UP, 1986.

Kahler, Maurice. *Decolonization in Britain and France: The Domestic Consequences of International Relations.* Princeton: Princeton UP, 1984.

Kanya-Forstner, A. S. *The Conquest of the Western Sudan: A Study in French Military Imperialism.* Cambridge: Cambridge UP, 1969.

Kaplan, Alice Yaeger. *Reproductions of Banality: Fascism, Literature, and French Intellectual Life.* Minneapolis: U of Minnesota P, 1986.

Karabel, Jerome. "Revolutionary Contradictions: Antonio Gramsci and the Problem of Intellectuals." *Politics and Society* 6 (1976): 123–72.

Katz, Jonathan G. "The Mauchamp Affair and the French Civilizing Mission." Unpub. paper, Society for French Historical Studies, Washington, DC, Mar. 1999.

Kedward, H. R., and Nancy Wood, eds. *The Liberation of France: Image and Event.* Oxford: Berg, 1995.

Kelley, Robin D. G. "Notes on Deconstructing 'The Folk.'" *American Historical Review* 97 (Dec. 1992).

Kelly, Gail Paradise. "Indigenous Society and School Practices: French West Africa and Indochina, 1918–1938." In *Education and the Colonial Experience,* ed. Philip G. Altman and Gail P. Kelly, 9–23. New Brunswick, NJ: Transaction, 1984.

Kenez, Peter. *Cinema and Soviet Society* New York: Cambridge UP, 1992.

Khuri, Fuad. "Parallel Cousin Marriage Reconsidered." *Man* 5 (1970).

Kiernan, V. G. *From Conquest to Collapse: European Empires, 1815–1960.* New York: Pantheon, 1982.

———. *The Lords of Humankind.* New York: Columbia UP, 1969.

Kittler, Glenn D. *The White Fathers.* New York: Harper, 1957.

Klarsfeld, Serge. *French Children of the Holocaust: A Memorial.* New York: New York UP, 1996.

Klier, John D., and Shlomo Lambroza, eds. *Pogroms: Anti-Jewish Violence in Modern Russian History.* Cambridge: Cambridge UP, 1992.

Knight, Melvin. *Morocco as a French Economic Venture: A Study in Open Door Imperialism.* New York: Appleton-Century, 1937.

Kobak, Annette. *Isabelle: The Life of Isabelle Eberhardt.* New York: Vintage/Random House, 1990.

Koerner, Francis. "Répercussions de la guerre d'espagne en Oranie, 1936–1939." *Revue d'histoire moderne et contemporaine* (July-Sept. 1975): 476–84.

Kofman, Sara. *Rue Ordener/Rue Labat.* Trans. Ann Smock. Lincoln: U of Nebraska P, 1996 [Paris: Galilée, 1994].

Kriegel, Annie. *Les communistes français dans leur premier demi-siècle, 1920–1970.* 2nd ed. Paris: PUF, 1985.

Kyrou, Adonis. *L'Age d'or de la carte postale.* Paris: Balland, 1966.

Lacoste, Yves, André Nouschi, and André Prenant. *L'Algérie passé et présent.* Paris: Sociales, 1960.

Lagny, Michèle, Marie-Claire Ropars, and Pierre Sorlin. *Générique des années 30.* Paris: PU de Vincennes, 1986.

Landau, Rom. *Moroccan Drama.* London: Hale, 1956.

Landy, Marcia. *Film, Politics, and Gramsci.* Minneapolis: U of Minnesota P, 1994.

———. *Cinemate Uses of the Past.* Minneapolis: U of Minnesota P, 1996.

Langer, William L. *Encyclopedia of World History.* 4th ed. Boston: Houghton Mifflin, 1968.

Larkin, Maurice. *France since the Popular Front: Government and People, 1936–1986.* Oxford: Clarendon, 1988.

Laskier, Michael M. *The Alliance Israélite Universelle and the Jewish Communities of Morocco, 1862–1962.* Albany: State U of New York P, 1983.

———. "Review: *Abitbol* and *Rodrigue.*" *International Journal of Middle East Studies* 2 (Nov. 1991): 636–40.

Lavisse, Ernest. *Histoire de France.* 21st ed. Paris: Colin, 1926.

Lazard, Didier. *Max Lazard, ses frères, et Lyautey: Lettres, 1894–1933.* Published by the author: Neuilly, 1990.

Le Bon, Gustave. *The Crowd.* Harmondsworth, UK: Penguin, 1977.

Le Glay, Maurice. *Badda: Fille Berbère.* Paris: Plon-Nourrit & Cie, 1921.

———. *Le Chat aux oreilles percées: Histoire Marocaine.* Paris: Plon, 1922.

———. *Chronique.* Paris: Berger-Levrault, 1923.

———. *Chronique marocaine.* Paris: Berger-Levrault, 1933.

———. "Ecoles françaises pour les berbères." *L'Afrique française* (Mar. 1921).

———. *Itto: Récit Marocain d'amour et de bataille.* Paris: Plon, 1923.

———. *La mort du Rogui.* Paris: 1926.

———. *Récits Morocains de la plaine et des monts.* Nancy: 1920.

———. *Les sentiers de la guerre et de l'amour.* Paris: Berger-Levrault, 1930.

Le Tourneau, Roger. *Fès avant le Protectorat.* Casablanca: 1949.

Le Révérend, André. *Lyautey.* Paris: Fayard, 1983.

Lebovics, Herman. *The Alliance of Iron and Wheat in the Third Republic, 1880–1914: Origins of the New Conservatism.* Baton Rouge: Louisiana State UP, 1988.

———. *True France: The Wars over French Cultural Identity, 1900–1940.* Ithaca: Cornell UP, 1992.

Leenhardt, Roger. "Encore *Le Mouchard* et *La Bandera.*" In *French Film Theory and Criticism,* ed. Richard Abel, 2:193–94. Princeton: Princeton UP, 1988.

Lefevre, Albert. "Observations on the French Left during the Algerian War." *Revolution* (spring 1984): 54–63.

Leiris, Michel. *L'Afrique fantôme.* Paris: Gallimard, 1988 [1934].

Lelieu, Anne-Claude, Bernard Mirabel, et al. *Négripub L'image des Noirs dans la publicité depuis un siècle.* Paris: Bibliothèque Forney Catalogue, 1988.

Lepp, Ignace. *Midi sonne au Maroc.* Paris: Aubier, 1954.

Leprohon, Pierre. *L'Exotisme et le Cinéma: Le "Chasseurs d'images" à la conquête du monde.* Paris: Susse, 1945.

Leprun, Sylviane. *Le Théâtre des colonies.* Paris: L'Harmattan, 1986.

Leps, Marie-Christine. *Apprehending the Criminal: The Production of Deviance in Nineteenth-Century Discourse.* Durham: Duke UP, 1992.

Lesbet, Djaffar. *Le Casbah d'Alger: Gestion urbaine et sociale.* Algiers: Offices des Publications Universitaires, 1985.

Lespes, René. *Alger.* Paris: Alcan, 1930.

———. *Oran.* Paris: Alcan, 1938.

Levin, Nora. *The Jews in the Soviet Union since 1917: Paradox of Survival.* 2 vols. New York: New York UP, 1988.

Levy Richard S. *Antisemitism in the Modern World: An Anthology of Texts.* Lexington, MA: Heath, 1991.

Lévy-Bruhl, Lucien. *La Mentalité primitive.* 11th ed. Paris: PUF, 1960.

———. *Les Fonctions mentales dans les sociétés inférieurs.* Paris: Alcan, 1910.

Lewis, Helena. *The Politics of Surrealism.* New York: Paragon House, 1988.

Lewis, Wyndham. *Journey into Barbary.* Santa Barbara: Black Sparrow, 1987.

Leyda, Jay. *KINO: A History of Russian and Soviet Film.* 3rd ed. Princeton: Princeton UP, 1983.

Lichten, Joseph. "Notes on the Assimilation and Acculturation of Jews in Poland, 1863–1943." In *The Jews in Poland,* ed. Chimen Abramsky, Maciej Jachimczyk, and Antony Polonsky. Oxford: Blackwell, 1986.

Liddell-Hart, B. H. "Armies." *New Cambridge Modern History* vol. 10, 320–21. Cambridge: Cambridge UP, 1960.

Linderman, Deborah. "*Pépé le Moko* and Orientalism." Unpub. NEH seminar paper, University of Iowa, 1990.

Linebaugh, Peter. *The London Hanged: Crime and Civil Society in the Eighteenth Century.* Cambridge: Cambridge UP, 1992.

Linke, Uli. "Formation of White Space." Unpub. paper, Center for Analysis of Contemporary Culture, Rutgers University, Nov. 1996.

Lombroso, Cesare. *L'homme criminel [Criminal Man.* Rome: 1876]. Paris: Alcan, 1887.

Lorcin, Patricia M. E. *Imperial Identities.* New York: St. Martin's, 1995.

Loti, Pierre. *Roman d'un spahi.* Paris: Calmann-Lévy, 1979 [1881].

———. *Vers Ispahan.* Paris: Calmann-Lévy, 1904.

Loutfi, Martine Astier. *Littérature et colonialisme.* Paris: Mouton, 1971.

———. "North Africa in the French Movies." In *Proceedings of the Fourth Meeting of the French Colonial History Society,* ed. James J. Cooke and Alf A. Heggoy. Washington, DC: UP of America, 1979.

———. "Imperial Frame: Film Industry and Colonial Representations." In *Cinema, Colonialism, Postcolonialism: Perspectives from the French and Francophone Worlds,* ed. Dina Sherzer. Austin: U of Texas P, 1996.

———. *Littérature et colonialisme: L'Expansion coloniale vue dans la littérature romanesque français, 1871–1914.* Paris: Mouton, 1971.

Lucas, Philippe, and Jean-Claude Vatin. *L'Algérie des anthropologues.* Paris: Maspéro, 1982 [1975].

Lustick, Ian. *State-building Failure in British Ireland and French Algeria.* Berkeley: Institute of International Studies Research Series No. 63, University of California, 1985.

———. *Unsettled States, Disputed Lands: Britain and Ireland, France and Algeria, Israel and Palestine.* Ithaca: Cornell UP, 1994.

Lutz, Catherine A., and Jane L. Collins. *Reading National Geographic.* Chicago: U of Chicago P, 1993.

Lyautey, Louis-Hubert. *Lyautey l'Africain: Textes et lettres.* Paris: Plon, 1953–57.

———. *Paroles de'action: Madagascar-Sud Oranais-Oran-Maroc, 1900–1926.* Paris: Colin, 1927.

———. "Du Rôle colonial de l'armée." *Revue des Deux Mondes* (15 Jan. 1900): 308–18.

MacMaster, Neil. *Colonial Migrants and Racism: Algerians in France, 1900–62.* New York: St. Martin's, 1997.

Madariaga, Maria Rosa de. "L'image et le retour du Maure dans la mémoire collective du peuple espagnol et la guerre civile de 1936." *L'Homme et la Société* 22 (Oct.-Dec. 1988): 63–79.

———. *L'Espagne et le Rif: Pénétration coloniale et résistances locales, 1909–1926.* 2 vols. Doctoral thesis, Université de Paris 1, Sorbonne, 1987.

———. "The Intervention of Moroccan Troops in the Spanish Civil War: A Reconsideration." *European History Quarterly* 22 (Jan. 1992): 67–97.

Malcolm X. *The Autobiography of Malcolm X*. New York: Grove, 1966.

Mannheim, Karl. *Ideology and Utopia*. Trans. Louis Wirth and Edward Shils. New York: Harcourt, Brace & World, 1966 [1936].

Mannheim, Karl G. "Introduction to Gramsci." *New Left Review* 48 (1970): 22–58.

March, Patrick, G. *Eastern Destiny: Russia in Asia and the North Pacific*. Westport, CT: Praeger, 1996.

Margueritte, Victor. *La Garçonne*. Paris: Flammarion, 1922.

Marquet, Jean. *Le Jaune et le blanc*. Paris: Monde Moderne, 1926.

Mariamov, A. *Vsevolod Pudovkin*. Moscow: MFLP, 1951.

Marrus, Michael. *The Politics of Assimilation*. Oxford: Clarendon, 1971.

Marrus, Michael, and Robert Paxton. *Vichy France and the Jews*. New York: Basic, 1981.

Marshall, Bruce. *The French Colonial Myth and Constitution: Making the Fourth Republic*. New Haven: Yale UP, 1973.

Martin, Benjamin. *Hypocrisy of Justice in the Belle Epoque*. Baton Rouge: Louisiana State UP, 1984.

Martinkus-Zemp, Ada. "Européocentrisme et exotisme: L'Homme blanc et la femme noire dans la littérature française de l'entre-deux-guerres." *Cahiers d'Etudes Africaines* 49 (1973) 60–81.

———. *Le Blanc et le Noir: Essai d'une description de la vision du Noir par le Blanc dans la littérature française de l'entre-deux-guerres*. Paris: Nizet, 1975.

Marty, Paul. *Le Maroc de demain*. Paris: Comité de l'Afrique Française, 1925.

Marzani, Carl, ed. *The Open Marxism of Antonio Gramsci*. Trans. Carl Marzani. New York: Cameron, 1957.

Massis, Henri. *Defense of the West*. Trans. Frank S. Flint. New York: Harcourt, Brace, 1928.

———. *Défense de l'Occident*. Paris: Plon, 1927.

Mauchamp, Emile. *La Sorcellerie au Maroc*. Paris: Dorbon-Ainé, 1911.

Mawdsley, Evan. *The Russian Civil War*. Boston: Allen & Unwin, 1987.

Mayeur, J. M. *Les Débuts de la Troisième République, 1871–1898*. Paris: Seuil, 1973.

Maza, Sarah. "Stories in History: Cultural Narratives in Recent Works in European History." *American Historical Review* 101 (Dec. 1996): 1493–515.

McCauley, Elizabeth Anne. *Industrial Madness: Commercial Photography in Paris, 1848–1871*. New Haven: Yale UP, 1994.

McCracken, Grant. *Big Hair: A Journey into the Transformation of Self*. Woodstock: Overlook, 1995.

McMillan, James F. *Housewife or Harlot: The Place of Women in French Society, 1870–1940*. New York: St. Martin's, 1981.

McNamara, JoAnn Kay. *Sisters in Arms: Catholic Nuns through Two Millenia.* Cambridge: Harvard UP, 1996.

McNeill, William H. "Mythistory, or Truth, Myth, History, and Historians." *American Historical Review* 91 (Feb. 1986).

———. "The Eccentricity of Wheels: Eurasian Transportation in Historical Perspective." *American Historical Review* 92 (Dec. 1987): 111–26.

———. *Plagues and Peoples.* Garden City, NJ: Anchor, 1976.

Megherbi, Abdelghani. *Les Algériens au Miroir du Cinéma colonial.* Algiers: SNED, 1982.

———. *The Koran Interpreted.* Trans. A. J. Arberry. New York: Macmillan, 1979.

Mekhaled, Boucif. *Chroniques d'un massacre, 8 mai 1945: Sétif, Guelma, Kherrata.* Paris: Syros, 1995.

Memmi, Albert. *The Colonizer and the Colonised.* New York: Orion, 1965.

Mendelsohn, Ezra. "Interwar Poland: Good or Bad for the Jews?" In *The Jews in Poland,* ed. Chimen Abramsky, Maciej Jachimczyk, and Antony Polonsky, 130–39. Oxford: Blackwell, 1986.

———. *The Jews of East Central Europe between the Wars.* Bloomington: Indiana UP, 1983.

Mendenhall, John. *French Trademarks: The Art Deco Era.* San Francisco: Chronicle Books, 1991.

Mernissi, Fatima. *Beyond the Veil: Male-Female Dynamics in a Modern Muslim Society.* Cambridge, UK.: Schenkman, 1975.

Mesguich, Félix. *Tours de marivelle: Souvenirs d'un chasseur d'images.* Paris: Grasset, 1933.

Michel, Marc. *L'Appel à l'Afrique.* Paris: UP Sorbonne, 1982.

Miller, Michael B. *The Bon Marché: Bourgeois Culture and the Department Store, 1869–1920.* Princeton: Princeton UP, 1992.

———. *Shanghai on the Métro.* Berkeley: U of California P, 1995.

Miller, Webb. *I Found No Peace.* New York: Simon & Schuster, 1936.

Minh-ha, Trinh T. *Woman, Native, Other: Writing, Postcoloniality and Feminism.* Bloomington: Indiana UP, 1989.

Mink, Gwendolyn. *The Wages of Motherhood: Inequality in the Welfare State, 1917–1942.* Ithaca: Cornell UP, 1995.

Mitchell, Timothy. *Colonising Egypt.* New York: Cambridge UP, 1988.

Mitry, Jean. *Ivan Mosjoukine.* Anthologie du cinéma, ser. no. 48 (Oct. 1969). Supplement to *L'Avant-scène du cinéma,* no. 96.

Monroe, James T. "The Hispanic-Arabic World." In *Américo Castro and the Meaning of Spanish Civilization,* ed. José Rubia Barcia, 69–90. Berkeley: U of California P, 1976.

Morales-Lezcano, Victor. "Marruecos en la guerra civil." *Historia 16* 5 (1986): 104–30.

Morand, Paul. *Paris-Tombouctou*. Paris: Flammarion, 1928.

Morgan, Janice. "In the Labyrinth: Masculine Subjectivity, Expatriation, and Colonialism in *Pépé le Moko*." *French Review* (Mar. 1994).

Morgan, Robin. *The Demon Lover: On the Sexuality of Terrorism*. New York: Norton, 1989.

Mosse, George. *Nationalism and Sexuality: Middle Class Morality and Sexual Norms in Modern Europe*. Madison: U of Wisconsin P, 1985.

———. *Towards the Final Solution: A History of European Racism*. Madison: U of Wisconsin P, 1985.

Mossuz-Lavau, Janine. *Les lois de l'amour: Les politiques de la sexualité en France de 1950 à nos jours*. Paris: Payot, 1991.

Moussinac, Léon. "Etat du cinéma international." In *L'Age ingrat du cinéma*, 331–54. Paris: Français Réunis, 1967.

Mouvement français pour le planning familial. *D'une révolte à une lutte: 25 ans d'histoire du planning familial*. Paris: Tierce, 1982.

Mulvey, Laura. "Visual Pleasure and Narrative Cinema." *Screen* 16 (autumn 1977): 6–18.

———. *Visual and Other Pleasures*. Bloomington: Indiana UP, 1989.

Mumford, Bryant W., with G. St. J. Orde-Brown. *Africans Learn to Be French*. London: Evans Bros., 1935.

Muret, Maurice. *Le Crépuscule des nations blanches*. Paris: Payot, 1925.

———. *Twilight of the White Races*. Trans. Mme Touzalin. New York: Scribner, 1926.

Murphy, George G. S. *Soviet Mongolia: A Study of the Oldest Political Satellite*. Berkeley: U of California P, 1966.

Murray, Roger. "The Algerian Revolution." *New Left Review*, no. 22 (Dec. 1963): 14–65.

Nandy, Ashis. *The Savage Freud and Other Essays in Possible and Retrievable Selves*. Princeton: Princeton UP, 1995.

Nestorenko, Geneviève. "L'Afrique de l'autre." In *Générique des années trente*, ed. Michel Lagny, Marie-Claire Ropars, and Pierre Sorlin. Paris: Vincennes, 1986.

Newsinger, John. "Lord Greystoke and Darkest Africa: The Politics of the Tarzan Stories." *Race and Class* 28, no. 2 (1986): 59–71.

Noiriel, Gérard. *Les Ouvriers dans la société française*. Paris: Seuil, 1986.

Norbert, Kathryn. "The Libertine Whore in French Pornography from Margot to Juliette." In *The Invention of Pornography: Obscenity and the Origins of Modernity, 1500–1800*, ed. Lynn Hunt. New York: Zone Books, 1993.

Nord, Pierre. *Paris Shopkeepers and the Politics of Resentment*. Princeton: Princeton UP, 1984.

Nye, Robert A. *Masculinity and Male Codes of Honor in Modern France.* New York: Oxford UP, 1993.

O'Brien, Charles. "The 'Cinéma Colonial' of 1930s France: Film Narration as Spatial Practice." In *Visions of the East: Orientalism in Film,* ed. Matthew Bernstein and Gaylyn Studlar. New Brunswick: Rutgers UP, 1997.

O'Brien, Justin. Introduction to *The Journals of André Gide,* ed. Justin O'Brien. 4 vols. New York: Random House, 1947–1956.

O'Donnell, Joseph Dean. *Lavigerie in Tunisia: The Interplay of Imperialist and Missionary.* Athens: U of Georgia P, 1979.

Offen, Karen. "Liberty, Equality, and Justice for Women: The Theory and Practice of Feminism in Nineteenth Century Europe." In *Becoming Visible: Women in European History,* ed. Renate Bridenthal, Claudia Koonz, and Susan Stuard, 335–74. Boston: Houghton Mifflin, 1987.

Oms, Marcel. "Un Cinéaste des années vingt: René le Somptier." *Cahiers de la cinémathèque,* nos. 33–34 (autumn 1981): 207–13.

Ossendowski, Ferdinand. *Beasts, Men, and Gods.* New York: Dutton, 1922.

Oved, George. *La Gauche français et le nationalisme marocain.* Paris: L'Harmattan, 1984.

Ozouf, Jacques, and Mona Ozouf. "Le thème du patriotisme dans les manuels primaires." *Le Mouvement social,* no. 49 (Oct.-Dec. 1964): 5–31.

Payne, Stanley. *Politics and the Military in Modern Spain.* Stanford: Stanford UP, 1967.

Pennell, Richard C. *A Country with a Government and a Flag: The Rif War in Morocco, 1921–1926.* Cambridgeshire, UK: Middle East and North African Studies Press, 1986.

Perec, Georges. *W, ou Souvenirs de l'enfance.* Paris: Denoel, 1975.

———. *W, or The Memory of Childhood.* Trans. David Bellos. Boston: Godine, 1988.

Perkins, Charles Alfred. "French Catholic Opinion and Imperial Expansion, 1880–1886." Ph.D. diss., Harvard University, 1964.

Perrot, Michelle. "L'Eloge de la Menagère dans le discours des ouvriers français au XIXe siècle." *Romantisme* 13/14 (1976): 105–21.

———. "The New Eve and the Old Adam: Changes in French Women's Condition at the Turn of the Century." In *Behind the Lines: Gender and the Two World Wars,* ed. Margaret Randolph Higonnet et al., 53–60. New Haven: Yale UP, 1987.

———. *Mythes et représentations de la femme française au XIXe siècle.* Paris: Champion, 1976.

Persell, Stuart Michael. *The French Colonial Lobby.* Stanford: Hoover Institutions Press, 1983.

Peyrefitte, Jacqueline. "Rehabilitating the Traumatized War Veteran: The Case of French Conscripts from the Algerian War, 1954–1962." In *War and*

Memory in the Twentieth Century, ed. Martin Evans and Ken Lunn, 73–85. Oxford, UK: Berg, 1997.

Phillips, H. *"Black October": The Impact of the Spanish Influenza Epidemic on South Africa.* Pretoria: Govt. Printer, 1990.

Pierre, Michel. "L'affaire Voulet-Chanoine." *L'Histoire,* no. 69 (1984): 67–71.

Pieterse, Jan Nederveen. *White on Black: Images of Africa and Blacks in Western Popular Culture.* New Haven: Yale UP, 1992.

Pomel, Auguste. *Des races indigènes de l'Algérie et du rôle que leur réservent leurs aptitudes.* Oran: Dagorn, 1871.

Porch, Douglas. *The French Foreign Legion. A Complete History of the Legendary Fighting Force.* New York: Harper Collins, 1991.

———. *Conquest of the Sahara.* New York: Knopf, 1984.

Pratt, Mary Louise. *Imperial Eyes: Travel Writing and Transculturation.* New York: Routledge, 1992.

Prédal, René. *La société française 1914–1945 à travers le cinéma.* Paris: Colin, 1972.

Prédal, René, and Robert Florey. *Rudolph Valentino, 1895–1926.* Supplement to *L'Avant-scène du cinéma,* no. 92 (May 1969).

Prochaska, David. *Making Algeria French: Colonialism in Bône, 1870–1920.* New York: Cambridge UP, 1990.

———. "The Archive of *Algérie Imaginaire.*" *History and Anthropology* 4 (1990): 373–420.

Prost, Antoine. *In the Wake of War: 'Les Anciens Combattants' and French Society, 1914–1939.* Trans. Helen McPhail. Providence, RI: Berg, 1992 [Paris edition: *Les anciens combattants et la société française, 1914–1939.* 3 vols. P Nationales françaises, 1977].

Pryne, Rudyers. *War in Morocco.* Tangier: 1927.

Pudovkin, V. I. *Film Technique and Film Acting.* London: Gollancz, 1929.

Rabinow, Paul. *French Modern: Norms and Forms of the Social Environment.* Cambridge: Harvard UP, 1989.

Ray, Joany. *Les Marocains en France.* Paris: Syrey, 1938.

Rebérioux, Madeleine. "La carte postale de grève: Propos sur une collection et une exposition." *Le Mouvement social,* no. 126 (Jan.-Mar. 1984): 141–44.

Renaudin, J. L. C., and L. Charpentier. *Petite histoire de France du jeune âge.* Paris: Boyer, 1908.

Rentschler, Eric., ed. *The Films of G. W. Pabst: An Extraterritorial Cinema.* New Brunswick: Rutgers UP, 1990.

Resnick, Charles. *Pleasures of the Belle Epoque.* New Haven: Yale UP, 1985.

Rey, Etienne. *La Renaissance de l'orgueil français.* Paris: Grasset, 1912.

Reynolds, Siân. *France Between the Wars: Gender and Politics.* London: Routledge, 1996.

Ripert, Alain, and Claude Frère. *La Carte Postale, son histoire, sa fonction social.* Lyon: PU Lyon, 1983.

Rivet, Daniel. "Mines et politique au Maroc, 1907–1914." *Revue d'histoire moderne et contemporaine* (Oct.-Dec. 1979): 558–59.

———. *Lyautey et l'Institution du Protectorat Français au Maroc, 1912–1925.* 3 vols. Paris: L'Harmattan, 1988.

Roberts, Mary Louise. "Samson and Delilah Revisited: The Politics of Women's Fashion in 1920s France." *American Historical Review* 98 (Jun. 1993): 657–84.

Robin, Pierre. "Review." *Commune,* no. 43 (Mar. 1937): 89–90.

Rodrigue, Aron. *De l'instruction à l'émancipation: Les enseignants de l'alliance israélite universelle et les juifs d'Orient, 1860–1939.* Paris: Calmann-Lévy, 1989.

Roger-Mathieu, J. J., ed. *Mémoires d'Abd el-Krim.* Paris: Libraires des Champs-Élysées, 1927.

Rogin, Michael. "'The Sword Became a Flashing Vision': D. W. Griffith's *The Birth of a Nation.*" *Representations,* no. 9 (winter 1985): 150–95.

Rosay, Françoise. *La Traversée d'une vie.* Paris: Laffont, 1974.

Rose, Phyllis. *Jazz Cleopatra: Josephine Baker in Her Time.* New York: Doubleday, 1989.

Rosello, Mireille. *Declining the Stereotype: Ethnicity and Representation in French Cultures.* Hanover: UP of New England, 1998.

Rosenblum, Mort. *Mission to Civilize: The French Way.* New York: Harcourt, Brace, Jovanovich, 1986.

Ross, Philip E. "Hard Words: Trends in Linguistics." *Scientific American* (Apr. 1991): 136–47.

Roud, Richard. Introduction to *Rediscovering French Film,* ed. Mary Lea Bandy, 29–31. New York: MOMA, 1983.

———. "Jean Grémillion and *Gueule d'Amour.*" In *Rediscovering French Film,* ed. Mary Lea Bandy, 121–23. New York: MOMA, 1983.

Rousso, Henry, and Eric Conan. *Vichy: Un passé qui ne passe pas.* Paris: Fayard, 1994.

———. *The Vichy Syndrome: History and Memory in France since 1944.* Trans. Arthur Goldhammer. Cambridge: Harvard UP, 1991. [Published in French as *Le Syndrome de Vichy.* Paris: Seuil, 1987].

Ruedy, John. *Modern Algeria.* Bloomington: Indiana UP, 1992.

Sabbah, Fatna. *Women in the Muslim Unconscious.* Trans. Mary Jo Lakeland. New York: Pergamon, 1984.

Sadoul, Georges. *Le Cinéma français, 1890–1962.* Paris: Flammarion, 1962.

Said, Edward. *Orientalism.* New York: Pantheon, 1979.

———. *Culture and Imperialism* New York: Pantheon, 1993.

———. "Orientalism Reconsidered." *Race and Class* 27 (fall 1985): 1–15.

Salinas, Michèle. *Voyages et voyageurs en Algérie, 1830–1930.* Toulouse: Privat, 1989.

Sánchez-Albornoz, Claudio. *España, un enigma histórico.* Buenos Aires: Sudamericana, 1956.

Sanders, Alan J. K. *Mongolia: Politics, Economics, and Society.* London: Pinter, 1987.

Sarmiento, Domingo F. *Viajes, 1845–1847: Collected Works.*

Sartre, Jean-Paul. *The Words.* New York: Braziller, 1964.

Saxton, Alexander. *The Rise and Fall of the White Republic.* New York: Verso, 1990.

Schalk, David L. *War and the Ivory Tower: Algeria and Vietnam.* New York: Oxford UP, 1991.

Scham, Alan. *Lyautey in Morocco.* Berkeley: U of California P, 1970.

Schilcher, Linda Schatkowski. "The Lore and Reality of Middle Eastern Patriarchy." *Die Welt des Islams* 28 (1988).

Schneider, William H. *An Empire for the Masses: The French Popular Image of Africa, 1870–1900.* Westport, CT: Greenwood, 1982.

———. *Quality and Quantity: The Quest for Biological Regeneration in Twentieth-century France.* Cambridge: Cambridge UP, 1990.

Schnitzer, Luda, and Jean Schnitzer. *Vsevolod Pudovkin.* Paris: Seghers, 1966.

Schor, Ralph. *L'Opinion francaise et les etrangéres en France, 1919–1939.* Paris: UP Sorbonne, 1985.

Schuker, Stephen A. *The End of French Predominance in Europe.* Chapel Hill: U of North Carolina P, 1976.

Schwartz, Vannessa. *Spectacular Realities: Early Mass Culture in Fin de Siècle Paris.* Berkeley: U of California P, 1998.

Segal, Daniel. "The European: Allegories of Racial Purity." *Anthropology Today* (Oct. 1991): 7–9.

Semidei, Manuela. "De l'Empire à la décolonisation à travers les manuels scolaires français." *Revue française des sciences politiques* 16 (Feb. 1966): 56–86.

Senghor, Léopold Sédar. *Poèmes.* Paris: Seuil, 1964.

Sheean, Vincent. *Personal History.* Boston: Houghton Mifflin, 1969 [1934].

Sherzer, Dina. *Cinema, Colonialism, Postcolonialism: Perspectives from the French and Francophone Worlds.* Austin: U of Texas P, 1996.

Shirer, William L. *The Collapse of the Third Republic.* New York: Simon & Schuster, 1969.

Shohat, Ella. "Gender and the Culture of Empire: Toward a Feminist Ethnography of the Cinema." *Quarterly Review of Film and Video* 13 (1991): 45–84.

Shohat, Ella, and Robert Stam. *Unthinking Eurocentrism.* London: Routledge, 1994.

Short, N. Robert. *Dada and Surrealism*. London: Calmann & Cooper, 1980.

Shulman, Irving. *Valentino*. New York: Simon & Schuster, 1968.

Silverman, Kaja. *Male Subjectivity at the Margins*. New York: Routledge, 1992.

Simon, Pierre. *La Contrôle de Naissances*. Paris: Payot, 1967.

Sirinelli, Jean-François. *La Guerre d'Algérie et les intellectuels français*. Paris: Institut d'Histoire du Temps Présent, 1988.

Sivan, Emmanuel. "Colonialism and Popular Culture in Algeria." *Journal of Contemporary History* 14 (Jan. 1979): 21–53.

———. *Communisme et nationalisme en Algérie, 1920–1962*. Paris: Fondation nationale des sciences politiques, 1976.

Sklar, Robert. *Film: An International History of the Medium*. Englewood, NJ: Prentice Hall, 1993.

Slavin, David H. "The Achilles Heel: The Republican Response to Morocco's Role in the Spanish Civil War." Unpub. paper, AHA Convention, Dec. 1986.

———. "Anticolonialism and the French Left: Opposition to the Rif War, 1924–1926." Ph.D. diss., University of Virginia, 1982.

———. "Colonial Film Before and After *Itto* (1934): From Berber Myth to Race War." *French Historical Studies* 27 (winter 1998).

———. "French Cinema's Other First Wave: Political and Racial Economies of Cinéma Colonial." *Cinema Journal* 37, no. 1 (fall 1997).

———. "The French Left and the Rif War." *Journal of Contemporary History* 26 (Jan. 1991): 5–32.

———. "Heart of Darkness, Heart of Light." In *Identity Papers*, ed. Tom Conley and Steven Ungar. Minneapolis: U of Minnesota P, 1995.

———. "Native Sons? White Blind Spots in Interwar French Cinema." Unpub. paper, NEH summer seminar, "The Cultures of the Popular Front," University of Iowa, 1991.

———. "Race Traitors in France?" *Race Traitor: Journal of the New Abolitionism* (Jan. 1995): 117–21.

Slotkin, Richard. *The Fatal Environment: The Myth of the Frontier in the Age of Industrialization, 1800–1890*. New York: Harper, 1994.

———. *Gunfighter Nation: The Myth of the Frontier in Twentieth-century America*. New York: Atheneum, 1992.

———. *Regeneration through Violence: The Mythology of the American Frontier, 1600–1860*. New York: Harper, 1996.

Smith, Alan K. *Creating a World Economy: Merchant Capital, Colonialism, and World Trade, 1400–1825*. Boulder, CO: Westview, 1991.

Smith, Dennis Mack. *Mussolini's Roman Empire*. New York: Penguin, 1976.

Smyth, Rosaleen. "The Development of British Colonial Film Policy, 1927–1939, with Special Reference to East and Central Africa." *Journal of African History* 20 (1979) 437–50.

Sorlin, Pierre. "The Fanciful Empire: French Feature Films and the Colonies in the 1930s." *French Cultural Studies* 2, no. 5 (Jun. 1991): 142.

Soucy, Robert. *French Fascism: The First Wave, 1924–1933.* New Haven: Yale UP, 1986.

Stam Burgoyne, Robert, and Sandy Flitterman-Lewis. *New Vocabularies in Film Semiotics.* London: Routledge, 1992.

Stanton, Gareth. "The Oriental City: A North African Itinerary." *Third Text,* nos. 3/4 (spring/summer 1988): 3–38.

Stavrianos, Leften S. *Global Rift: The Third World Comes of Age.* New York: Morrow, 1981.

Steinberg, Stephen. "The Politics of Memory." *New Politics* (winter 1991): 64–70.

Stoddard, Lothrop. *The Rising Tide of Color.* New York: Scribner, 1920.

Stora, Benjamin. *La gangrène et l'oubli: La mémoire de la guerre d'Algérie.* Paris: Seuil, 1991.

———. "Les Algeriens dans le Paris de l'entre-deux-guerres." In *Paris des étrangères,* ed. André Kaspi and Antoine Marès. Paris: Imprimerie nationale, 1989.

———. *Histoire d'Algérie Coloniale.* Paris: La Découverte, 1991.

———. *Ils Venaient d'Algérie: L'immigration algérienne en France, 1912–1992.* Paris: Fayard, 1992.

Stora-Lamarre, Annie. *L'Enfer des la IIIè République: Censeurs et Pornographes, 1881–1914.* Paris: Imago, 1990.

Stovall, Tyler. *The Rise of the Paris Red Belt.* Berkeley: U of California P, 1990.

———. "The Color Line behind the Lines: Racial Violence in France during the Great War." *American Historical Review* 103 (Jun. 1998): 737–69.

Stowasser, Barbara. "Women's Issues in Modern Islamic Thought." *Arab Women: Old Boundaries, New Frontiers.* Ed. Judith E. Tucker. Bloomington: Indiana UP, 1993.

Strauss, David. "The Rise of Anti-Americanism in France: French Intellectuals and the American Film Industry, 1927–1932." *Journal of Popular Culture* 10 (spring 1977).

Stroebel, Elizabeth Grottle. *French Social Cinema of the 1930s.* New York: Arno, 1980.

Studlar, Gaylyn. *Variety Film Reviews, 1907–1980.* New York: Garland, 1983.

———. *This Mad Masquerade: Stardom and Masculinity in the Jazz Age.* New York: Columbia UP, 1996.

Suleiman, Susan Rubin, ed. *The Female Body in Western Culture.* Cambridge: Harvard UP, 1986.

Swearingen, Wil D. *Moroccan Mirages: Agrarian Dreams and Deceptions, 1912–1986.* Princeton: Princeton UP, 1987.

Szyliowicz, Irene L. *Pierre Loti and the Oriental Woman*. New York: St. Martin's, 1988.

Talbott, John. *The War Without a Name: France in Algeria, 1954–1962*. New York: Knopf, 1980.

Theweleit, Klaus. *Male Fantasies*. Trans. Stephen Conway. Minneapolis: U of Minnesota P, 1987.

Thom, Deborah. "Play and Gestures: Child Guidance in Inter-war England." In *In the Name of the Child: Health and Welfare, 1880–1940*, ed. Roger Cooter, 200–19. London: 1992.

Thomas, Hugh. *The Spanish Civil War*. New York: Harper & Row, 1977.

Thompson, E. P. *Customs in Common*. New York: New Press, 1992.

Thompson, Leonard. *A History of South Africa*. New Haven: Yale UP, 1990.

Tillion, Germain. *Republic of Cousins: Women's Oppression in Mediterranean Society*. London: Al Saqi, 1983.

Tinker, Hugh. *A New System of Slavery: The Export of Indian Labor Overseas, 1830–1920*. London: Oxford UP, 1974.

Tocqueville, Alexis de. "Deux Lettres sur l'Algérie." In *Oeuvres complètes*, vol. 3. Paris: Gallimard, 1951–1989.

Torgovnick, Marianna. *Gone Primitive: Savage Intellects, Modern Lives*. Chicago: U. of Chicago P, 1990.

Tremayne, Sydney. *Twelve Years in the Foreign Legion*. Sydney, Aust.: Angus & Robertson, 1933.

Trice, Thomas Granville. "Spanish Liberalism in Crisis: A Study of the Liberal Party during Spain's Parliamentary Collapse, 1913–1923." Ph.D. diss., University of Wisconsin, 1974.

Tristan, Anne. "France admette massacre sécrète en Paris." *Manchester Guardian Weekly*, 3 Nov. 1991, 20–21.

Tristan, Anne, et al. *Le Silence du Fleuve*. Bezons: Au Nom de la Mémoire, 1991.

Troy, William. "Blood and Glory." *Nation*, 30 Jan. 1935, 139–40.

Truffaut, François. Introduction to *French Cinema of the Occupation and the Resistance: The Birth of a Critical Aesthetic*, by André Bazin, trans. Stanley Hochman. New York: Ungar, 1981.

Tual, Denise. *Le Temps Dévoré*. Paris: Fayard, 1980.

Tucker, Judith E. "The Arab Family in History: 'Otherness' and the Study of the Family." In *Arab Women: Old Boundaries, New Frontiers*, ed. Judith E. Tucker, 195–207. Bloomington: Indiana UP, 1993.

Turin, Yvonne. *Femmes et religieuses au XIXe siècle: Le féminisme en religion*. Paris: Nouvelle Cité, 1989.

Turner, Adrian. *The Making of David Lean's "Lawrence of Arabia."* Limpsfield, Eng.: Dragon's World, 1994.

Ullman, Richard. *Anglo-Soviet Relations, 1917–1921*. 3 vols. Princeton: Princeton UP, 1968–72.

Ungar, Steven. "*La Maison du Maltais* as Text and Document." In *Cinema, Colonialism, Postcolonialism: Perspectives from the French and Francophone Worlds*, ed. Dina Sherzer, 31–50. Austin: U of Texas P, 1996.

Vaillant-Couturier, Marie-Claude. Article on women's rights. *L'Humanité*, 9 Mar. 1956.

Valois, Georges. *L'homme qui vient*. Paris: Nouvelle Libraire Nationale, 1906.

Vandevoort, Bruce. "The French CGT, German Labor, and the First Moroccan Crisis." Ph.D. diss., University of Virginia, 1986.

Vayo, Julio Alvarez del. *Freedom's Battle*. New York: Knopf, 1940.

———. *The Last Optimist*. New York: Viking, 1950.

Vegh, Claudine. *Je ne lui ai pas dit au revoir: Des enfants de déportés parlent*. Paris: NRF/Gallimard, 1979.

Verne, Jules. *The Mysterious Island*. New York: Dodd, Mead, 1958.

Vignaud, Jean. *Sarati le Terrible*. Trans. Judy Davis. London: 1927 [1919].

———. *Notre enfant, l'Algérie*. Paris: Broché, 1947.

———. *La Maison du Maltais*. Paris: Plon, 1926.

Vincendeau, Ginette. "French Cinema of the 1930s: Social Text and Context of a Popular Entertainment Medium." Ph.D. diss., University of East Anglia, UK, 1985.

———. "Daddy's Girls: Oedipal Narratives in 1930s French Films." *IRIS* 5 (1988): 74.

———. "Community, Nostalgia, and the Spectacle of Masculinity." *Screen* 26 (1985): 18–38.

———. "Melodramatic Realism: On Some French Women's Films in the 1930s." *Screen* 30 (summer 1989): 51–69.

Waldman, Harry. *Paramount in Paris: Three Hundred Films Produced at the Joinville Studios, 1930–1933*. Lanham, MD: Scarecrow Press, 1998.

Waltraud, Ernst. "European Madness and Gender in Nineteenth-Century British India." *Social History of Medicine* 9 (1996): 357–82.

———. *Mad Tales from the Raj: The European Insane in Nineteenth Century British India, 1800–1858*. London: Routledge, 1991.

Weber, Eugen. *Peasants into Frenchmen*. Stanford: Stanford UP, 1976.

Weinstein, Frida Scheps. *A Hidden Childhood: A Jewish Girl's Sanctuary in a French Convent, 1942–1945*. Trans. Barbara Loeb Kennedy. New York: Hill & Wang, 1985.

———. *J'habitais rue des Jardins Saint-Paul*. Paris: Balland, 1983.

Weitz, Eric D. "The Heroic Man and the Ever-changing Woman: Gender and Politics in European Communism, 1917–1950." In *Gender and Class in Modern Europe*, ed. Laura L. Frader and Sonya O. Rose. Ithaca: Cornell UP, 1996.

Whitaker, Ian. "Familial Roles in the Extended Patrilineal Kin-group in Northern Albania." In *Mediterranean Family Structures,* ed. J. G. Peristianty. Cambridge: Cambridge UP, 1976.

White, Hayden. *Tropics of Discourse.* Baltimore: Johns Hopkins UP, 1978.

Williams, Alan. *Republic of Images: A History of French Filmmaking.* Cambridge: Harvard UP, 1992.

Wilson, Stephen. *Ideology and Experience: Antisemitism in France at the Time of the Dreyfus Affair.* Rutherford, NJ: Fairleigh Dickinson, 1982.

Wolf, Eric. *Europe and the People without History.* Berkeley: U of California P, 1982.

Woolman, David. *Rebels in the Rif.* Stanford: Stanford UP, 1968.

Wright, Gwendolyn. *The Politics of Design in French Colonial Urbanism.* Chicago: U. of Chicago P, 1991.

Yacine, Kateb. *Le cadavre encerclé.* Paris: Seuil, 1959.

———. *Nedjma.* Paris: Seuil, 1956.

Yezuitov, N. *Pudovkin, Creative Paths.* Moscow: MFLPH, 1937.

Zangger, Eberhard. *The Flood from Heaven: Deciphering the Atlantis Legend.* New York: Morrow, 1992.

Zeldin, Theodore. *France 1848–1945: Ambition and Love.* New York: Oxford UP, 1979.

Filmography: Feature Films Cited

Algiers (U.S., 1938)

L'Ame du bled (Jacques Séverac, 1929)

L'Appel du silence (Léon Poirier, 1936)

L'Atlantide (Jacques Feyder, 1921; Georg-Wilhelm Pabst, 1932)

L'Aventurier (Maurice Mariaud and Louis Osmont, 1924)

La Bandera (Julien Duvivier, 1935)

Le Belle équipe (Julien Duvivier, 1936)

Le Bled (Jean Renoir, 1929)

Bouboule 1er, roi nègre (Léon Mathot, 1933)

Bourrasque (Pierre Billon, 1935)

Brazza, ou l'Epopée du Congo (Léon Poirier, 1939)

Cinq Gentlemen maudits (Luitz Morat, 1920; Julien Duvivier, 1930)

La Comtesse Marie (Benito Perojo [Franco-Spanish], 1927)

Le Crime de M. Lange (Jean Renoir, 1935)

Dans l'Ombre du harem (Léon Mathot and André Liabel, 1927)

L'Esclave blanche (Augusto Genina, 1927; Marc Sorkin, 1939)

Les Fils du soleil (Renée Le Somptier, 1924)

Garden of Allah (U.S., 1936)

Le Grand jeu (Jacques Feyder, 1934)

Gueule d'Amour (Jean Grémillon, 1937)

L'Homme du Niger (Jacques de Baroncelli, 1939)

Les Hommes nouveaux (Violet and Donatien 1922; Marcel L'Herbier 1936)

Les Hommes sans nom (Jean Valle'e, 1937)

In'ch' Allah! (Frantz Toussaint, 1922)

Itto (Jean Benoit-Lévy and Marie Epstein, 1934)

Le Lion des Mongols (Jean Epstein, 1924)

Maman Colibri (Julien Duvivier, 1929; Jean Dréville, 1937)

La Maison du Maltais (Henri Fescourt, 1926; Pierre Chenal, 1938)

La Marseillaise (Pierre Renoir, 1937)

Morocco (*Coeurs Brûlés*: U.S., 1930)

L'Occident (Henri Fescourt, 1927 and 1937)
La Pente (Henri Andreani, 1928)
Pépé le Moko (Julien Duvivier, 1937)
Princesse Tam-Tam (Edmond T. Gréville, 1935)
Quai des brumes (Marcel Carné, 1938)
Le Roman d'un spahi (Michel Bernheim, 1936)
Le Sang d'Allah (Luitz-Morat 1922)
Sarati le Terrible (Louis Mercanton, 1923; André Hugon, 1937)
Le Sergent X (Vladimir Striyewski, 1931)
Le Simoun (Firmin Gémier, 1933)
La Sirène des tropiques (Henri Etievant and Mario Nalpas, 1927)
Sirocco (Jacques Séverac, 1930)
La Sultane de l'amour (René Le Somptier and Charles Burguet, 1919)
Sur les Toits de Paris
La Symphonie pathétique (Henri Etievant and Mario Nalpas 1929)
Tempête sur l'Asie (*Storm over Asia*: V. I. Pudovkin, 1929)
Les Terres d'or (Renée Le Somptier, 1924)
La Vie est à nous (Pierre Renoir, 1935)
Un de la Légion (Christian-Jaque, 1936)
Zouzou (Marc Allégret, 1934)

Index